Restorative Approaches to Conflict in Schools

Drawing on recent international developments in criminal justice, *Restorative Approaches to Conflict in Schools* highlights the long-term ineffectiveness of punitive models of discipline in education contexts and examines an alternative approach, underpinned by the principles of restorative justice. This approach provides an opportunity for adults and young people to engage with a range of processes such as group conferencing and peer mediation, whereby:

- conflict and harm are confronted and repaired;
- a future rather than past orientation is developed;
- relationships are built upon the values and attitudes of respect, inclusion and equality;
- pupils learn interpersonal and problem-solving skills as well as social responsibility;
- staff develop skills and confidence in working restoratively;
- the risk of future/repeat problems is minimised;
- a positive school ethos is developed.

These approaches have proven to be highly effective in criminal justice systems around the world, and are beginning to be applied more widely in educational contexts. This edited volume draws together for the first time contributions from an interdisciplinary field of international experts and practitioners on the subject, and offers both critique and guidance in order that the implementation of restorative approaches in schools may be undertaken thoughtfully and sustainably. This exciting new text will be a key reference book for locating contemporary, international and interdisciplinary debate in the field.

Edward Sellman is Lecturer in Education at the University of Nottingham, UK.

Hilary Cremin is Senior Lecturer in Education at the University of Cambridge, UK.

Gillean McCluskey is Senior Lecturer and Deputy Head of the Institute of Education, Community and Society at the University of Edinburgh, UK.

Restorative Approaches to Conflict in Schools

Interdisciplinary perspectives
on whole school approaches
to managing relationships

Edited by
Edward Sellman, Hilary Cremin
and Gillean McCluskey

 Routledge
Taylor & Francis Group

LONDON AND NEW YORK

First published 2013
by Routledge
2 Park Square, Milton Park, Abingdon, Oxon OX14 4RN

and by Routledge
711 Third Avenue, New York, NY 10017

Routledge is an imprint of the Taylor & Francis Group, an informa business

© 2014 Edward Sellman, Hilary Cremin and Gillean McCluskey

The right of the editors to be identified as the authors of the
editorial material, and of the authors for their individual chapters,
has been asserted in accordance with sections 77 and 78 of the
Copyright, Designs and Patents Act 1988.

British Library Cataloguing in Publication Data
A catalogue record for this book is available from the British
Library

Library of Congress Cataloging in Publication Data
A catalog record for this book has been requested

ISBN: 978-0-415-65609-2 (hbk)
ISBN: 978-0-415-65611-5 (pbk)
ISBN: 978-1-315-88969-6 (ebk)

Typeset in Galliard
by Saxon Graphics Ltd, Derby

MIX
Paper from
responsible sources
FSC
www.fsc.org   FSC® C013056

Printed and bound in Great Britain by
TJ International Ltd, Padstow, Cornwall

For my father, Frederick George Sellman
  – *Edward Sellman*

For my husband, Tim
  – *Hilary Cremin*

For my mum, Elisabeth McCluskey
  – *Gillean McCluskey*

Contents

PART III
Catalytic?

15 Restorative approaches in schools: Necessary roles of
    cooperative learning and constructive conflict   159
    DAVID W. JOHNSON AND ROGER T. JOHNSON

16 Peacebuilding through circle dialogue processes in primary
    classrooms: Locations for restorative and educative work   175
    KATHY BICKMORE

17 Challenging the punitive turn in youth justice through
    restorative approaches in schools?   192
    NATASHA DU ROSE AND LAYLA SKINNS

18 Creating the restorative school part 1: Seeding restorative
    approaches in Minnesota   207
    NANCY RIESTENBERG

19 Creating the restorative school part 2: The impact of
    restorative approaches on roles, power and language   217
    EDWARD SELLMAN

20 Creating the restorative school part 3: Rethinking neutrality
    and hierarchy   231
    SHELAGH McCALL

21 Who misses out? Inclusive strategies for students with
    communicational difficulties   240
    MARY MEREDITH AND EDWARD SELLMAN

22 Speaking the restorative language   253
    RICHARD HENDRY, BELINDA HOPKINS AND BRIAN STEELE

    Pamphlet text: Restorative approaches in schools   264
    RICHARD HENDRY, BELINDA HOPKINS AND BRIAN STEELE

    Index   269

Figures and boxes

Figures

Boxes

Contributors

Kathy Bickmore is Professor of Curriculum, Teaching and Learning and Comparative International and Development Education at the Ontario Institute for Studies in Education, University of Toronto, Canada. She teaches initial teacher education courses on managing conflict, and graduate courses on comparative democratic citizenship education, conflict resolution education and curriculum studies. Her research addresses peace building (including restorative approaches), incorporating controversial issues, and educating for democracy and social justice in schools. Recent publications appear in *Educational Policy, Journal of Teaching and Learning, Social Education* and the book *Debates in Citizenship Education*.

David J. Carruthers worked as a lawyer and a district court judge before chairing the New Zealand Parole Board between 2005–2012. He was knighted in 2009 and appointed as the chairman of the New Zealand Independent Police Conduct Authority in 2012. He has maintained an interest in prisoner rehabilitation and restorative justice throughout his working life.

Helen Cowie is Emeritus Professor and Director of the UK Observatory for the Promotion of Non-Violence at the University of Surrey, in the Faculty of Health and Medical Sciences. She has conducted extensive research in the areas of cooperative group work, peer support, bullying prevention and the promotion of emotional health and well-being in children and young people. She has written guidance material on implementing peer support, managing violence in schools and dealing with cyber-bullying alongside co-writing a bestselling undergraduate textbook on child development, now in its fifth edition.

Hilary Cremin is a Senior Lecturer in the Faculty of Education at Cambridge University, and works with graduate students from all over the world. She researches, publishes and teaches citizenship education, peace education and conflict resolution in educational and community settings. She has worked in the public, private and voluntary sectors as a schoolteacher, educational consultant, project coordinator, mediator and academic. Her goal is to work towards new models of global education in which learning is a grounded, authentic, life-long process and young people are prepared for the physical, emotional, moral and logistical challenges that they will face in the twenty-first century.

Wendy Drewery is Associate Professor in the Faculty of Education at the University of Waikato in Hamilton, New Zealand. She was part of a team that developed a conferencing process for schools, based on restorative justice, Māori huitanga, and narrative approaches to anti-colonising ways of speaking at the turn of the millennium. She has taught counselling and health development and currently teaches postgraduate programmes in restorative practice and human development. She has also co-authored the textbook, *Human Development: Family, Place, Culture*, now in its fourth edition.

Natasha Du Rose is a Lecturer in Criminology and Sociology in the Department of Social Sciences at the University of Roehampton. Her PhD research examined the impact of drug policy while working as a volunteer coordinator at a women's therapy centre in Bristol. Natasha's research activities have focused on the governance of socially excluded, marginalised and/or vulnerable individuals such as drug users, women and young people. She has been involved in various research projects including restorative approaches in schools and drug policy.

Carol Hayden is Professor of Applied Social Research at the Institute of Criminal Justice Studies, University of Portsmouth. She has conducted research about the use of family group conferences in education and the use of restorative approaches with children in residential care. This connects to a wider programme of research focused on addressing the needs of children who present problematic behaviour in schools, the care system and/or the community. She has written books on crime, anti-social behaviour and schools as well as implementing restorative approaches in children's residential care settings.

Richard Hendry is Additional Support Needs Education Officer for the Highland Council in Scotland. He taught for 20 years in secondary education, establishing Scotland's first Peer Mediation service and subsequently developing a Restorative Alternative to Exclusion Programme between 1996 and 2002. He has since worked as SACRO's (Safeguarding Communities – Reducing Offending) National Restorative Practice Consultant/Trainer from 2006–2013, as a postgraduate tutor for the University of Edinburgh and as a consultant/trainer with Local Education Authorities, youth justice, social work and police services. He has written a book about building and restoring respectful relationships in schools, which is also published by Routledge.

Belinda Hopkins is Director of Transforming Conflict, the National Centre for Restorative Approaches in Youth Settings, UK, founded in the 1990s and now a widely-respected provider of advice and training nationally and internationally. Her recently completed doctoral research was on the implementation of a whole school restorative approach. She remains an active restorative practitioner but also facilitates training, provides change consultancy and writes a variety of books, articles, conference presentations and training resources. Her books *Just Schools* and *Just Care* were amongst the first to be written about restorative approaches in educational and residential child care settings, both published by Jessica Kingsley.

David W. Johnson is Emeritus Professor of Educational Psychology at the University of Minnesota and Co-Director of the Cooperative Learning Center. He has received numerous professional awards from the American Psychological Association, the American Educational Research Association, the International Association of Conflict Management and other professional organisations. He is a past-editor of the *American Educational Research Journal* and has authored over 500 research articles, books and book chapters, many with his brother, Roger, about conflict and cooperation within education.

Roger T. Johnson is Professor of Education at the University of Minnesota and is Co-Director of the Cooperative Learning Center. He has been honoured with several national teaching awards. He has provided consultancy to schools around the world and authored numerous research articles, book chapters and books. Alongside David, his brother, their research interests include the study of social interdependence (cooperation and competition), conflict resolution (constructive controversy and integrative negotiations), peace psychology and restorative justice.

Jean Kane was a Senior Lecturer in Education at the University of Glasgow, Scotland. Previously, she was a teacher in secondary schools in England and Scotland, a teacher educator and a researcher in the area of inclusive education. Her research examined the processes of inclusion and exclusion in schooling with particular reference to social class and gender. She has utilised restorative practices as a means of supporting the developing practices of schools in their efforts to enable higher levels of student participation and more inclusive school cultures.

Mirriam Lephalala is a Lecturer in the Department of English Studies at the University of South Africa. Her research interests are in the areas of promoting student access to education at both school and higher education levels for disadvantaged groups. She has worked in various projects related to student access, including critical reading and writing in second- and foreign-language contexts, promoting reading for fun in the classroom and exploring restorative approaches as an alternative to addressing conflict and violence in schools.

Gwynedd Lloyd is an Honorary Fellow at Moray House School of Education, University of Edinburgh, Scotland as well as an independent researcher and consultant. She was previously Head of Educational Studies and Director of the Scottish Traveller Education Programme at the University of Edinburgh. She has written widely about restorative approaches, young people in trouble, gender and ethnicity in relation to exclusion/inclusion and the medicalisation of behaviour.

James MacAllister is a Lecturer in Education at the University of Stirling, Scotland, where he coordinates the first year undergraduate programme in education studies. His research concerns how philosophy and theory does, and might, influence and inform education. His publications to date include philosophical exploration of the following areas: school discipline, teacher authority, ethics in education and educational research, emotion education, and physical education. He is also interested in the philosophical underpinnings of innovative school discipline practices, such as restorative approaches.

Shelagh McCall is a Commissioner at the Scottish Human Rights Commission and a part-time sheriff. Previously, she studied law and was called to the Scottish Bar in 2000. Her current role focuses on human rights, criminal law and public law. She is also a trained mediator with a particular interest in conflict resolution systems design, including those in school communities.

Gillean McCluskey is a Senior Lecturer and Deputy Head of the Institute for Education, Community and Society, within the School of Education at the University of Edinburgh, Scotland. She has researched and published widely on restorative approaches in schools, and on issues surrounding exclusion, discipline and the challenges faced by marginalised children and young people in education.

Mary Meredith is Assistant Headteacher responsible for inclusion at an 11–16, all-ability high school in rural Lincolnshire. She developed an interest in restorative approaches through her work with young people who were at risk of exclusion because of their behavioural difficulties. The school has developed a Behaviour and Relationship Management Policy, which has restorative approaches at its heart. Inspection in September 2012 applauded the school's 'dramatic' reduction in exclusions and the support it now provides for its most vulnerable learners.

Brenda Morrison is an Associate Professor and the Director of the Centre for Restorative Justice in the School of Criminology, Simon Fraser University, Canada. She is a social psychologist with field experience in outdoor education, government administration and restorative justice. Her teaching and research interests include restorative justice, responsive regulation, school safety, shame-management and social identity.

Sheila Riddell is Professor of Inclusion and Diversity, Director of Research and Knowledge Exchange, and Director of the Centre for Research in Education Inclusion and Diversity at the Moray House School of Education, University of Edinburgh, Scotland. Her research interests are in the broad field of equality and social inclusion, with particular reference to gender, social class and disability in education, training, employment and social care. She is currently working on projects investigating the experiences and outcomes of disabled students in higher education, life-long learning policy, and special and inclusive education across Europe.

Nancy Riestenberg is the School Climate Specialist for the Minnesota Department of Education in the United States. She provides support to school districts on a variety of topics including violence and bullying prevention, inclusion and school culture. Her work with school districts, community organisations and individuals has involved applying the principles and practices of restorative justice in schools as a means of building community, improving teaching and holding students accountable, summarised in her book, *Circle in the Square: Building Community and Repairing Harm in Schools.*

Edward Sellman is a Lecturer in Education at the University of Nottingham, England. Previously, he has worked with young people experiencing social, emotional and behavioural difficulties as well as providing training to schools in conflict resolution. His research interests include the arts and social inclusion, whole-school change and restorative approaches to conflict in schools. He has published widely on all of these topics.

Lucio Sia is a programme specialist at UNESCO's Division for Teachers and Higher Education as well as Academic Adviser at the American Graduate School in Paris. He is involved in conflict resolution and peace building activities and Global Citizenship education projects around the world. As a representative on the Task Force for International Cooperation on Holocaust Education, Remembrance and Research between 2009–2010, he was also responsible for UNESCO's publication 'Combating Intolerance, Exclusion and Violence through Holocaust Education'. He has also published a range of guidance materials for teachers on behalf of UNESCO.

Layla Skinns is a Senior Lecturer in Criminology at the Centre for Criminological Research, School of Law, University of Sheffield, England. She has conducted a wide range of research and authored a number of publications on policing, crime prevention, multi-agency criminal justice partnerships, drug users and the criminal justice system, as well as restorative approaches in schools.

Joan Stead is an Honorary Fellow at the University of Edinburgh, Scotland. She has extensive experience of working with schools and with parents/carers, children and young people, especially with those who may be viewed as vulnerable and/or marginal to mainstream schooling. Her research expertise is in qualitative/ interpretive methods and methodologies, and her research interests include restorative approaches in schools, disciplinary exclusion from school, multi-agency working in schools and ADHD (Attention Deficit Hyperactivity Disorder), publishing widely on these topics.

Brian Steele has been a psychologist for over 40 years in both education and social work contexts. He has been active in the field of restorative practices since 2001 as a practitioner, trainer and supervisor. He contributed to the Scottish Government's Positive Behaviour Team in promoting restorative practices and positive behaviour approaches to school discipline and has also helped develop a range of training materials for use at individual, school and education authority levels. He has a particular interest in assisting organisations develop cultures necessary for the successful implementation of restorative practices.

Daniel W. Van Ness is Executive Director of the Center for Justice and Reconciliation at Prison Fellowship International, based in the United States. The Center helps its 128 affiliates and others address criminal justice challenges using restorative approaches and human rights initiatives. Restorative justice has been his major professional interest for over 30 years. He has explored and promoted restorative justice as a public policy advocate, programme designer, writer and teacher. He was also closely involved in the development of the UN Declaration of Basic Principles on the Use of Restorative Justice Programmes in Criminal Matters, endorsed in 2002.

Elisabet Weedon is Deputy Director of the Centre for Research in Education Inclusion and Diversity at the Moray House School of Education, University of Edinburgh, Scotland. Her main research interests are in the area of social justice and equality in education. She is currently involved in projects on widening access to higher education and educational experiences and outcomes for Muslim pupils in England and Scotland.

Derick Wilson is Reader Emeritus in Education at the School of Education, University of Ulster, Coleraine, and a commissioner with the Equality Commission for Northern Ireland. Recipient of a MBE, he has been an active advocate and researcher of integrated schooling, organisational change, youth and community work, peace education and reconciliation in Northern Ireland.

About the editors

Edward Sellman is a Lecturer in Education at the University of Nottingham, Hilary Cremin is a Senior Lecturer in Education at the University of Cambridge and Gillean McCluskey is a Senior Lecturer and Deputy Head of the Institute of Education at the University of Edinburgh. All former teachers, each of them have conducted extensive research in citizenship education, social inclusion and restorative approaches to conflict in schools.

Praise for the book

Restorative justice raises complex and yet compelling questions, sometimes difficult to define, let alone resolve. They are at the core of debates about the justice system generally and wherever and whenever there is conflict and dispute. This collection of essays is timely for that reason and offers a distinctive contribution, given its focus on restorative approaches in schools; while the perspectives it offers are refreshingly comparative and international. Based on a seminar series supported by the Economic and Social Research Council, based in the UK, the book brings together a number of relevant themes and offers an analysis that is of value both theoretically and practically. The organisation of the book according to the categories, contextualised, contested and catalytic, reflects the intentions of the editors and their contributing colleagues to stimulate debate and reflective practice. The diversity of perspectives offered is also impressive, enabling the volume to appeal to a very wide range of readers interested in the potential of restorative approaches in schools. The bibliography provided by the articles offers a further tool for research and understanding of the important issues raised. I recommend this volume to its readership wholeheartedly.

Professor W. John Morgan,
Chairman of the United Kingdom National Commission for UNESCO
UNESCO Chair of Political Economy and Education
School of Education, University of Nottingham, England

Foreword

Ten years ago, as head teacher of a large primary school in a significant area of deprivation, I found myself constantly dealing with conflict and trying to sort out what had gone wrong. Many of the challenges giving rise to conflict appeared to stem from the relationships, or rather a breakdown in relationships, between children. Misunderstanding and miscommunication often escalated, leaving both parties feeling angry. At that time I was looking for a better way to support children, as on many occasions unresolved issues would spill over into class, affecting learning. It was at this time that I was fortunate to access training in restorative practice through my local authority. This training has had a major influence on my professional practice over the last 10 years. In working with children it has skilled me to better support them in taking responsibility for the harm they have caused, without further shame or humiliation. I also began to understand the importance of involving the children who had been harmed and others who had been affected by what had happened. Changing the language I used and following a restorative script enabled me to facilitate restorative conversations, which focused on the thoughts and feelings of those involved. Empathic listening and the reframing of what has been said are important skills in the restorative process. Developing children's own skills in managing conflict led to the introduction of peer mediation training for upper primary pupils and the setting up of a peer mediation service during break times. Within the school, staff, pupils and parents were involved in the implementation of a restorative approach from the very start. Ensuring all staff had a real awareness of this approach and further training for key staff were essential. Opportunities to involve staff in restorative circles and meetings contributed to the development of a restorative ethos within the school and a real understanding of the process.

In 2004, I took part in a Scottish Government's pilot study of restorative practice being researched by Edinburgh and Glasgow Universities. This was an important development in measuring the impact within the school and helped to set the direction in continuing to embed this approach. The importance of fostering positive relationships became the foundation of the school's promoting positive behaviour policy.

As a head teacher I have seen the difference that restorative practice made in my school, putting relationships at the very heart of everything we do. Now, as a member of the Rights, Support and Wellbeing Team, I continue to lead the development of restorative approaches nationally. This edited book makes a topical and very welcome contribution to the continuing development of restorative approaches.

Lorraine Hunter
Head Teacher: Lawmuir Primary School
Bellshill, North Lanarkshire, Scotland

Acknowledgements

The editors wish to express their gratitude to the Economic and Social Research Council for funding of the seminar series, which took place at the House of Lords, Universities of Cambridge, Edinburgh and Nottingham, 2010–11. We would also like to acknowledge the core group members who attended each seminar and contributed to lively discussion on each theme.

Abbreviations

ESRC	Economic and Social Research Council
EWS	Educational Welfare Service
FGC	Family Group Conference
NGO	Non-Governmental Organisation
RA	Restorative Approach
RAiS	Restorative Approaches in Schools
RJ	Restorative Justice
RP	Restorative Practice
SDQ	Strengths and Difficulties Questionnaire
UN	United Nations
UNESCO	United Nations Educational, Scientific and Cultural Organisation

Chapter 1

Contextualised, contested and catalytic

A thematic introduction to the potential of restorative approaches in schools

Edward Sellman, Hilary Cremin and Gillean McCluskey

Introduction

This edited book addresses the ways in which educational settings and their communities can best encourage and promote positive behaviour and relationships. It examines the potential of restorative approaches in schools as an alternative to the proliferation of policies and practices recommending punitive and zero tolerance responses to 'misconduct', which growing evidence indicates is ineffective in the long-term (Skiba *et al.* 2008).

Restorative approaches are closely related to restorative justice, with the latter referring to a process used in the criminal and youth justice sectors where harm has been caused. It involves an impartial third party facilitating a process whereby an 'offender' (or 'wrong-doer') is held accountable and makes some form of reparation to his or her 'victim'. The victim is placed at the centre of the process, and is given the opportunity to express the ways in which s/he has been affected and to ask questions about the offence (typically – 'Why me?', 'Am I safe?'). Some cases eventually involve a face-to-face meeting, although it is also common for parties to choose shuttle mediation. It has been positively evaluated, and shown to be very effective in diverting young people from crime and reducing re-offending (Sherman and Strang 2007).

In educational and care settings, restorative approaches have been advocated by many as a means of bringing young people in conflict together, to undertake a deeper enquiry of the incident, including who has been affected and who is obliged to make amends, before agreeing their own long-term solution to the problem. A range of processes (e.g. mediation, conferencing) are used to encourage reflection and seeking answers to questions like: What happened? Who has been affected? What were you feeling at the time, and now? How is the other person feeling? What can you do, if applicable, to put things right? It has been seen as an effective complement to behaviour management strategies in schools, and may well contribute to more inclusive and harmonious school cultures (Cremin 2007, Hendry 2009, Hopkins 2004, McCluskey *et al.* 2008, Sellman 2011). Research carried out by Skinns *et al.* (2009) has shown that it can have a positive impact on pupils who are confronted with the consequences of their actions for the first time. It can provide new insights for teachers into the complexities of bullying and conflict between peers and enhanced feelings of empowerment, emotional literacy, and respect amongst teachers and pupils. It has also been shown to improve the quality of relationships, and to restore friendships, or enable young people to simply learn to live with each other (McCluskey *et al.* 2008).

This book will pool together, for the first time in an edited volume, a range of perspectives from international and interdisciplinary theory and practice on restorative approaches to conflict in schools. It draws together the work of key international academics and practitioners who have implemented restorative approaches in educational settings and have lessons to share or questions to raise. Many of these chapters emerged from a seminal and highly successful seminar series, Restorative Approaches to Conflict Resolution in Schools, organised by the editors and funded by the Economic and Social Research Council in the UK (see Cremin *et al.* 2012). This took place between 2010 and 2011, hosted initially at the House of Lords, London, then at the Universities of Cambridge, Edinburgh and Nottingham. The contributions to this book drew on this seminar and upon perspectives from the academic disciplines of education, criminology, law, human rights, philosophy, psychology, psychotherapy, sociology and social policy to examine the nature and potential of restorative approaches in schools.

The book has three main moves, which relate to the thematic structure of the book. In the first section, restorative approaches will be positioned as highly contextualised. It will share practice and insights from around the globe, examine the disciplinary impact of various fields upon assumptions, definitions and implications for practice and show how behaviour in schools is deeply rooted in social, cultural and institutional contexts. The contested nature of restorative approaches will be examined in the second section, debating the assumptions, aims, terminology and implications of applying restorative principles, themselves diverse in origin, in educational settings. The third section addresses the catalytic, or transformative, nature of restorative approaches in schools. It will question whether transformative practice is achievable in educational contexts and share the learning of researchers and practitioners who have successfully implemented restorative approaches. All of the sections will raise critical questions for theory and practice. These include:

*   What are the merits and limitations of various ways of conceptualising restorative approaches?
*   How do cultural and environmental factors influence understanding of restorative approaches in schools?
*   To what degree do different moral and ethical values, and accepted norms and practices, in different academic disciplines, policy and practice contexts impact upon the implementation of restorative approaches?
*   What is the relationship between retributive and restorative approaches to conflict and justice in different academic disciplines and policy contexts, and their implications for schools?

- To what extent can/should restorative approaches be voluntary, non-directive and non-judgemental?
- What is it about the socio-political context of schools that makes it challenging/ possible for restorative approaches to become embedded and effective?
- How can restorative approaches be sustainable within current and future educational policy and practice contexts internationally?

There will be several issues that overlap this thematic structure and are hence examined throughout the text. Here follows a brief introduction to each theme and an overview of the chapters contained within each section.

Contextualised

Howard Zehr – a genuine pioneer in the field – has made it clear that restorative justice is not a particular programme or a blueprint. Whilst it can be seen as a compass pointing in a direction, there is no pure model that can be seen as ideal or that can be simply implemented in any community. Writing in 2002, he noted that:

> The most exciting practices that have emerged in the past years were not even imagined by those of us who began the first programmes, and many more new ideas will surely emerge through dialogue and experimentation. Also, all models are to some extent culture-bound. So restorative justice should be built from the bottom up, by communities, in dialogue assessing their needs and resources and applying the principles to their own situations.
> (Zehr 2002, p. 10)

He values a context-oriented approach that emerges from debate and takes account of local needs and traditions. He is cautious about top-down strategies for implementing restorative justice. In the light of this, the first section of the book takes context as its central organising factor.

Restorative approaches in schools draw upon recent international developments in criminal justice but also upon lessons learned through the study of indigenous communities and the work of truth and reconciliation commissions in post-conflict societies. Lucio Sia begins this section by providing an international overview of how the United Nations and its agencies have applied restorative approaches around the world. He emphasises the contextual nature of the examples included by sharing how policy, legislation, culture and language frame both conflict and its response. This chapter also introduces some key terminology, useful for the rest of the book. The journey of restorative approaches from criminal justice to education is then charted by Judge David Carruthers, who draws upon seminal work in New Zealand to untangle some of the issues concerning the application of principles from one field to another. This chapter is then complemented by Dan Van Ness, who traces the roots of restorative approaches back further to spiritual and tribal communities. In so doing, he argues for a communitarian view with implications for those wishing to inaugurate restorative approaches in schools. He argues the need to move away from an instrumental conceptualisation of intervention, which focuses on programmes and techniques, to greater attention to the cultural nature of institutions, a recurring theme throughout the book.

Three chapters follow by Wendy Drewery, Mirriam Lephalala and Derick Wilson, who discuss restorative approaches in schools from New Zealand, South Africa and Northern Ireland respectively. Drewery's historical analysis of the case for restorative approaches in New Zealand schools raises questions about the relationship between the disciplinary and educative functions of schools. Lephalala discusses 'Ubuntu', a term originating from the Bantu languages of southern Africa that is used for a traditional and time-tested process for resolving conflict in South Africa. She argues that the introduction of Ubuntu and restorative approaches challenge punitive models of discipline in schools. Wilson discusses the broader role of citizenship education as a means of developing trust and understanding for a more secure future in Northern Ireland – a society deeply affected by ethnic and religious conflict in the past.

Two further chapters by Helen Cowie and Carol Hayden, reflect on restorative approaches in schools and care homes. Cowie draws upon psychological perspectives to highlight the positive impact restorative approaches can have in schools but emphasises that such impact is augmented by all members of a peer group playing a role. Finally, Hayden compares the implementation of restorative approaches in educational settings and care homes, discussing the transferability of such approaches from context to context, particularly those also under performance management pressures.

Contested

From a theoretical perspective, restorative justice is essentially a contested concept (Acorn 2004, Cremin *et al.* 2012). It is unlikely that there will ever be one agreed definition. Some theorists have seen the different approaches and practices of restorative justice as forming a continuum (Zehr 2002), whilst others have grouped them into different categories (Johnstone and Van Ness 2007).

Some argue that restorative approaches are beneficial whilst others argue that they can cause harm (e.g. Acorn 2004). Most recognise that much depends on context and on the ways in which it is used (Cremin *et al.* 2012). Several questions present themselves. For example, to what extent are young offenders, or pupils in schools (or their workers and teachers) 'empowered' in any aspect of the judicial process or in processes of schooling? What is meant by the empowerment of the young, the poor and the dispossessed when it comes to the dispensation of 'their' crimes or misdemeanours? Are restorative approaches appropriate when there is a case for transforming the antecedents of the conflict? To what extent can adults in youth offending settings and schools – responsible for the safety, well-being, and educational achievement of large numbers of young people – facilitate in a neutral, non-judgemental and non-directive way? Is it possible for strategies in educational settings that are proactive and preventative to be classed as restorative? And perhaps most significantly, what precisely is being restored?

James MacAllister begins this section by arguing from a philosophical perspective that some present-day attempts to formulate a concept of restorative justice are logically paradoxical. He questions whether 'transformative restoration' is possible, and whether proactive restoration is a useful concept. He draws this together by arguing that advocates of restorative approaches might be well advised to make modest and specific claims about what is distinctive about the contribution of restorative approaches in schools. Hilary Cremin and Brenda Morrison both argue from a social psychological point of view that restorative approaches can cause harm if they attribute misconduct with 'deficient' individuals rather than with the socio-cultural and economic factors that create the conditions of crime, cultural resistance and poverty. There is a real danger of pathologising and criminalising the poor and the dispossessed if, as Van Ness argues in the previous section, restorative procedures and processes are taken off the shelf, rather than embraced in the full spirit of their indigenous and spiritual roots.

Finally, Gillean McCluskey argues that restorative approaches offer the opportunity for a radical re-imagining of the relationship between teachers and students in schools, but that this brings significant challenges to school structures that are often deeply conventional and resistant to innovation, a theme revisited in the final section of chapters. McCluskey *et al.* then conclude this section with a reflection on research approaches that are congruent with restorative values. They question to what extent evaluation, which is positioned 'inside' pilot projects and owned by stakeholders, can be of value to others wanting more standardised research methods and findings? Indeed, are standardised approaches appropriate to evaluate restorative practices at all?

Catalytic?

The final section considers the ways in which restorative approaches provide a catalyst for change or whether such change is necessary before restorative approaches can be implemented (Hopkins 2004). The section begins with a discussion by David and Roger Johnson, who argue that restorative approaches such as peer mediation must be complemented by everyday educational experiences of cooperative learning and constructive controversy in order to augment their impact and prepare young people with the necessary skills to resolve conflict both now, and as adults. This theme is further developed by Kathy Bickmore, who explains how restorative approaches in schools can vary in their degree of depth. She distinguishes between peacekeeping, peacemaking and peacebuilding, arguing that only the latter goes beyond reacting to the symptoms of conflict to transformative practices where conflict is managed more creatively and constructively. She also emphasises the need for everyday educational practices, such as circles, for developing the necessary attitudes and skills to embrace conflict in this way.

Three chapters follow, which address the requirements of creating the restorative school. In the first of these, Nancy Riestenberg draws upon her experience supporting the implementation of restorative approaches in numerous schools in Minnesota, US. She discusses the challenges to implementation faced by regional and institutional policies, particularly those limiting funding and advocating punishment. Edward Sellman then discusses the impact that effective implementation of restorative approaches in schools can have upon teacher and student roles, power relationships and language. He argues that schools frequently underestimate the degree of cultural transformation required for restorative approaches to be both successful and sustained. Shelagh McCall then questions how restorative approaches and hierarchical structures in schools will dovetail and critiques the requirement of facilitators to remain neutral during restorative processes. Drawing upon Ury (2000), she suggests the concept of 'omni-partiality' as an alternative, which encourages facilitators to be on multiple sides at the same time.

In the penultimate chapter, Mary Meredith and Edward Sellman raise the question 'Who misses out from restorative approaches in schools?'. Using students with communication difficulties and the restorative conference as examples, they argue that those who often most need restorative approaches are those who experience the greatest challenge in participating fully. They suggest some considerations for making such processes more inclusive. Finally, Richard Hendry, Belinda Hopkins and Brian Steele reflect on the process of clarifying and communicating the key principles of restorative approaches to schools. They share a text they have developed with this precise aim in mind, which also serves as a quick introduction to terminology for readers not familiar with the aims and characteristics of restorative approaches in schools, located at the end of this volume.

A brief note on terminology

Throughout this volume there will be a tendency to avoid acronyms, unless it is necessary to the economy of individual chapters. With respect to individuals, this is to recognise the agency of young people and to avoid any collusion with labelling of groups. Acronyms are also generally avoided when describing initiatives as to avoid the impression that restorative approaches can be packaged and branded into neat programmes.

As discussed in several chapters, the concept of restorative justice itself has developed within criminal justice and its terminology is thus not easily transferable to the school context. Hence, in schools, there has thus been a preference for the term 'restorative approach' or 'restorative practices' in place of 'restorative justice', to 'fairness' in preference to 'justice' and 'harmer' and 'harmed' rather than 'victim' and 'offender'. In some chapters it will be necessary to use a range of terms to clarify and enhance debate but otherwise the term 'restorative approaches in schools' will be used throughout the text, subsuming restorative justice, practices and related terminology.

Finally, different terms are used to describe various levels of schooling and the nature of their funding in different countries. This can be confusing, so to aid clarity, the terms primary and secondary will be used generically to refer to schools for pupils under and over 11 years of age respectively. The term 'state', rather than 'public' school will be used to refer to any school funded by local, regional and/or national government, as in some contexts public actually means private.

A brief note on how to read this book

The contributors to this book include leading academics and educators and thus there is a good balance between theory and practice. This volume will therefore have a broad appeal to initial teacher training courses and postgraduate education courses as it engages with core issues; particularly behaviour and citizenship. It will also appeal to relevant modules on law and social policy degrees. It shares contemporary research, thinking and practice and hence will be extremely valuable for researchers, policymakers and educators interested in considering restorative approaches in educational contexts or wishing to further improve such services.

As previously indicated, the book has been carefully organised to a thematic structure so we hope you feel able to read the whole book. However, each chapter stands by itself and can be read independently. Chapters by Sia, Cowie, and Johnson and Johnson provide a particularly helpful introduction for anyone unfamiliar with restorative terminology and approaches. This is particularly the case with the final chapter by Hendry, Hopkins and Steele, who share a pamphlet written for schools as a means of introducing key values, concepts and approaches. If you've never read anything about restorative approaches to conflict in schools before, we suggest you read this pamphlet first.

References

Acorn, A. (2004) *Compulsory Compassion: A Critique of Restorative Justice*. Vancouver: UBC Press.

Cremin, H. (2007) *Peer Mediation: Citizenship and Social Inclusion Revisited*. Milton Keynes: Open University Press.

Cremin, H., Sellman, E. and McCluskey, G. (2012) 'Interdisciplinary Perspectives on Restorative Justice: Developing Insights for Education'. *British Journal of Educational Studies*, 60 (4), 421–437.

Hendry, R. (2009) *Building and Restoring Respectful Relationships in Schools: A Guide to using Restorative Practice*. Abingdon: Routledge.

Hopkins, B. (2004) *Just Schools: A Whole School Approach To Restorative Justice*. London: Jessica Kingsley Publishers.

Johnstone, G. and Van Ness, D. (eds) (2007) *Handbook of Restorative Justice*. Cullompton: Willain Publishing.

McCluskey, G., Lloyd, G., Kane, J., Stead, J., Riddell, S. and Weedon, E. (2008) 'Can Restorative Practices in Schools make a Difference?'. *Educational Review*: Special Issue: Truancy, Disaffection, Anti-social behaviour and the Governance of Children. 60(4): 405–417.

Sellman, E. (2011) 'Peer Mediation Services for Conflict Resolution in Schools: What Transformations in Activity Characterise Successful Implementation?' *British Educational Research Journal*, 37, 1, 45–60.

Sherman, L.W. and Strang, H. (2007) 'Restorative Justice: The Evidence, London: Smith Institute'. Available from: <www.esmeefairbairn.org.uk/docs/RJ_full_report.pdf>.

Skiba, R., Reynolds, C. R., Graham, S., Sheras, P., Conoley, J. C. and Garcia-Vazquez, E. (2008) 'Are Zero Tolerance Policies Effective in the Schools?', *American Psychologist*, 63, 852–862.

Skinns, L., Du Rose, N. and Hough, M. (2009) *An Evaluation of Bristol RAiS*. London: Institute for Criminal Policy Research, Kings College London.

Ury, W. (2000) *The Third Side: Why We Fight and How We Can Stop*. New York: Penguin.

Zehr, H. (2002) *The Little Book of Restorative Justice*. Intercourse: Good Books.

Part 1

Contextualised

Chapter 2

Restorative justice

An international perspective

Lucio Sia

Introduction

Restorative justice and restorative processes focus on redressing the harm done to the victims, holding offenders accountable for their actions and often engaging the community in the resolution of conflict. Participation of the parties is an essential part of the process that emphasises relationship building, reconciliation and the development of agreements around a desired outcome between victim and offender. The victim, the offender and the community regain some control over the process. The process itself can often transform the relationship between the community and the justice system as a whole. Restorative justice processes can be adapted to various cultural contexts and the needs of different communities. This chapter illustrates how restorative justice and restorative approaches are contextual. It cites the work and the contribution of the United Nations and its agencies in this field and provides examples of applied restorative approaches around the world.

Context certainly plays a primary role in any conflict or dispute resolution as it determines the best way to proceed in achieving justice. The success of restorative justice initiatives depends on the context, and several considerations must be accounted for to ensure successful outcomes. The different parties involved will directly or indirectly influence the process and resolution of the issues at hand. Context involves the community, be it the smaller community of secondary victims (people who may have suffered because of the nature of their relationship with the victim or offender), communities of support (those who may not be directly linked to the offender or the victim but have an ongoing concern) or a broader group of neighbours or local government representatives. The nature of the offence, the conditions and inclinations of those involved and actual or potential risks have to be evaluated when conceiving the appropriateness or benefits of engaging the community.

Context also concerns culture and tradition, which play an essential part in the pursuit of justice. A classic example is the South African Truth and Reconciliation Commission, where the spirit of 'Ubuntu'; the 'healing of breaches, the redressing of imbalances and the restoration of broken relationships' (Roche 2006: 2) provided a foundation for the country's restorative justice process. Likewise, in New Zealand, an effective implementation of restorative justice can be found through the family conferencing approach, patterned on traditional Maori and contemporary practices, evolving into a mandatory model for juvenile justice. In these family conferences, the young offender, teachers, social workers, family, victims and others join together to determine and agree upon payments (financial or non-financial payments), service, apologies and behaviour plans as an alternative to incarceration. Another example, also in New Zealand, involves the settlement process of the Treaty of Waitangi,[1] where emphasis of the settlement is on the restoration of tribal power and prestige, as opposed to lands and resources. The focus is not on the full restoration of Maori land or financial compensation. Instead, the settlements account for apology, the restoration of the tribal economic base and the return of significant sites and other forms of cultural repair. Reconciliation and the restoration of dignity are given priority over material gains or allocation of resources (Gibbs 2006).

Other examples of cultural differences as they relate to restorative justice involve the understanding of the concept of 'human rights' and the concept of 'crime'. The Western concept of human rights focuses on the individual who is allocated a specific legal status, as opposed to an extended family, community or language group. The European concept of 'crime' is viewed by the Navajo tribes of North America as 'disharmony'. Navajo justice customarily believes that the victim and the offender must be restored to a state of harmony. The emphasis is on finding the origins behind the injustice instead of laying blame, in order to address the root causes of disharmony. The conferences or circles do not aim to find guilt or blame but to determine how to best compensate or rehabilitate the victim and how to treat and reintegrate the offender. In this case, the seat of power does not lie in the hands of a single judge and restorative approaches are decided collectively with less formal rules and standards. Some conferences or circles may be referred to more formal legal proceedings if the victim is not satisfied with the redress.

Hence, restorative justice may be practiced in a variety of ways depending on context. Reconciliation, confrontation and communication may be either direct or indirect between victims and offenders. For instance, in the wake of certain serious crimes, allowing face-to-face communication can make matters worse or cause excessive pain, as in cases of murder or sexual crimes. Restorative justice may also be private and confidential as in the Truth and Reconciliation Commissions (see the Truth and Reconciliation website www.justice.gov.za/trc/).

As noted from above, differing contexts and diverging world views of justice are important considerations in the application of the principles and philosophy behind restorative justice. Understanding the cultural context of the group where the offence has been committed may assist in developing an appropriate intervention as group-based rights systems may have greater significance in non-Western or indigenous contexts. Restorative justice is recognised in its capacity to repair systemic harm, particularly in inequitable societies such as indigenous communities, because it considers social and cultural norms and social sanctioning elements that form the core of many indigenous justice systems.

As an approach, restorative justice has extensive implications and potential and can provide an opportunity for indigenous values to obtain internationally recognised legitimacy and application. The United Nations (UN) and its different agencies have recognised this potential, and have consequently developed substantive work on restorative justice. During the Tenth United Nations Congress on the Prevention of Crime and Treatment of Offenders, the *Vienna Declaration on Crime and Justice: Meeting the Challenges of the Twenty-first Century* (2000) advocated the 'development of restorative justice policies, procedures and programmes that are respectful of the rights, needs and interests of victims, offenders, communities and all of the parties' (Vienna Declaration on Crime and Justice 2000).

In August 2002, the UN Economic and Social Council adopted a resolution calling upon Member States implementing restorative justice programmes to draw on a set of *Basic Principles on the Use of Restorative Justice Programmes in Criminal Matters*. In 2005, the declaration of the Eleventh UN Congress on the Prevention of Crime and the Treatment of Offenders (2005) urged Member States, for very practical reasons, to recognise the importance of further developing restorative justice policies, procedures and programmes that include alternatives to prosecution. This is so because restorative justice programmes can be used to reduce the burden on the criminal justice system, or divert cases out of the system and provide a range of constructive sanctions instead.

UNESCO's Asia Pacific Network for International Education and Values Education (APNIEVE) has been active in restorative justice processes in the classroom, particularly in Australian schools, through the Victorian Association for Restorative Justice and the Association of School Councils in Victoria. The UNESCO Office in Brasilia promotes the use of RJ processes for youth in Brazil. The UNESCO Chair and Institute of Comparative Human Rights in the University of Connecticut, in its human rights education, promotes the understanding of the processes and relevance of restorative justice. UNESCO's Associated Schools Project Network (ASPnet) supports and encourages innovative programmes such as restorative practice projects in different schools worldwide.

Features and conceptions of restorative justice

There are many terms that are used to describe the restorative justice movement. These include communitarian justice, making amends, positive justice, relational justice, reparative justice, community justice and restorative justice. Restorative justice gives as much importance to the process as to the outcome. In Europe and in many parts of the world the process is often referred to as 'mediation' as distinct from legal adjudication.

The UN Handbook on Restorative Justice Programmes (2006) mentions some features of RJ programmes:

- A flexible and variable approach that can be adapted to the circumstances, legal tradition, principles and underlying philosophies of established national criminal justice systems.
- A particularly suitable response to crimes, where juvenile offenders are involved and in which an important objective of the intervention is to teach the offenders some new values and skills.
- A response that recognises the role of the community as a prime site of preventing and responding to crime and social disorder.

The UN handbook also delineates underlying assumptions of restorative justice programmes:

- the response to crime should repair as much as possible the harm suffered by the victim;
- offenders should be brought to understand that their behaviour is not acceptable and that it has some real consequences for the victim and community;
- offenders can and should accept responsibility for their action;
- victims should have an opportunity to express their needs and to participate in determining the best way for the offender to make reparation;
- the community has a responsibility to contribute to this process.

A key feature of restorative justice is that the response to criminal behaviour focuses not only on the offender and the offence. Peacemaking, dispute resolution and rebuilding relationships are viewed as the primary methods for achieving justice and supporting the victim, the offender and for interests of the community. It can also be helpful for identifying underlying causes of crime and developing crime prevention strategies. Several different conceptions or ideas about what restorative justice is have emerged.

One understanding is what has been called the 'encounter' conception (Johnson and Van Ness 2006). This focuses on the meeting together of parties to discuss the crime, its consequences and what should be done to rectify the situation. Persons who work within this conception could suggest that restorative processes be used even when there has not been a crime, such as when neighbours have a conflict or whenever a family needs to solve a problem.

A second idea is the 'reparative' conception. This focuses on the need to repair the harm resulting from crime. People who work within this conception agree that this is best done in a restorative process (encounter) but are willing to find other ways to repair the harm even if there is no encounter process, for instance if the offender is never caught or the victim is unwilling to participate.

The third idea has been called the 'transformative' conception. This is the broadest perspective as it not only embraces encounter and reparation, but also focuses on structural and individual injustice. For instance, it draws attention to structural injustice by identifying and attempting to resolve underlying causes of crime such as poverty or idleness. However, it also challenges individuals to apply restorative justice principles in their interaction with those around them and to their environment. This can even generate internal spiritual transformation as it calls for external societal transformation.

Should everything be labelled as 'RJ' (Restorative Justice) or are there aspects that are complementary but different? Controversies on what restorative justice is or what it is not arise. For instance the following questions have been raised in the UN handbook:

Is there a role for punishment in restorative justice? Some argue that there is none because the purpose of restorative justice is to repair harm and not to cause more harm. Others, while agreeing with this, think that restorative processes have many features of punishment such as having to pay a price for violation.

Are victim support services and offender reintegration programmes restorative justice? If there is no encounter, those who have an encounter perception would say that while victim support services and offender reintegration programmes are valuable, they are not restorative justice. Those working on reparative and transformative conceptions would likely say that they are restorative.

What happens if a victim or offender is not willing or able to participate in a restorative process? There are a number of ways that a party might participate. If victims cannot participate personally, they can participate indirectly e.g. sending a representative or communicating their views in writing or in some other way. If they are not interested or are unable to participate even indirectly, those who work in the encounter conception would conclude that there is no suitable restorative response. Those who work in the reparative and transformative conception would explore other reparative options such as victim support services and offender reintegration programmes and the possibilities of inviting victims to meet with other offenders – not necessarily their own offender – to discuss general issues of crime and justice.

Can there be restorative justice in an unjust world? Some people are long-term victims of systemic injustice. Can violators be held accountable for injustice without taking substantial steps to address the underlying injustice? Those who work within the transformative conception would say that systemic injustices as well as individual injustices must be confronted. Those who work within the encounter and the reparative conceptions would say that restorative justice does not compel this.

The use of restorative justice for certain types of offences is more controversial than for others. What is most controversial in a given context depends on a number of factors, including the characteristics of the community, the cultural context or the nature of the programme. The use of restorative justice in cases of domestic violence and sexual assault, for instance, is often controversial. Some advocates of restorative justice see it as appropriate, subject to carefully thought out practices and safeguards, for all types of offences and advocate the extension of restorative justice programmes to domestic violence and sexual assaults. Others, including some women's organisations, have expressed concerns that a restorative approach may re-victimise women victims and not provide adequate denunciation of the offending behaviour (UN 2006).

Restorative approaches and restorative justice across cultures

Aspects of the restorative justice approach are found in many cultures. The first ESRC seminar discussed practices in Australia and Canada, where indigenous informal participation in sentencing procedures has been occurring in remote communities for some time. Many of them are informal. In many African countries, customary law may provide a basis for rebuilding the capacity of the justice system, where restoration of social responsibility, reconciliation between the offender and the victim and a sense of justice are the primary aims. In south-eastern Nigeria and many parts of West Africa, the 'age grade' systems encourage reconciliation within communities through peer group interventions. In Uganda, the local council courts have the power to grant remedies such as compensation, restitution, reconciliation or apology, as well as more coercive measures. In the Philippines, the *Barangay* justice system consists of a locally-elected *Barangay* captain and a 'peacekeeping committee' who hear cases involving conflicts between residents. There is a mediation session that is facilitated by the captain or another member of the committee. Agreements reached through this process are legally binding and are recognised by the courts.

Victim–offender mediation programmes were among the earliest restorative justice initiatives. In the Czech Republic, the Probation and Mediation Service is involved in pre-trial and court proceedings in an attempt to mediate effective and pro-social resolutions to crime-related conflicts. Mediation may only be carried out with the voluntary consent of the two parties. Mediators are skilled in effective negotiations. They help the disputing parties to settle their conflict and to find a mutually acceptable solution to the situation. Their task is to manage the negotiation process, to create conditions allowing understanding between the participants and to reach a solution that takes both parties' interests into account.

In New Zealand in 1989, a community and family group conferencing model was adopted into national legislation and applied to the youth justice process. The majority of cases are now handled by the police through restorative caution and by police-directed or court family group conferencing. It is based on the dispute resolution traditions of the Maori. This model is now also widely used in modified form as a police initiated diversion approach in South Australia, South Africa, Ireland, Lesotho, as well as in the US cities of Minnesota, Pennsylvania and Montana. Each conferencing process has a convenor or facilitator. It brings together the family and friends of both the victim and the offender and sometimes also other members of the community to participate in a professionally facilitated process to identify desirable outcomes for the parties, address the consequences of the crime and explore appropriate ways to prevent the offending behaviour from reoccurring. The mandate of family group conferencing is to confront the offender with the consequences of the crime, develop a reparative plan and, in more serious cases (in the New Zealand model), determine the need for more restrictive supervision or custody. In Australia and the US, police officers generally serve as primary gatekeepers, while in South Africa it is the prosecutors who fulfil this role. Community conferencing is also used sometimes as an alternative measure to which an offender can be diverted from the criminal justice system. Such programmes tend to be managed by community groups or agencies with or without financial support from the government. The offender's compliance with the terms of agreement may or may not function under the direct supervision of law enforcement or justice officials.

Peacemaking committees operate in Zwelethemba (South Africa). The process started as an experiment in 1997, aimed at mobilising local knowledge and capacity on issues of dispute resolution and community building. The peace committees are made up of local township residents who undertake both peacemaking and peace building. Peacemaking involves resolving specific conflicts while peace building addresses the underlying problems in the community such as poverty or lack of access to services. Peacemaking activities deal with a range of legal disputes, including both civil and criminal matters. The peace committees initially received almost all of their referrals directly from the community, not from the police or the courts. As the project evolved, there has been increased interaction with state agencies, notably the police. The peacemaking process does not involve adjudication but rather focuses on discovering what can be done to reduce or eliminate the problem. The outcomes of peacemaking meetings are restorative in nature: apologies, restitution and compensation.

Sentencing circles are conducted in many aboriginal communities in Canada. In circle sentencing, all participants: the judge, defence counsel, prosecutor, police officer, the victim and the offender and their respective families and community residents, sit facing one another in a circle. Circle sentencing is generally available to those offenders who plead guilty. Discussions among those in the circle are designed to reach a consensus about the best way to resolve the conflict and dispose of the case, taking into account the need to protect the community, the needs of the victims, and the rehabilitation and punishment of the offender. The sentencing circle process is typically conducted within the criminal justice process, includes justice professionals and supports the sentencing process. The outcome of the circle is generally submitted to the judge, who may or may not have participated directly in the circle, and is not binding on the court. Circle sentencing is an example of how the principles of restorative justice can be applied within a holistic framework in which justice system personnel share power and authority with community members. In contrast to the formal and often adversarial approach to justice, circle sentencing can help reacquaint individuals, families and communities with problem-solving skills, rebuild relationships, promote awareness and respect for values and the lives of others, address the needs and interests of all parties – including the victim, and focus action on causes, not just symptoms of problems.

Restorative justice around the world

Africa

Restorative justice in Africa has been highlighted by the recovery of indigenous justice practices, the use of community service to address chronic prison overcrowding, national restorative responses to genocide and civil war, and the South African Truth and Reconciliation Commission.

Asia

In Asia, interest in restorative justice has particularly focused on juvenile justice, on regularising indigenous practices and on peacemaking and reconciliation in divided societies.

Europe

Restorative justice in Europe is characterised by experimentation in different areas with input from both government and community actors. With a diversity of systems and cultures in the region, the development of restorative initiatives has been used to address issues as diverse as juvenile justice in many countries, alternatives to paramilitary violence in Northern Ireland, and justice reform needs in Eastern Europe.

Latin America

Latin American experiments with restorative justice developed in response to a variety of needs including justice reforms to counteract increasing rates of crime and violence while increasing citizen confidence in justice systems; national reconciliation efforts after years of civil war; and communities looking for alternative ways of addressing violence and conflict to create a 'culture of peace'.

Middle East

Restorative justice experiments are beginning in the Middle East. Some are related to the use of traditional processes for conflict resolution while others deal with child welfare and juvenile justice issues.

North America and the Caribbean

Restorative justice in North America has arisen out of various sources such as indigenous practices of First Nations people, a discontent with the justice system, and a need to meet the needs of victims. It is currently being applied in various areas from prison to schools to child welfare issues.

Pacific

In the Pacific region, restorative justice is well established as a manner of responding to crime. With roots in indigenous practices, restorative justice is being used to address crime, school discipline, and other types of conflicts.

Source: http://www.restorativejustice.org/university-classroom/02world

Examples of restorative programmes for youth: Restorative practices in schools

Many programmes have been developed for use with youth in conflict with the law and have also provided the basis for the subsequent development of programmes for adult offenders. Restorative programmes offer effective alternatives to the formal and alienating youth justice measures. Because of their educational value, they are particularly useful in diverting youth from incarceration or expulsion from schools and provide alternative measures that would otherwise deprive a young person's liberty. Many such programmes offer opportunities to create a community of care around youth in conflict with the law. Gaining public support for restorative justice programmes for youth is relatively easier. In many countries, juvenile justice legislation provides specifically for the creation of diversion programmes for youth, which can be developed in line with restorative justice principles. Moreover, many programmes developed completely outside of the criminal justice system, in schools or in the community, can provide an opportunity for the community to respond appropriately to minor offences and other conflicts without formally criminalising the behaviour or the individual. A number of programmes including peer mediation and conflict resolution circles already exists in schools that facilitate a response to minor youth crime (such as fights, violent bullying, minor theft, vandalism of school property, extortion of pocket money) that may otherwise have become the object of a formal criminal justice intervention.

Restorative approaches include peer mediation, circles (peacemaking circles) and community conferencing. Practical steps include: training key staff in process skills; enhancing peer mediator and/or similar programmes; providing forums to introduce restorative practices to members of the school community; appointing one or more staff members to programme-coordinator positions; developing community-based partnership with local providers of social services such as parenting workshops.

Conferencing has now been used extensively in schools in Australia and New Zealand, Canada, the US, the UK and other parts of Western and Central Europe, and in some pilot programmes in South East Asia. The process has had various titles but 'group conferencing' or 'community conferencing' are now probably the most widely used. The results from early-evaluated programmes have largely been replicated, with high levels of participant satisfaction in process and outcome, and high levels of compliance with agreements. Brenda Morrison, then of the Australian National University provided her overview of current practices:

> ...education systems in a number of countries are realising that a whole school approach to behaviour management requires (i) that members of a school community have access to practices that support pro-social behaviour; (ii) systems to support practices; (iii) data to support policy making about systems.
>
> (Morrison 2000)

The ensuing discussion illustrates some initiatives that have been developed worldwide. These programmes are in line with UNESCO's Associated Schools Network (ASPnet) goal to promote peace and international cooperation through education. Schools that are part of the ASPnet undertake projects that prepare young people to meet current challenges. ASPnet teachers and students work together to develop innovative educational approaches, methods and materials at the local, national and global levels.

The Society for Safe and Caring Schools and Communities (SACSC) in Canada, has special programmes and projects such as Peer Mentoring and Youth Action Programmes which conduct research among their peers and then develop, implement and evaluate projects that address the issues and interests they reveal. The SACSC 'offers knowledge and skills for educators, parents, and community helpers to respectfully work with children in a safe, non-coercive environment to help them learn self-discipline and become productive, principled citizens. This restorative approach helps participants understand their behaviour and provides problem-solving skills that strengthen people as they learn to fix their mistakes, repair relationships, and return balance to their lives. Self-discipline results in improved self-esteem, healthier relationships, and increased achievement. In schools where the SACSC Restorative Justice approach is implemented as a part of the SACSC comprehensive programme, it is expected that discipline incidents will continue to decline, school attendance increase, grades improve, and students, staff and parents enjoy a more caring school community. Negative behaviour does not need to be criminal to benefit from this approach, but simply cause an issue that negatively impacts individuals, classrooms or the school as a whole' (SACSC www.sacsc.ca/special_programs.htm). The SACSC Restorative Justice Program was developed through funding from the Alberta Solicitor General and Ministry of Public Security.

The UNESCO office in Brasilia is collaborating actively on restorative justice programmes in the country. There are a number of youth-centred mediation and conferencing projects throughout Brazil that incorporate the philosophy and principles of restorative justice, for instance, the Youth Justice System in Porto Alegre. This system is experimenting with conferencing for young offenders. The Children and Adolescent Act of 1990 allows the presiding youth court judge to suspend the legal proceedings for first-time offenders involved in less serious crimes and for the use of sanctions such as community service and reparation. The Porto Alegre youth justice system is piloting use of this restorative process for young offenders.

Youth Offenders Panels operate in England and Wales. A widely-used method which has some restorative features is the 'referral order'. Young offenders, aged 10–17, appearing in court for the first time, are referred to youth offender panels (unless their offence is so serious as to require custody). A panel consists of two trained members of the community, one of whom acts as the chairperson and one professional. The panels are attended by the young person and a parent or guardian. The victim, if any, and a person who may have a good influence on the young person may also be invited. The panel decides on an action plan through which the young person can make reparation and address his or her problems. The panel meets again at the end of the order to assess progress. Young persons who offend again may be given a reparation order. The victim may be invited to meet the offender to express his or her feelings about the offence and consider what form reparation should take, but the decision remains with the court (Newburn *et al.* 2001).

Building on customary justice practices

In many countries, especially in rural and post-conflict countries, the justice system has collapsed and people have to rely on their own practices to settle disputes. It is possible to build on customary justice practices based on the application of restorative justice principles. In the Democratic Republic of Congo, due to the absence of courts, most people consult their chiefs and elders for settlements of disputes including serious criminal matters. The State justice is used mostly when an official stamp is needed (e.g. in civil matters concerning guardianship and adoption). Owing to the displacement of communities and corruption of traditional chiefs and elders, new mechanisms have been developed by NGOs (Non Governmental Organisations) and faith groups to assist people in dispute resolution. For instance, *Héritiers de la Justice*, a non-governmental organisation, has set up a committee for *Mediation and Defence*. The members of the committees are trained in human rights and mediation skills and provided with basic introduction to the relevant laws.

In Bangladesh, a traditional dispute resolution mechanism at the village level (*salish*) involving village headmen or elders, actively engage the offender and the victim in settling the dispute, with the goal of reaching a mutually agreed solution. The process is highly participatory and results are usually complied with because they have been agreed to by both sides, and because there is community pressure from the villagers who ensure compliance.

In conclusion, restorative justice is gaining worldwide momentum owing to its adaptability to different cultures and contexts, its ability to resolve conflicts constructively and its capacity to provide viable alternative solutions.

Note

1 The 1840 Treaty of Waitangi involved British and Maori groups, where vast amounts of land were ceded to the British with little understanding from the Maori chiefs of property ownership or sovereignty.

References

Gibbs, M. (2006) 'Justice as reconciliation and restoring mana in New Zealand's Treaty of Waitangi settlement process', *Political Science*, 58 (2): 15–27.

Johnson, G. and Van Ness, D. (eds) (2006) 'The Meaning of Restorative Justice', *The Handbook on Restorative Justice*. Cullompton: Willan Publishing.

Morrison, B. (2000) *From Bullying to Responsible Citizenship: A Restorative Approach to Building Safe School Communities*. Sydney: Federation Press.

Newburn, T., Masters, G., Earle, R., Golfie, S., Crawford, A., Sharpe, K., Netten, A., Hale, C., Uglow, S. and Saunders, R. (2001) *The Introduction of Referral Orders into the Youth Justice System*. London: Home Office, RDS Occasional Paper No. 70.

Roche, D. (2006) 'Dimensions of restorative justice', *Journal of Social Issues*, 62 (2): 217–238.

UN Handbook on Restorative Justice Programmes (2006) Criminal Justice Handbook Series, UN: New York.

Vienna Declaration on Crime and Justice: Meeting the Challenges of the Twenty-first Century, 10th United Nations Congress on the Prevention of Crime and the Treatment of Offenders, Vienna, 10–17 April 2000, A/CONF. 184/4/Rev.3, para.29.

Chapter 3

The journey from criminal justice to education

Utilising restorative justice practices in schools in New Zealand

David J. Carruthers

New Zealand is a world leader in adopting restorative justice practices in the youth justice system. The Children, Young Persons and their Families Act 1989 heralded the introduction of the Family Group Conference (FGC). Experience with these led to similar restorative practices being legislatively recognised in the adult criminal justice system. Recently, educators have started applying the principles of restorative justice to discipline in schools. Common sense suggests what works in one area should work equally well in the other. This paper outlines the restorative justice system in New Zealand, before considering the congruity of these ideas in the school system.

Restorative justice in New Zealand courts

Many consider New Zealand to be a country that leads the world in this area. The Māori population has always had a well-developed system of custom and practice that ensured the stability of their societies, one that had much in common with restorative philosophy. There were a number of important elements to this. When there was a breach, community process enabled a consideration of the interests of the *whanaungatanga* (social group) and ensured the integrity of the social fabric. Through *whanau* (family) or *hapu* (wider family) meetings, and on occasion *iwi* (tribal) meetings, the voices of all parties could be heard, and decisions could be arrived at by consensus (*kotahitanga*). The aim was to restore the *mana* (prestige/ authority) of the victim, the victim's family and the family of the offender, and to ensure measures were taken to restore the future social order of the wider community. Because these concepts were given meaning in the context of the wider group, retribution against an individual offender was not seen as the primary mechanism for achieving justice. Rather, the group was accountable for the actions of the individual (*manaakitanga*) and for compensation of the aggrieved. This could even take the form of *utu* (balancing the scales) that involved the offended party and their kinsmen acting as a raiding party and plundering the offender and their kin of an agreed amount of food or other resources.

It is certainly ironic that 150 years after Europeans abolished the Māori customary system by introducing adversarial British criminal justice, Parliament legislated for a system that operates from the same restorative philosophy in which the Māori system was grounded.

Restorative justice in the youth court

The enactment of the Children, Young Persons and their Families Act 1989 introduced a philosophical sea change in the youth justice system. Prior to this legislation, many youth offenders were sent to child welfare institutions, or in serious cases, detention centres, borstals or corrective training institutions; places where they would further develop their 'bad boy/girl' image and learn new anti-social and criminal behaviours. While there was some reform of the court system in 1974, (particularly notable was the introduction of diversion) these procedures were seen as not working, and the new Children's and Young Persons Court was consequently too active. The failure of the system to prevent re-offending, and the manner in which it encouraged dependency on the welfare of the State, can be seen as major defects of the previous system. Further factors that influenced calls for change are summarised by Maxwell:

> Concern for children's rights; new approaches to effective family therapy; research demonstrating the negative impact of institutionalism on children; inadequacies in the approach taken in the 1974 legislation to young offenders; the failure of the criminal justice system to take account of issues for victims; experimentation with new models of service provision and approaches to youth offending in the courts; and concerns raised by Māori about the injustices that had been involved in the removal of children from their families.
>
> (Maxwell, 2007: 46)

These factors converged and saw the incoming Labour government of 1984 establish a working group to overhaul the youth justice system. Legislation introduced in 1986 was, however, widely criticised, particularly by Māori, as being too paternalistic. The government listened to the criticisms and a Select Committee travelled the country to hear submissions on how the Bill needed to be changed. In the meantime, the youth court itself had launched restorative initiatives; one of these led by Judge (soon to be Principal Youth Court Judge) M.J.A. Brown. Those initiatives, not then seen as restorative, were inclusive of victims, family and community and drew their inspiration from early experiments in family decision-making.

A report by Mike Doolan, Chief Social Worker at the Department of Social Welfare, was also highly influential. It suggested utilising Family Group Conferences as a diversionary process that would allow community ownership of decision-making. The radically altered Bill passed its second and third readings, becoming the Children, Young Persons and their Families Act 1989 and coming into force on 1 November 1989.

Currently, in the youth justice sphere, about one-third of conferences are not directed by the court. They are diversionary conferences initiated and attended by the police, although, unlike in some parts of Australia, Canada and the United Kingdom, the police do not run the conferences. There is always an independent facilitator in charge. If agreement on an outcome can be reached that does not involve the laying of charges, then no charges are laid – so long as the outcome is implemented. The youth court nearly always accepts such plans, recognising that the scheme of the Act places the primary power of disposition with the FGC. However, in serious cases, the court can use a wide range of court-imposed sanctions, the most severe being three months residence in a social welfare institution, followed by six months supervision; or the court may convict and refer the young person to the District Court for sentence under the Criminal Justice Act 1985 (s 283(o)), which can include imprisonment for up to five years.

As with other diversion schemes, if the plan is carried out as agreed, the proceedings are usually withdrawn; if the plan breaks down the court can impose its own sanctions. Thus the court acts as both a backstop (where FGC plans break down) and a filter (for patently unsatisfactory recommendations). The key restorative device is the FGC. It is important to note that these FGCs are mandatory for virtually all youth offender cases and that the FGC, not the court, determines the manner in which the offending should be addressed. Full decision-making power is therefore devolved to the community in which the offending took place.

The origins of restorative justice in the adult court

The absence of legislative backing for restorative justice in adult courts did not deter those (such as Judge McElrea in 1984) who put forward the idea of utilising restorative processes from the youth court in the adult setting. From 1995, adult courts began accepting restorative justice conference recommendations, which started filtering through on an ad hoc basis. The conferences themselves were delivered through community groups with support by the local judiciary. A common theme in the successful adoption of restorative justice processes in New Zealand has been the involvement of the local community, and the utilisation of groups already in existence and working to right problems in local communities. For the most part the necessary infrastructure exists; it simply needs to be supported by the State through the provision of the necessary training and/or funding. The State does not necessarily need to be directly involved in the provision of restorative justice.

All this was admittedly without legislative basis, but in 1998 a case before the Court of Appeal affirmed the right of the New Zealand courts to take account of restorative justice processes. The defendant had been charged with wounding with intent to cause grievous bodily harm. In the District Court there had been a restorative justice conference prior to sentencing at which the victim accepted an apology and made clear that a payment of reparation was preferable to imprisonment (as the latter would have prevented recovering any of the former). The offender had agreed to pay reparation. The District Court Judge took account of that agreement in eventually imposing a suspended two-year sentence with a substantial reparation and community work component. *R v Clotworthy* (1998) 15 CRNZ 651 CA was the Crown appeal from that sentence. The Crown alleged the penalty was insufficient for the offence of wounding with intent to cause grievous bodily harm. While the Court of Appeal substantially agreed, it noted that restorative justice processes should be taken into account when sentencing, and indicated that they can have an impact on the length of sentences to be imposed.

Legislative recognition of restorative justice in the adult criminal justice system was soon to follow. In 1997, the government released a discussion document entitled Sentencing Policy and Guidance. Before the work consequent on that discussion document could be completed, a citizen's initiated referendum was held in conjunction with the 1999 election. It asked: 'should there be a reform of our justice system placing greater emphasis on the needs of victims, providing restitution and compensation for them, and imposing minimum hard labour for all serious violent offences?'

The question is a little ambiguous and perhaps is a good reflection of both restorative and retributive influences in the New Zealand criminal justice system. As one might expect, 91 per cent of voters responded with a 'yes'. The new Labour government committed itself to a reform of sentencing practice and policy which saw the eventual enactment of the Sentencing Act 2002 and Victims Rights Act 2002. The Act contains a number of provisions that acknowledge and encourage the restorative practices which had been occurring on a voluntary basis.

In many ways, the provisions in the Sentencing Act simply reflected what the judiciary and community had been doing in practice for some time, lending legitimacy to those practices. Those practices reflected positive experiences with similar processes adopted in the youth court. As a consequence, when the provisions came into force, the infrastructure, mostly in communities and through community groups, was already in place.

Role of the Ministry of Justice in adult restorative justice

Unlike the Ministry of Social Development whose staff administer the youth justice FGCs, the Ministry of Justice do not have staff directly involved in the delivery of adult restorative justice conferences. Instead, the Ministry of Justice's role is primarily that of a funding body, which also performs a role in supervising the quality of the restorative justice services that an external provider delivers. The Ministry of Justice has been working towards a quality performance supervision role and is developing standards for restorative justice based on the principles of best practice. These aim to provide assurance for victims, offenders, members of the judiciary, public sector stakeholders (such as police) and members of the public about the quality and robustness of restorative justice processes. The standards provide guidelines for:

- Code of ethics.
- Safety.
- Confidentiality and privacy.

- Feedback and complaints.
- Cultural respect.
- Member selection.
- Facilitator training.
- Supervision and debriefing.
- Performance management.
- Criminal records and convictions.

Reflections on the New Zealand experience

It will be noted that there are some key differences between restorative justice practices in the adult and youth justice settings (Consedine 1999). The youth court FGCs are mandatory for virtually all cases, whereas adult restorative justice is accessible only if all involved agree to participate. In the adult court a guilty plea or acceptance of guilt is seen as essential for the restorative justice conference to happen (but not legislatively required), whereas an FGC occurs when an offence is proved or admitted, so there can be cases where the youth may have maintained their innocence throughout. The youth FGC is State-funded and administered, whereas the adult restorative justice processes, evolving without legislative support, have relied heavily on community volunteers and other initiatives. Adult restorative justice conferences are run through independent community groups who receive funding from the Ministry. Judge McElrea suggests that the provision of State funding in the FGC meant that all the professionals involved received training in the relevant principles and philosophies. The judges, lawyers and police officers concerned with the FGC are all specialists in youth justice. In the adult arena the commitment to restorative justice principles among those involved is much more varied. Another difference is the source of referrals to restorative justice. In the youth area a significant proportion of referrals are made even where no charge has been laid in court, whereas only a handful of adults are so referred. The police adult diversion scheme's utilisation of restorative justice as a means to develop the plan 'to make right the wrong' could be expanded further in this respect.

The differences between youth justice and adult justice in the delivery of restorative processes are interesting to note, presenting two potential models for reform and development in education. But perhaps the most substantial difference is that the FGC is mandatory for virtually all youth offenders, while uptake in the adult setting is much more sporadic, depending as it does on the agreement of all involved for it to occur. It may be that in the future, restorative justice conferences should become mandatory for even adult offenders, unless there are strong and good grounds not to do so.

Restorative justice in education

There are clear similarities between the ways we have historically sought to regulate behaviour in the wider community and in the school community. For many years school disciplinary procedures were similar to the procedure traditionally followed by European courts, both in the way responsibility was established and in the way consequences were visited upon those found guilty. Perhaps the most fundamental similarity has been the belief that a tariff-based deterrent sentence is necessary to prevent future offending by the culprit and others in the respective communities. Meting out negative consequences following undesirable conduct has been the primary approach.

The focus in both arenas has therefore traditionally been on finding a suitable punishment for the offender. Little focus has been given to the cause of the offending, and little if any focus has been on teaching new positive behaviours. If we measure success as preventing further offending by the present offender and others in society, both systems have traditionally been found lacking. We must recognise that after the punishment has been exacted, the offender will almost always return to life in the respective community. In what condition do we want that person to return? In the school setting, the final consequences (suspensions and exclusions) prevent the offender from receiving one of the most fundamental tools for building their future; an education. Involvement in education is crime prevention at its best. Finally, both systems have tended to neglect the victims of the offending, both in addressing the harm caused to them and giving them a voice in determining the way in which the wrong committed against them can be righted.

The perceived shortcomings outlined above have all influenced the adoption of restorative justice practices in New Zealand's criminal court systems. Since the same shortcomings can be identified in the education setting, it was inevitable that restorative justice practices would be extended into the school setting.

The New Zealand experience of restorative justice in schools

Restorative justice conferencing was formally introduced into schools in New Zealand in late 1990 as part of a Ministry of Education initiative called the Suspension Reduction Initiative. (There had been many such private initiatives). A group from Waikato University (see Drewery in this volume) was contracted to provide conferencing processes into five schools initially, with 24 schools subsequently sending their staff for training. The group drew on the FGC concept. Suspension in those schools went down. In 2005, Sean Buckley and Dr Gabrielle Maxwell conducted an examination of the experiences of 15 schools in New Zealand who were utilising restorative practices. They reported that there were five common restorative practice methods being employed:

1   *The restorative chat* is a one-on-one private conversation between staff and student where an issue is discussed using a series of questions based on a restorative approach that aims to explore the events, their consequences and how any harm can be repaired (that is, 'What happened?', 'What were you thinking at the time?', 'Who do you think has been affected?', 'How could you have acted differently?' and 'What do you need to make things right?').

2   *The restorative classroom* is an open dialogue held within the classroom to discuss specific conflicts as they arise and how members of the class should approach potential conflict situations before they happen. Often, a class will write down its agreed set of guiding principles and display these within the classroom. At any stage, the class can revisit these principles and make changes. The restorative thinking room is a room specifically set aside for students who have become involved in a conflict situation and who may need time away from peers to regain their composure. Time is spent in the restorative thinking room working through several restorative questions with a staff member and discussing the conflict and how to repair any harm caused.

3   *A restorative mini conference* is held for more serious conflict situations. It includes the victim, the offender, a staff member and perhaps one other individual. The number of those in attendance is limited in order to make it easier for the conference to be quickly arranged and held. The full restorative conference is loosely based on the youth justice family group conference. It may take several days or weeks to organise, because participants are likely to include, though not limited to, victims, offenders, staff, family/*whanau*, officials, and other support personnel. Conferences are used for the most serious of conflict issues and can take several hours.

Buckley (2007) notes that, much like the adult criminal justice system, some of the schools have been unable to secure the funding required to move to a fully restorative practice and so have been forced to operate between management paradigms, either reverting to one based on exclusionary processes or mixing this with a restorative process when only limited support exists for restorative options. That has also been the experience in the adult court system, however, and it should not necessarily be seen as a disadvantage. The brief outline of the different ways restorative justice is used in the New Zealand court system illustrates the different ways restorative justice can and is being used in the school setting while co-existing with the existing exclusionary processes.

4   *As a diversionary procedure.* A restorative justice conference is convened in suitable cases prior to and as an alternative to a formal disciplinary investigation being launched. In the criminal system police are utilising restorative justice conferences to develop a plan for 'righting the wrong' as part of their adult diversion schemes. In the education setting a restorative justice conference is convened to develop a similar plan, the successful completion of which would mean that disciplinary procedures need not be invoked.

5   *As a procedure to be used to determine a suitable sentence/punishment/plan (or to present such exclusion).* In the youth court there is a separation to be found between (a) adjudication upon liability, i.e. deciding whether a disputed charge is proved, and (b) the disposition of admitted or proved offences. The adversary system is retained for the former, while a FGC, a key restorative practice, is utilised for the latter. Something similar is already used in schools. The school could, if it wishes, conduct its usual investigations in order to be

satisfied that the conduct occurred. The next step, (as in the youth court) would be to have a restorative justice conference to which decision-making power in respect of disposition can be devolved. The school board could meet periodically to supervise compliance with the plan developed at the conference, as the youth court does.

The final and full vision of restorative justice in schools envisages a fully restorative approach (whole of culture) to the entire way the school orders itself in all its relationships and every aspect of its functioning; a fully restorative therapeutic learning community. Some schools around the world have already achieved this final form. For others, it will be a step too far and smaller steps need to be taken before espousing wholesale change. One thing is certain, the experience of the criminal justice system in New Zealand has given birth to a new approach to relationship problems in many New Zealand schools. Other countries have had similar successful experiences. Both justice and education have, in this area, much to learn from each other about a process which will always be dynamic, changeable and challenging.

Conclusion

As alluded to in the introduction, despite an international reputation for breaking ground in the restorative arena, New Zealand remains a strongly retributive or punitive society. It has one of the highest rates of imprisonment in the Western world. Faced with crime, the instinct is to punish the offender, to see them suffer for the harm they have caused others, predominantly through imprisonment. Alarmingly, it is said that based on current projections the prison population will continue to rise to the extent we shall need to build more and more prisons. Along with high rates of imprisonment there is disenchantment, particularly on the part of victims of crime but also among defendants, with the criminal justice system itself. Against this view Professor Howard Zehr advocates restorative justice processes as providing a mechanism through which victims' rights may receive greater recognition. Incorporating restorative justice as a mandatory practice at all court events might go some way to lowering our imprisonment rate, and improving on re-conviction rates. It clearly has positive effects for victims, helping them understand the offending action and move on with their lives.

Restorative justice conferences can be a better place than courtrooms for identifying and addressing the underlying causes of crime. In this way restorative justice conferences can be a conduit between the offender and the necessary state agency to provide the services needed for an offender to turn away from crime and/or drug dependency. This is not to say that there should be no punishment for criminal offending, the worst and most dangerous offenders are likely to require incarceration in some form. However, there is support in New Zealand to tilt further still in favour of a restorative approach over a retributive approach to criminal justice in the adult arena. The advantages of restorative justice processes have to do with bringing home wrongdoing in a personal way to the offender himself so that consequences and accountability are foremost. They have to do with meeting the needs of victims so that they can be victims no longer and they have to do with preventing reprisals and revenge. In short they have to do with restoring some peace to communities after terrible things have happened. Restorative justice can be seen to have a most crucial part to play in all of that. The New Zealand experience is that it makes a real difference.

References

Buckley, S. (2007) *Respectful Schools: Restorative Practices in Education. A Summary Report*. Wellington: Office of the Children's Commissioner and The Institute of Policy Studies, School of Government, Victoria University.

Consedine, J. (1999) *Restorative Justice: Healing the Effects of Crime*. Ploughshares, Judge FWM McElrea, 'Customary Values, Restorative Justice and the Role of Prosecutors: A New Zealand Perspective' presented to the Restorative Justice and Community Prosecution Conference, Cape Town, South Africa, 23 February 2007.

Maxwell, G. (2007) 'The Youth Justice System in New Zealand: Restorative Justice Delivered Through the Family Group Conference in Restorative Justice and Practices in New Zealand' (Institute of Policy Studies, VUW).

Thorsborne, M. and Vinegrad, D. (2002) *Restorative Justice Practices in Schools: Rethinking Behaviour Management*. Queenscliff, Victoria: Inyahead Press.

Chapter 4

Restorative justice as world view

Daniel W. Van Ness

Introduction

There is a tendency in the West to view restorative justice/approaches in terms of programmes or techniques. The definition of restorative justice as the meeting of parties to a crime or conflict to arrive at a solution contributes to this understanding because of the questions it raises: Who is present at the meeting? Who convenes and runs it? How are human rights of defendants protected? etc. But for the indigenous peoples who have inspired several well-known restorative practices, these are the natural manifestation of world views that are different from those found in most of Europe and North America (Hadley 2001). Schools attempting to introduce restorative approaches would do well to consider their cultures and to initiate cultural change as they inaugurate restorative approaches to discipline.

A decade ago I chaired the drafting committee for what eventually became the UN Basic Principles on the Use of Restorative Justice Programmes in Criminal Matters (2002). One of the challenges we faced was how to define restorative justice. The Council of Europe had produced guidelines (1999) for its countries on the use of mediation, and we drew from that excellent document in a number of ways. But because their guidelines addressed a particular kind of restorative programme – mediation – and not restorative justice generally, it did not offer much help in defining the broader concept.

It will not surprise you that we had trouble agreeing on a broader definition. In the end we avoided the issue by stating that the guidelines would address restorative justice *programmes*, defining those as either restorative processes or restorative outcomes. For the meaning of restorative processes we adapted the Council of Europe's language:

> any process in which the victim and the offender, and, where appropriate, any other individuals or community members affected by a crime, participate together actively in the resolution of matters arising from the crime, generally with the help of a facilitator. Restorative processes may include mediation, conciliation, conferencing and sentencing circles.
>
> (Council of Europe 1999, par. 3)

What was our justification for taking this approach? First, we needed to offer draft guidelines that Member States, NGOs and individual experts who supported restorative justice could unite behind. They would support a definition of restorative programmes, but did not agree on a definition of the larger concept itself. Second, the rationale for UN action on restorative justice was that restorative processes, being informal and often conducted out of the public's eye, could result in human rights abuses of both offenders and victims. So the need was for guidelines on how to conduct restorative encounters that were relational and informal without violating the rights of the parties. Finally, the UN is probably the last place the restorative justice movement should ask for an authoritative and clear definition of restorative justice since its practitioners, advocates and researchers cannot offer one themselves.

Several years later, as Gerry Johnstone and I discussed the lack of consensus on definition, he recalled an idea from political philosophy called 'essentially contested concepts' (Gallie 1962, Connolly 1993). These are concepts around which there is general agreement about meaning but little if any likelihood of consensus forming around a precise definition. 'Democracy' is an essentially contested concept, for example. Common characteristics of essentially contested concepts are that they are viewed as positive (one wants the label), they are internally complex, and our understanding of them changes over time based on experience and developments.

We identified three basic conceptions of restorative justice that have emerged. The first is the *encounter* conception: people with a stake in a crime or misconduct come together, often with a facilitator's assistance, to discuss what happened, how it affected them and what needs to be done about it. Victim–offender mediation, conferencing, and peacemaking circles are programmatic examples of encounter. The second is the *reparative* conception: crime and misconduct cause a number of kinds of harm and a just response works to repair that harm. Restitution, in-kind services and sometimes community service are examples of this understanding. The third is the *transformative* conception: restorative justice is more than a process and/or outcome. It offers a perspective that changes how we view ourselves, others around us and the structures that influence and constrain us. One begins to think more relationally, for example, which results in modification of everyday behaviour and recognition of systemic injustices that must also be addressed (Johnstone and Van Ness 2007).

There is considerable overlap between these conceptions, enough that we can say that they refer to the same basic idea, but the overlap is not complete. We can imagine an encounter that fails to repair, a reparative response that fails to transform, and transformation that does not include encounter. In general, the scopes of the conceptions are different. Encounter is the most narrowly-focused conception, which is one reason it is possible to draft guidelines about its use. Repair is somewhat broader in scope. And neither has the potential expansiveness of the transformative conception. Restorative justice can become a way of life, certainly a way of seeing life.

So when we speak of restorative approaches, do we have the encounter, reparative or transformative conception in mind, or some combination of the three? The definition of restorative justice that I use most frequently draws from and orders all three:

> Restorative justice seeks to repair the harm caused by crime and misconduct. This is best done by the affected parties as they meet voluntarily to cooperatively find a resolution. When that happens, transformation of people, perspectives and structures can follow.

The primary conception is reparative, but there is a high value given to encounters as the best way to repair all the dimensions of harm. Finally, the definition anticipates, without prescribing, the possibility for transformation to take place.

Restorative cultures

This is a Western, or Northern, definition. It is useful because it holds the focus of restorative justice to the level of policy and programmes. Therefore it can be integrated into existing criminal, juvenile and civil justice systems and to employment, academic and other forms of disciplinary processes without requiring society to adopt or embrace a new world view. This is a criticism made by those who hold to the transformative conception. The aim, they argue, should be to precede, not follow, destructive acts with restorative justice. It should be to 'transform structurally violent, unjust societies into structurally non-violent, just ones' (Gil 2006). In such societies, repair and encounter would be natural responses to wrongdoing.

It is well known that practices reflecting some restorative values at least have been used for thousands of years and continue to be used in indigenous and aboriginal cultures today. While some of the values and practices of these cultures violate modern sensibilities, in those cultures restorative practices are not intriguing, new interventions; rather, they flow naturally from a clear world view.

What is that world view? Sawatsky (2009) studied three communities that self-consciously pursue what he called 'healing justice' in response to wrongdoing (healing justice is very much like restorative justice). The Hollow Water Community in Manitoba, Canada consists of four villages, one of which is made up of Anishinabe or Ojibway people and the other three of Métis peoples (these are people whose parentage is mixed European and First Nations. Canada acknowledges them as an aboriginal group in their own right along with the Inuit and First Nations). The Iona Community was founded in 1938 in Scotland but over time has become a network of Christian peace and justice activists living primarily in Britain. Plum Village is a Buddhist Monastery and training centre in France founded by the Vietnamese Buddhist Monk Thich Nhat Hanh. The purpose of Sawatsky's research was to identify what he called the 'common imagination or logic' (Sawatsky 2009, p. 239) of those communities, which he then contrasted with the imagination or logic of cultures in which contemporary criminal justice flourishes. He concluded that there were six major areas of difference between the two:

- The first has to do with the source of justice. In criminal justice it flows from the government and institutions of society. In healing justice it flows from the Spirit and from the land.
- The second concerns the intentions of justice procedures. In criminal justice it is to observe the relevant rules and to follow established processes. In healing justice the procedures are more concerned with the outcome sought than with correct process.
- The third has to do with responses to harm. Criminal justice looks at it as a problem to be addressed. Healing justice responds with loving kindness to teach those who have forgotten how to act with loving kindness.
- The fourth has to do with identity. Criminal justice labels the victims, offenders and justice professionals. Healing justice focuses on helping them find their essential nature.
- The fifth refers to the place of the individual. Criminal justice focuses on the individual as an autonomous decision maker. Healing justice views the individual in the context of his/her relationships.
- The sixth addresses the response to the offender. Criminal justice responds with punishment and violence. The objective of healing justice is that offenders as well as victims (indeed all members of the community) should heal.

Contrasting the logics: criminal justice and healing justice		
Criminal justice		**Healing justice**
Logic of states and institutions	1	Logic of creator and creation
Logic of rules and processes	2	Logic of transforming patterns (the sacred)
Logic of problem-responsiveness	3	Logic of cultivating loving-kindness
Logic of nouns	4	Logic of finding true identity
Logic of individual autonomy	5	Logic of interdependent relationships
Logic of punishment and violence	6	Logic of healing for all

Box 4.1 Contrasted logics: Criminal and healing justice (based on Sawatsky 2009)

Implications for restorative approaches

So what fate awaits restorative approaches such as encounter and repair when they are introduced into settings characterised by the logic and imagination of criminal justice? A pessimistic view is that they will change so as to reflect the existing logic and imagination. Repair will become punitive as all harm to direct and indirect victims is punitively totted up into restitution orders that geometrically exceed the benefits gained by the offender and the losses experienced by the direct victim. Encounters will become occasions for shame that stigmatise rather than reintegrate. Victim–offender mediation, conferencing and circles will join the penitentiary, probation, parole and other now-familiar and too often oppressive institutions of criminal justice that were launched by good people for benevolent purposes.

Several years ago Sherman and Strang (2007) released a meta-analysis of well-designed studies that compared restorative justice with criminal justice interventions. In all instances but one the impact of restorative justice on re-offending was as good as or better than that of criminal justice. The one exception was a subgroup analysis of a small number of Aboriginal young people under 18 who were sent to an Australian programme in which police officers were the facilitators. The repeat offending rate of those young people was much higher than those who were sent to ordinary criminal courts. Why? Sherman and Strang (2007) do not draw conclusions, but a reasonable hypothesis is that Aboriginal youth believed that the 'logic and imagination' of the police was significantly different from that of their own, more restorative, cultures.

But there is another possibility. It may be that in some settings restorative approaches can contribute to a cultural transformation that generates greater support for healing justice, which would in turn increase the demand for restorative practices. A number of people have suggested that schools might offer such a setting. Morrison (2003) proposes a three-level implementation strategy that begins with helping students develop competencies in conflict resolution so that they can address disputes when they first arise. The second level uses restorative justice circles to deal with conflicts that involve more people or are more entrenched. The third involves restorative justice conferences with more people – including parents, social workers and others – to address serious offences.

Hopkins (2004) agrees. It is not enough to respond to particular instances of conflict or wrongdoing, such as bullying, with a restorative intervention because the values and benefit of that intervention will not reach the school's culture. This is a problem because the victim and the bully will both need to return to the school community and that community will not be prepared to receive them in a restorative manner.

Therefore, she suggests that the school must first become a 'listening school'; a place where empathic listening is valued and listening skills are taught and modelled. Then it is ready to move to 'restorative conversations' in which students are taught to effectively express their perspectives, feelings and needs with others using their listening skills. These are foundational for creating a school in which relationships are built. When those are threatened by conflict and harm, she suggests that mediation, conferencing and circles can be used to repair the harm and restore relationships.

Claassen and Claassen (2008) propose that at the beginning of the year teachers should lead their students in development of a 'respect agreement', a set of guidelines that define the classroom behaviour that everyone agrees show respect to one another. This list is eventually divided into four categories: 1) student respecting student; 2) student respecting teacher; 3) teacher respecting student; and 4) all respecting equipment and facilities. When each student and the teacher are satisfied, they sign the agreement.

The teacher helps the students learn active listening and I-messages (similar to Hopkins' listening school and restorative conversations) so that they are prepared to use both when problems arise. Claassen and Claassen (2008) also recommend that a four-options model of dispute resolution be explained to the students, with discussion about the relative advantages and disadvantages of each. The first option is for one of the disputing parties to decide how it will be resolved. The second is for an outside party to make the decision. The third is for an outside party to help the disputing parties make the decision. The fourth is for them to do that without outside help.

The first two options are familiar in school settings: a teacher faced with a disruptive student decides how the disruption will be handled, or sends the student to the administrator responsible for discipline. But they advise that as many decisions as possible, even those between teachers and students, are resolved using options three and four. This requires skill and patience on the part of the teacher but in the end yields better, and better-kept, solutions because both have arrived at them.

The International Institute of Restorative Practices has trained school administrators and teachers to use restorative processes in encouraging communication generally and in dealing with disciplinary issues. Lewis (2009) offers brief case statements of ten schools in the US, Canada and UK that have adopted restorative disciplinary practices. The data presented shows a reduction in offences and in suspensions after the introduction of restorative practices, suggesting that the school climate – at least as demonstrated in the behaviour of students, teachers and administrators – has changed.

What might that school climate look like? The following are my suggestions of what the 'logic and imagination' of whole school adoption of restorative justice might be:

Contrasting the logics: Criminal justice, healing justice and restorative schools			
	Criminal justice	Healing justice	Restorative schools
1	Logic of states and institutions	Logic of creator and creation	Logic of consensus and covenant
2	Logic of rules and processes	Logic of transforming patterns (the sacred)	Logic of effective communication
3	Logic of problem-responsiveness	Logic of cultivating loving-kindness	Logic of learning communities
4	Logic of nouns	Logic of finding true identity	Logic of emotional and relational maturity
5	Logic of individual autonomy	Logic of interdependent relationships	Logic of interdependent relationships
6	Logic of punishment and violence	Logic of healing for all	Logic of constructive responses

Box 4.2 Criminal justice, healing justice and restorative schools

Conclusion

Restorative approaches to schools must include all three conceptions of restorative justice: repair of harm, encounter of the affected parties and transformation of relationships and culture. Because they are contained institutions within the broader community, it may be possible to build a world view within schools that is conducive to restorative conversations and practices. According to the sources cited in this article, this could be approached by teaching students to listen and express themselves in ways that build relationships, to use processes that focus on repair of harm through conversation, and by establishing the necessary programmatic and administrative support.

A whole-school approach to restorative approaches must be supported within the larger educational structure and its surrounding police and judicial environments. This means that laws, regulations and policies that are conducive to building a restorative culture should be viewed as important and natural steps in the process of embracing restorative approaches. These should be reinforced, or at the very least not obstructed, by the youth justice system. Ultimately, one would seek a restorative community in which restorative values and practices are understood, used and nurtured.

References

Claassen, R. and Claassen, R. (2008) *Discipline that Restores: Strategies to Create Respect, Cooperation, and Responsibility in the Classroom.* South Carolina: BookSurge Publishing.

Connolly, W.E. (1993) *The Terms of Political Discourse*. 3rd edition. Oxford and Cambridge, MA: Blackwell.

Council of Europe. Committee of Ministers (1999) *Recommendation No. R (99) 19: Mediation in Penal Matters and Explanatory Memorandum*.

Gallie, W.B. (1962) 'Essentially contested concepts', in M. Black (ed.) *The Importance of Language*. Englewood Cliffs, NJ: Prentice Hall (originally published in *Proceedings of the Aristotelian Society, 1955–6, 56*).

Gil, D.G. (2006) 'Toward a "radical" paradigm of restorative justice', in Sullivan, D. and Tifft, L. *Handbook of Restorative Justice: A Global Perspective*. London and New York: Routledge.

Hadley, M. (ed.) (2001) *The Spiritual Roots of Restorative Justice*. New York: State University of New York Press.

Hopkins, B. (2004) *Just Schools: A Whole School Approach to Restorative Justice*. London and New York: Jessica Kingsley Publishers.

Johnstone, G. and Van Ness, D.W. (2007) 'The meaning of restorative justice', in Johnstone, G. and Van Ness, D.W. *Handbook of Restorative Justice*. Cullompton, UK: Willan Publishing.

Lewis. S. (2009) *Improving School Climate: Findings from Schools Implementing Restorative Practices*. Bethlehem, PA: International Institute for Restorative Practices.

Morrison, B. (2003) 'Regulating safe school communities: Being responsive and restorative', *Journal of Educational Administration*, 41(6): 689–704.

Sawatsky, J. (2009) *The Ethic of Traditional Communities and the Spirit of Healing Justice: Studies from Hollow Water, the Iona Community, and Plum Village*. London and Philadelphia: Jessica Kingsley Publishers.

Sherman, L. and Strang, H. (2007) *Restorative Justice: The Evidence*. London: The Smith Institute.

United Nations (2002) '2002/12: Basic Principles on the Use of Restorative Justice Programmes in Criminal Matters'. United Nations, Economic and Social Council. Substantive Session 2002. (1–26 July 2002).

Chapter 5

Restorative approaches in New Zealand schools

A developmental approach

Wendy Drewery

Introduction

You can see the history of Aotearoa New Zealand playing out in the story of restorative approaches in our schools. Indeed, understanding the historical context of this country is important to enabling appreciation of this story. Many commentators on restorative approaches refer to the fact that indigenous peoples around the world used something akin to restorative practice to resolve conflict well before contact with Europeans and colonisers. In this chapter, I shall argue that the introduction of restorative approaches in schools offers an opportunity for further historical development and change in this country. I see it, hopefully, as a story about the ongoing role of education in colonisation: a story better understood as developing capability and potentially restoring dignity – to all parties.

A historical backdrop

Aotearoa New Zealand was settled in around 1300 AD by people who sailed and paddled canoes, called waka,[1] from islands in the Pacific. Māori lived in different iwi[2] or nations around the country. Some readers may have learned that New Zealand was 'discovered' by the Dutch sailor Abel Tasman, and then by the British sailor Captain Cook. In the early days of contact, traders, sealers and whalers moved across from Australia. Some of these (mainly British) settlers became a problem for the Māori, and when George Grey proposed a treaty in 1840, many Māori chiefs signed, though not without serious and prolonged discussion, and a significant number of abstentions. A common interpretation of this move is that they saw this as a chance for Queen Victoria to take control of her unruly subjects (King 2003). The settlers brought diseases with them, and by 1900 there were an estimated 49,000 Māori, when there had been up to 100,000 before 1840 (Durie 1994). In 2012, New Zealand had a population of 4.4 million, of whom 16 per cent or over 673,000 are Māori; at the 2006 Census, the latest data available, 7.2 per cent were from Pacific Islands, and 9.7 per cent from Asia – including China, India, and Korea. We have a small number of immigrants and refugees from the Middle East and Africa. The population of Māori has proportionately more children and fewer older people compared with the population of European extraction, called Pākehā[3] (Statistics New Zealand 2012). Increasing numbers of respondents claim multi-ethnicities (Kukutai 2008). So the ethnic shape of the country is changing. There is a growing proportion of Māori children in our schools, and the efforts of Māori to offer a more indigenous education are also growing apace.

Today, education is widely recognised as a tool for development, but in the 19th century it was no different in this country. Early missionaries taught in the Māori language. But the Native Schools Act 1867 made schooling a responsibility of the state, and teaching in English became the norm. By the end of the century, the decimation of the indigenous population through illness was so catastrophic that the race was not expected to survive. In schools, Māori children were punished for speaking in their own language (see for example Edwards 1990). Seeing this, their parents and grandparents also stopped using their own language at home, as it was widely considered – by Māori – that Pākehā education was useful. As a result, generations of Māori did not grow up speaking their language. Combined with a drift from rural to urban living, the alienation of many Māori from their homelands, language and culture was effectively accomplished within a little over a century of the signing of the Treaty. Today, there is much discussion about what to do to revive the language. Some blame education policy for this situation, and some look to education, by Māori, to retrieve it. At my university campus, te reo[4] can often be heard, which is a big change from 30 years ago. In a variety of ways, education is still fully implicated in this situation.

Introducing restorative approaches into New Zealand schools

Initially, I became involved in restorative practice in 1999, when the New Zealand Ministry of Education commissioned a team from the University of Waikato to develop and trial a process for conferencing in schools, using restorative justice principles. This was in part a response to concerns about escalating suspensions from schools, prompted and supported by judges in the Youth Court (McElrea 1993; 1996). Our team developed and trialled a process for formal conferencing after serious misdemeanour (The Restorative Practices Development Team 2004). Our process drew on indigenous practices of huitanga[5] and restorative justice (Zehr 1990; 1994), as well as aspects of narrative therapy (Morgan 2000; White 2007). We realised quickly that the learning careers of young people in our conferences required intervention much sooner, and our attention turned to school culture and teacher–student relationships.

Training in restorative approaches in New Zealand schools originally ran under the heading of 'behaviour management', though more recently this was translated into 'relationship management' (Thorsborne and Vinegrad 2008). Participants learn a scripted restorative conference process that they are encouraged to adapt for the classroom, for smaller disciplinary conversations and for formal conferences.

As is clear from the brief for our original project, the initial assumption was that restorative approaches are intended for disciplinary purposes and that they address behaviour difficulties of individual students. I would guess that now it is presumed that restorative approaches primarily help teachers with 'classroom management'. Although there is widespread recognition that the approaches may require a whole-school culture change, a one-off professional development programme cannot address the nature and processes of change required in an ongoing way in schools that embrace the approaches. This kind of change cannot be achieved by a single teacher, however skilful she or he may be, without the understanding and support of the school leadership; and it takes a long time to develop. In fact, over the last decade I have seen schools take on, lose, and regain some form of the approaches. The uptake, quality and understanding of the approaches that claimed to be restorative are mixed across the education sector. Nevertheless, the tenacity of those involved has produced a growing appreciation of what the approaches can and cannot do. In my view, although there has to be a set of common values, there is no single 'standard' of practice, nor should there be; and the approaches cannot simply be implemented in a linear fashion. On the contrary, every school has its own people, with their own quirks, strengths and weaknesses, and its own history of relationships both within and outside the school. So both the approaches themselves, and the processes of introduction, are likely to look different in every school.

Restorative values

Our team's understanding of restorative values is grounded in uncompromising respect for individuals' right to be here, and the presumption that relationships are the basis of human interaction. We used White's (2007) idea that the problem is the problem, not the person, and we adapted a 'narrative' therapy approach to therapeutic conversation to show how problematic identities can be deconstructed and rebuilt. We strongly believe that identities are never fixed, and people can always change. There is a mixed understanding among policymakers, teachers and principals about the values underlying these approaches, and not all would agree with our position. My experience is that most begin with the expectation that the approaches will make students behave as the teacher requires. Nevertheless, as individual teachers use the approaches in their daily interactions with students, some begin to see that speaking differently can stop trouble before it happens. Others take the script and do conversations by rote, perhaps learning that the steps do make a difference as they go. Yet others are concerned that using the approaches means relinquishing their power as a teacher. I stand with those who see the values as fundamental to whole-school culture, and promote a focus on respectful relationships across the school. I believe respectful relationships are made through respectful ways of speaking.

It seems to me that restorative approaches operate at the intersection of the disciplinary and pastoral care functions of a school, and hence they are fundamentally about how we understand the purpose of education. Just as parents are expected to teach their children how to live in a community and observe its rules, a school has similar responsibilities, acting in loco parentis, and carrying out its educational function on behalf of society – producing the citizens of the future. So I have begun to think that restorative approaches are not simply therapeutic or remedial or even disciplinary. It is a productive process capable of developing a caring culture where the values of respect for diversity are what we agree to strive for. In this sense, it is a form of just social practice. School is a great place for this to emerge.

Successful restorative approaches in New Zealand schools

We know that suspensions do still occur in schools who take on the philosophy, and the evidence for the success of restorative approaches in schools in New Zealand is growing, though much is still anecdotal. It is reasonably well-established that timely use of 'small' conversations in the classroom can de-escalate conflict before it has time to flourish. A deputy principal in a school I was visiting told me that since their teachers have been learning to use this approach, there are fewer referrals to the central disciplinary system. She believes teachers are defusing issues before they escalate. Another deputy principal in an Intermediate School told me that of 25 formal conferences for serious misdemeanour run over three years by the school, 'not one has come back' – none of the young persons have reoffended.

Colleagues at another college developed a form of classroom meetings as their predominant mode of restorative practice. Teachers could ask for classroom meetings when they found that the dynamics of the class were interfering with the smooth running of their lessons, so there is a disciplinary motivation for these meetings. The meetings took a developmental form, focusing on students' identities as learners (Kaveney and Drewery 2011; Kecskemeti 2011). Teachers who were outside the project told me that they noticed a major change in the tone of the school: students were quieter and the whole school felt calmer. Here too, referrals to the deputy principal reduced significantly.

Restorative approaches and the New Zealand Curriculum

In 2007, the Ministry of Education published the new New Zealand Curriculum (Ministry of Education 2007; 2010). This document was consulted widely, both within and outside the Education sector, and has been very well received. Rather than prescribing exact objectives for learning at each year level, it describes the learning objectives in general terms, leaving the specifics of learning programmes to schools and teachers. A feature of this document is the Principles that underpin it. The Principles include the Treaty of Waitangi, cultural diversity, inclusion and community engagement. Thus the document is explicitly intent on preparing young people for citizenship in diverse communities. It also names five 'Key Competencies': Thinking; Using language, symbols and texts; Managing self;

Relating to others, and Participating and contributing. With others, I have come to think that some restorative approaches can teach these key competencies.

At a school I worked with, one of the deans studied the video records of classroom meetings held through 2009 (Gray and Drewery 2011). She showed that, where initially many preferred not to speak, or grunted monosyllabic comments at their turn in the circle, by the last meeting most were contributing in full sentences, looking directly at others, and making useful points. She argues that this demonstrates not only that the students learned to speak more clearly and more confidently, but also that they learned to relate to others and to contribute and participate in the whole-class discussion. She suggests that the deconstructive meeting process they developed not only addresses students' learning identities, but also offers both a way of addressing relationship difficulties and an effective teaching tool for developing the key competencies.

Different understandings

I think it is likely that schools who take on the philosophy and values of respect, rather than simply the disciplinary tool, and who pay attention to the quality of their relationships across all levels of the school, are the ones who have had most success in reducing suspensions and exclusions. To enable this, the 'buy-in' of not only the principal and the whole staff is required, but also the Board of Trustees (who are charged with the legal governance of the school), and often, parents' associations as well. However, when asked by senior managers and enthusiastic teachers who are struggling with the 'problem' of not having influential colleagues 'on board', I do not suggest that they put all efforts on hold until they have 'permission', but that they can begin to use the practices of conversation within their own sphere of influence, whether this is the classroom or the dean's office.

I am relatively relaxed about this because it does not cost any money or contravene any regulations to speak respectfully to students or to use a different form of conversation. But if the matter is about serious behaviour issues that require referral to a higher authority in the school, then the disciplinary system in the school is activated, and it is at this level that confusion can be generated. In my view, it is not appropriate for some parts of a school to operate a system of restorative conferencing without this being mandated within the structure of the school. If it is not mandated that the outcomes of restorative conferences must be taken into account at disciplinary hearings in our schools, students and their families can go through a conference, produce a good outcome, and then they can find that the school requires a suspension hearing, and a punishment quite different from that agreed upon in the conference may be handed down. I do not believe it is necessary to force the exclusive adoption of either a punitive or a restorative approach to discipline in schools. The two approaches are not mutually exclusive. After all, sometimes punishment is deemed appropriate and agreed upon by the perpetrator as an appropriate outcome of a restorative conference. Because of the potential for confusion it is important that the school has policies and understanding of how discipline can be wielded across the whole school if they want to incorporate a restorative approach.

Links with justice: Challenging disengagement and school disaffection

As noted earlier, the introduction of restorative approaches in New Zealand began in direct relationship with suspensions. From this perspective, the restorative project in schools, as in Welfare and in Justice, has its origins in concerns about disengaged youth. Our initial project was part of the Suspension Reduction Initiative; this project evolved into the Student Engagement Initiative. Recently, the Ministry of Education identified restorative approaches as part of the Positive Behaviour for Learning Action Plan (http://www.minedu.govt.nz/theMinistry/EducationInitiatives. aspx). This development is, I believe, largely due to the persistence of teachers whose positive experiences of restorative approaches could not be denied, despite the initial evidence being regarded as 'soft' by policymakers. The Ministry of Education has documented the accumulated evidence, which is now deemed reliable, and is proceeding to develop a service delivery model and a process to pilot its implementation (M. Corrigan, personal communication, 3 August, 2012).

Because of disparities in student outcomes, Ministry of Education policy initiatives have an underpinning motivation to keep young people from disengaging too early from school – especially Māori and Pacific Island youth. The earliest reference to this problem in relation to restorative justice was a plea from Senior Judge of the Youth Court, Judge McElrea (McElrea 1993; 1996), who pointed out that most of the young people coming before him had dropped out from school early. Judge McElrea went on to champion the introduction of restorative justice in New Zealand schools. Still more recently, the Principal Youth Court Judge Andrew Becroft made a similar appeal, for schools to work harder to keep these young people in school. So, 'disengaged' youth are an important focus of the 'restorative' project in both justice and education in this country. Judge Becroft estimates that there are between 900 and 1,500 such 14–16 year olds in New Zealand: 'We know their names. We know their families' (Ministry of Social Development 2009). My examination of the disciplinary referrals for a whole year level in a secondary school revealed that about 20 per cent of students were the subject of over 80 per cent of the referrals. The Ministry of Education (2012) states that in 2011 only .5 per cent of the student population were suspended, and stand-downs (being formally removed for no more than five days) affected just 1.8 per cent. So, the overall numbers of students who drop out is quite small. I believe there is also a much larger group who stay, but who are not convinced that school is for them. This form of disaffection shows up in the achievement statistics.

In spite of the interest of the judges in the general problem, there has been little systematic study of the 'careers' of excluded students – with the notable exception of a large Australian study by Smyth and Hattam (2004). Their project proposed a correlation between the relational style of a school and student drop-outs. But it is not sufficient to keep them from dropping out: we also want them to achieve. Te Kotahitanga (Bishop, Berryman, Tiakiwai and Richardson 2004) is a major educational initiative originating in New Zealand, aimed at improving educational outcomes for Māori students. It is based on the assumption that students learn best when they have a good relationship with their teacher (Bishop, Berryman, Cavanagh and Teddy 2007) and it aims to change the ways teachers work with Māori students. This project has been critiqued for its inherent blaming of teachers: but it cannot be denied that the results from schools in the project show strong increases in achievement by Māori students (see http:// tekotahitanga.tki.org.nz/). Its objectives include intentional development of teachers' interactions with these students, as well as increasing teachers' appreciation of the contexts of the students' lives and relationships with their whānau.[6] In some senses, *Te Kotahitanga* is clearly a restorative project. However, I would prefer not to call it a restorative approach because, in my view, restorative values are more inclusive than the focus on teaching Māori students would suggest. At the same time I think that the traditional protocols of Māori meetings, manners of greeting and address, and general demeanour towards others, offer excellent examples of respectful relationship. Pākehā have benefitted hugely from this inherent Māori cultural value, often without recognising that acceptance of hospitality also brings obligation.

How should we think about 'relationship'?

We want our students to achieve, and we also want them to be happy at school. It is well accepted in the field of education that teacher–student relationships are fundamental to learning but, apart from the Kotahitanga project, little attention is paid to how to produce such relationships. Most teacher education seems to be concerned with teaching curriculum, meaning *subjects*. There is plenty of (negative) psychology about the individual and some work in the therapy literature on how relationships affect individuals and how individuals can do relationships better. I think we know little about what produces 'good' relationship as a basis for learning. We know a lot about the conditions for children's growth and development in families, but even this huge body of work does not pay much direct attention to how 'quality' is brought about in a teaching–learning relationship. In fact, we mostly assume we know what quality relationship means, because we can recognise it when we see it, but we do not examine it. The focus of psychology, including in relation to behaviour difficulties, is generally on how the individual, whether parent, child or teacher, conforms to euro-western norms.

Expectations of individual control over their own behaviour and self management are currently very dominant ideas about behaviour management in New Zealand education. Restorative approaches introduce a very different paradigm with which to think about and address the problems of behaviour, disengagement and underachievement. In the managerial approach, which I will call a modernist paradigm, disengagement is seen as a failure of students to control their own behaviour, or a failure of parenting, or a failure of teachers to control their classrooms. Some of the versions of restorative practice that have developed in New Zealand schools include the 'Restorative Thinking Room', or the 'Reflection Room'. There is great store set on the idea that if students think rationally, they will not behave in inappropriate ways. But different peoples and cultures have different ways of thinking – and not all people understand individual responsibilities or the responsibilities of teachers and schools in the same way.

I do not hold much hope for approaches that require certain ways of thinking and behaviour without engaging with how a person experiences the world, and I do not accept that education should manipulate minds without consideration of the culturally-informed presuppositions of students and their families. This does not seem to me to be relational practice. To work relationally with cultural diversity, a different attitude is required: not power over, but power *with*. To theorise this, I find that a different psychological paradigm is useful. I take a critical ecological approach to human psychology, which means that I believe there is an interactive relationship between the environment in which a person lives, and their sense not only of what is right, but of their own identity/ies (Claiborne and Drewery 2010; Rogoff 2003). Becoming a person is not a solo performance over which one has unique control, nor is it necessarily one that is ever finished. Personal identity in this account is not a singular, one-off achievement. Restorative approaches feature inquiry about the real experiences of those involved, and this aspect of the practices accords very well with a critical ecological approach to development. In Aotearoa New Zealand, such a clash of paradigms around the responsibilities of care, discipline, and even education and authority, lives on. It reaches very deeply back to our historical roots.

My perception is that Māori pay attention to the quality of relationships as a way of life (and politics): underlying this value is a deep sense of personal honour, pride and self respect, which in turn is strongly connected with iwi and whānau[7] relationships and histories. Mana, variously translated as status, respect, dignity, strength, power, authority (and a wide range of similar words), is central to this code of honour, which is profoundly linked with a historical sense of tribal affiliation to ancestors and land. Colonisation, by contrast, is a process that eventually subsumes the identity of a people into the identity of another, and it is not at all what Māori thought they were signing up to. Having experienced their power, many Pākehā have deep respect for Māori cultural practices and traditions. But, perhaps unwittingly in many cases, we have all (including Māori, historically) participated in the exclusion of Māori identities through our educational practices. As Pākehā we don't have to notice how educational practices do this, but many Māori students must feel assailed, at some level, at almost every turn. If I could expand on this I would argue that the modernist aspiration for human control over the world, spawned by 'enlightenment' thinking, represents a relationship with knowledge that is inherently alien to many indigenous peoples. Cultural difference is not just a matter of how you hold a fork.

Fostering respectful relationships across difference

Many people accept that restorative approaches are about managing relationships rather than behaviour. Central to this is establishing respectful relationships throughout the school and its communities. Within this commitment, the most important principle is respect for the dignity, or as Māori would say, the mana, of each person. Mana cannot be considered in isolation from whānau, hapū,[8] or whenua.[9] My euro-western way of understanding this is to think about the moral stature of the person, which cannot be achieved in isolation. A 'restorative' school is one where respectful relationships predominate. And respect has to be commonly understood.

Ways of speaking can compel the other into the frame of reference of the speaker: a colonising stance. Or they can invite a conversation that does not require the submission of one speaker's meaning-making to that of the other: a respectful stance (Drewery 2004; 2005). Respectful speakers engage with the mana of the other, and inquire about how they are making meaning. I think some teachers assume that a student's presence in school means submission to the teachers' educational values. This is a mistake, one which is repeated all around us. For example, in New Zealand media we hear daily now in radio and television interviews with members of the Māori Party, who are in coalition in government in 2012, rejection of forms of inquisition by journalists that are invitations to disrespect and patient reframing of the party members' positions. Being in parliament does not mean acceptance of the oppositional approach to politics, or anything else. But respectful engagement is so unfamiliar in such contexts. I am sure most teachers would protest that they do have deep respect for all their students. Even so, as Pākehā we have some way to go to appreciate the impact of our direct and often objectifying ways of speaking, diagnosing and exerting power over others – particularly but not only in our approach to education. Learning this is a necessary step in addressing the ravages of the nineteenth century. I think that embracing restorative approaches to conflict can help.

Conclusion

My argument draws what may seem to be tenuous connections across a range of ideas. I continue to build my own understanding of the restorative project. I think that the philosophy of restoration offers a basis for living peaceably in a diverse society. I do not see conflict as problematic, but rather as inevitable in a society that is dynamic and constantly changing. After all, peace is not about everyone agreeing: it is about having processes for getting through when we do not agree, even when we do not understand the other at all. In my view, not every approach that claims the name 'restorative' is in fact worthy of it, but there is a job to do to understand what is the essence of the practices (though I would go so far as to claim that the restoration and/or maintenance of mana is a central piece). I have invested myself in studying, theorising and teaching about the practices because I think they can enable reparation where otherwise there could be ongoing disgruntlement, if not declared conflict. I believe I know that restorative conversation can show us not only how to repair damaged mana, but how to produce respectful relationships as well. I think the disciplinary function is part of this, because conflict happens at the boundaries of what is socially acceptable. Teachers and senior managers in many schools across New Zealand have appreciated this, and have enabled the development of a variety of different practices, many loosely based on restorative principles. Like many of them, I believe that restorative approaches can help educate our children for citizenship in diverse communities. Perhaps it can also begin to change euro-western hubris: make us find spaces to listen, as well as tell. This project is, and should always be, a work in progress, hiccupping along, born as much of our history as formative of it. Insofar as education is the biggest social project we undertake, learning to hear others who are very different from oneself, especially children, is more than a worthwhile project. In an increasingly diverse world, it is utterly necessary.

Notes

1 Waka are large canoes, often hewn from tree trunks.
2 Iwi is the word for tribe or people. There are many Māori tribes, which they prefer to call nations, since they were originally independent and self-governing.
3 Pākehā is the name given by Māori to people who came mainly from Britain. There is another word Tauiwi, for people who have come lately.
4 Te reo: literally, the language; commonly used to refer to the Māori language.
5 Huitanga means the cultural practices of doing hui, or formal meetings, in Māori culture.
6 Whānau is a Māori word for a broad and extended family.
7 Whānau is roughly translated as family, but it refers to a group who share a broad range of genetic and historical relationships.
8 Kinship group.
9 Land.

References

Bishop, R., Berryman, M., Tiakiwai, S. and Richardson, C. (2004) *The Experiences of Year 9 and 10 Māori Students in Mainstream Classrooms*. Hamilton, Tauranga: Ministry of Education.
Bishop, R. Berryman, M., Cavanagh, T. and Teddy, L. (2007) *Te Kotahitanga Phase 3: Establishing a Culturally Responsive Pedagogy of Relations in Mainstream Secondary School Classrooms*. Ministry of Education. Available at: <http://www.educationcounts. govt.nz/publications/maori_education/9977>.
Claiborne, L., Baird, B. and Drewery, W. (2010) *Human Development: Family, Place, Culture*. 3rd edition. Sydney: McGraw-Hill.
Drewery, W. (2004) 'Conferencing in schools: Punishment, restorative justice, and the productive importance of the process of conversation', *Journal of Community and Applied Social Psychology*, 14: 332–344.

—— (2005) 'Why we should watch what we say: Position calls, everyday speech, and the production of relational subjectivity', *Theory and Psychology*, 15(3): 305–324.

Durie, M. (1994) *Whaiora: Māori Health Development*. Auckland, N.Z.: Oxford University Press.

Edwards, M. (1990) *Mihipeka: Early Years*. Auckland: Penguin.

Gray, S. and Drewery, W. (2011) 'Restorative practices meet key competencies', *International Journal on School Disaffection*, 8(1): 13–21.

Kaveney, K. and Drewery, W. (2011) 'Classroom meetings as a restorative practice', *International Journal on School Disaffection*, 8(1): 5–12.

Kecskemeti, M. (2011) *A Discursive Approach to Relationship Practices in Classrooms: An Exploratory Study*, Unpublished PhD Thesis, University of Waikato, Hamilton, NZ.

King, M. (2003) *The Penguin History of New Zealand*. Auckland, NZ: Penguin Books.

Kukutai, T. (Tahatū Consulting) Statistics New Zealand (2008) *Ethnic Self-prioritisation of Dual and Multi-ethnic Youth in New Zealand*, Wellington: Statistics New Zealand. Available at: <http://www.stats.govt.nz/browse_for_stats/population/census_counts/review-measurement-of-ethnicity/>. Retrieved 25 July 2012.

McElrea, F. (1993) 'A new model of justice' in *The Youth Court in New Zealand: A New Model of Justice*. Legal Research Foundation.

—— (1996) 'Education, discipline and restorative justice', *Butterworths Family Law Journal*, 2(4): 91–94.

Ministry of Education (2007) *The New Zealand Curriculum for English Medium Teaching Years 1–13*. Wellington, NZ: Learning Media.

—— (2010) *The New Zealand Curriculum Online*. Wellington, NZ. Available at: <http://nzcurriculum.tki.org.nz/>. Retrieved 25 July 2012.

—— (2012) *Stand-downs, Suspensions, Expulsions and Exclusions from School*. Wellington, NZ. Available at: <http://www.educationcounts.govt.nz/indicators>. Retrieved 25 July 2012.

Ministry of Social Development (2009, July) 'Making a difference early on is where it counts most', *Rise*, Issue 7. Available at: <http://www.msd.govt.nz/about-msd-and-our-work/publications-resources/>. Retrieved 25 July 2012.

Morgan, A. (2000) *What is Narrative Therapy?* Adelaide: Dulwich Centre Publications.

Rogoff, B. (2003) *The Cultural Nature of Human Development*. Oxford, UK: Oxford University Press.

Smyth, J. and Hattam, R. (2004) *'Dropping Out', Drifting Off, Being Excluded*. New York: Peter Lang.

Statistics New Zealand (2007) *QuickStats National Highlights 2006 Census*. Department of Statistics. Wellington, NZ. Available at <http://www.stats.govt.nz/Census/2006Census HomePage/>. Retrieved 25 July 2012.

—— (2012) *Population Clock*. Available at: <http://statistics.govt.nz/>. Retrieved 25 July 2012.

The Restorative Practices Development Team (2004) *Restorative Practices in Schools: A Resource*. Hamilton, NZ: School of Education, University of Waikato.

Thorsborne, M. and Vinegrad, D. (2008) *Restorative Practices in Classrooms: Rethinking Behaviour Management*. Buderim, Qld: Margaret Thorsborne & Associates.

White, M. (2007) *Maps of Narrative Practice*. New York: W.W. Norton & Co.

Zehr, H. (1990) *Changing Lenses*. Scottdale, PA: Herald Press.

—— (1994) 'Justice that heals: the vision', *Stimulus*, 2(1), 2.

Chapter 6

Merging past and present? Conflict resolution in South African township schools

An Ubuntu-restorative approach

Mirriam Lephalala

Introduction

The increasing incidence of violence in South African state schools located in townships has raised concerns from various sectors. One of the main concerns is that despite policies abolishing corporal punishment, schools still tend to resort to this mode of punishment or other equally harsh disciplinary measures as a means of enforcing discipline. Indications are that state schools, and society, seem to be trapped in the legacy of the apartheid system that was characterised by discriminatory laws that were mainly enforced through harsh and inhuman disciplinary measures. As a result, discipline in schools remains mainly punitive and concerns regarding aggression among learners are rising.

While schools struggle to develop effective ways of addressing conflict, government and public bodies have, in contrast, come up with a strong call for reassertion of humanitarian and traditional values based on Ubuntu to bring about harmony and reconciliation in the country. For example, it was in the spirit of Ubuntu that the first president of a free and democratic South Africa, President Mandela, led his new government in 1994, with the aim of bringing about racial harmony and establishing an ethos of nation-building. Similarly, various policy changes in South Africa at government level have been driven by and centred along Ubuntu principles to advocate humanitarian values and redress past apartheid policies.

The aim of this chapter is to explore the extent to which the notion of Ubuntu can address the violence in township schools in South Africa and how restorative approaches can complement that process. It seeks to respond to the following questions: To what extent can the principles of Ubuntu, a traditional value system, be applied proactively to stem the present tide of violence and conflict in township schools? Can both Ubuntu and the principles of restorative approaches be adopted as complementary approaches to address the violence in schools such that the basic human dignity of all involved is protected? This chapter responds to these questions by first examining the concept of Ubuntu, drawing on personal experiences of growing up and living in a South African township. The chapter then examines Ubuntu as a possible approach to resolving the current wave of violence in township schools. Finally, it considers how the traditional principles of Ubuntu fit with restorative approaches and how they can be adopted as complementary approaches to positively stem the conflict in schools.

The past: What is Ubuntu?

Over the years, the concept of Ubuntu has been used in a general sense to refer to an African philosophy of life (Mokgoro 1997). It originates from the African idioms, 'Motho ke motho ka batho ba bangwe' and 'Umuntu ngumuntu ngabantu' which, loosely translated, mean 'A person is a person through other persons', or, 'I am because we are; we are because I am' (Goduka 2000; Ramose 1999). Research reveals that although the concept originates in rural settings in pre-colonial Africa and is linked with indigenous ways of knowing and being (Swanson 2007), it is not easily definable because it tends to be thought of in diverse forms depending on the social context (Mokgoro 1997; Anderson 2003). As a result, various definitions and descriptions of Ubuntu abound. These include 'an African philosophy of humanity and community' (Skelton 2002); 'an African cultural world-view' (Murithi 2006, 2009); and 'a philosophy of becoming human' (Swanson 2008). These definitions and descriptions depict the complex, elusive and multifaceted nature of the concept of Ubuntu. Thus Ubuntu mirrors the multiple and shifting insights into African society and human relationships and confirms Mokgoro's (1997: 3) argument that 'its social value will always depend on the approach and the purpose for which it is depended on'. It is clear that while on one hand there seems to be a common understanding of Ubuntu and what it stands for as a value system, on the other hand this meaning is not fixed because it can mutate and offer different meanings depending on the social context.

However, despite these complexities, it is commonly understood that at the core of Ubuntu is the recognition of a value system that acknowledges communities as social, and individuals as co-dependent beings. This is an ideal that expresses the need for a basic respect and compassion for others (Louw 2003), promotes 'communalism and interdependence' (Mapadimeng 2007: 258) and confirms that 'all human beings are connected not only by ties of kinship but also by a bond of reciprocity rooted in the interweaving and interdependence of all humanity' (Goduka 2000: 70). Thus Ubuntu espouses values that enhance societal well-being. These include consensus, agreement and reconciliation, compassion, human dignity, forgiveness, transcendence and healing (Tutu 1995; Mokgoro 1999). Such values resonate strongly with the principles of restorative approaches.

With the advent of the post-Apartheid era in South Africa, the notion of Ubuntu as a lived and commonly-accepted value system was extended to incorporate notions of nation-building, transformation, reconstruction and transition into democracy (Mbigi 1995; Skelton 2002; Swanson 2007). Ubuntu principles are central to and underlie the restructuring of South Africa as a new democracy and have influenced various policies in government, public and economic sectors. Key government and judiciary policies informed by Ubuntu values include:

- the Child Justice Bill of 2008 on juvenile justice reform which advocates the rehabilitation of children who violate the law and their reintegration into society (Skelton 2002);
- the abolition of the death penalty: adopted by the constitutional court as an Ubuntu principle in 1995 (Anderson 2003); and
- the Truth and Reconciliation Commission: incorporated the values of peacemaking as advocated in Ubuntu as part of a national drive to bring about socio-political reconciliation across racial lines (Mapadimeng 2007; Murithi 2006; Ramose 1999).

These developments indicate that although viewed as a traditional notion, Ubuntu is seen to have the capacity to inform and shape modern South African society and societal well-being. Importantly, it is not considered a 'one-off' process, but as an integral aspect of the new democracy.

The concept of Ubuntu exemplifies positive and affirming practices of co-existence between individuals, families, communities and societies. Examples of such practices abound in South African communities. For instance, in the past it was commonly understood and accepted that as neighbours, families should co-operate and support each other in different ways. The word 'moagisane', a North Sotho word meaning 'neighbour', has deeply ingrained notions of communal well-being. It requires unconditional co-operation and support for each other from individuals, families, neighbours and communities. For instance, it is common practice to expect 'moagisane' to ask for what could be considered simple items such as a spoon of salt, a cup of sugar, an onion or two potatoes because as neighbours there is an understanding of the silent and unwritten code: 'I am able to support and help you today and that tomorrow or next week I might need your assistance, and I know that you or someone else will do the same for me'. This code also applies to and extends to various occasions and celebrations in the community. These include weddings and funerals, where without any formal invitation, neighbours are expected to attend in order to lend a hand and assist the affected family financially with preparations of cooking for and feeding visitors as well as cleaning up afterwards.

Personally, growing up as a black female in a township, one of the practices I have come to value and now also practise myself is when women come together in groups commonly referred to as 'societies'. These women support each other in various ways, including financially and emotionally. In the harsh years of Apartheid, men were often absent from the lives of their communities, for instance they were in jail or in exile. 'Societies' were a means of survival for township women. It meant that women could provide for their children's education because they knew 'societies' would assist with funds to pay school or university fees. Currently, these practices seem to be waning but pockets still exist, and in some instances are being revived as communities come to recognise the value of Ubuntu: 'I am because we are; we are because I am'.

The present: Ubuntu and the school system

The important issue now facing South Africa is how to develop schools based on these principles of Ubuntu so that schools are places where, for example, notions of 'moagisane' (neighbour) have real meaning for all members of the school community.

The school system in South Africa has been under pressure for decades, particularly under the Apartheid government where schools were often used to advance the government's political agenda, for instance, in the ways they were racially categorised, divided and unequally funded. It was not surprising that schools often turned into battlegrounds between police, students and teachers. Thus, although many seem to view the present wave of violence in schools as unexpected, it is closely related to past experiences and the practices of an inhumane apartheid system. In addition, and significantly, corporal punishment, which in itself could be viewed as exemplifying violence, was adopted as the main and in most instances the only mode of discipline in schools.

Ubuntu offers an alternative and more humane set of possibilities for resolving some key tensions in the school system. The conflicts in schools often emanate from a lack of an appropriate and agreed set of processes to help address challenges and individual differences adequately, as well as offering appropriate support for both victim and perpetrator. Ubuntu could offer a starting point for accommodating both sides and for finding agreed solutions which espouse the motto: 'I am because we are; we are because I am'.

However, while Ubuntu espouses values that aim to bring about harmony and promote the collective well-being of society, the concept cannot be advocated uncritically, as Swanson (2007: 59) cautions. Of particular concern for schools is that Ubuntu tends to entrench some of the existing and unchallenged discriminatory practices that are based on age, gender and social standing (Mduli 1987), that is, the very practices the younger generation tends to find problematic and would seek to challenge. For instance, the value of respect is sometimes abused to justify superiority based on age differences, gender and social positions to entrench the existing societal power imbalances between men and women, adults and children, as well as the rich and poor (ibid. 1987). Thus, one of the main criticisms raised against the Truth and Reconciliation Commission, for instance, is that it bowed to pressure from legislative concerns and time constraints at the expense of the concerns and fears raised by, in particular, the individual women concerned (Chapman 2007). These are genuine concerns, which have serious implications for the younger generation and especially the school system. The principles espoused in Ubuntu, a traditional value system, might be problematic when applied in school settings because, as Nzimande (1988) warns, youth tends to view culture-based values as 'adult business', and as such they are seen as old-fashioned and not applicable to them. Therefore, there is a need to re-examine and apply Ubuntu principles more critically as an alternative approach to conflict resolution in schools to avoid entrenching some of the negative traditional views that characterise adult–child relations and tend to discriminate against and disempower the youth. Such an examination will entail empowering learners as human beings and acknowledging them as significant and valuable members of society by drawing in and incorporating their views through negotiations.

Another key criticism of Ubuntu that has implications for schools and learners is that its emphasis on values where 'the collective supersedes the individual' (Khoza 2006) and its tendency to view 'the community and not the individual at the centre' (Goduka 2000) mean that Ubuntu as a value system tends to enforce conformity (Marx 2002). The contention is that by enforcing conformity, existing imbalances and power relations between the individual and the community are in turn reinforced and perpetuated (Sono 1994; Mbigi and Maree 1995; Marx 2002). In promoting societal well-being uncritically, Ubuntu tends to enforce group solidarity at the expense of individual well-being. The danger with forced conformity is that it can create an environment of repressive conformity and compulsory loyalty thus discouraging any questioning of authority and/or resistance of domination (Mduli 1987: 67–69). Of concern, as Louw (2003) and Sono (1994) point out, is that very often noncompliance is met with harsh punitive measures resulting in the individual being marginalised and/or disempowered as a being. But in an 'Ubuntu school' it should be expected that these concerns are not ignored but challenged because they are disruptive and are likely to promote and bring about inequality and disharmony. In a school that upholds Ubuntu as a value, every stakeholder in the school, and learners in particular, should be made aware of this and reassured that they can bring these concerns to the fore where they will be addressed without fear of being discriminated against because of their age, gender or standing in society.

As Bruner (1996) argues, societal contexts, which comprise family norms, values and culture, tend to be highly influential and can impact on young people's thinking and behaviour in critical ways. The values of Ubuntu, like those of any other culture, are not inborn but are acquired in society and transmitted from one generation to another by various means, including day-to-day practices and language (Kamwangamalu 1999). The challenge for schools, therefore, is to find the appropriate medium through which to introduce, strengthen and embrace Ubuntu principles as well as adapt them to fit their own specific contexts as well as community values. Schools could start by adopting Ubuntu as a way of life, that is, as a community where everyone is affirmed and supported to be the best they can be.

Thus, as an existing and tested cultural approach to conflict resolution, Ubuntu can offer useful insights to alternative ways for more humane understandings of discipline, resolving violations and conflict as well as building an ethos of 'a person is a person because of others' in schools. As Murithi (2006: 20) affirms: 'As a traditional conflict resolution method and custom, Ubuntu is part of a time-proven social system, in which the objective is more than just settling a case – but is oriented towards the reconciliation and maintenance or even improvement of social relationships'. Aimed at maintaining and improving social relations and enhancing practice, Ubuntu, as embodied by the former President of South Africa Nelson Mandela, is part of the traditional practices that have stood the test of time and as such can offer valuable lessons on how to resolve the current wave of violence to youth and school communities.

Ubuntu and restorative approaches

Because Ubuntu and restorative approaches share qualities that emphasise the importance of humanity and societal well-being, they offer complementary ways to address conflict in schools. Ubuntu, as Murithi (2006) argues, gives insights into how the principles of empathy, sharing and co-operation can be utilised to resolve day-to-day issues that tend to impact negatively on human relations. Both Ubuntu and restorative approaches advocate the use of co-operative efforts to address the imbalances created by an individual's conduct and aim at bringing about agreement and harmony (Anderson 2003). The four stages Murithi (2006: 23) identifies as Ubuntu processes, 'acknowledging guilt, showing remorse and repenting, asking for and giving forgiveness, and where required paying compensation or reparations as a prelude to reconciliation', are consistent with the principles of restorative approaches (RA). In addition, as noted earlier, the same values promoted in Ubuntu, consensus, agreement and reconciliation, equally embody the principles of conflict resolution advocated in restorative approaches (Anderson 2003; Murithi 2009).

Research on restorative approaches confirms existing similarities between these approaches and Ubuntu (McCluskey and Lephalala 2010; Lloyd and McCluskey 2008), suggesting that both approaches offer possibilities for school communities to start building a culture of mutual respect between the various stakeholders: staff and students as well as parents, staff and students; and more importantly allow them to develop with common agreed solutions in their own unique ways, which can bring about harmony in the school (McCluskey and Lephalala 2010). Ubuntu, like RA, is aligned to the philosophy and practices of restorative justice, which put repairing harm done to relationships and people over and above the need for assigning blame and dispensing punishment. Both include values that are aimed at creating an ethos of respect, inclusion, accountability and taking responsibility, commitment to relationships, impartiality, being non-judgemental, collaboration, empowerment and emotional articulacy (ibid. 2010). Some of the key and valuable skills that should be applicable and useful in school settings include empowering learners to take ownership of problems which require active listening, facilitating dialogue and problem-solving and expressing emotions in a safe environment.

Conclusion

This chapter has shown that the concept of Ubuntu has been embraced as a useful compass for transcending the apartheid legacy and as a guiding principle at both government and community level. While one has to acknowledge that Ubuntu, as a cultural approach, might not be an instant or 'fix-it-all' solution to the diverse challenges faced by schools in South Africa, it can however, as a lived experience, be adopted as one of the possible approaches that could offer hope and open up alternatives to conflict resolution in schools. But Ubuntu should not be applied uncritically in schools; as Nzimande (1998) and Khoza (2006) caution, it is a traditional value system that can sometimes be used to discriminate against individuals according to age, gender and class. It is of vital importance that issues of context, age, gender and class are addressed with sensitivity from the onset. Similarly, restorative approaches can offer practical guidelines for addressing the current tide of student conflict and violence that tends to characterise township school communities. Hence both Ubuntu and restorative approaches can offer effective conflict resolution possibilities in schools because they share common principles that aim to bring about consensus, agreement and reconciliation. More importantly, since both Ubuntu and restorative approaches acknowledge the complexities and importance of resolving conflict, they can offer useful insights into the more subtle and extensive meanings of discipline that are unique to individual school communities and thus challenge the use of corporal punishment and other punitive measures as the main and sometimes only mode or alternative to resolving conflict.

References

Anderson, A.M. (2003) 'Restorative justice, the African philosophy of Ubuntu and the diversion of criminal prosecution'. Available at: <http://www.restorativejustice.org/articlesdb/articles/3862>. Accessed 7 February 2013.

Bruner, J. (1996) *The culture of education.* Cambridge, MA: Harvard University Press.

Goduka, I.N. (2000) 'Indigenous/African philosophies: Legitimizing spirituality centred wisdoms within academy' in Higgs, P., Vakalisa, N.C.G., Mda, T.V. and Assie-Lumumba N.A. (eds) *African voices in education.* Landsdowne: Juta and Co. Ltd.

Hoppers, C. Odoro (2002) 'Recognising, promoting, protecting and integrating IKS into the mainstream: critical concerns and challenges at policy and institutional levels in South Africa'. Paper presented to *World Summit on Sustainable Development,* Ubuntu Village, Johannesburg, 29 August 2002.

Kane, J., Lloyd, G., McCluskey, G., Riddell, S., Stead, J. and Weedon, E. (2007) *Restorative practices in Scottish schools.* Edinburgh: Scottish Executive.

Kamwangamalu, N.M. (1999) 'Ubuntu in South Africa: A sociolinguistic perspective to a pan-African concept', *Critical Arts: South-North Cultural & Media Studies* 13(2): 24–41.

Khoza, R. (2006) *Let Africa lead: African transformational leadership for 21st century business.* Johannesburg: VesUbuntu Publishing.

Lloyd, G. and McCluskey, G. (2008) *Restorative approaches in Scotland: Impact of National Pilot Projects and recent developments.* Edinburgh: Scottish Government.

Louw, D.J. (2003) *Ubuntu and the challenges of multiculturalism in post-Apartheid South Africa.* Sovenga, South Africa: University of the North.

—— (2005) 'The African Concept of Ubuntu and Restorative Justice'. In Sullivan, D. and Tifft, L. (eds) *Handbook of Restorative Justice: a global perspective.* Abingdon: Routledge.

Mapadimeng, M.S. (2007) 'Ubuntu, the work-place and "Two Economies". *Africanus* 37(2): 257–271.

Marx, C. (2002) 'Ubu and Ubuntu: on the dialectics of apartheid and nation building'. *Politikon*,29(1):49–69.Availableat:<http://dx.doi.org/10.1080/02589340220149434>. Accessed 7 February 2013.

Mbigi, L. (1995) *Ubuntu: a rainbow celebration of cultural diversity*. Pretoria: Ubuntu School of Philosophy, Tshwane.

McCluskey, G. and Lephalala, M. (2010) 'A person is a person because of others': challenges to meanings of discipline in South African and UK schools. *Power and Education* 2(1) 2010: 18–30.

McCluskey, G., Lloyd, G., Kane, J., Stead, J., Riddell, S. and Weedon, E. (2008) 'Can restorative practices in schools make a difference?', *Educational Review* 60(4): 405–417.

Mdluli, P. (1987) 'Ubuntu: Inkatha's "people's education"', *Transformation* 5: 60–77.

Mokgoro, J.Y. (1997) 'Ubuntu and the law in South Africa'. Paper presented to *First Colloquium on Constitutional Law*, Potchefstroom, South Africa, 31 October 1997.

—— (1999) 'The protection of cultural identity and constitution at the creation of National Unity in South Africa: A contradiction in terms?' *SMU Law Reviews* 52: 1549–1562.

Morrel, R. (2000) 'Corporal punishment in South African schools: A neglected explanation for its persistence', *South African Journal of Education* 21: 292–299.

Morrison, B. (2007) *Restoring safer school communities*. Sydney: Federation Press.

Murithi, T. (2006) Practical Peacemaking wisdom from Africa: Reflections on Ubuntu. *The Journal of Pan African Studies* 1(4): 25–34.

—— (2006) 'Approaches to building peace and social solidarity'. *African Journal on Conflict Resolution* 6(2): 9–35.

—— (2009) *The ethics of peace building*. Edinburgh: Edinburgh University Press.

Nzimande, B. (1988) 'African life and the "hidden abode" of mental health: Some unasked questions about "tradition" and progressive social services in South Africa'. Paper presented to *The Organisation for Appropriate Social Services in South Africa*, 9 September 1988.

Skelton, A. (2002) 'Restorative justice as a framework for juvenile justice reform: A South African Perspective'. *The British Journal of Criminology*, 42: 496–513.

Sono, T. (1994) *Dilemmas of African intellectuals in South Africa*. Pretoria: University of South Africa.

Swanson, D.M. (2007) 'Ubuntu: an African contribution to (re)search for/with a "humble togetherness"', *Journal of Contemporary Issues in Education* 2(2): 53–67.

Tutu, D. (1999) *No future without forgiveness*. NY: Doubleday.

—— (1999) *Ubuntu: putting ourselves back together*. London: Tutu Foundation. Available at: <http://www.tutufoundationuk.org/Ubuntu.html>. Accessed 7 February 2013.

Chapter 7

A restorative challenge

Can citizenship trump identity in Northern Ireland?

Derick Wilson

Introduction

The restorative task in Northern Ireland is deeply entwined with promoting and securing citizenship as a primary identifier over identity itself, in the wake of an inclusive political agreement and a devolved legislature. Making peace with people from different, and often opposed, traditions is not easy yet is deeply restorative. Patterns of identity group belonging have become aligned with a historical ambivalence to violence that has excused 'my violence as provoked' but has rejected 'your violence as unacceptable', meaning that now the restorative task is about opening people up to trust, as equal citizens, those they have previously seen as 'the enemy'. Restoring an openness to those previously seen as the enemy in an ethnic frontier area (Wright 1987), as well as an openness to those who are new citizens, demands the following: that citizenship, not group identity, is established as the primary point of identification; that people find relationships and civic and political structures, which enable all to deal more openly with the legacy of the past; that core values are established at the heart of public and civic life about treating one another equitably, appreciating the diversity each brings and promoting our mutual interdependence (Eyben *et al.* 1997); and that public, civic and political society spaces empower people to create a more civil society. This chapter examines ways in which citizenship can trump identity in Northern Ireland and how restorative learning can lead to ease with different others.

The legacy of the long historical past

The restorative task is relational, intergenerational and institutional. The need for citizenship education for children and young people needs to be couched within a wider intergenerational commitment to see one another as equal citizens of one place and not primarily as members of opposed identity groups. The restorative task is to empower and support people of all ages in making lasting changes towards a shared society a reality, equipping them with both the knowledge and experience that virulent circles of pessimism, avoidance, communal deterrence and local essentialism can be dissolved through building ease with different others. Restorative practice involves promoting commitments between people and groups that establish and sustain 'transformative platforms' within the society that address 'both the symptoms and causes of historic polarisation...support constructive change...and bring together strategic, often improbable, alliances' (Lederach 2007, p. 6):

'Between 1969–2001, 3523 people were killed as a result of the conflict. Almost 60 per cent were killed by Republicans, almost 30 per cent by Loyalists and 10 per cent by the British and Irish Security Forces' (Consultative Group on Acknowledging the Past 2009, accessed 31.12.12). In an ethnic frontier, the past always has the capacity to invade and destroy present-day hope because history always lies close to the surface of daily life. The normal rituals of more secure societies that allow past and hurtful events to be both acknowledged and, over time, placed at a distance from day-to-day life, do not work. As the society seeks to move on through new political agreements and mutually owned institutions, it takes time and deep commitment to build new institutions that propel people forward and build mutual ownership and cohesion.

Ethnic frontiers are contested places where, in a flash, the daily lives of people and the energies of political parties can be consumed in a vortex of emotions and destructive actions across a fear/identity line (Wright 1987). In such societies the distinctions between 'legitimate force' and 'violence' and the ability of the law to criminalise effectively are eroded. Establishing an agreed criminal justice system is a major restorative task.

Established in the wake of an exhausted Britain winning World War One, partition (in Ireland) in many ways represents the balance of forces that prevailed in Ireland at that time, and the line of least resistance for the decisive power, which, in this case, was the United Kingdom. Critically, in Northern Ireland self-determination and democracy for Unionists was simultaneously ongoing British rule and the betrayal of democracy to Nationalists, and in particular to Sinn Fein.

The ethnic frontier of Northern Ireland was a vortex where, for those from the pro-British Unionist traditions who wished it and secured it in 1921, the state became a form of liberation and a security. For those from the Irish Nationalist tradition, forced to accept the 1921 partition, the state became a tyranny.

Northern Ireland was a space where it was impossible to experience anything close to what metropolitan societies called peace. In Wright's (1987) analysis, daily life was often fuelled by a force field of antagonism, nourished by unaddressed historical inequalities. The restorative task of nurturing new energy and vitality (Jenkins 2006) in relationships, between generations, and within structures has to acknowledge but not be overwhelmed by the potential of fear to invade, and even destroy, every potential meeting across lines of difference.

Building a more restorative culture in society is to enable people to transgress traditional boundaries and meet; to build a new practice that works critically and reflectively within existing traditions and institutions; to support existing organisations re-envision their role in the light of a new and agreed political dispensation; and to set free initiatives that are transformative because of their inclusive structures or the focus of their work.

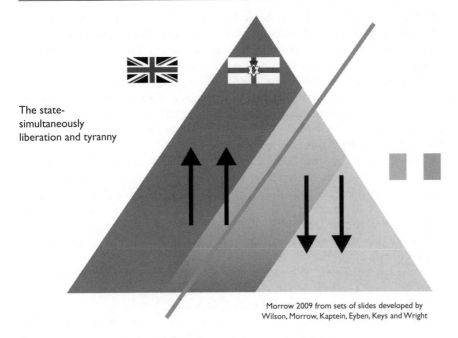

The state-
simultaneously
liberation and tyranny

Morrow 2009 from sets of slides developed by
Wilson, Morrow, Kaptein, Eyben, Keys and Wright

Figure 7.1 Ethnic frontier dynamics

Restorative challenges: Unveiling asymmetries and establishing a restorative principle

In Northern Ireland a vortex of asymmetries of experience make mutual understanding difficult. Historically, there was asymmetrical access to the state internally and with the aligned cosmopolitan neighbours – the Unionists to Britain, the Nationalists to Ireland (see Figure 7.1). A second asymmetry has been the differential impact of the conflict. The direct experience of violence fell on people primarily from the border areas between Northern Ireland and the Republic of Ireland; contested rural areas of mid-Ulster, the urban areas with high levels of poverty in Belfast and Derry; on business people and staff in the security forces, policing and the criminal justice system. A third asymmetry exists between those who want their hurt acknowledged and those who refuse to remember.

The considerable initiatives to assist healing of those impacted by the conflict, whilst singularly important, have revealed the often large gulf in understanding of the same events between people with diverse political and religious traditions as well as an element of 'a refusal to remember' (Czelaw Milocz 1980) on the part of others.

In a recent review of how victims and survivors, former combatants, local politicians and the British and Irish governments might deal with the past, the Consultative Group on Acknowledging the Past arrived at a transcending restorative principle: 'The past should be dealt with in a manner which enables society to become more defined by its desire for true and lasting reconciliation rather than by division and mistrust, seeking to promote a shared and reconciled future for all' (Consultative Group on Acknowledging the Past 2009, p. 1).

The hasty dismissal by diverse and opposed political, religious and victims groups of this report unveiled this deep asymmetry of understanding. However, some restorative working principles, outlined next, still flowed from this as well as some positive intercommunity responses to the Saville Enquiry (2010) about Bloody Sunday (1972) are more positive signs.

A fourth asymmetry that needs restorative attention is that of different groups demanding that 'others' acknowledge their violence without acknowledging their own. It is important, and painful, to recognise the circles that one's own traditions are caught within. In ethnic frontier society conflicts many, on all sides, wish for a one-sided acknowledgement by the others of their violent actions, without acknowledging their own. The only way to break the circular pattern of the endless demands for 'the others' acknowledgement first, matched by a refusal to acknowledge 'their own', is if the demand for acknowledgement is free from the accusation that it is one-sided and free from a wish to re-write history in a certain manner by pre-determining the evidence that is used.

When acknowledgement is given by all, the circular bind is broken. Then the mutual acknowledgement is seen as a process of dealing with the past and moving forward as well as then dealing with other violent actions that, for identity reasons, have been ignored. Dealing with the past in such a dynamic force field of relationships means having to face many uncomfortable truths within and between all sides to the conflict. The recently-established pilot Victims and Survivors Forum has argued for the addition of 'the Effect of the Conflict on Women and Children', an often forgotten theme that is identified in more recent local and international research in post-conflict societies.

Restorative tasks: Promoting 'Ease with difference' in spaces, relationships and structures

A restorative task is to promote spaces and relationships where people experience being at ease with different others. Such relational work is made much easier when supported by wider institutional structures promoting trust as a societal imperative.

In public institutions, moving beyond combative relationships with enemies means to promote robust relationships that engage with sharing responsibility for public institutions; that embed a political culture focused on social and economic issues rather than identity politics; and that secure more open and shared public spaces for all ages in cities, towns and villages. Through such initiatives and agreed structures, the move to a society based on the primacy of the citizen rather than the group gradually becomes a new reality.

Diverse civil society institutions (Edwards 2004) also have their part in promoting a new, shared civil society characterised by an ease with difference, the 'good society' and the 'public good' being explored, new forms of diverse citizen association being experienced and building a robust and open society beyond antagonism and asymmetry (such as in the Inclusive Neighbourhood Project: http://www.nicras.btck.co.uk/PartnerOrganisations/InclusiveNeighbourhoodProject).

Political institutions have the structural potential for a new political reality that can dissolve the old dynamics of antagonism and asymmetry to evolve. However, public and civic engagement with politicians is essential to this restorative engagement (Strang and Braithwaite 2001) if we are to move towards 'a better future for all – a society which is at ease with itself and where everyone shares and enjoys the benefits of this new opportunity' (Programme for Government, Office of the Minister and the Deputy First Minister, Northern Ireland 2007).

In moving the restorative agenda forward, the establishment of the Commission for Victims and Survivors (2008) and the establishment of the pilot Victims and Survivors Forum in 2009 model a new restorative engagement between public and political institutions on one hand, and civil society, on the other. Dealing with the past requires all sides of the conflict to face many uncomfortable truths. These emerging institutions model relational, intergenerational and structural attempts to promote greater acknowledgement of the legacy of victims and survivors in this society, their need for long-term services and support, as well as supporting victims and survivors in making their still considerable contribution to future civil society.

Restorative learning for a shared future

The 'peace process' drew heavily on specially convened mixed residential learning experiences, locally and internationally. It is important that local people from diverse backgrounds still come together in a contested society, especially in residential learning settings, and that they have opportunities to work together, meet together, build lasting relationships and build a sense of common purpose between them, beyond fear (Wilson 1994).

People can share the same space but these same spaces can be hostage to a wider dynamic of preferring 'separation' and silence, 'avoidance' where people are in the vicinity of one another or 'politeness' where people have to share the same space. In such a climate, the space for meeting the other in depth is narrowed and so the space for mutual understanding work can become small.

There are at least two broad 'restorative learning tasks'. One is to assist people to understand the present-day dynamics that are influenced by the diverse asymmetries mentioned previously and that continue to feed mutual antagonism and, in some cases, fear in daily life. The second is to practically learn to dissolve antagonism and fear through the promotion of more open relationships and structures.

In work since 1979, drawing on Girard's mimetic hypothesis (1997), Wilson with colleagues explored these dynamics within reflective learning groups and, at the same time, offered participants the opportunity to experience how new relationships and structures may be built beyond distrust and fear. The dynamics

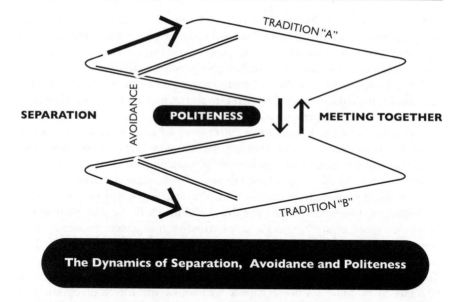

Figure 7.2 Separation, Avoidance or Meeting Together? Adapted from Eyben, Morrow and Wilson with Robinson 2002 © *The Future Ways Programme, University of Ulster*

that feed mutual distrust are explored visually with citizens, groups and institutions and the models are offered after listening to storytelling about life in this place or sometimes taught experientially through guided group exercises (Wilson and Morrow 1994). The work is located within an approach that invites participants to examine how much, or little, of their lives and the organisational cultures they belong to, are caught up in avoidance, politeness or silence and to what extent the potential for really meeting one another is taken. In ethnic frontier societies there can be no eventual outright winner, peace within the boundaries is an uneasy tranquillity and 'left/right politics' is usually trumped by identity politics. Over time, the lines between the different traditions become blurred as all become long-term residents even though each does not often see the other as an equal citizen. A central restorative theme today is 'to promote an ease with different others'.

Deep mutual distrust still pervades many relationships between people from all social backgrounds. These draw on historical reservoirs of distrust and the more recent challenges of accepting more recent residents as equals (Police Service of Northern Ireland 2011). Space to morally re-evaluate each tradition's actions needs the experience of deep learning where hard, but respectful, conversations take place in diverse company and through which people re-evaluate their positions and understandings. This deep learning deals with the complexity of hurt, distrust and misunderstanding between us, going beyond the spectacles of cultural identity that so many have grown up with.

Supporting 'critical lovers of traditions'

Shriver (2005) argues that for societies to become strong and future-oriented they must have people who are 'critical lovers of their traditions'. He argues that closed societies have many who opt out as 'loveless critics of their traditions' or who are 'uncritical lovers of their traditions'. He refers to the words of historian Yahuda Bauer that are inscribed on the US Holocaust Memorial in Washington DC: 'Thou shalt not be a victim. Thou shalt not be a perpetrator. Above all thou shalt not be a bystander' (Shriver 2005, p. 108).

There is a need to promote active experiences that carry the message that 'change is possible'. Some people hold the view that the past cannot be changed. It is not that facts can be changed but that, in the midst of a contested society, we grow to understand that each person can see the same event through very different eyes and come to very different positions. In such ways we can experience change.

Acknowledging that dealing with the past is a task for more than the dispersed community of victims and survivors, we need a layered approach by many people and institutions to ensure that the violence done to people is acknowledged on all sides. This is a societal task to harness goodwill and bind diverse people into some new common reality capable of withstanding the violent urges for retaliation and revenge that still emerge. It is important to acknowledge the civic courage of the many small groups and individuals both outside and within the political mainstream that, until now, have kept these themes alive when there was an absence of mainstream political will to address them (Tyrell and Wilson 1995). There is also a need to understand that truth telling, justice and empathy between diverse people can assist healing. In a review of diverse truth and reconciliation processes, Shriver identified four aspects of truth (Shiver 2007) that heal rather than divide, arguing for an understanding of justice that repairs rather than revenges. This includes the development of more restorative approaches within communities as well as within the court system. He also argues for a societal culture of empathy that expands rather than constricts the ties that bind a political community.

Alongside this, there is a need to dissolve a culture of what might be called 'pessimistic common sense', that readily dominates ethnic frontier societies and frustrates restorative actions such as risk-taking and the building of trust between people. In the creation and sustaining of the Victims and Survivors Forum, where people from all sides meet together, there is an experience of being nurtured whereby members challenge this pessimistic culture and assist the wider society 'mourn some features of our...past with new present awareness that we must never repeat such events in our future' (Shriver 2009, p. 5).

In systems thinking exercises undertaken with diverse mature student groups since 1973, Wilson and colleagues (Wilson and Eyben 2006) consistently identified a deep ambivalence about the value of 'promoting trust with different others' as a central, hidden constraint undermining the development of better community relations in Northern Ireland. In the presence of fear people preferred 'their own tradition' and generated their understandings of the other through the stories of 'their community' and the myths of 'the dangerous other'. The violence of the other side, real or potential, dominated. The threat or actual use of violence was often used to communally deter the others. Those who were open to meeting were often, and are still, branded 'traitors' and relationships across the traditions were not readily tolerated. Faith leaders, community leaders and local politicians were often subject to veto by those willing to be the most violent.

Emerging from these experiences, deterrence relationships make for uneasy and unstable agreements and truces between groups. An act of violence has a communal meaning; private acts of violence are rare. In a conflict, acts of violence against an individual are rarely read as random acts but are seen as communal acts of violence by a member of one group against all members of the other group. A collective identity is readily affixed to both victim and victimiser. In ethnic frontier areas, once started, revenge and tit-for-tat cycles of retaliation quickly generate their own logic. In such cycles, each side only sees the part of the other in starting things. It always sees its own actions as provoked and justified: 'My violence is understandable and your violence is unacceptable' becomes the mantra.

The restorative learning task is to alert people to these dynamics and to give them some distance and discernment: how people caught up in a conflict always have their 'cultural good reasons' for doing actions; and how every emotional outburst can ignite burdens of history in us that we can use to justify revenge and even violence.

Restorative values to underpin a shared society: Equity, diversity and interdependence

Equity, diversity and interdependence are principles emerging from extensive research with individuals, groups and organisations in Northern Ireland in terms of how they understood and committed themselves to improve community relations (Eyben *et al.* 1997). These principles became the fundamental principles for the 'Shared Future' policy produced by Government in 2005 (Office of the First Minister and Deputy First Minister). In restorative terms, the challenge is to build a societal commitment to the values that underpin a shared society, create relationships, places and structures where mutual regard is experienced, acknowledgement and regret expressed, and interdependence can flourish. In such ways, ease with difference is secured and a culture that is open to people from minority ethnic communities in our midst, who often have had to behave in an invisible manner, is also generated.

Above and apart from the compliance base of equality and good relations legislation, it is also important to develop humanising, transgressing, envisioning and transformative work that builds new commitments to and structures that support a shared society. A restorative aspect is to empower people and groups to move, hopefully together, beyond the different asymmetries of experience and to live boldly and move beyond experiences of mutual distrust. A restorative learning possibility is to promote and secure spaces in which people commit to treating one another well, promoting the norm of respect. Such generative platforms work at 'both the symptoms and the causes of historic polarisation…support constructive change… and bring together strategic, often improbable alliances' (Lederach 2007, p. 6).

The principles of equality, diversity and interdependence are capable of informing the daily work of teachers, youth workers, social workers and community workers in a contested society in order that they stay free of serving partisan and narrow interests. Thoughtful practitioners, working to an intercultural vision, can use these principles to measure whether their practice promotes this wider vision. Managers and policymakers can ensure that the vision, structures and policies associated with their agencies are explicitly and implicitly committed to building an interdependent society (Wilson 2007a), applying these principles to ensure that need is the focus of agency community work policy and practice. An organisation could review its goals (Wilson 2007a) against the extent to which they address inequality (the equity theme), challenge narrow practices that exclude (the diversity agenda) and consider how they could secure a shared society (the interdependence drive): the end point to which everything else works.

Restoring communities of invitation and inclusion

Pavlich (2004) speaks of the often hidden and violent edges of traditional models of community. In a contested society these violent and exclusionary edges are often very evident. In contrast, the learning groups or communities that restore or reconcile tend to have boundaries that are more shaped by hospitality and invitation; they are more open, inclusive, permeable and future-oriented.

Identities can become too localised and may become future prisons that limit opportunity and imagination for adults and children alike. Local essentialism tends to close people to difference. Ethnic Irishness or Britishness have been easily tenable on the fringes of those historic cultures yet such positions reflect little of the growing diversity at their centres. Also at this time, some secure states are now experiencing the growth of ethnocentric groups in their midst, unwilling to share with different others. Such dynamics feed excluding cultures and a politics of 'ethnic essentialism' (Sondhi 2004) that 'only my group and my place counts above all else'. Here, the metropolitan centres of secure states can learn from the ethnic frontiers.

As citizens within an expanded Europe, restorative historical healing is necessary around Islamic, Christian and Jewish relations and other expressions of distrust and violence that links restorative reconciliation practice in Northern Ireland with central European 'silences'. Promoting good relations between people of different religious beliefs, political opinion, racial groups, sexual orientation, diverse abilities and social backgrounds are modern challenges for citizens in all societies.

The restorative challenge is to ask, 'Have our existing cultural and political formations the space and openness to different others or do major traditions only want others if they assimilate into *our* existing ways?' Such restorative spaces are opportunities to resolve the challenge of creating safety and security for all, inviting all to change our behaviour and change the views of others different to us by class, religion, gender, ability, race or political identity.

Promoting restorative platforms for learning anew

Educationally, restorative practices are about generating new experiences that contrast with the old adaptive ways (Eyben *et al.* 2002). Generative change means transforming organisational structures so that people communicate in new ways.

The challenge now is to promote a restorative civic and public culture (Wilson 2009) that moves people beyond the important compliance base established in law (Northern Ireland Act 1998) and promote a commitment to treating all fairly, building a new culture of ease with different others. The conversations that are needed are about the quality of relationships that exist between us as human beings, and the level of trust that allows people to acknowledge and value each other's experiences, cultures and insights. This means creating new restorative platforms, spaces that facilitate such conversations, irrespective of religion, race, politics or other differences. This means attending both to the internal relationships and the external links organisations have with diverse members of the communities they serve.

Promoting, developing and sustaining new 'process structures'

In the traces of reconciliation practice before and during the conflict in Northern Ireland (Montville 1990, 1993) there has been a stubborn refusal to give into despair and distrust and a wish to create a sense of interdependence. Such interdependence may only be a level of listening to the other, while still disagreeing, yet when such meetings develop further they nurture imagination and gain a life of their own. Examples of this include the history of Corrymeela; the growth of Integrated Schools; WAVE, NI Mixed Marriage Association, Counteract. Lederach (2003) refers to these acts as process-structures. They are the outworking of generative meetings between people and certainly one aspect of the healing processes needed post-conflict (Lederach 2007).

Such platforms are the basis of reconciliation practice between people from diverse backgrounds and include victims (Towards Understanding and Healing 2004); people who have committed violence and wish to reconsider their views and actions (Fitzduff 1987); young people from diverse histories of mutual distrust (Wilson 2007a); people of all ages examining the need to address poverty and inequality in new and non-partisan ways; people from diverse faith traditions (Northern Ireland Association for Mental Health); police and security personnel (Mediation Northern Ireland and Future Ways 1998, 2004; Morrow et al. 2000; Wilson and Morrow 2013); public servants, local and first-level politicians (Civic Leadership Report 2002; Eyben *et al.* 2006); school children and diverse professionals from teaching (Magill *et al.* 2009; Wilson 2006); social work (Central Council for Education and Training in Social Work 1999); youth work (Wilson 2007a); probation (Wilson 2007b); health and community development (Fay *et al.* 1999).

A critical question then arises: with so many involved in peace building, why is the society still relatively fragile about embracing the securing of a shared society?

An openness to the different 'other' as a gift, is a reality for some but not yet a societal norm. Here we return to the deep ambivalence that exists about trusting the other. Essentially separatist political ideologies implicitly underpin the dominant and opposed major political parties. The ability of these parties to act in a mature, political manner and understand the views of those opposed to them is only in their infancy (Shriver 2005). There have also been dominant theological strands of 'a chosen people' and 'a sacrificial theology' in Protestant and Catholic traditions that have subordinated a more liberating and inclusive theology of reconciliation, with notable exceptions. However, there is a significant intergenerational body of people of who have participated in 'meeting the other'. In a sense, many citizens have more experience of meeting different others than their political representatives. There may be a critical mass developing of diverse people from diverse backgrounds that know deeply that 'making friends with the enemy' (Atran 2010), or at least meeting them, is the only way forward.

Excluding practices are now illegal. Platforms of minimum compliance standards and agreed public institutions now exist. Under the 1998 Belfast Agreement, internationally recognised by the British and Irish Governments and assented to by a plebiscite on the whole island, there are now agreed public structures under the devolved NI Assembly that are responsible for all areas, including law and order. There are minimum compliance standards underpinned by the equality and good relations laws that govern fair treatment and challenge actions of a sectarian, politically exclusive or racist nature (Northern Ireland Act 1998).

The restorative task around children and young people in a society emerging from conflict

The restorative task is to work for a shared society based on the principles of equity, diversity and interdependence within the 'process-structures' of everyday life, to empower voice, to promote new norms and to promote and secure values at work. There are specific ways of being with one another that need to be promoted and embedded, that are practical tasks to be promoted within the old, as well as the new, structures. Creating a shared society is a deeply restorative task that needs to be promoted in the relationships, policies and structures of everyday life (see Eyben *et al.* 2002, 2003).

Some restorative learning practices from the past years of reconciliation practice are as follows. Firstly, that developmental and innovative work on the edge has to be balanced by patient and dogged work at the centre of institutional, structural and civic life. It is to seek some very incremental gains at the centre and reconfigure that centre, however difficult, so that more learning from the developmental edge can be incorporated there (Eyben *et al.* 2003). Secondly, that self-interest must be used unselfishly if the broader body of people are to buy into the new shared society project. The interests of adults for their children and grandchildren, for greater safety in the communities and societies and for the well-being of older people must be used as levers if we are to bring more people to the shared society table. Thirdly, a shared society is a practical gift to people in terms of everyone wishing that there is no bullying of 'different others' in schools, and that fairer treatment for all means a more equitable use of public and civic resources, especially in a time of financial need.

Building a more restorative culture where children and young people experience themselves as equal yet different citizens of a society is to engage in strands of work that change the character of engagement between people from different traditions so that people meet as citizens rather than members of identity groups. Citizens, children, young people and adults are then seen as assets not problems. Whether children and young people attend separated or integrated schools or youth programmes, the 'others' they are with and the 'different others' they meet are also acknowledged as assets. This demands that formal and informal educators work energetically to promote a culture open to difference, where 'the other' is experienced or referred to as an equal citizen and where the language and practices of 'shared spaces' and 'the common good' infuse events when people come together in diverse groups.

Promoting ease with difference and establishing low levels of inequality are two elements that are 'non-economic' but nevertheless essential to the economic development of sustainable regions. Children and young people meeting across lines of difference contribute religiously, politically and culturally to this wider societal agenda. In such meetings, the experience of the common good and shared spaces grow within them and between them. This demands that adult educators work to a shared value base (Wilson and Morrow 2013) around inter-cultural understanding and are personally at ease with this task. This creates and motivates 'critical lovers of traditions' (Shriver 2005) who are willing to challenge their cultures to live to values that respond to diversity and inclusion and discard those values that do not do so in this modern interdependent age.

Traditionally, educationalists have both a reproductive and reconstructive function (Connell 1981). Currently, it appears that the reproductive function dominates the education profession in Northern Ireland (Wilson 1994), at least implicitly. Higher education tutors hold an important bridging position in terms of their freedom to ask critical questions of teachers and informal educators in training and on refresher courses. For the foreseeable future the educational structures of the NI devolved assembly will primarily offer formal education through separate identity strands, whilst encouraging a small, integrated sector and a range of shared programmes between schools (see Education and Training Inspectorate 2010; Queen's University Belfast 2012). This means that people primarily still meet 'their own side' more readily. The new agreed political structures must not cement these separations. There is cause for concern that in recent policy decisions the Department of Education, whilst being committed to a more diluted form of community relations policy (Department of Education 2011) than that of 2005 (Office of the First Minister and Deputy First Minister 2005), is ambivalent about promoting and securing deep and lasting institutional engagement between people from the diverse traditions (Morrow 2012). In the long run, we must hope that the financial pressures to cluster resources plus the positive developments of the digital age and youth culture horizontally linking young people across lines of difference grow and that parents make different choices in support of a more open, restorative, societal culture.

Building a more restorative culture in society is to work on a number of axes.

Axis 1 *Relational and intergenerational: empowering and connecting voices*

It is important that formal and informal educators empower voice, promote new norms that make mutual understanding an explicit goal and use language that envisions and secures a shared society. Publicly-funded programmes with children and young people which are relevant to the broader experience of citizenship (see Changemakers Programme; Community Relations in Schools 2012 and WIMPS. tv 2013) and understanding recent history (see The Corrymeela Community 2013) need to fully use the new, forward-looking NI Curriculum (Council for the Curriculum, Examinations and Assessment 2013) around these themes. The voices of all children and young people need to be heard in a society where the full diversity of experience and background is not yet heard (Youth and Society 43: 2 2011). Giving time and voice to children and young people who experience being diminished is important (Zeldin *et al.* 2011). Promoting more restorative spaces for those in care (www.voypic.org) as a priority is also essential to this axis. Enabling a more diverse base of children and young people to be visible and acknowledged in wider society here is the goal (see NICCY 2009).

It is also important that young people are empowered and supported in undertaking new youth–adult partnership working (Zeldin 2004) to experience that the possibilities for change are real and that civic engagements enable adults and young people to advocate for change and understand the complexity of social change.

Axis 2 *Institutional practice: humanising, transgressing, envisioning and transforming work*

'Humanising work' is the act of building a more open set of relationships within groups and organisations. 'Transgressing work' assists people in moving beyond the often-limiting boundaries of strong cultures to meet different others and supporting them in questioning aspects of these cultures. 'Envisioning work' is re-orienting existing organisations around the theme of whether the group or organisation addresses and promotes a more open and shared society. 'Transforming work' is creating new groups and organisations that model new ways of being together across lines of difference.

Axis 3 *Integrating work across relationships, generations and institutions*

Building a more restorative culture in society involves supporting people as they engage politically and challenge public and civil society cultures in order to underpin a shared society. The restorative task requires people to articulate the importance of building a more open society secured by the values of equity, diversity and interdependence; it promotes and supports any willingness to meet and engage openly and robustly, never losing sight of the human cost of the recent conflict and being committed to ensuring that we never return there; and it must ensure that children and young people are equipped, through the governance cultures of formal and informal educational organisations, to experience being at ease with different others and encouraged to put relationships right in a restorative manner, rather than let relationships and grievances fester for too long.

Conclusion

Reconciliation practice over many years has been restorative, incubating relationships between unexpected people so that they, with others, can soar above distrust and fear. It is important that these restorative relationships, with their capacity to restore hope and possibility between diverse and often separated people, are now used in the practical task of restoring equity, promoting trust and securing agreed, commonly owned and non-partisan civic, public and political structures within which people of all ages can move more freely and at ease with different others.

As more secure societies evidence identity groups forming in opposition to established laws or around claims of being unfairly treated, the restorative learning from contested societies has a relevance for the relational, institutional and structural patterns being established between different others in these societies as well. The primacy of equal citizenship, not identity, has to be a goal if we are to be at ease with different others and release all our abilities for the common good.

References

Atran, S. (2010) *Talking to the enemy*, New York: Harper Collins.
Central Council for Education and Training in Social Work (1999) *Getting off the fence: Challenging sectarianism in personal social services.* London: Belfast.
Community Relations in Schools (2012) Available: <http://www.cris-ni.org.uk/>. Accessed 2 Jan 2013.
Connell, W.F. (1981) *A history of education in the 20th century world.* New York: Teachers College Press.
Corrymeela Community (2013) 'The Facing History Programme'. Available at: <http://www.corrymeela.org/programmes/our-programmes.aspx>. Accessed 2 Jan 2013.
Council for the Curriculum, Examinations and Assessment (2012) Available at: <http://www.nicurriculum.org.uk/>. Accessed 30 Dec 2012.
Department of Education (2011) 'Community relations, equality and diversity in education'. Available at: <http://www.ycni.org/downloads/CRED/cred_policy_doc1.pdf>. Accessed 30 Dec 2012.
Education and Training Inspectorate (2010) Available at: <http://www.etini.gov.uk/index/international-fund-for-irelands-sharing-in-education-programme.htm>. Accessed 2 Jan 2013.

Eyben, K., Keys, L. and Wilson, D.A. (2006) 'A new shape for one of the oldest professions? Politics and civil society, the good relations task'. Belfast: Belfast City Council.

Eyben, K., Morrow, D. and Wilson, D.A. (1997) *A worthwhile venture: Practically investing in equity, diversity and interdependence in Northern Ireland?* Coleraine: University of Ulster.

—— (2002) *The equity, diversity and interdependence framework: A framework for organisational learning and change.* Coleraine: University of Ulster.

Eyben, K., Wilson, D.A. and Morrow, D.J. (2003) *Investing in trust building and good relations in a public sector organisation.* Coleraine: University of Ulster.

Fay, M.T., Morrissey, M., Smyth, M. and Wong, T. (1999) *The cost of the troubles study. Report on the Northern Ireland Survey: the experience and impact of the troubles.* Londonderry: INCORE.

Fitzduff, M. (1987) 'From ritual to consciousness', DPhil Thesis, University of Ulster.

Lascaris, A. (2008) *Healing Europe.* The Netherlands: Dominicaans Studiecentrum voor Theologie en Samenleving.

Lederach, J.P. (2003) *The little book of conflict transformation.* Intercourse, PA: Good Books.

—— (2007) 'From truce to transformation'. Available at: <www.nicrc.org.uk>. 23 November 2007. Accessed 2 Jan 2013.

Magill, C., Smith, A. and Hamber, B. (2009) 'The role of education in reconciliation'. A report for the EU Peace and Reconciliation Fund. Coleraine: University of Ulster.

Mediation Northern Ireland & Future Ways (1998) 'Policing Our Divided Society'. A report to The International Commission on Policing in Northern Ireland (The Patten Commission).

—— (2004) Unpublished.

Milocz, C. *Nobel Lecture*, Nobel Prize in Literature, Nov 1980.

Montville, J. (1990) *Conflict and peacemaking in multiethnic societies.* Lexington, MA and Toronto: Lexington Books.

—— (1993) 'The healing function in political conflict resolution' in Sandole, D.J. and van der Merwe, H. (eds) *Conflict resolution theory and practice: Integration and application.* New York: Manchester University Press.

Morrow, D. *The practice, progress and failings of community relations work in Northern Ireland.* Institute for Research in Social Sciences, University of Ulster, Seminar Paper, May 2012. Available at: <www.ulster.ac.uk/IRiSS>. Accessed 2 Jan 2013.

Morrow, D., Wilson, D.A., McAllister, B. and Campbell, J. (2000) *Policing Our Divided Society, 1997–2000.* Ulster: University of Ulster. Mediation Network of Northern Ireland and Future Ways.

Northern Ireland Act (1998) 'Equality and good relations', Section 75(i) and (ii). London: The Stationery Office.

Northern Ireland Commissioner for Children and Young People (2009) Available at: <www.niccy.org/>. Accessed 30 Dec 2012.

Office of the First Minister and Deputy First Minister (2005) *A shared future.* Belfast: OFMDFM.

Pavlich, G. (2004) 'Restorative justice's community: Promise and peril' in Toews, B. and Zehr, H. (eds) *Critical issues in restorative justice.* New York: Criminal Justice Press, pp. 173–190.

Queen's University Belfast (2012) Centre for Shared Education. Available at: <http://www.qub.ac.uk/research-centres/CentreforSharedEducation/>. Accessed 2 Jan 2013>.

Shriver, D. (2005) *Honest Patriots.* New York: OUP.

—— (2007) 'Truths for reconciliation: An American perspective', NI Community Relations Council; Public Lecture, Belfast 16 October 2007.

Sondhi, R. (2004) 'The Middle Way: On Being Indian in Britain Today'. Presentation to Oxford Centre for Hindu Studies. Available at: <http://www.ochs.org.uk/news/evening-ranjit-sondhi-cbe-launches-ochs-leicester>. Accessed 2 Jan 2012.

Towards Understanding and Healing. Available at: <www.thejunction-ni.org/towardsunderstandingandhealing.htm>. Accessed 2 Jan 2012.

Tyrell, G. and Wilson, D.A. (1995) 'Institutions for conciliation and mediation' in Dunn, S. (ed.) *Facets of the conflict in Northern Ireland*. Dublin: Macmillan Press.

Wilson, D.A. (1994) *Learning together for a change: the evolution of an educational model for cross-community meetings between adults in a divided society*. DPhil Thesis, Coleraine, NI: University of Ulster.

—— (2006) *Paper for principals of integrated schools*. Belfast: Northern Ireland Council for Integrated Schools.

—— (2007a) 'Coming of age at last', *Youth Studies Ireland* 2(1): 55. Available at: <http://eprints.ulster.ac.uk/998/1/2._Coming_of_Age_at_last_PDF.pdf>.

—— (2007b) 'Probation practice and citizenship, good relations and the emerging European intercultural agenda', *Irish Probation Journal* 4(1): 46–62.

—— (2009) *Platforms for a restorative culture in Northern Ireland*. Available at: <http://www.restorativejustice.org/10fulltext/Platforms%20for%20a%20Restorative%20Society%20Dec%2009.doc/view>. Accessed 7 Feb 2013.

Wilson, D. and Morrow, D. (2013) *Understanding works too*. Belfast: Understanding Conflict Trust.

Wilson, D.A. and Eyben, K. (2006) 'Fit for purpose?' Future Ways Programme, Coleraine, NI: University of Ulster.

WIMPS (Where is My Public Servant?) (2013) Available at: <http://wimps.tv/>. Accessed 2 Jan 2013.

Wright, F. (1987) *Northern Ireland: a comparative analysis*. Dublin: Gill & Macmillan.

Zeldin, R. (2004) 'Youth-adult relationships in community programs: Diverse perspectives on good practices', *Journal of Community Psychology* 33(1): 121–135.

Zeldin, S. Wilson, D.A. and Collura, J. (eds) (2011) 'Creating Restorative and Intergenerational Cultures for Youth: Insights from Northern Ireland and the United States', *Youth and Society* 43 (2): 481–582. Available from Sage Publishing at: <http://yas.sagepub.com/content/43/2.toc>. Last Accessed 23 April 2013.

Chapter 8

Restorative approaches in schools

A psychological perspective

Helen Cowie

Introduction

Schools that put a restorative philosophy into practice typically use a range of methods. Whatever form these take, at their core is the concept of a caring, inclusive community. When conflicts, bullying and social exclusion arise – as inevitably they will – restorative approaches have the potential to engage the perpetrators, those harmed and the bystanders in a collective process of problem-solving whose aim is reparation of damage, restoration of the quality of relationships and the reintegration of participants in the conflict back into the school community.

What are restorative approaches in schools?

In the past, much research focused on the individual aspects of conflict and aggression by exploring the individual characteristics of perpetrators and targets, so overlooking the powerful influence of the social context. While an understanding of the personal aspects of the perpetrator–target relationship is important, it only addresses part of the issue since it is experienced within a group of peers who adopt a range of participant roles, whether as active agents, targets, bystanders or defenders, and who experience a range of emotions. Salmivalli *et al.* (1996) first proposed a participant-role approach to the study of traditional bullying. (See also Salmivalli 2010 for a recent review of the participant role approach.) They argued that perpetrators seldom act alone but are usually supported by their immediate group of *assistants* and *reinforcers*. The bullying escalates further as a result of the responses of the bystanders, acting as *outsiders*, whether they react with indifference to the plight of the victim or implicitly condone what is happening. Only a small proportion of bystanders will act in the role of *defenders* who offer emotional support or protection to those harmed. Salmivalli's pioneering research shows how essential it is to take account of the social context in which bullying acts occur and the key role played by the whole group in shaping how children and young people respond to aggression and violent behaviour.

In schools which adopt a restorative approach the work is not only done with the individual perpetrators and those harmed but with the whole school, through, for example, circle time, problem-solving, conflict resolution, peer mediation, circle of friends and conferencing. In other words, this is a challenge for all members of the school community if attitudes and perspectives are to be changed (Cameron and Thorsborne 2001; Cowie and Jennifer 2008; Hopkins 2004; Morrison 2003; Wachtel and McCold 2001). From the restorative perspective, it is essential to involve all members of the school community in reflecting on the effects of aggressive or cruel behaviour on not only targets and perpetrators but also on the bystanders.

Zero tolerance is often proposed as a tough deterrent but despite its 'face value' appeal there is no evidence to suggest that zero tolerance works. In fact, this approach can be counterproductive. Skiba *et al.* (2008), in their report to the American Psychological Association Zero Tolerance Task Force (APA 2008), concluded that zero-tolerance policies actually fail to make school environments safer. In this study, zero-tolerance policies predicted higher rates of misbehaviour and suspension among students; schools with zero-tolerance policies rated lower on school climate and had higher school drop-out rates. Additionally, these schools had lower rates of academic achievement. There were other serious outcomes. They observed that zero-tolerance policies were construed as racist in the local community since particular ethnic groups appeared to be targeted. Children with disabilities, especially those with emotional and behavioural disorders, were suspended at rates disproportionate to their representation in the population. Additionally, the task force found that zero-tolerance policies increased referrals to the criminal justice system and created what they call 'a school-to-prison pipeline'. Furthermore, these systems were more likely to be perceived as unjust by young people and their families.

Skiba *et al.* (2008) concluded that far more emphasis needs to be placed on non-punitive strategies to promote school safety, including restorative approaches. Zero-tolerance strategies, they conclude, should only be used in the most extreme and severe cases and even then they should be applied with great thought for the needs and rights of all the individuals involved, including the perpetrators. They recommended restorative programmes since these actively promote a cooperative rather than a punitive process in which there is scope for reconciliation and some form of closure or resolution. Most importantly, they argue, restorative approaches in schools have the potential to create a safe and supportive learning environment that expresses positive values in the school community. Morrison (2007) confirms that not only does zero tolerance fail to work, it also promotes intolerance and discrimination, since such a policy works to discriminate against a minority of pupils with emotional and behavioural difficulties and fails to meet children's rights as set out in the United Nations *Convention on the Rights of the Child* (UN 1989). From this perspective, in contrast to traditional punitive approaches to discipline, restorative approaches place more emphasis on pupils themselves resolving conflicts and so build a stronger sense of community in the long term.

This does not mean, however, that schools should not adopt some sanctions against bullying and other forms of aggressive behaviour. In fact, Ttofi and Farrington (2011) report that 'disciplinary methods' are strongly associated with *decreases* in bullying and being victimised. But we need to be clear about what such disciplinary practices mean. In the particular context of bullying, Pepler *et al.* (2004) evaluated the effectiveness of sanctions. They acknowledged that some sanctions will always be part of a school's policy to counteract bullying. However, they found that when schools promoted an emphasis on positive relationships and created an ethos of care and responsibility, the need for strict, punitive sanctions declined. When sanctions *were* applied, the perpetrators were more likely to perceive them as fair and meaningful. The reason for this was that the students had been included in the process of creating the school rules and had been made aware that negative behaviour, such as bullying, had consequences for all.

In a further analysis of reactive strategies used by schools in England, Thompson and Smith (2011) found a range of what they called 'direct sanctions' including verbal reprimand, meetings involving parents, temporary removal from class, withdrawal of privileges, school community service, internal exclusion, short-term exclusion – through to permanent exclusion. Almost all schools used verbal reprimands and meetings with parents, at least in some cases. However, in three-quarters of the schools surveyed, these direct sanctions were combined with other approaches, including restorative approaches.

Working with the relationship

The core principles of counselling psychology provide insights into how restorative approaches might work. Rogers (1955; 1965) proposed that people have the ability to find solutions to interpersonal difficulties through the support of a warm, person-centred relationship in which the focus is on problem-solving. The very process of problem-solving shifts the person away from introspecting negatively about the circumstances that are causing them distress or avoiding responsibility for their actions by blaming others. It is the quality of the relationship that is the catalyst for therapeutic change. The core conditions in this relationship are congruence, empathy and unconditional positive regard, with the counsellor having a non-judgemental attitude.

The person-centred approach is in harmony with the application of restorative justice principles in schools. Braithwaite (1989, 2003) proposed the need for 'reintegrative shaming' – disapproval of the aggressive act but at the same time respect for the person. This is in marked contrast to stigmatisation – a form of disrespectful shaming that leads to humiliation, hardening of attitudes and a distancing of perpetrator from the pain caused by their actions. Through a series of vignettes, Ttofi and Farrington (2008) confirmed this finding when they asked 182 10–12-year-olds about the emotions they would have felt, including anger, shame, remorse or guilt, if they observed a peer being bullied. The children who scored high on disintegrative shaming also scored high on items that measured maladaptive forms of shame management.

Using a qualitative narrative method, Jennifer and Cowie (2012), in a study of 10–11-year-olds' moral and emotional attributions of bullying, found that the children typically characterised the bystanders as 'worried and ashamed'. These children described a range of emotions, to include concern for the person harmed and fear of the consequences if they intervened, as well as conflicting emotions of moral disengagement (in terms of the personal gain of not becoming the bully's next victim), empathy (in terms of moral responsibility towards those harmed) and shame (in terms of their inability to act in defence of the victim). The children were also able to distinguish attributes of pride and indifference on the part of the bully, in contrast to shame and worry if they imagined finding *themselves* in the role of bully. Such findings offer some explanation of the observation that, although many bystanders experience shame at their inaction, their reluctance to intervene may be due to their understanding of the risks that may ensue if they offer protection to those harmed and the pressure that they are under to conform to group norms. Jennifer and Cowie (2012) emphasise the importance of taking account of the strong emotions aroused by witnessing or experiencing aggressive behaviour. They recommend that schools should provide more opportunities for children to reflect on how these feelings arise, to consider where emotions of shame and guilt are located and to explore different ways of resisting negative behaviour that targets vulnerable peers.

The study by Jennifer and Cowie (2012) indicates the value of using narrative methods when trying to capture the complexity of children's responses to difficult or distressing situations. In a similar way, narrative therapy offers interesting parallels with restorative approaches through its focus on story-telling as a fundamental means for people to communicate and make sense of experience (McLeod 1997; White and Epston 1990). Essentially the argument is that people find it helpful to tell their story in a context where what they have to say is accepted and valued by others. As McLeod (2000, p. 345) writes: 'The basic experience of another person becoming a witness to one's account of troubles is meaningful and worthwhile'. By being given time and space to tell their story in a supportive place, the person is, in the process, given an opportunity to reflect on their story and to consider whether it could be understood or expressed in different ways. Narrative therapists also propose the concept of externalising the story. From this perspective, the person has a relationship with their own story and is in conversation with the issues that feature in it. Thus, there is potential for editing and changing the ways in which the story unfolds and for exploring the layers of meaning that are embedded within it. The listeners too are in dialogue with the story. The experience of hearing different accounts of the same episode provides an opportunity to understand why the protagonists behaved as they did. This is a significant part of the restorative process, with potential for change, including forgiveness and acknowledgement of causing hurt. For example, when peer mediators are trained to engage in conflict resolution with peers in dispute, each person tells their side of the story and the mediator reflects back each account and, in the process, gives each an opportunity to reflect on their story and consider whether it could have happened in a different way.

Involving young people in improving their social context

Restorative approaches also aim to create a safer community. One way in which this can be achieved is by developing systems of peer support (Andrès 2007; Cowie *et al.* 2002, 2008; Cremin 2007; Hutson and Cowie, 2005; Lane-Garon and Richardson 2003; Smith and Watson 2004). Andrès *et al.* (2005) report on a longitudinal study in two secondary schools in Spain, an experimental school that had developed a system of peer support to enhance the school's ethos and a control school in the same catchment area. The study took place in a context of major difficulty with a large influx of families from different cultures and an on-going concern about rising levels of violence, both in the community and in the school itself. In each class of the experimental school the students democratically elected classmates to act in the role of peer helpers. The elected students were then given training that enabled them to intervene directly to resolve peer conflicts, with a particular brief to intervene in cases of bullying and the abuse of power.

Andrès *et al.* (2005) found that the peer support activity had a very positive impact on the social development and personal qualities of those who participated as peer helpers, with boys demonstrating greater gains than girls. The programme indicated how important it is to give young people a framework in which to develop pro-social behaviour, self-efficacy and emotional literacy. The greatest impact of the programme was on psychological or indirect bullying. Social exclusion decreased dramatically in the experimental school during this study and there was interview-based evidence that the whole ethos of the experimental school improved substantially. This restorative programme has been running for over eight years and has become an integral part of the school culture, indicating that a whole community can change.

Conclusion

There are many advantages for schools that develop restorative approaches. There are fewer student suspensions and improved ratings on positive school climate. There is also a reduced likelihood of retribution or repeat offending, so preventing the escalation of violence. For example, trials of conferencing in Australian schools (Cameron and Thorsborne 2001) indicated that the majority of participants were positive about the experience of taking part in a restorative conference, those harmed felt safer after the conference and perpetrators felt cared for during the conference and more able to make a fresh start after the conference.

From a psychological perspective, there is evidence that school climate is greatly improved by increasing young people's understanding of rules and enhancing trust in how these rules are applied. This is likely to result in more positive relationships between peers and adults, as well as more confidence in acting pro-socially to defend vulnerable peers. Studies of peer support indicate that this approach gives children and young people deeper understanding of the reasons why perpetrators act the way that they do. Experiential training, with its emphasis on the emotional aspects of relationships, enables young people to explore the nature of empathy for another person's distress and to become more aware of the complex processes that underlie social interactions. By putting restorative principles into practice, young people develop greater insights into the factors that lead to conflict and violence.

Finally, the chapter proposes that it is crucial to work with peer relationships in order to address the problem of aggression and violent behaviour at school. This should be part of a much wider concern for self-awareness and understanding of group processes. All members of the peer group have a part to play and in a restorative context they are more likely to take action against aggressive behaviour rather than remaining as passive bystanders. In the process, they gain deeper insights into themselves.

References

American Psychological Association Zero Tolerance Task Force (2008) 'Are zero tolerance policies effective in the schools?', *American Psychologist*, 63(9): 852–862.

Andrès, S. (2007) 'Peer support systems as instruments for increasing *convivencia* in schools: an evaluation'. Unpublished PhD thesis, Universidad Autonoma, Madrid.

Andrès, S., Gaynard, S. and Martin, E. (2005) 'Evaluation of social competence in the school context: the experience of a programme of peer support in secondary schools' in J. A. del Barrio and I. Fajando (eds) *New Psychological and Social Contexts in Education*. Santander: INFAD, Psioex, 17–32.

Braithwaite, J. (1989) *Crime, Shame and Reintegration*. Cambridge: Cambridge University Press.

—— (2003) 'Restorative justice and a better future' in E. McLaughlin, R. Fergusson, G. Hughes and L. Westmarland (eds) *Restorative Justice: Critical Issues*. London: Sage, 54–65.

Cameron, L. and Thorsborne, M. (2001) 'Restorative justice and school discipline: mutually exclusive?' in H. Strang and J. Braithwaite (eds) *Restorative Justice and Civil Society*. Cambridge: Cambridge University Press, 180–194.

Cowie, H. and Jennifer, D. (2008) *New Perspectives on Bullying*. Maidenhead: Open University Press.

Cowie, H., Naylor, P., Talamelli, L., Chauhan, P. and Smith, P. K. (2002) 'Knowledge, use of and attitudes towards peer support', *Journal of Adolescence*, 25: 453–467.

Cowie, H., Hutson, N., Oztug, O. and Myers, C. (2008) 'The impact of peer support schemes on pupils' perceptions of bullying, aggression and safety at school', *Emotional and Behavioral Difficulties*, 13(1): 63–71.

Cremin, H. (2007) *Peer Mediation*. Milton Keynes, UK: Open University Press.

Hopkins, B. (2004) *Just Schools*. London: Jessica Kingsley.

Hutson, N. and Cowie, H. (2008) 'Setting up an e-mail peer support scheme', *Pastoral Care in Education*, 25(4): 12–16.

Jennifer, D. and Cowie, H. (2012) 'Listening to children's voices: moral emotional attributions in relation to primary school bullying', *Emotional and Behavioural Difficulties*, 17(3): 229–241.

Lane-Garon, P. and Richardson, T. (2003) 'Mediator mentors: improving school climate – nurturing student disposition', *Conflict Resolution Quarterly*, 21: 47–69.

McLeod, J. (1997) *Narrative and Psychotherapy*. London: Sage.

—— (2000) 'Narrative therapy' in C. Feltham and I. Horton (eds.) *Handbook of Counselling and Psychotherapy*. London: Sage, 343–347.

Morrison, B. (2003) 'Regulating safe school communities: being responsive and restorative', *Journal of Educational Administration*, 41(6): 689–704.

—— (2007) *Restoring Safe School Communities: A Whole School Response to Bullying, Violence and Alienation*. Sydney: The Federation Press.

Pepler, D., Smith, P. K. and Rigby, K. (2004) 'Looking back and looking forward: implications for making interventions work effectively' in P. K. Smith, D. Pepler and K. Rigby (eds). *Bullying in Schools: How Successful Can Schools Be?* Cambridge: Cambridge University Press.

Rogers, C. R. (1955) *Client Centered Therapy*. Boston: Houghton-Mifflin.

—— (1965) *Client Centered Therapy: Its Current Practice, Implications and Theory*. Boston: Houghton-Mifflin.

Salmivalli, C. (2010) 'Bullying and the peer group: A review', *Aggression and Violent Behaviour*, 15, 112–120.

Salmivalli, C., Lagerspetz, K., Björkqvist, K., Österman, K. and Kaukiainen, A. (1996) 'Bullying as a group process: Participant roles and their relations to social status within the group', *Aggressive Behavior*, 22, 1–15.

Skiba, R., Reynolds, C. R., Graham, S., Sheras, P., Conoley, J. C. and Garcia-Vazquez, E. (2008) 'Are Zero Tolerance Policies Effective in the Schools?', *American Psychologist*, 63, 852–862.

Smith, P. K. and Watson, D. (2004) *Evaluation of the ChildLine in Partnership with Schools (CHIPS) programme*. Research Report RR570, DCSF Publications.

Thompson, F. and Smith, P. K. (2011) *The use and effectiveness of anti-bullying strategies in schools*. Research Brief DFE-RB098 (2011) Available at: <https://www.education.gov.uk/publications/RSG/AllRsgPublications/Page10/DFE-RR098>.

Ttofi, M. M. and Farrington, D. P. (2008) Reintegrative shaming theory, moral emotions and bullying, *Aggressive Behavior*, 34(4), 352–368.

—— (2011) 'Effectiveness of school-based programs to reduce bullying: a systematic and meta-analytic review', *Journal of Experimental Criminology*, 7, 27–56.

United Nations (1989) *Convention on the Rights of the Child*. Geneva, Switzerland: Office of the United Nations High Commissioner for Human Rights. Retrieved March 9, 2007. Available at: <http://www.unicef.org/crc>.

Wachtel, T. and McCold, T. (2001) 'Restorative justice in everyday life: beyond the formal ritual' in H. Strang and J. Braithwaite (eds) *Restorative Justice and Civil Society*. Cambridge: Cambridge University Press, 114–129.

White, M. and Epston, D. (1990) *Narrative Means to Therapeutic Ends*. New York: Norton.

Chapter 9

Reflections on researching restorative approaches in schools and children's residential care

Carol Hayden

Introduction

This chapter reflects on the use of restorative approaches (RAs) with children in two different types of institutional context, as well as the challenges inherent in researching their impact. It draws on two research projects in different settings that use different restorative approaches: Family Group Conferences (FGCs) in mainstream schools (see Hayden, 2009) and Restorative Justice (RJ) in children's residential care (Hayden and Gough, 2010). As the key findings of these studies are already published they are not reproduced in full here. Instead, this chapter sets out to consider how the approaches used in these two institutional settings demonstrated key values and practices associated with RAs. In so doing the chapter considers the transferability of RAs to different contexts that work with and care for children. Considerations to do with research design and 'findings' are presented to encourage discussion about how we go about researching RAs in a climate where performance management strongly influences 'success' criteria and how Children's Services in the UK have to operate.

Two approaches: FGCs and RJ (later referred to as RAs)

In characterising the great variety of practices that are used by RJ practitioners, McCold and Watchel (2003) view FGCs as 'fully restorative' because 'victim reparation', 'offender responsibility' and 'communities of care and reconciliation' are all present. Using the same conceptualisation, the way that RJ was used as a values and practice framework for working in children's residential care could be seen as 'largely restorative', paying most attention to 'offender responsibility' and 'communities of care and reconciliation'; but with less attention to 'victim reparation'. However, we are already in trouble with this use of language when applied to the two types of institutional setting that inform this article. The way that FGCs in schools were used strongly resisted any connection to the language of 'justice', 'victim' and 'offender' and did not seek to implement 'reparation'. The users of RJ in children's residential care also quickly rejected concepts associated with the criminal justice system, and the term 'Restorative Approaches' (RAs) was adopted within the first year after staff training; although the concept of reparation in the residential care setting was viewed as *sometimes* appropriate. Do these departures from key RJ concepts matter? Are these two approaches still within the RJ suite of approaches? I would argue that despite the differences and departures from key aspects of RJ as used in relation to criminal justice, they are both examples of how the values and practices of RJ have evolved in different contexts; and specifically when applied to working with children and young people. What these two restorative approaches share in common is the desire to change the way we respond to children and young people who display problematic behaviour and/or who are in conflict with others. Both approaches set out to move away from punishment and towards the resolution of problems through encounter and planning for continued attempts to include the child or young person more successfully in school (FGCs) or in the residential care home (RJ/RAs).

However, the starting point for the two approaches is different (see Box 9.1). The FGCs in education service was focused on families and significant others coming together to address problems presented in schools – specifically attendance and behaviour problems (sometimes leading to exclusion from school). At the time of the research (2003–2004), FGCs were already well-established in the local authority and had been used in child protection cases since the early 1990s. In this well-established model, conferences are set up by an independent co-ordinator and paid for by the FGC service within the local authority. Independent co-ordinators spend time talking to the child and immediate carers; through which they identify the family network and significant others. Invitations to a FGC are issued and participants are prepared for the event by the co-ordinator.

Values underpinning the FGC approach include the belief that families (rather than professionals) are best placed to help understand and address their children's problems; that families have the best interests of their child in mind; that children can participate meaningfully in such conferences and that professionals will be willing and able to agree and act on the plan put forward by the family. The service evolved out of its established use in child protection in this local authority. 'Empowering' families is a key underpinning aim. Having an independent co-ordinator to set up and 'mediate' the FGC event (or encounter) is crucial in this model. The principle of voluntarism is also fundamental. Schools and families have the choice to offer or ask for a FGC (or not) and withdraw after an initial period of willingness. Indeed, about a quarter of referrals in the research did not go as far as a conference, after some hours of work from the co-ordinator. Overall, this way of being restorative could be seen as based on a service model, wherein the external FGC service could be brought in to the school, but without any wider contact with or adjustments to values across the school staff.

In contrast, the work in children's residential care was about whole-service change, with ambitions to influence agencies outside the residential care environment. So, for example, a protocol was agreed with the police in relation to how they responded to calls from children's residential care units. This approach started by using the language of the criminal justice system and was originally referred to as RJ (rather than RAs); with a focus on reducing conflict and offending behaviour as the key indicators of success. The research in this setting was undertaken between 2006–2008, starting in the year after all staff had received training. Like the FGC work, this initiative built on a longer period of changing practice in the local authority. All the residential homes had already completed training in the Team-Teach approach (Team Teach, 2003), which includes conflict resolution, as well as 'positive handling strategies': so staff were used to the concept of consistency of approach, as well as the values that underpin conflict resolution. The focus in children's residential care was on using RAs to resolve conflict and reduce offending behaviour. The wider objective was to create a more positive living and working environment for young people and staff. The local authority emphasised from the outset that this approach was not seen as a 'quick fix'; it was seen as part of a long-term programme of culture change.

All care staff in the ten children's homes in this local authority were trained over a one year period. The initial training for staff communicated the idea that a 'gold standard' of restorative justice was the formal scripted restorative conference with the established roles of the *victim*, the *offender* and the trained *mediator*. Care staff soon realised that such formal scripted approaches would have limited the impact upon the care environment and would possibly make relationships between young people and staff even more problematic. As a result, care staff decided that more fluid restorative processes would have to be developed and this resulted in what has been called 'stand up RJ' or 'corridor' RJ in work with schools (see for example, Morrison, 2001). By the second period of field research most staff referred to restorative *approaches*, rather than restorative justice, because they wanted to emphasise the difference in what they did in comparison with the youth justice system. Furthermore, most of the behaviour responded to with a restorative approach was not necessarily criminal. The most frequent situation was interpersonal conflict, mostly between young people, sometimes involving staff.

The values underpinning the adoption of a RJ approach included a commitment to change in staff culture and a belief that RJ was a better way of resolving conflict than 'sanctions' or punishment. Thus this work was based on homes 'owning their own conflict' (see Christie, 1977) and reducing reliance on external help; in this case calls to the police, out-of-hours service or incident records sent to management. However, the principle of voluntarism was compromised for staff, who were *expected* to adopt this approach. Also, there was no funding for external or additional staff to act as mediators in an encounter; although certain individual staff took on this role in particular homes.

	FGCs (established in Child Protection cases in 1994; in education in 1998)	RJ (all staff trained during autumn 2005/spring 2006)
The model	Formal – Full conference External service part funded by short-term grants. 80 conferences funded per year. *Evolved from use in Child Protection.*	**Continuum of approaches, mostly informal** An approach to be used by all staff in children's residential care, with attempts to liaise with external agencies (e.g. YOT). Underpinned by a Police Protocol on RJ. *Trainers and language came from a Criminal Justice background.*
Roles: relevance of 'victim' 'offender'	**Victim and offender roles not relevant** Focused on the individual child and the need for support to change.	**Blurred – not always clear,** e.g. Staff could be victims, offenders or mediators. Relationships, history and interpersonal conflict very relevant to both staff and young people in the residential care setting.
External mediator	Independent 'co-ordinator' as mediator.	**No external staff** Some homes had members of staff who regularly acted as the mediator in formal conferences.
Reparation	Not the focus	**Often, but not always**
Cultural change in schools/homes	Not the focus	**Strong focus**
Links across agencies	Part of the local authority support services to schools: **co-ordinators worked across agencies using FGCs.**	Attempts made via a **steering group, e.g. Youth Offending Team** in particular, who later developed RJ differently. **Protocol with the Police**
Period of research	2003–2004	2006–2008

Box 9.1 The two approaches: FGCs and RJ (1)

The research projects

Both research projects were commissioned by a local authority, so the design in each case was developed and agreed with the local authority. Both commissioners wanted a fairly 'hard-nosed' look at the outcomes they had to address in terms of performance management. Both commissioners were well aware of the evidence available about whether or not participants tended to prefer this sort of approach to traditional and other ways of addressing problem and conflict in the lives of children and young people. The FGC work in this local authority was already well established and valued. The RJ project had a different starting point: it had a strategic manager who believed that achieving values and cultural change in children's care homes was the most important objective. The performance management indicator that focused on records of offending and children in care was just the organisational hook to get the change underway. The key aspects of the research design and data collection in each piece of research are summarised in Box 9.2.

	FGCs (2003–2004)	RJ (autumn 2006–2008)
Design	Quasi experimental (41 FGC and EWS comparison group 37). 78 children in all	Natural experiment (before and after, informed by a realist approach). 10 residential care homes
Outcomes data	All children: percentage attendance and whether excluded. FGCs: 24 cases teacher and parents SDQs.	All homes: 2001–2007 percentage offending; incident records; police call outs; out-of-hours service. Cohort study (n=46)
Staff viewpoints	Referral agents (n=60) EWS staff team (n=9) FGC co-ordinators (n=20)	Care staff (2006: n=99; 2007: n=71) Managers (2006: n=10; 2007: n=8)
Young people's viewpoints	Young people's experiences of a FGC (n=27).	After staff training and one year later: how staff responded to conflict (n=43).

Box 9.2 The two research projects: FGCs and RJ (2)

FGCs in education

As this was to be a study comparing outcomes from FGCs with the EWS (Educational Welfare Service) there was much discussion at the outset of the possibility of random allocation – to either a FGC or the EWS service only. However, there was resistance to this amongst practitioners who felt that they did not want their assessments compromised. There were also concerns to do with the special project status of FGCs and the possibility that random allocation could interfere with the number of FGCs convened in a year. Other concerns centred on the specific requirement that referrers and families were 'committed' to the FGC process; a practical issue that could make random allocation difficult, if not impossible to achieve in practice. Other research has illustrated the difficulties in achieving random allocation because of practitioner resistance to random allocation (see Brown, 2003; Little *et al.*, 2004).

At the time the research began (2003), this was already an established service, having provided FGCs in education since 1998 (and in Child Protection since 1994), experiences of the process were generally positive. The education service had funding for up to 80 FGCs a year and a crucial question for them was how and where in the lives of children and families these conferences might operate. The local authority as a whole had created a pool of FGC co-ordinators for use across services/issues (at the time of the research this included child welfare, youth justice, domestic violence and schools). However, the central concern of the research reported upon here (and the education service funding it) was to take a harder look at outcomes and also investigate the potential of FGCs as a way of enhancing support systems for children in difficulty at school. The EWS as a long established support service to schools was also one of the main referral agencies to FGCs, alongside schools themselves. The research sought to investigate whether FGCs in education could set a framework for working with families in relation to improving pupil attendance and behaviour in school, and as such whether they were a potential way of working for the EWS. What we wanted to know was whether FGCs set a *more* or *less* effective framework for working with families on these issues than would otherwise be the case in the way the EWS has traditionally worked.

Key aspects of the FGC and EWS referral forms were harmonised for the purposes of the research. Official records of attendance and exclusion were part of the way we wanted to compare the FGC and EWS groups. In practice, referrers did not always use the new FGC forms and even if they did, they did not always supply data in the same way. Therefore all attendance and exclusion data was verified from local authority records in exactly the same way and for the same timescale before and after a referral at the end of data gathering. At this point, it is worth reflecting for a moment upon whether levels of attendance and amount and duration of exclusions *are* the best comparative outcome measures for the study and indeed whether they are a *fair way* of establishing the impact of a FGC. The main defence for using these measures was the pressure on the FGC and EWS services to focus on these performance indicators and their consequent desire to have some answers on this in the research.

In the event, only 30 of the planned 41 FGCs were convened (that is the conferences went ahead) but we followed up the attendance and exclusion data for those individuals who did not have a FGC, despite some time spent with the co-ordinator. We reported on the SDQ (Strengths and Difficulties Questionnaires, see Goodman, 1997) for convened FGC cases only; as insufficient SDQ questionnaires were completed in the EWS comparison group. SDQ data from teachers was the most complete and enabled a useful 'before' and 'after' comparison to be made for 24 children (80 per cent of 30) who were the focus of convened FGCs from the perspective of those working directly with the children and young people on a daily basis. Survey and interview data in this research was used to help provide more insight into where and how FGCs in education are perceived as being successful or unsuccessful. Children were consulted about their experiences of taking part in a FGC.

RJ in children's residential care

The field research in care homes was undertaken during autumn 2006 and 2007, with organisational data being analysed over a longer period (2001–2007). The research was an evaluation, involving the collection and triangulation of a range of types of data: before, during and after the implementation of a Restorative Justice approach across all children's residential units in one local authority. In a sense, this provided the opportunity for a natural experiment, in which any change could be tracked over both an extended (2001–2007) as well as a more focused time period (2006 and 2007); with the latter time period being after all care staff had been trained in the same RJ approach. Like most natural experiments conducted in a service setting, this study presented lots of complexity and potential for multiple influences and measures of 'success' or 'failure'. For this reason we were influenced by the way a realist evaluation recognises the complexity of 'real world' settings and avoids the use of single measures of effectiveness (Pawson and Tilley, 2004, p. 8).

Although our study does not meet the full criteria for a realist evaluation, we have borrowed concepts from this approach because it helps make sense of the complexity of the research setting and data collected. It also helps situate the implementation of the RJ approach in children's residential care. Pawson and Tilley (2004) argue that programmes or interventions (in the current research, Restorative Justice) are based on a vision or theory of change, which can be explained by the *context-mechanism-outcomes configuration,* as shown in Box 9.3 in relation to the RJ study.

The research tracks both process and outcomes from training all residential care staff in this approach; as well as the changes over time in a range of secondary data available from within the local authority. The key changes that were investigated in the fieldwork were staff attitudes towards the use of restorative justice and the way in which it was being used. Other parts of the research use existing organisational data (from 2001 to 2007) to track any evidence of changes in resolving conflict that may relate to how RJ is being used, both across the service (for example, by looking at the pattern of police call-outs and incident reports) and in relation to individual children (by conducting a cohort study as well as individual case studies). We also interviewed children about the way RJ was used in their homes.

Contexts: (*those features of the conditions in which programmes that are relevant to the operation of the programme mechanisms are introduced*)
Different types of children's residential care homes (secure, open, long-stay, short-stay, younger children 9–13, teenagers 13+) as places where conflict and offending behaviour might occur or emanate. All staff have the requisite training, but will have different attitudes towards, experiences and understandings of young people's behaviour. Attitudes, experiences and understandings of agencies external to residential care will also vary (e.g. police, YOT, schools).

Mechanisms: (*what it is about programmes or interventions that is likely to bring about an effect*)
Young people, through the actions and responses of staff trained in the use of a RJ approach will develop more empathy for others, learn to resolve conflict and address offending behaviour through the RJ encounter and process. They will learn to take responsibility and make amends for wrongdoing through the process of reparation. In turn, staff will have a way of resolving more conflicts without resorting to external help, particularly the police.

Desired outcomes: (*what the adoption of a RJ approach is trying to achieve*)
Reductions in conflict and offending behaviour; residential homes become a better place to live and work.

Box 9.3 RJ in children's residential care – Context–Mechanism–Outcome configuration

Contact with care staff from homes prior to starting the field research revealed that some were uncomfortable with the criminal justice language of 'victim' and 'offender' and indeed with the concept of Restorative *Justice*. However, the local authority used the term 'Restorative Justice' in their promotional literature and clearly saw the adoption of the process as something they were trying to do *with* other agencies, such as the Youth Offending Team (YOT). The local authority's promotional literature clearly explained the key restorative concepts of 'responsibility, reparation and reintegration'. The training literature referred to both Restorative *Justice* and Restorative *Approaches* in relation to what they were doing, with an emphasis very much on the more formal use in meetings and conferences.

Reflections on key findings

As both pieces of research were evaluating the impact of the practical application of different types of restorative approach they had to come up with conclusions on whether these approaches had worthwhile results. Neither research study started with a commitment to either approach per se on the part of the researcher. However, these two studies followed on from earlier work on conflict resolution (Hayden and Pike, 2004) and, with hindsight, became part of a process of change in the researcher's understanding of the common value base of these approaches and the responsibility of researchers to reflect on what they do when they evaluate the 'impact' or 'outcomes' of this sort of work.

The evidence in the FGC study overall was that FGCs had demonstrable impact (better attendance, improved SDQ scores, no further exclusion) in some cases but not in most. FGCs were clearly not the panacea hoped for and sometimes believed to be by some of the local authority practitioners at the start of the research. Part of the issue here is about whether what the FGC is trying to achieve is possible through the FGC mechanism; and, whether it can happen quickly enough. We also have to consider how we measure this and whether the measure is valid. In relation to FGCs, we already knew from existing research that families willing to commit to a FGC generally have positive experiences of the process, but there was no evidence that FGCs could set in motion the kind of support that would lead to the changes that agencies working with families are expected to bring about (improved school attendance and avoidance of exclusion from school in particular in this study). Furthermore, the schools had to be willing to allow time for change to happen. But in relation to behaviour, it appeared that some schools were impatient (or 'making a point', or maybe they were 'at the end of their tether') and excluded children within weeks of a FGC referral. When looking at interventions that try to harness the resources and support of the family for children and young people it is important to consider whether this can happen quickly enough and in a way that also meets the remit and performance targets of the agencies tasked with providing a service.

RJ in children's residential care had some positive (and measurable) impacts and it fitted well with the existing practice of most homes and most staff. There was a reduction in call outs to the police, calls to the out-of-hours service, as well as a reduction in incident reports. But there was no change in the rate of official records of offending. Also, in the year following the formal implementation of the approach the differences between institutions and within staff groups became more marked. External issues limited the potential of the work done in these homes: a somewhat hostile external climate towards youth crime, a lack of agreement within key external agencies who had the power to act restoratively (or not) and changes in the residential care service all hampered the realisation of the full potential of the approach. The conclusion to the study acknowledged that cultural change takes much longer than could be captured in the two years of this research study and was able to reflect back on earlier research in the same local authority. Earlier research was undertaken in residential care homes in the mid 1990s, when 'physical restraint' was the focus of the research (Hayden, 1998) and 'sanctions', 'punishment' and 'loss of activities and opportunities' was the language used. Taking this longer perspective it was clear that there had been significant improvements in the way these homes worked with and related to children and young people and that RAs were (for most) a logical step in their development. Furthermore, we concluded that the values and practices underpinning a restorative approach were a better way of working with vulnerable children who have already missed out on and lost so many opportunities; making a 'sanctions' approach one that can lead to the replication of harms already suffered before entry into care.

Data types and sources	Conclusions
Outcomes data (attendance and exclusion)	FGCs not successful overall in helping to increase attendance or prevent exclusion – in comparison with the EWS – although some success in individual cases.
SDQ (Strengths and Difficulties Questionnaire) for 24 children who had an FGC.	For a few children – change in total difficulties score. Reduced 'sense of burden' – for both teachers and parents. Increased 'pro-social behaviour' – parents and teacher assessments.
Referral agents	Often positive about the idea of FGCs. Outside help popular with schools.
EWS team	Saw the potential and wanted the option in some cases.
FGC co-ordinators	Last resort status of FGCs in schools. Very reliant on individual change of the child, compared with other uses of FGCs.
Children	Self conscious – didn't like the number of adults in meetings, especially those from school. Wanted a friend in the meeting; some schools would not allow this in school time. Most children's SDQs illustrated the perception of difference in relation to themselves, also found in the adult SDQs on the same children.

Box 9.4 FGCs in education: summary of findings

Translating the research findings into the framework of 'Context–Mechanism– Outcomes', presented earlier in Box 9.3, creates the following 'realist conclusions'.

Contexts: (*those features of the conditions in which programmes are introduced that are relevant to the operation of the programme mechanisms*)
RJ was implemented in very different types of children's residential care home; it was 'a useful tool' in all types of home, but met with more success in homes with staff that saw the broader relevance of the approach. Care staff working with younger children did not always like/see the relevance of the focus on offending behaviour. Care staff working in the secure home were more confident in the use of the approach and voluntarism was not seen as an option: children were expected to resolve conflict within a RJ encounter. The timing in the use of RJ was crucial in all settings, it had to be immediate enough (as people had to go on living and working together) but also timely in relation to the young person being calm enough and willing to talk things through.

Mechanisms: (*what it is about programmes or interventions that is likely to bring about an effect*)
Most staff used informal RJ as a style or way of communicating or in impromptu conferences or 'encounters' to help resolve everyday conflicts within children's homes. This approach was viewed both as a way of resolving conflict as well as modelling wanted or pro-social behaviour.

Desired outcomes: (*what the adoption of a RJ approach is trying to achieve*)
Some reduction in conflict but no reduction in official records of offending behaviour; some improvement in perceptions of residential homes as better places to live and work; evidence of staff/homes 'owning more of their conflicts' by reduced calls to the police, incident records and calls to the out-of-hours service. But, it appeared that any learning for young people, in terms of managing conflict or behaving in a pro-social manner, did not transfer to outside the home, partly because the response of people outside the home could not be controlled or predicted.

Box 9.5 Realist conclusions to the RJ research

Conclusion

Researching real-world interventions is an inherently political act: the choices that are made in terms of research design, any outcome measures and so on can have an important effect on the perceived success (or otherwise) of a practical project. Although both evaluations collected data on experience and perception from operational staff as well as children and young people; senior managers focused most on 'hard outcomes' that related more to performance management criteria than to the wider objectives of the services and context in which they were working. However, both pieces of research ended with some consideration of values and whether the approach was simply one alternative amongst others, or a *better* way of responding to conflict or problem behaviour in schools or residential care homes.

When the two approaches are compared, 80 externally facilitated FGCs looked like a luxury item in a mass service like schools; whereas RJ had informed and developed the expertise of all care staff in how they responded to conflict with children placed in the residential care environment. As such, the latter was sustainable and did not rely on major funding to continue being used. In contrast, the FGC approach in schools looked like a drop in the ocean in relation to the scale of the issues of poor attendance and problem behaviour in schools. All schools have children and families with a poor record of attendance and difficult behaviour; it was difficult to rationalise where the 80 conferences a year should be used when there were hundreds of schools in the local authority. Probably because only a small number of FGCs were available to schools they became a last resort for some schools and the way that this approach was brought in from outside did little to change school culture. Perhaps this led to frustration and a tendency to exclude children when the FGC was slow to materialise or did not 'work'. FGCs were a good idea that had some impact in some cases and SDQ data showed that they reduced the 'sense of burden' for participants. However, they did not have an overall impact on measurable outcomes – attendance and exclusion. It is not unreasonable to comment that attendance and exclusion were perhaps the wrong measures for the impact of FGCs in any case. But the service had set itself up to address these issues and so became subject to the same performance measures that other services had to address in this area of work.

RAs (as they became known) in children's residential care were more successful because they were more pragmatically adopted and resonated with existing practice for many staff. Adopting this approach did not reduce offending behaviour though – the key performance management criteria. The adaptation of RJ in children's residential care compromised some key principles associated with RJ – such as the independence of the mediator role and the principle of voluntarism in the parties involved in an encounter, but it did adhere to key characteristics of encounter and often (but not always) reparation.

References

Brown, L. (2003) 'Mainstream or margin? The current use of family group conferences in child welfare practice in the UK', *Child and Family Social Work*, 8: 331–340.

Christie, N. (1977) 'Conflicts as Property', *British Journal of Criminology*, 17: 1–15.

Crow, G. (1999) *Family Group Conference in Education*. Interim Report: Process and early outcomes. University of Sheffield.

Goodman, R. (1997) 'The Strengths and Difficulties Questionnaire: A research note'. *Journal of Child Psychology and Psychiatry*, 38: 581–586.

Hayden, C. (1998) 'The Use of Physical Restraint in Children's Residential Care', *Social Services Research*, 3: 36–46.

—— (2009) 'Family Group Conferences – are they an effective and viable way of working with attendance and behaviour problems in schools?', *British Journal of Educational Research*, 35 (2): 205–220.

Hayden, C. and Pike, S. (2005) 'Including "positive handling strategies" within training in behaviour management – the "Team-Teach" approach', *Emotional and Behavioural Difficulties*, 10(3): 173–188.

Hayden, C. and Gough, D. (2010) *Implementing Restorative Justice in Children's Residential Care*. Bristol: Policy Press.

Little, M., Kogan, J., Bullock, R. and Van Der Laan, P. (2004) 'An experiment in multi-systemic responses to persistent young offenders known to children's services', *British Journal of Criminology*, 44: 225–240.

McCold, P. and Watchel, T. (2003) 'In Pursuit of Paradigm: A Theory of Restorative Justice', IIRP Canada. Available at: <http://canada.iirp.edu/articles.html?articleId=424> [Accessed 13 July 2012].

Morrison, B. (2001) 'Developing the School's capacity in the regulation of civil society' in Strang, H. and Braithwaite, J. (eds) *Restorative Justice and Civil Society*. Cambridge: Cambridge University Press.

Pawson, R. and Tilley, N. (2004) 'Realist Evaluation'. Paper funded by the British Cabinet Office. This paper develops ideas from the well-known book: Pawson, R. and Tilley, N. (1995) *Realistic Evaluation*. London: Sage.

Team-Teach (2003) *Team-Teach Workbook*. St. Leonards-on-Sea: Steaming Publications.

Part II

Contested

Chapter 10

Restoration, transformation or education?

A philosophical critique of restorative approaches in schools

James MacAllister

Introduction

In this chapter, the conceptual foundations of restorative approaches in education will be scrutinised. Initially, it will be acknowledged that the recent adoption of 'restorative justice' principles in schools is not without promise. However, it will be argued that some attempts to explain: 1) the meaning of restorative justice; and 2) how restorative approaches might contribute to social and emotional education – are riddled with ambiguity. It will be suggested that a philosophical analysis might help to clear away some of the muddle. In particular, it will first be argued that Johnstone and Van Ness's concept of 'transformative restoration' (see Chapter 4) is logically paradoxical. Their terms 'encounter' and 'reparation' better capture what would seem to be the core functions of restorative justice. However, 'education' probably more aptly describes the more preventative or pro-active functions of restorative processes. In reference to Aristotle, it will secondly be argued that it is not obviously apparent there is a natural state of 'positive' emotion that educational processes can restore pupils to. It will, rather, be maintained that social and emotional education should involve helping pupils to learn through various painful and pleasant sentiments, including (controversially) shame, so that they can moderate these where necessary. It will be concluded that restorative approaches may be able to contribute to such social and emotional development. Indeed, the merit of restorative approaches may become most evident if proponents of it restrict themselves to modest and specific claims about its educational potential.

The myth of Diana and Actaeon

> *Diana and Actaeon*
> Destiny, not guilt, was enough
> For Actaeon. It is no crime
> To lose your way in a dark wood
>
> (Hughes, 1997, p. 105)

I would like to begin with a myth – one of transformation and restoration. A myth that involves anger at a slight perceived and shame from the excessive nature of the retaliation. In book III of Ovid's *Metamorphoses* (2008), the poet recounts the tale of Actaeon, who, tired from the day's hunting in the woods, stumbles into a cavern. In the cavern is a waterfall and pool where the Goddess Diana secretly bathes under the watchful protection of her nymphs. Diana becomes enraged with Actaeon upon spotting him peering towards her unclothed body. She hurls some water in the huntsman's face and challenges him to tell anyone else how he came to see her naked. Upon Diana's words Actaeon undergoes metamorphoses. He sprouts a rack of antlers, hooves replace his hands and powerful legs his arms – he swiftly turns into a stag. Dizzied with shame at his unexpected transformation he leaps, terror stricken, back into the forest. There he finds the pack of hounds he used to lead on in the hunt. Now being without voice he cannot call them off. In a bitter irony the hounds savagely catch, kill and eat their former master unaware of who he so recently was. Only then, it is said, did the remorseless anger of Diana find peace (Hughes, 1997, p. 112). Only with violent retribution was her anger restored to calm.[1]

The ancient parable of Actaeon may seem like an odd place to start a discussion on the nature and possible benefits of restorative approaches in schools. However, I believe the poem can help to bring home (albeit somewhat fantastically) the harm that can result when someone vengefully reacts to feelings of anger, in a reckless and disproportionate way. After all, Actaeon did not as Hughes[2] puts it 'commit a crime'; but he suffered the ultimate penalty of his life anyway. It is possible that restorative approaches in schools may be able to help reduce the likelihood of extreme and unjustified actions resulting from angry feelings; especially in instances where harm (apparent or real) is apprehended. It has certainly been claimed that restorative approaches can repair harm (Morrison, 2007), restore relationships, and enable a more thoughtful and constructive way of addressing conflict in schools (McCluskey *et al.*, 2007 and Cremin in this volume). Restorative approaches, perhaps, restore relationships through seeking apology and appropriate 'reparation' rather than 'punishment' (McCluskey *et al.*, 2007). Still, while I am broadly sympathetic to the basic idea that creating a safe space for dialogue might improve relationships where they have, for whatever reason, broken down; the theoretical foundations of restorative approaches do seem more than a little unsteady.[3] Cremin gets to the nub of a central conceptual confusion in her chapter in this volume on the adaptation of restorative approaches and principles to schools. Why champion 'restoration' when it is far from clear that the harmony sought ever really *was* in the first place?[4] Why return to a destination whose (moral?) value may now be questionable?

> If the bottom layer of...restorative approaches...is concerned with everyone in schools developing social and emotional skills and attitudes to prevent and deal constructively with conflict, one has to ask what this has to do with restoration – restoring to what? To an idealised notion of...societies in which everyone took responsibility for their own actions...? It is hard to imagine that such communities ever really existed. And if they did, is it really desirable to go back to pre-modern times?
>
> (Cremin, 2010, p. 4)

In this chapter, I would like to examine the theory that underpins some latter-day accounts of restorative approaches in education.[5] I will reflect upon Cremin's question: is it really desirable to go back to pre-modern times? It is of course pellucid that we cannot return and *live* in history, no matter how much we may (or may not) want to. However, I do think that the philosophers of Ancient Athens conceived of the emotions in a nuanced way that might lend clarity to contemporary debate about how to best educate them. It will be suggested that sensitively mediated restorative approaches may help to foster virtuous sentiments in school pupils; sentiments that are valuable because of their likely relation to human flourishing. However, it will be maintained that educational approaches that are distinctively 'restorations' are probably reactive rather than preventative in nature as a 'restoration' typically involves responding to and repairing some harm or damage that has already been caused. What, though, is educational philosophy and how might it help to provide clarity to debate about restorative approaches in education?

How might educational philosophy contribute?

Although a diverse range of famous philosophers since antiquity have turned their hand to educational problems, the philosophy of education did not really emerge as a distinct discipline until the twentieth century (Archambault, 1968; Blake *et al.*, 2003; Hirst and W. Carr, 2005). D. J. O'Connor (1957) was one of the first to employ the methods of philosophical analysis to specifically educational problems. He argued that philosophy was an 'activity of criticism and clarification' (O'Connor, 1957, p. 4) that could be exercised on any subject matter. The phrase 'philosophy of education' refers to 'those problems of philosophy that are of direct relevance to educational theory' (O'Connor, 1957, pp. 14–15).

While there is far from contemporary consensus about the precise nature of educational philosophy, many agree that conceptual analysis is possibly the principal tool at the educational philosophers disposal. O'Connor (1957), Archambault (1968), Reid (1968), Best (1968), Peters (1970), Hirst and Peters (1975), Blake *et al.* (2003), Curren (2007) and Holma (2009) all concur on this in their different ways. What, though, should educational philosophers be trying to gain from a more profound grasp of concepts? Archambault observes that processes of philosophy often lead to a more coherent set of educational aims. Holma suggests that the newly clarified concepts ought to be fed back into wider educational dialogue. Biesta (2007), Archambault (1968) and Reid (1968) all broadly think that philosophical clarity can support wise practical decision making in education. It seems that a vital function of educational philosophy is to employ logical inquiry to resolve conceptual and linguistic ambiguities where they occur, so as to support the development of sound theory, policy and practice in education. Arguably, there are at least two such central ambiguities in the literature of restorative approaches and education. It is to these that discussion now turns. First, what is meant by restoration and transformation? Second, how exactly may such restoration and/or transformation support emotion education?

Philosophical analysis of 'restoration' and 'transformation'

In his chapter in this volume, Van Ness maintains that restorative justice is a deeply contested concept: there is not likely to be (indeed perhaps should not be) a single conception of it. Nonetheless, he does propose three possible conceptions, implying that each may overlap the other in practice: namely, encounter; reparative; and transformative (see also Johnstone and Van Ness, 2007). In the 'encounter' notion the focus is placed upon those involved in a crime meeting and making a collective judgement about the best way to respond to the crime. In the 'reparative' version of restorative justice the emphasis is placed upon the offender repairing the harm caused by the commission of that crime. It is asserted that in 'the *transformative* conception, restorative justice is conceived as a way of life we should lead' (Johnstone and Van Ness, 2007, p. 15). Johnstone and Van Ness indicate that individual people are all inextricably connected to each other in complex social networks. They seem to construe 'transformative restoration' as an aspiration, as an ideal type of human relation, 'guided by a vision of transformation of people, structures and our very selves' (ibid, p. 17). How useful are these suggested concepts in clarifying restorative justice and its influence on education?

Taking first of all the concept of transformation – can *any* educational process (restorative or otherwise) truly 'transform' people and social structures and *should* education aspire to such transformations in the first place? What does transformation actually mean? The *Oxford English Dictionary* indicates that to 'transform' is to 'make a thorough and dramatic change in the form of outward appearance or character' (OED, 1991). It similarly defines a 'transformation' as a change in form or 'metamorphoses' (OED, 1991). It seems that a person is 'transformed' if they become changed into something that they were not previously. In contrast, 'restorative' means either a 'tending to restore to health' or a bringing 'back or attempt to bring back to the original state by rebuilding, repairing' (OED, 1991). Thus restoration and transformation seem to refer to very different processes: the essence of a restoration involves something being *returned to how it was before,* whereas at its core, a transformation entails something *becoming different and new.* Furthermore, while a 'transformation' suggests a sudden, swift and perhaps radical alteration, 'restoration' implies a more gradual process. Given these differences it is probable that 'restoration' and 'transformation' are words that cannot be used to describe the same activity or goal without a distortion of the very meaning of these words. Thus, the very idea of a *transformative restoration* arguably hinges on a logical (or at least a linguistic) paradox.

If restoration and transformation are mutually incompatible descriptive terms, which one captures better the core functions of restorative approaches in schools? Morrison (2007) remarks that, by far and away the most common model of restoration actually employed in schools is a face-to-face conference, or as Van Ness and Johnstone would put it, an 'encounter'. School-based encounters might take the form of community or family conferences, or they may involve less formal peer mediation or problem solving circles (ibid, 2007). Morrison adds that schools often adapted the vocabulary employed by the criminal justice system to better reflect the purposes of education. Instead of the terms 'victim', 'crime' and 'offender' schools seemed to prefer to speak of 'students who have been harmed or caused harm' (Morrison, 2007). It has similarly been observed that the borrowing of legalistic phrases such as 'victim' and 'perpetrator' 'may reinforce a discourse that demonises and criminalises young people, and should be avoided' (McCluskey et al., 2008, p. 204). Thus, restoration through informal encounter appears to be the concept that is most useful in schools. What happens though when the move away from notions of 'victims' and 'perpetrators' extends to situations where no clear harm has occurred? Can restoration still take place?

Although Scottish secondary schools tended to perceive restorative approaches as a method for resolving 'particular incidents where relationships had broken down' (Kane et al., p. 102); primary schools in the same study construed such practices as capable of 'permeating school culture and providing a vehicle for the development of school ethos' (ibid, p. 102). Similarly, Morrison notes that today many schools are adopting 'pro-active, as well as reactive restorative measures. The broad aim is to build the social and emotional intelligence and skills within the school community' (2007, p. 326). It has also been implied that restorative approaches might prevent harm from arising in the first place by seeking to promote emotional literacy in pupils (McCluskey et al., 2008). What should be made of these claims? Restorations can be pro-active and preventative? While a process of restoration may perhaps lead to eventual positive change in a person over time,[6] it certainly appears mistaken to describe individual restorative encounters as 'transformative', given the necessarily dramatic nature of a transformation. Furthermore, once educational practices become focused on the 'pro-active' rather than the 'reactive' they arguably cannot be, at base, 'restorative' either. A restoration does, after all, seem to necessarily require effort to make good some pre-existent harm, damage or deterioration in state. Therefore it seems to me that distinctively restorative approaches to education hinge on: 1) some harm having already been caused; and 2) attempts being made to repair this harm. Arguably, educational encounters specifically designed to restore relationships and/or repair harm caused by conflict may be properly described as restorative. When educational ends become more pro-active however, the term restoration appears to be less apt. This is not to dispute that restorative *approaches* might aid the social and emotional education of pupils; it is only to say that it is rather perverse to speak of a 'pro-active restoration'. For a 'pro-active restoration' arguably necessitates both the active prevention of deterioration on the one hand and the actual facilitation or permission of such deterioration on the other. Thus, to my mind social and emotional education, or even just 'education' captures much better than 'restoration', the idea of pro-actively cultivating the emotional development of pupils. In this regard, what do proponents of restorative approaches mean by 'emotional intelligence' and 'emotional literacy'? *How* might emotions be restored and/or educated and *what* emotions should be so restored and/or educated?

Emotions as restorations to a natural state of harmony?

It has been supposed that restorative approaches in schools can help pupils to build emotional skills and intelligence (Morrison, 2007; McCluskey *et al.*, 2008 and Cremin in this volume). However, to the best of my knowledge there has been relatively little debate in the restorative approaches literature about exactly what sort of phenomena *the emotions are*. Cremin suggests in Chapter 11 that restorative justice involves an integration of thought and emotion for the wider purpose of human flourishing. Her view may not be without promise or substance but it does perhaps invite further clarification. Is Cremin suggesting here that a more balanced and moderate integration of thought and feeling is educationally and/or morally desirable; and that restorative approaches might support the social and emotional education of pupils in something like this way? Or is she rather implying that emotions are, at some important level, unruly, non-moral feelings that are devoid of thought and in need of rational control?

While the restorative approaches literature may not provide much specific detail about the sort of emotional intelligence aimed for; Goleman's[7] concept of emotional intelligence has recently come into question. Kristjánsson (2006, 2007) and Macleod *et al.* (2010) have suggested that educators should try to promote 'virtuous' rather than 'intelligent' emotions. Notably, they claim that emotion-virtues, unlike emotional intelligence involve: 1) proper and moderate, rather than rationally controlled feelings; and 2) actions that have distinctively moral ends. I certainly think it is unhelpful, from an educational perspective, to conceptualise the emotions as mere physiological sensations or disturbances that are divorced from cognition and/or morality. If emotions do not entail mental activity then can they be readily *educated* through dialogue with others? Can conversation about past feelings positively alter a person's future affection and behaviour? Perhaps, but such dialogue would seem to require some sort of capacity to rationally reflect on feelings and conduct. To be sure, William James (2007), one of the founders of modern psychology, did famously construe the emotions in largely physiological terms. However, in Ancient Athens a very different cognitive theory of emotion was developed. 'What is characteristic of all emotions is a single feature: namely thought or belief as the efficient cause' (Fortenbaugh, 2008, p. 116). In the opening pages of his influential text, *Aristotle on Emotion*, Fortenbaugh (2008) chronicled a period when members of Plato's academy, including Aristotle, conducted a groundbreaking inquiry into the emotions. The investigation culminated in a theory, fully articulated in Aristotle's *Rhetoric*, according to which thought and/or belief came to be construed as 'efficient causes' (Fortenbaugh, 2008, p. 12) of emotion. Fortenbaugh suggests that the Academy's investigation of emotion was first evident in Plato's *Philebus*. Fortenbaugh claims the *Philebus* raises questions about the emotions, but it is Aristotle that directly addresses and answers these questions in the *Rhetoric*. A significant feature of Aristotle's account, Fortenbaugh argues, was the creation of a new educational theory for the emotions. Frede (1996), however, argued that

Plato in the *Philebus* developed a theory of emotion as restoration to the natural state. Given the language used to describe recent 'restorative approaches' in schools, the theory of emotion Frede attributes to Plato would seem to be of contemporary relevance and interest. In the *Philebus*, Plato does, to be sure, suppose that there is a natural state of harmony in all living creatures that disintegrates when they experience emptiness (Philebus, 31d-32c). It is painful, he says, to suffer the decay and destruction of this natural state (Philebus, 42c8-d3). He adds that the pain brought about by the disintegration of the natural state can be removed by the filling up of whatever has been lacking.

Crucially, Plato actually defines *pleasure* at this point, as such a restoration to the natural state. As he puts it, 'when things are restored to their own nature again, this restoration, as we established in our agreement among ourselves, is pleasure' (Philebus, 42d5-6). There would appear to be sound textual evidence then, in support of Frede's declaration that Phileban *pleasures* are 'always the restoration of some disturbance or the filling of a lack' (Frede, 1996, p. 262). However, Frede's claim that Plato developed a theory of *emotion as restoration* is less well supported by the text. If Plato did intend to develop a general theory of the emotions in the *Philebus*, one of its distinctive features would seem to be that they are *free* of bodily feelings – they are entirely cognitive judgements or mental events. Letwin concurs with this reading and observes that Phileban passions are occurrences that are 'psychological rather than physiological in character' (1980, p. 196). Importantly, I do not think that it is educationally prudent to imply that the emotions are feelings that can be restored to a natural state of harmony. For one, as Letwin (1981) notes, Plato leaves unanswered, in the *Philebus*, the question of whether or not the pleasures Frede takes to be constitutive of emotions are essentially *private* events or *public* ones, specifiable in a shared community of discourse. For another, in the *Philebus*, pleasures are not so much to be educated but rationally limited. For Aristotle, in contrast, moderate emotions were a necessary feature of moral virtue and the exercise of virtue was, in turn, necessary for the flourishing[8] life (eudaimonia). Aristotle thought that the emotions are neither free of thought, nor pure thought – but rather, feelings that are infused with thought, and as such, educable. In this respect, Cremin (2010, p. 1) may have done well to base her account of human thriving on Aristotle rather than Seligman. It is arguably unduly restrictive to classify pleasure as 'positive emotion'. As we shall see in the subsequent section, some emotions that are painful in the short term may be positive over all. Importantly, Aristotle also maintained that human flourishing requires the exercise of virtue rather than the pursuit of pleasure.

Educated emotions and the flourishing life

> Emotions are those things by the alteration of which men differ with regard to those judgements which pain and pleasure accompany, such as anger, pity, fear and all other such and their opposites.
>
> (*Rhetoric*, 1378a24-26, p. 141)

In Section 6 of the *Rhetoric* Aristotle discusses a range of emotions in depth: anger, calm, friendship, enmity, fear, confidence, shame, favour, pity, indignation, envy and emulation. To be sure, at least some of these emotions appear to be aiming at some sort of restoration. Calmness, for example, is defined as the 'suspension and placation of anger' (Rhetoric, 1380a8-9). However, Aristotle stipulates that *three* elements must be present for an emotion to become manifest. He takes the example of anger and says that it must be established, *what state* persons are in when they are angry, *who* they are angry with and in *what circumstances* (Rhetoric, 1378a). Pathos (passion or emotion, taken from the verb to suffer or experience), Konstan suggests, 'looks to the outside stimulus to which it responds' (Konstan, 2007, p. 4). Arguably, when we *suffer* emotions, we are at least partly, passive, in regard to them. It is the aspect of passivity that takes them beyond the realm of what we can *wholly* choose. However, Aristotle holds that an emotion is not just a passive alteration but also a judgement about pleasure and pain. Importantly, these judgements are at least partly cognitive and as such, susceptible to persuasion under the sage advice of others. His emphasis on persuasion not only marks a significant departure from the Phileban view of pleasure and emotion; it also perhaps offers a theory about how restorative approaches like conferencing and/or mediation might enable emotion education through verbal exchange and dialogue.

Unlike Plato, Aristotle seemed to think that our emotions can dispose us to act out of virtue. Kosman (1980) and Kristjánsson (2006 and 2007) both suggest that moral virtue often entails a certain reciprocity between passionate reaction and action (pathos and praxis). To be sure, people may suffer emotions in that they are centrally passive in regard to them, but *dispositions* of feeling need not be passive. We do not, perhaps, choose to become angry about something in a specific moment, or during an episode of feeling, but we can shape how we respond to things more broadly, through the habits of feeling we acquire. Sherman and White (2007) have recently suggested that we are more than merely 'indirectly responsible' for our emotions, in so far as we choose our dispositions. Our emotional habits, they say, are open to revision in social interaction with others. Sherman and White think Aristotle did *not* hold the view that people are essentially passive in regard to their emotions; a perspective they say resides implicit in Aristotle's *Rhetoric*. Indeed, it seems to me that Aristotle regarded persuasion as a quite legitimate educational tool.[9] Certainly, the *Rhetoric* does not find Aristotle explicitly stating that persuasion is a means that *should* be used to aid the development of virtue, in the young. However, Aristotle's discussion of the role of emotional appeal, in political and legal settings, strongly suggests that he held the view that persuasion *could* improve the judgements of young people. Moreover, Aristotle seemed to think that we could learn through feelings of shame and emulation[10] too.

'And since shame is an imagination connected with disrepute, and felt for its own sake and not for its consequences...one must needs feel shame before those whom one *holds in regard*' (Rhetoric, 1384a 31-34). Aristotle maintains that shame (aiskhunê) is a type of pain felt when one's reputation is being, or might be, sullied (Rhetoric 1383b11-15). Moreover, shame is at its most acute when one's behaviour is witnessed by others (Rhetoric, 1384a 43-b), especially those that one admires (ibid. 1384a 35-36 and 1384b 37-39). Thus, shame is arguably a distinctively moral[11] emotion that is intimately connected with public standards or norms, of acceptable behaviour. Konstan (2007) argues that in modernity shame has been derided as only a primitive form of guilt. In restorative approaches in education it has certainly been suggested that it 'is clear that notions of shame are not helpful' (McCluskey, 2008, p. 207). However, Aristotle implied that shame is a distinctive virtue of the learner.[12] Through feeling moderate shame young people can arguably become: 1) acquainted with the moral values of their community (moral values that may come to serve them well in the long term); and 2) moved to act to work towards acquiring these values themselves. Thus there is perhaps a need to distinguish between excessive public shaming and feeling justified shame.[13] Crippling, cruel public shaming of the sort experienced by Actaeon would seem to have no place in schools, but justified and tolerable shame might be morally educational.[14] In any case, shame would not appear to be an emotion that is inherently unhelpful in education. Far from it: feelings of shame that are justified, comparatively mild and understood (by teacher and pupil alike) may actually move pupils to change their future actions in more ethically desirable directions. While I would certainly not want to suggest that social and emotion education (and restorative approaches that may support this) should be restricted to the cultivation of shame, I do not think this emotion should be considered off limits either. For Aristotle, human thriving involved the moderate experience of a range of pleasant and painful emotions. Importantly, he thought that some painful emotions (like shame) are educational and valuable because of their particular capacity to engender long term human flourishing.

Transformation, restoration or old-fashioned education?

In this chapter it has been argued that some present-day attempts to formulate a concept of restorative justice have failed to convince. It has been suggested that: 1) the notion of a transformative restoration is logically paradoxical; and 2) the idea of a pro-active restoration is ill-considered. However, it has also been suggested that restorative approaches may, in practice, be able to contribute to a broader Aristotelian sentimental education. It is hoped the philosophical clarifications offered here will be perceived by practitioners not as a 'sniping from the side-lines'; but rather as an attempt to engage in dialogue so as to strengthen the theoretical foundations of the field. In this respect, it seems to me that advocates of restorative justice might be well advised to make modest and specific claims about what distinctively restorative approaches might realistically achieve in schools. Much of the actual practices described as 'transformative' and/or 'pro-active' might be more aptly characterised by a much older word – education.

In fairness, to Johnstone and Van Ness, they do acknowledge there may be 'other and better names' (2007, p. 20) to describe the concept of restorative justice than the ones they put forward. In the case of transformation I would be particularly inclined to agree. By their very rapid nature, transformations, for good or ill, tend to only occur in mythology.

Notes

1 This is a brief recap of events told much more poetically, first by Ovid (2008) and later by Ted Hughes (1997) and Robin Robertson (2006).
2 In his adaptation of the poem 'Actaeon' (Hughes, 1997).
3 Cremin (2010) notes Braithewaite's comment that the literature in relation to restorative justice is 'immature' and lacking in 'theoretical sophistication'.
4 It has also been recorded that some Scottish head teachers are beginning to ask: 'What are we restoring to?' (McCluskey *et al.*, 2008, p. 213).
5 In particular, the views of Morrison (2007); Kane (Kane *et al.*, 2008); McCluskey (McCluskey *et al.*, 2008) and Cremin (2010) will be discussed.
6 As (McCluskey *et al.*, 2008) do certainly, broadly suggest.
7 Goleman is of course, one of the first and arguably the most notable advocates of emotional intelligence.
8 See the *Nicomachean Ethics* (2004), Kristjánsson (2006 and 2007) and Carr (2009) for explanations of the need for moderate emotions within the virtuous and flourishing life.
9 Konstan (2007, p. 97) and Kristjánsson (2007, p. 19) also interpret the *Rhetoric* in a similar light.
10 See Kristjánsson (2006b and 2007) for a detailed explanation of why emulation is moral emotion characteristic of learners.
11 Konstan remarks that shame has a fundamentally ethical character (2007, p. 104).
12 See Burnyeat (1980) and Kristjánsson (2007) for discussion of how shame is a semi-virtue of the learner.
13 Even if shame should not be directly cultivated by educators it seems to me that some pupils may experience it anyway. Surely in such cases it would be educational to help pupils understand this shame and put it in the right perspective.
14 Indeed, when educators utter phrases such as 'I am disappointed in your behaviour' they are perhaps trying to instil feelings of shame in the person concerned in the hope that this shame will be morally educational; in the hope that the same behaviour will not be repeated again. If such phrases are uttered sensitively and with genuine concern for the person involved then the shame invoked need not, it seems to me, become damaging or excessive.

References

Allen, R. OED (1991) *The Concise Oxford Dictionary of Current English*. 8th edition. Oxford: Oxford University Press.
Archambault, R. (ed.) (1968) *Philosophical Analysis and Education*. London: Routledge and Kegan Paul.
Aristotle (2004) *The Nichomachean Ethics*. 3rd edition. London: Penguin.
—— (2004) *The Art of Rhetoric*. London: Penguin.

Best, E. (1968) 'Common Confusions in Educational Theory' in R. Archambault (ed.) *Philosophical Analysis and Education*. London: Routledge and Kegan Paul, pp. 39–56.

Biesta, G. (2007) 'Why 'WHAT WORKS' Won't Work: Evidence-Based Practice and the Democratic Deficit in Educational Research', *Educational Theory*, vol. 57, Issue 1, 1–22.

Blake, N., Smeyers, P., Smith, R. and Standish, P. (eds) (2003) *The Blackwell Guide to the Philosophy of Education*. Oxford: Blackwell Publishing.

Burnyeat, M. (1980) 'Aristotle on Learning to be Good' in A. Rorty (ed.) *Essays on Aristotle's Ethics*, pp. 69–92.

Carr, D. (2009) 'Virtue, Mixed Emotion and Moral Ambivalence', *Philosophy*, vol. 84, 31–46.

Carr, W. (2004) 'Philosophy and Education', *Journal of Philosophy of Education*, vol. 38, 1, 55–73.

Cremin, H. (2010) 'Do restorative approaches in schools work? The evidence'. Paper presented at *ESRC Seminar Series: International Perspectives on Restorative Approaches in Schools*, House of Lords, 4 February 2010.

Curren, R. (ed.) (2007) *Philosophy of Education: An Anthology*. Oxford: Blackwell.

Curzer, H. (2002) 'Aristotle's Painful Path to Virtue', *Journal of the History of Philosophy*, vol. 40, no. 2, 141–162.

Dewey, J. (2008) *Democracy and Education*. UK: Filiquarian Publishing.

Fortenbaugh, W. (2008) *Aristotle on Emotion*. 2nd edition. London: Duckworth.

Frede, D. (1993) *Philebus Introductory Essay*. Indiana: Hackett, pp. xiii–lxxx.

—— (1996) 'Mixed feelings in Aristotle's Rhetoric' in A. Rorty (ed.) *Essays on Aristotle's Rhetoric*, pp. 258–285.

Hirst, P. and Peters, R. (1975) *The Logic of Education*. London: Routledge and Kegan Paul.

Hirst, P. and Carr, W. (2005) 'Philosophy And Education – A Symposium', *Journal of Philosophy of Education*, vol. 39, 4, 615–632.

Holma, K. (2009) 'The Strict Analysis and the Open Discussion', *Journal of the Philosophy of Education*, vol. 43 (3), 325–338.

Hughes, T. (1997) *Tales from Ovid*. London: Faber & Faber.

James, W. (2007) *What is an Emotion?* Milton Keynes: Wilder Publications.

Johnstone, J. and Van Ness, D. (2007) 'The meaning of restorative Justice' in G. Johnstone and D. Van Ness (eds) *The Handbook of Restorative Justice*, Devon: William Publishing, pp. 5–23.

Kane, J.* (2008) 'Collaborative Evaluation: Balancing Rigour and Relevance in a Research Study of Restorative Approaches in Schools in Scotland', *International Journal of Research & Method in Education*, vol. 31, No. 2, July 2008, pp. 99–111, also* written by G. McCluskey, S. Riddell, G. Lloyd, J. Stead and E. Weedon.

Konstan, D. (2007) *The Emotions of the Ancient Greeks; Studies in Aristotle and Classical Literature*. Toronto: University of Toronto Press.

Kosman, L. (1980) 'Being Properly Affected: Virtues and Feelings in Aristotle's Ethics' in A. Rorty (ed.), *Essays on Aristotle's Ethics*, pp. 103–116.

Kristjánsson, K. (2006) '"Emotional intelligence" in the classroom? An Aristotelian critique', *Educational Theory*, vol. 56 (1), 39–56.

—— (2006b) 'Emulation and the Use of Role Models in Moral Education', *Journal of Moral Education*, vol. 35 (1), 37–49.

—— (2007) *Aristotle, Emotions, and Education*, Aldershot: Ashgate.

Leighton, S. (1996) 'Aristotle and the Emotions' in A. Rorty (ed.), *Essays on Aristotle's Rhetoric*, pp. 206–237.

Letwin, O. (1981) 'Interpreting the Philebus', *Phronesis*, vol. 26 (3), pp. 187–206.

Macleod, G.* (2010) 'Emotion Education as Second Language Acquisition', *International Journal of Emotion Education*, vol. 2 (1), pp 34–38, also* written by J. MacAllister and A. Pirrie.

McCluskey, G.* (2008) '"I was Dead Restorative Today": From Restorative Justice to Restorative Approaches in School', *Cambridge Journal of Education*, vol. 38 (2), pp. 199–216, also* written by G. Lloyd, J. Stead, J. Kane, S. Riddell and E. Weedon.

Morrison, B. (2007) 'Schools and Restorative Justice' in G. Johnstone and D. Van Ness (eds) *The Handbook of Restorative Justice*. Devon: William Publishing, pp. 325–350.

Nussbaum, M. (1996) 'Aristotle on Emotions and Rational Persuasion' in A. Rorty (ed.), *Essays on Aristotle's Ethics*, pp. 303–323.

O'Connor, D. J. (1957) *An Introduction to the Philosophy of Education*. London: Routledge and Kegan Paul.

Ovid (2008) *Metamorphoses, A New Translation*. Translated by A. D. Melville. Oxford: Oxford University Press.

Peters, R. S. (1970) *Ethics & Education*, London: George Allen & Unwin Ltd.

—— (1972b) 'The Education of the Emotions' in R. Dearden, P. Hirst and R. Peters (eds) *Education and the Development of Reason*. London: Routledge and Kegan Paul, pp. 466–483.

Plato (1993) *Philebus*, Indiana: Hackett.

Reeve, C. (1996) 'Philosophy, Politics, and Rhetoric in Aristotle' in A. Rorty (ed.) *Essays on Aristotle's Rhetoric*, pp. 191–205.

Reid, L. (1968) 'Philosophy and the Theory and Practice of Education' in R. Archambault (ed.) *Philosophical Analysis and Education*. London: Routledge and Kegan Paul, pp. 17–37.

Robertson, R. (2006) *Swithering*. London: Picador.

Ruitenberg, C. (2009) 'What do Philosophers of Education do? (And how do they do it?)'. *Journal of Philosophy of Education Special Issue*, vol. 43 (3), 315–470.

Sherman, N. and White, H. (2007) 'Intellectual Virtue: Emotions, Luck and the Ancients' in De Paul, M. and L. Zagzebski (eds) *Intellectual Virtue, Perspectives from Ethics and Epistemology*. 2nd edition. Oxford: Clarendon, Oxford, pp. 34–53.

Chapter 11

Critical perspectives on restorative justice/restorative approaches in educational settings

Hilary Cremin

Introduction

In recent years there has been growing interest in the ways in which restorative justice (RJ) might have a contribution to make in the education sector (Thorsborne and Vinegrad, 2008; Hendry, 2009; Cremin, 2008; DCSF, 2007). Many proponents of RJ from the youth justice sector have argued that its timely introduction into schools might have upstream effects that could reduce educational exclusion and youth offending. Others have argued that these matters are more complex, and that concepts taken from the youth justice sector translate badly into school settings. In this chapter I will critically review similarities and differences between RJ in the criminal justice sector and RJ (or restorative approaches, 'RA') in schools, drawing on different conceptions of RJ and RA that might illuminate benefits and challenges. The chapter draws in part from papers from the Economic and Social Research Council (ESRC) funded seminar series on Restorative Approaches in Schools that is at the heart of many chapters in this book.

In a school setting, McCluskey *et al.* (2008, p. 200) have defined restorative approaches as, 'Restoring good relationships where there has been conflict or harm and developing school ethos, policies and procedures to reduce the possibility of such conflict and harm arising'. Proactive approaches alongside reactive approaches to conflict are seen as embedded in the very definition of RA in schools. Even at a definitional level, however, questions immediately present themselves. To what extent are young offenders, or students in schools (or their workers and teachers) 'empowered' in any aspect of the judicial process or in processes of schooling? What is meant by the empowerment of the young, the poor and the dispossessed when it comes to the dispensation of 'their' crimes/ misdemeanours? What is meant by 'facilitation'? To what extent can adults in youth offending settings and schools – responsible for the safety, well-being, and educational achievement of large numbers of young people – facilitate in a neutral, non-judgemental and non-directive way? What is meant by 'community'? Whose community is it? Is it possible for strategies in educational settings that are proactive and preventative to be classed as restorative? And finally, (and perhaps most significantly) what is being restored, and to whom?

Some RJ theorists have seen the different approaches and practices of RJ as forming a continuum (Zehr, 2002), and others have grouped them into different categories. Van Ness, earlier in this book, and Johnstone and Van Ness (2007) suggest three different but overlapping categories: the encounter conception; the reparative conception and the transformative conception. What follows uses the framework of the first two of these conceptions of RJ to respond to some of the above questions, critically analysing ways in which RJ and RA are theorised and applied, and making tentative suggestions for possible ways forward both in educational and youth justice settings. The transformative conception of RJ and RA are discussed in MacAllister's chapter in this book.

The encounter concept of RJ

The encounter concept of RJ is grounded in victim–offender mediation. It argues that the strength of RJ lies in its ability to bring victims, offenders and stakeholders in a case together outside formal, professional-dominated settings such as the courtroom, and to support them to engage in meaningful dialogue. Values, including the central role of communication and recognition of emotion (particularly feelings of hurt and loss) are important in ensuring that encounters remain restorative (Zehr, 2002). The heart of this process, the restorative conference, enables those involved to increase awareness of self and others, forging an integration of the public and the private, self and other, thought and emotion. An example provided by Charlie Falconer, the former UK Lord Chief Justice in Tony Blair's government, shows why RJ (and the process of encounter in particular) captured the interest of New Labour. In a case in Liverpool a 'chaotic drug user' was diverted from future offending through a meeting with a widowed lady in her seventies whom he had burgled. He agreed to spend time helping her in her garden, and benefitted from getting to know her. She was able to get answers to questions about why she was targeted, and was no longer traumatised and fearful when she saw how 'pathetic' he was (Falconer, 2010).

There are, however, challenges in implementing the encounter concept of RJ, and there are those who have argued that it can be unjust, or even harmful (Ashworth, 2002: Roche, 2003). The informality of RJ enables offenders to show their best side, but it also enables them to show their worst. As Roche (2003, p. 2) points out: 'Just as people can empathise, reconcile, repair, reintegrate and forgive, so too can they scold and stigmatise, hector and humiliate, dominate and demoralise'. There is a real risk of poor facilitation leading to victims being re-victimised through badly-managed restorative processes (Cossins, 2008). The key here is in the skill of the facilitator, but this varies, particularly with the mainstreaming of RJ and its integration into existing systems of criminal justice. In a study of a family group conferencing project for juvenile offenders in the south-east of England, Zernova (2007) found that the main aim of the funding body (the Youth Justice Board) to reduce youth offending sometimes interfered with the project's stated aim of prioritising victims. Only victims of juveniles were offered the service, for example, conferences never took place when the offender was not present (although they did when the victim was not present) and some victims complained of a 'party atmosphere' detracting from the seriousness of the crime. One victim stated that: 'It did make me feel as though [the offender] hadn't done anything wrong, though. It did. It did feel like they [i.e. conference organisers] were sticking up for her' (Zernova, 2007, p. 499). Victims had very little say over how the crime should be responded to in this project, and yet, by allowing them to attend conferences, express emotions, ask offenders questions and receive an apology, 'an illusion might be created that victims play an active role in the criminal justice process, and that the restorative process "belongs" to them' (Zernova, 2007, p. 503). Zernova argues that the only real driving force behind restorative processes was the criminal justice system itself, which stayed in charge, while creating an impression that conference participants were key decision makers.

As shown above in relation to victims, offenders can also be marginalised through the dominance of the criminal justice system's priorities. The power of processes of encounter can be limited by direct or indirect manipulation of offender's responses. During observations of family group conferences, Zernova (2007) found that facilitators encouraged and subtly pressured offenders to adopt particular self-identities – the identities of repentant individuals who have understood the wrongfulness of their past actions, and wish to put right their wrongs and not repeat their mistakes. This was achieved through skilful questioning, probing, reframing and rephrasing offenders' statements, focusing offenders on certain issues and praising and encouraging them. If conference facilitators successfully achieved this, offenders were likely to state that they attended a conference and apologised to victims because they wanted to do so.

In a similar vein, Zernova (2007) found that restorative conferences were not as open as was claimed. Pre-conferencing reports tended to be directive, providing a detailed description of why the offender got into trouble, and a series of suggestions for how the family might support the offender to stay out of trouble in the future. This works against the idea that those most directly affected by crime should be empowered through a retreat of the state. In interviews, offenders were divided in their understanding of whether the encounters were mandatory or voluntary, and one young man apologised for something in an encounter that he claimed before and afterwards he had not done. There seemed to be a feeling amongst some of the offenders that they might go back to court if they did not attend and participate in the process in the ways that were expected of them. This is a long way from the voluntariness that many proponents of RJ claim is central to the process.

Claims of neutrality and non-directiveness in restorative conferences are compromised by these practices. Rose (2000) has drawn on Foucault's concept of governmentality to suggest that the state's role in the control and regulation of conduct has shifted to become more diffuse and complex, with government done at a distance and the problem of crime de-centred from 'codes, courts and constables' (Rose, 2000, p. 324). Within this 'new politics of conduct' a plethora of 'control workers' take up the role of managing communities on the margins, encouraging their 'responsibilisation' for their own needs and behaviour. 'Responsibilisation' reformulates the problems of offenders as moral or ethical problems, and, 'this ethical reformulation opens the possibility for a whole range of psychological techniques to be recycled in programmes for governing "the excluded"' (Rose, 2000, p. 334). Offenders can take up more pro-social identities through encounter and adoption of the values of RJ (openness, repair of harm, accountability) and in doing so can transfer from Rose's 'circuits of exclusion' to 'circuits of inclusion'. The social structures that maintain these circuits, however, remain intact and unchallenged by restorative processes (Gray, 2005).

Thus, RJ can worsen or leave unchallenged the stigmatisation and social exclusion of the offender in the hands of inexperienced or unreflective facilitators who consciously or unconsciously take on a morally superior stance (Braithwaite, 2002). Ashworth (2002) has expressed concern about a lack of consistency, and therefore lack of fairness, in restorative practice that relies on the willingness of victims to participate in a restorative meeting, and in the degree of reparation that is agreed in each individual case. It has even been argued that there are times when RJ can work against natural justice and human rights. Cossins (2008) points out that the use of RJ to divert sex offenders from court, together with the risk of re-victimisation and the leniency of agreements, could affect victims', offenders' and the public's perception of the seriousness of child sex offences compared with the efforts of the last three decades to improve social and legal awareness of the prevalence and effects of child sexual abuse. For this reason, she suggests that, 'the prosecution of child sex offences should not become a private conference process, with varying outcomes and no follow-up in relation to offender compliance. Arguably, such prosecutions should continue to be a public process with assured and measureable outcomes' (Cossins, 2008, p. 375). Thus the foregrounding of the 'encounter' element of responding to crime can lead to procedural difficulties and a lack of equality. RJ is nothing if it is not applied, and theorists and proponents of RJ must do more than complain that poor practice should not define the field (Morris, 2002).

The encounter concept in educational settings

Initiatives to develop RJ in educational settings are often grounded in notions of 'encounter'. Students are encouraged to develop understanding of the consequences of their actions through dialogue with those who have been affected. This may be in the form of a formal restorative conference involving a student who might otherwise enter the youth justice system or be expelled from school, but it is more likely to take an informal turn, through practices such as peer mediation and restorative dialogue with teachers (Morrison, 2007; Hendry, 2009).

Some of the objections that have been raised above in the context of criminal justice may perhaps be less applicable to educational settings. In many ways the role of school is precisely to educate young people into the values and norms of wider society, and processes of encounter can be a powerful way of achieving this. Falconer (2010) draws a sharp distinction:

> The education system provides a learning experience that is designed to improve and do something for pupils, helping them to develop a sense of responsibility. The criminal justice system, including the youth justice system, is not for that purpose. Its purpose is to provide protection for the public from crime. Its purpose is also to ensure that the public accept that the State is there to provide punishment and retribution in relation to crime.
>
> (Falconer, 2010, p. 1)

Thus, Falconer argues that the education system has an important function of inducting young people into the social and moral norms of society, and its punitive function must be moderated if it conflicts with this first aim. As I have argued elsewhere (Cremin, 2010) bringing young people together to talk about conflict and its effects is a useful way of encouraging social and moral awareness. Restorative approaches can provide an antidote to behaviourist methods in schools, which risk reproducing the retributive function of the criminal justice system. Schools have increasingly relied on behaviourist methods of behaviour management (especially for those students who find it hardest to engage with activities that they find boring or irrelevant) to achieve the function of getting students to do well in tests. Behaviourist methods (e.g. Cantor, 1989) have grown out of behaviourist psychology, and experiments on animals, most famously Pavlov's dogs (classical conditioning) and Skinner's rats (operant conditioning). They entail the manipulation of rewards and punishments to encourage desirable behaviour and to reduce unwanted behaviour. These methods rely on teacher-imposed discipline, and deny young people opportunities to develop empathy and moral reasoning through encounter with those they have harmed. If self-discipline is the goal of education, then educational settings need to provide learning environments that enable young people to learn from their mistakes, and to reflect on that learning. This is the promise of restorative approaches in educational settings, and encounters between perpetrators and those who have been harmed in particular.

Lewis (2009) quotes from an evaluation of RA in a High School in Pennsylvania by a principal who clearly felt that the programme had encouraged meaningful encounters between students: 'We didn't really believe that we could get our kids to the point where they could express remorse, sympathy and respect. Now the kids have embraced restorative practices even more than the adults' (Lewis, 2009, p. 6). The evaluation of the Restorative Approaches in Schools (RAiS) programme in Bristol by Skinns, Du Rose and Hough (2009) is perhaps the most independent and rigorous evaluation of RA in schools to date. Quantitative data concerning project secondary schools was collected from the local authority pre- and post-intervention, alongside data from control schools. Measures included attendance, exclusions and educational attainment. Qualitative data were collected from interviews with staff and pupils at four schools that had implemented RAs (two schools withdrew). A total of 34 staff and 26 pupils participated in semi-structured interviews. The programme was perceived to have many benefits in the schools that had made the most effective use of it (two of the original six). Restorative approaches were found to have had a positive impact on some pupils who were confronted for the first time with the consequences of their actions. Teachers gained insight into the complexity of conflicts between peers through the conferencing process and were more aware of both sides of the story, and the need to avoid a bully–victim divide. RA was seen to improve communication, both between peers and between teachers and pupils. This led to 'closing loops' that had previously been disconnected because of a lack of dialogue. Pupils benefitted from hearing the perspectives of teachers, and learnt to respect those who were prepared to listen to them. Friendships were restored, or even created, through the restorative process and some young people simply learnt to live with each other better, or keep out of each others' way. The emotional literacy of some teachers and pupils was improved through the habitual use of restorative language, greater empathy, problem-solving skills and more reflection on the consequences of behaviour. One 14-year-old pupil spoke about how bullying that had led to suicidal thoughts had been stopped through a restorative encounter:

> They said that they didn't really know the effect it had on me, because at the time I was saying that I wanted to kill myself and stuff, and like the police came out, and they had to get my counsellor. It was like really bad, and I said that to them in the meeting, but they didn't think it would have that amount of effect on me. They thought it was just like a joke or something.
>
> (Skinns *et al.*, 2009, p. 43)

One Head of Year asserted that every one of the conferences that she had facilitated had worked, and that despite being tempted to offer solutions to young people 'they actually sort it out themselves' (Skinns *et al.*, 2009, p. 30). One 14-year-old student's comments about the way the conferencing process had made her feel, suggests that RA can improve self-discipline through a more child-centred, no-blame approach, 'The way the meeting came across it felt like you, well you were in the wrong obviously, but you weren't in trouble like'.

Although many of the objections to RJ in the criminal justice system are less applicable to educational settings, some do remain, and these mirror the objections to its use in the criminal justice sector. With regards to encounter processes, concerns have been expressed about students feigning contrition to avoid sanctions, re-victimisation in conferences, and the loss of gains in placing bullying firmly in the public arena through a return to more informal processes. Rigby (2010) points out that, far from being isolated loners, most young people who engage in bullying are popular within their peer group. Processes of encounter sometimes fail because there is a false assumption that a sense of belonging comes uniquely from being part of a group that is good and compassionate, and that young people who have bullied others need to be 'reintegrated'. The evaluation of the RAiS project in Bristol shows that both teachers and pupils recognised the limitations of RA for people who do not accept the harm that they have caused. A Head of Year in one of the schools said that it didn't work for students who deny the harm they have caused, or who don't care. A 13-year-old pupil felt that, 'If the people actually don't care about what the other person is thinking, and don't really care if they're being horrible to someone, and if they're sort of winning, in a way, then it doesn't work, maybe they should get in trouble' (Skinns et al., 2009, p. 31). A victim of racist bullying in another school was not happy with the outcome of a conference because the person responsible was not punished, and a 15-year-old pupil admitted to engaging in the process in a tokenistic way, 'Me writing on a piece of paper isn't going to stop me from hitting her again, it's just making them shut up basically' (Skinns et al. 2009, p. 34).

There are also concerns about procedural difficulties with RA in schools and a lack of time and resources. It is clear that after years of struggle to bring into the public arena, both sexual abuse and domestic violence in the criminal justice sector, and school bullying in the education sector, there are dangers that gains made through zero tolerance policies may be lost in favour of more informal policy and practice.

The reparative concept of RJ

The reparative concept of RJ is grounded in the idea that the harm caused (for example, by crime) to people and relationships needs to be repaired. Adherents to this view argue that when an encounter is not possible (perhaps the victim does not wish to participate) a restorative process can still occur through, for example, the imposition of reparative sanctions ordered by the court. Braithwaite (2002) has suggested that RJ gains its power through reintegrative shaming, which involves disapproval of a harmful act within a continuum of respect for the offender and rituals of reparation and forgiveness that have their origins in many indigenous communities.

Practices of reparation and reintegrative shaming are associated in RJ literature with indigenous communities in New Zealand, Canada and Australia. These communities have been characterised as high-context cultures, where conflict interaction unfolds according to cultural and social controls (Ausburger, 2002). In high-context cultures, group values of harmony, solidarity, interdependence, honour, and the maintaining of 'face' aim to preserve hierarchy and status differentials. In cultures with low-contextual influence (i.e. urban Western cultures) the individual exercises his/her rights within a legalistic framework. Whereas in high-context cultures people are more likely to possess a non-confrontational, indirect, triangular resolution style, in low-context cultures people aim to preserve social mobility and individual freedom through liberal values of individualism, autonomy, independence, self-reliance, self-esteem, equality, and egalitarianism. In individualistic, low-context cultures people are much more likely to utilise a confrontational, direct-address, one-to-one negotiating style, or at least believe that that is the final way to resolve differences (Ausburger, 2002).

There are those who have argued that care must be taken in introducing models of justice that are culturally distant from most low-context industrialised societies. Restorative justice has taken root in the youth justice sector in New Zealand, but this has been the result of political pressure to reinstate traditional Mäori methods of conflict resolution (Carruthers, 2010). In 1989, nearly 150 years after Europeans abolished the Mäori restorative system and introduced adversarial British criminal justice, the New Zealand Parliament legislated for a system that operates from restorative Mäori philosophy. In New Zealand, then, there has been a return to more traditional models of justice, but it does not necessarily follow that these methods are universally applicable in Western contexts. The two social codes – honour and shame – that characterise Ausburger's high-context cultures are, 'reciprocal forces that serve to unite groups, police the boundaries, define who is included and excluded, and enforce conformity' (Ausburger, 2002, p. 103). Whilst it may be desirable to strengthen community cohesion in low-context Western societies that have become fragmented, it is perhaps less desirable to advocate a sense of community in which everyone knows their place and few transgress. Sen (2006) has argued that all communities are made up of individuals with differential access to power and justice to a greater or lesser extent, and that false notions of community can be used to promote conflict and violence just as easily as to promote community cohesion.

Critics of RJ have pointed to a lack of clarity about concepts of community amongst RJ proponents (Cossins, 2008). Zehr (2002) acknowledges controversy about the meaning of community, and about whom to involve in restorative conferences. Both he and Braithwaite (2002) advocate a focus on communities of care, or micro-communities, that may or may not be geographically defined. This still leaves, however, the question of how wider structural inequalities within communities are addressed. Ultimately the question remains – who is required to make reparation to whom? In 2005, Gray found that concepts of reparation and reintegration of socially excluded young offenders into mainstream society were false because most were never integrated to begin with. His study of a RJ programme in the south-west of England used qualitative and quantitative methods to investigate a sample of 240 young offenders and their victims. It found that, in the current penal climate, the principles of RJ had been narrowed to give undue weight to the responsibility of young offenders, and perceived deficits in their moral reasoning. The exclusionary socio-economic constraints that limited young people's choices and ability to reintegrate had been obscured. Findings showed that nearly three-quarters of the young offenders interviewed were experiencing moderate to high or high to very high levels of interpersonal and social difficulties, and that they ranked family, health and school issues highest in terms of problem severity. Restorative justice interventions did little to tackle these wider issues. Morris (2002) suggests that RJ is not 'restoring' offenders if they cannot access programmes to address their drug and alcohol abuse, and it is not 'restoring' victims if they cannot access long-term support or counselling if they need it.

The reparative concept of RJ in educational settings

Many teachers in schools that consider themselves to be restorative would argue that they use reparative processes to support young people to access feelings of guilt, shame, empathy and generosity, and to make amends to their peer group and others who have been hurt by their actions. As Hendry (2009) points out, restorative approaches can have a meaningful and sustainable impact on school climate and ethos by moving policy and practice for behaviour management away from a focus on rules, sanctions and rewards towards a focus on positive relationships. Costello, Wachtel, and Wachtel (2009) argue that restorative approaches support teachers and others to do the following: foster understanding about what underlies problem behaviour; repair harm done; enable genuine apology (from young people and from adults where appropriate); attend to the needs of everyone affected by a conflict (including teachers); and to actively involve everyone in its resolution. When young people are involved in a reparative process, 'their reparative actions and apologies allow them to feel pride. They are no longer merely objects of our anger and disapproval but fully-fledged human beings who are capable of making things right' (Costello *et al.*, 2009, p. 64). This was in evidence in the Bristol RAiS research project. One of the teachers reported that RA in the school had resulted in students feeling more empowered to resolve their difficulties:

> I think that this gives them a voice, it gives them some power, and that in most cases that is much more likely to produce an outcome which has got a lasting effect, and from which the pupils themselves are learning, so that they're learning about how to become independent and manage their own issues, rather than dependant on external forces, offering punishments as a reason why they should be behaving in the way that we want them to.
>
> (Skinns, *et. al.*, 2009, p. 44)

A teacher in another school felt that it had impacted positively on students' sense of well-being:

> I guess it's good for kids to realise, to actually get the opportunity to say sorry, or to say how they felt, because I think that can be quite a release, can't it, if you've been able to apologise to somebody, and you're given that opportunity. So I think in terms of well-being, I think that's helped a lot of children, yes, rather than keeping it all in.
>
> (Skinns, *et. al.*, 2009, p. 44)

Punitive and non-reparative responses to indiscipline, however, continue to dominate policy and practice in most educational settings. This is troubling for many reasons, not least because punitive methods often don't 'work'. As Hendry points out, those who are most exposed to punishment are usually those who transgress the most. Punishment rarely has an impact on behaviour, other than to teach young people the importance of avoiding detection! Skinns *et. al.*, (2009) found that RA was taken up in one of the Bristol project schools because punitive methods, including fixed-term exclusions, were not felt to be working. One member of staff described how, far from seeing day-long exclusions as a deterrent, many students had come to see them as a 'duvet day'. A teacher in another project school described how it was usual for some pupils to take an extra day or so on top of their exclusion to re-assert feelings of control. Students in this school not only stated that punitive methods don't work; they went further to express feelings of rejection when teachers over-used them. A 15-year-old student spoke about how she feels when detentions are given out by teachers, 'It's just like, "Here you go. Here's a detention. Here's your punishment, go"' (ibid: 32). A 12-year-old pupil in the same school simply stated, 'A lot of the teachers though are actually quite lazy. They can't be bothered to be dealing with people' (ibid: 39).

There may, therefore, be clear benefits in replacing at least some punitive practices with more restorative practices in many schools, especially as punitive methods can be of limited value. Nevertheless, it is the case that restorative approaches are seen as more time-consuming than punishments and sanctions, and that many teachers feel insecure when sanctions are withdrawn. A senior manager interviewed in one of the main RA project schools in Bristol spoke of concern from some staff in his school following the implementation of RA.

> It's caused some issues, you know, particularly in November, December, in the end of the Autumn term, you know, when staff are tired, you know, 'Nothing's being done about these children', 'There are no sanctions', 'The children are in charge', you know, type of thing.
>
> (Skinns *et al.*, 2009, p. 31)

Staff in all Bristol RAiS research project schools reported that many of their colleagues had resisted restorative approaches because they threatened the existing climate for learning in which they had power to discipline and punish badly behaved pupils. In all schools staff and pupils felt that there was an on-going role for punishment, especially for those young people who failed to acknowledge the harm that they had caused. Some older students felt that their aggressive behaviour was keeping them safe and that it was a part of their identity that they were reluctant to change, although they could see that younger pupils might benefit from restorative conferencing.

Given the current dominance of the standards agenda and high stakes testing in most Western countries, it is perhaps inevitable that some teachers lack the training, motivation and support for dealing restoratively with various social, emotional and behavioural problems – issues that are increasingly out-sourced to educational paraprofessionals and support workers. As I have argued elsewhere

(Cremin, 2010) schools are complex and multifaceted institutions. RJ interventions can't be used as cheap and easy solutions to complex social and political problems. Cultures of schooling are notoriously difficult to change and the restorative tail cannot be used to wag the unrestorative dog. There was evidence in the Bristol RAiS research project that some staff, although well-intentioned, had misunderstood principles and practice of RAiS and had, for example, not given young people the choice of whether or not to participate in a conference or had gone ahead with a conference when a young person had not admitted to causing harm. One 15-year-old pupil described how he was shouted at during a conference, 'They say they're conferences, but they are just going to sit you down and shout at you' (Skinns *et al.*, 2009, p. 22). It is a matter of concern that poorly-executed restorative approaches could be seen as more harmful than the punitive processes they are set to replace, given that the latter at least have the advantage of being perceived as clear and transparent.

As shown above in relation to notions of community in the field of criminology, ideas of schools as communities are often confused. Although it is common for national and local education policy to refer to schools as communities, it is not clear which model of community is being referred to, nor how those who have harmed others are to be 'reintegrated' in school when they are not 'integrated' into the mainstream communities surrounding the school. Processes of schooling have been seen to reproduce social inequality (Gilbourn and Mirza, 2000) and yet restorative approaches focus on holding young 'wrong-doers' accountable to their 'victims' in isolation of wider processes of social exclusion. Schools are unequal places, and access to different kinds of school is not shared equally within society. Following an extensive review of primary education funded by the Esmée Fairbairn Foundation between 2006 and 2009, involving over 1,000 written submissions, thousands of emails, over 200 national and regional soundings meetings Alexander notes that:

> The contrasts in children's lives were thought to be massive and widening. Those born into familial stability and economic comfort fare well, many exceptionally so. For others, deprivation is profound and multi-faceted: economic, emotional, linguistic and cultural. Our community witnesses believed that the accident of birth profoundly and often cruelly divides the nation's children.
>
> (Alexander, 2009, p. 14)

Alexander (2009) concludes that schools can and do make a difference in alleviating social and educational inequality, but that this is nowhere near as prevalent nor as consistent as it should be. This is not a problem that is limited to the UK. In the context of violence in schools in France, Debarbieux (2003) has argued that middle-class parents work hard to avoid ordinary schools and to keep their social privileges. He suggests that young people in the underprivileged suburbs of Paris who commit acts of violence are doing so, 'in order to reduce the grip of negative school verdicts on themselves' (Debarbieux, 2003, p. 23). Where, in this case, should shame be located? Should it be located with those socially excluded young people who commit acts of violence? Or should it be with the 'urban schools market' (Debarbieux, 2003) and with policy-makers, teachers, other professionals and parents who contribute to, or at least collude with, inequality and structural violence in social and educational settings? (Harber, 2009). This presents a real challenge for restorative approaches that are grounded in ideas of moral and just communities. Without these communities, it is hard to conceptualise how reintegrative shaming might work. As Zehr (2002, p. 31) points out, 'Crime might be a response to – an effort to undo – a sense of victimisation'. In Foucauldian terms, there is perhaps a danger that reintegrative shaming could be used to 'get inside the heads' of young people, encouraging them to use self-surveillance to police their own actions, and to conform to social norms that are shaped by discourses within society that favour those with power and influence (Foucault, 1979). The same issues arise here in the context of education that have been highlighted elsewhere in the context of criminology and social justice more generally.

Conclusion

In summary, both support and objections to RJ have been raised in the field of criminology, and these are surprisingly similar to the support and objections that have been raised in the field of education. The core concepts of encounter and reparation provide a useful way of reviewing these, and are equally applicable in education as they are in criminology. The challenges for educational settings appear to mirror those in youth justice settings. Issues of power, control, consistency and support emerge in all settings, as do more procedural and pragmatic considerations. It is useful for those who champion RJ with young people to take account of these findings from different contexts in order to consider how RJ can best be operationalised in ways that prioritise the needs of victims and offenders (people who have been harmed and those who have harmed) without compromising social justice. Restorative justice interventions in educational settings need to take account of the complexity of educational institutions, and the different ways in which they are embedded within diverse local, national and global communities. Restorative approaches in schools need to be grounded in an expanded view of conflict and justice, and a reinvigoration of student voice and Citizenship Education. Enabling student voice, and involving young people in the resolution of their own conflicts in schools can begin to articulate difference, revealing and challenging the ways in which divisions of power and opportunity have become obscured. As Braithwaite argues, 'disputing over daily injustices is where we learn to become democratic citizens. And the learning is more profound when those daily injustices reveal deeply structured patterns of injustice' (2002, p. 131). At its best RJ can enhance accountability as a two-way process. It can make offenders accountable for their crimes, and it can make educational and youth justice institutions more accountable to the diverse young people they serve. This is the real potential of RJ interventions in schools and elsewhere. As Roche (2003) points out, 'just as restorative justice requires the oversight of the state, the state requires restorative justice, with restorative justice offering the potential to reinvigorate democratic governments and their laws' (Roche, 2003, p. 24). Systems of encounter and reparation can contribute to the education and social inclusion of diverse young people, and, when used wisely and in more ambitious ways, they can contribute to the creation of more just and responsive communities. The detail of how this is done is yet to be worked through.

References

Alexander, R. (2009) *Introducing The Cambridge Primary Review*. London: Esmée Fairbairn.

Ashworth, A. (2002) 'Responsibilities, Rights and Restorative Justice', *The British Journal of Criminology*, 42 (4), 578–595.

Ausburger, D.W. (1992) *Conflict Mediation across Cultures: Pathways and Patterns*. Louisville: Westminster John Knox Press.

Bickmore, K. (2001) 'Student Conflict Resolution, Power "Sharing" in Schools, and Citizenship Education', *Curriculum Inquiry*, 32 (2), 137–162.

Braithwaite, J. (2002) *Restorative Justice and Responsive Regulation*. Oxford: Oxford University Press.

Cantor, L. (1989) 'Assertive discipline: More than names on the board and marbles in the jar', *Phi-Delta Kappa*, 71, 57–61.

Carruthers, D. (2010) 'Utilising Restorative Justice practices in school disciplinary procedures (the journey from criminal justice to education)'. Paper presented as part of the *Restorative Approaches to Conflict in Schools* seminar series, London, February 2010. Available at: <http://www.educ.cam.ac.uk/research/projects/restorativeapproaches/seminarone/>.

Christie, N. (1977) 'Conflicts as Property', *British Journal of Criminology*, 17 (1), 1–15.

Cossins, A. (2008) 'Restorative Justice and Child Sex Offences: The theory and the practice', *British Journal of Criminology*, 48, 359–378.

Costello, B., Wachtel, J. and Wachtel, T. (2009) 'The Restorative Practices Handbook', Bethlehem: IIRP.

Cremin, H. (2008) *Peer Mediation: Citizenship and Social Inclusion Revisited*, Buckingham: Open University Press.

Curtis-Fawley, S. and Daly, K. (2004) *Gendered Violence and Restorative Justice: The Views of Victim Advocates*. Available at: <www.gu.edu.au/school/ccj/kdaly_docs/vaw_paper.pdf>.

Debarbieux, E. (2003) 'France', in P.K. Smith (ed.) *Violence in Schools: The Response in Europe*. London: RoutledgeFalmer.

DFES (2007) *Social and Emotional Aspects of Learning for Secondary Schools (SEAL) Guidance Booklet*. London: DfES.

Falconer, C. (2010) 'Restorative Justice and Restorative Approaches to Conflict in Schools'. Paper presented as part of the *Restorative Approaches to Conflict in Schools* seminar series, London, February 2010. Available at: <http://www.educ.cam.ac.uk/research/projects/restorativeapproaches/seminarone/>.

Foucault, M. (1979) *Discipline and Punish: The Birth of the Prison*, (tr. A. Sheridan) Harmondsworth: Penguin.

Gilbourne, D. and Mirza, H. (2000) *Educational Inequality: Mapping Race, Class and Gender*. London: HMI.

Gray, P. (2005) 'The Politics of Risk and Young Offenders' Experiences of Social Exclusion and Restorative Justice', *British Journal of Criminology*, 45, 938–957.

Harber, C. (2004) *Schooling as Violence: How Schools Harm Pupils and Societies*. London: RoutledgeFalmer.

Hendry, R. (2009) *Building and Restoring Respectful Relationships at School, a Guide to using Restorative Practice*. London: Routledge.

Johnstone, G. and Van Ness, D.W. (2007) 'The meaning of restorative justice' in G. Johnstone and D.W. Van Ness (eds) *Handbook of Restorative Justice*. Cullompton: Willan Publishing.

Lewis, S. (2009) *Improving School Climate: Findings from schools implementing restorative practices*. Bethlehem: IIRP Graduate School.

McCluskey, G., Lloyd, G., Stead, J., Kane, J., Riddell, S. and Weedon, E. (2008) "I was dead restorative today" from 'Restorative Justice to Restorative Approaches in School', *Cambridge Journal of Education*, 38 (2), 199–217.

Morris, (2002) 'Critiquing the Critics: A Brief Response to Critics of Restorative Justice', *British Journal of Criminology*, 42, 596–615.

Morrison, B. (2007) 'Schools and restorative justice' in G. Johnstone and D.W. Van Ness (eds) *Handbook of Restorative Justice*, Cullompton: Willan Publishing.

Rigby, K. (2010) *Bullying Interventions in Schools: Six basic approaches*. Camberwell: Australian Council for Educational Research.

Roche, D. (2003) 'The rise and risks of restorative justice', *Accountability in Restorative Justice*. Clarendon Studies in Criminology. Oxford: Oxford University Press, pp. 1–24.

Rose, N. (2000) 'Government and Control', *British Journal of Criminology*, 40, 2, 321–339.

Sandra, V. and Cochran, K.M. (2000) 'The development of conflict resolution skills in children: Preschool to adolescence' in M. Deutsch and P.T. Coleman (eds) *The Handbook of Conflict Resolution: Theory and Practice*, San Francisco: Jossey-Bass.

Sen, A. (2006) *Identity and Violence: The Illusion of Destiny*, London: Penguin Books.

Sherman, L.W. and Strang, H. (2007) *Restorative Justice: The Evidence*, London: The Smith Institute. Available at: <www.esmeefairbairn.org.uk/docs/RJ_full_report.pdf>.

Skinns, L., Du Rose, N. and Hough, M. (2009) *An evaluation of Bristol RAiS*, London: ICPR, King's College London.

Thorsborne, M. and Vinegrad, D. (2008) *Restorative Practices in Classrooms*. Milton Keynes: Speechmark Publishing.

Zehr, H. (2002) *The Little Book of Restorative Justice*. Intercourse PA: Good Books.

Zernova, M. (2007) 'Aspirations of Restorative Justice proponents and experiences of participants in Family Group Conferences', *British Journal of Criminology*, 47, 491–509.

Chapter 12

Beyond the bad apple

Analytical and theoretical perspectives on the development of restorative approaches in schools

Brenda Morrison

Introduction

> If people are good only because they fear punishment, and hope for reward, then we are a sorry lot indeed.
>
> Albert Einstein

The idea of restorative justice is nuanced by its history. Many argue that it is both new and old (Pranis *et al.*, 2003), providing a rich landscape of history and discovery. In terms of recent history, the theory and practice of restorative justice developed within the field of criminology, offering a critical perspective on crime, safety and justice. In contemporary criminology the focus, in the name of justice, has largely been to improve processes involved in sentencing and punishing the offender; in other words, to develop and test normative and explanatory theory in order to understand and respond to the 'bad apple' of society. We punish the 'bad apple' for the sake of the common good, to differentiate and separate the good from the bad. This system of social control regulates behaviour through the use of strong institutional sanctioning systems, grounded in normative frameworks of distributive, adversarial and retributive justice, which dominate current thinking about managing criminals and other 'bad apples'. It is a system that has, for the most part, shaped our history as individuals and institutions. And yet, individually and collectively we can contemplate change. Ideas and practices, such as restorative justice shape history too. The practice of restorative justice is both process and product of institutional culture. Through the opportunity afforded to us through engaging with writing chapters for this book, and the ESRC-funded seminars that preceded it, we have the opportunity to embrace the current history of restorative justice and expand that history to new horizons. This chapter reflects on the costs of normative frameworks of distributive, adversarial and retributive justice, and asks what could be achieved if we shift our focus from the 'bad apple' to the bad barrel, and even to the bad barrel-maker?

Phil Zimbardo, social psychologist and principal researcher of the Stanford Prison Experiment, has been studying how good apples turn bad, or how good people turn evil, for at least three decades. Aptly, he calls the transformation from good to bad the 'Lucifer Effect' (Zimbardo, 2007). Through a commitment to his own history and dedication to building understanding of how and why human behaviour turns bad, Zimbardo (2007) models for us how to learn from our own failures. The initial experiment of 1971, over 40 years ago, was deemed one of the most unethical studies ever carried out. It was stopped, by one person only six days into the experiment. This 'failed experiment' has given rise to much controversy but also much debate about issues of power, control and justice.

What have we learnt from the Stanford Prison Experiment? The striking evidence from those few days the experiment ran shows that the behaviour of everyday citizens (deemed to be mentally healthy through a battery of psychological tests) can be transformed, within particular institutional conditions, to bring out the worst in us. The power of the situation revealed the Lucifer Effect: individuals randomly assigned to the role of prison guards began to systematically abuse their power; individuals randomly assigned to the role of prisoners began to suffer mental breakdowns. In that initial experiment, Zimbardo challenged us to look beyond dispositional (internal) attributes in understanding human behaviour (the fundamental attribution error) and consider the situational (external) factors that are predictive of behaviour. The experiment showed that situational variables trumped dispositional variables in understanding behaviour patterns in a prison context, be it guard or prisoner. Zimbardo has now further developed his analysis, following the replication of the Stanford Prison Experiment in England (Haslam and Reicher, 2003; Reicher et al., 2006) and being called as an expert witness in the Abu Ghraib trial in the US, where the torture of Iraqi prisoners by US army personnel in 2003–4 was attributed to a few 'bad apples'. Zimbardo now concludes three levels of analysis are important to understanding human behaviour 'gone bad': dispositional (bad apple); situational (bad barrel) and systemic institutional power structures (the bad barrel-makers). Zimbardo (2007, p. 326) called 'the system' to trial in understanding the abuses of Abu Ghraib and the assertion of General Myers (principal military advisor to the President, the Secretary of Defense, and the National Security Council during the earliest stages of the War on Terror) that the abuse was not systemic but the 'isolated work of a handful of "rogue soldiers"', the 'bad apples':

> There was something troubling about this authoritative declaration to absolve the System and blame the few at the bottom of the barrel. His claim was reminiscent of what police chiefs tell the media whenever police abuse of criminal suspects is revealed – blame the few rotten-apples-bad-cops – to deflect the focus away from the norms and usual practices in the back rooms of police stations or the police department itself. This rush to attribute a 'bad-boy' dispositional judgment to a few offenders is all too common among the guardians of the System. In the same way, school principals and teachers use the device to blame particularly "disruptive" students instead of taking the time to evaluate the alienating effects of boring curricula and poor classroom practices of specific teachers that might provoke such disruptions.
> (Zimbardo, 2007, p. 326)

While Zimbardo's assertion may be a bold leap from one institutional culture to another, it seems a worthy cause to take the time and effort to better understand the potential alienating effects of contemporary educational institutional culture, for the evidence suggests that we are expelling increasingly more 'bad apples' from the schools system.

For example, in the United States, zero-tolerance policies, which mandate automatic suspension and expulsion for a range of infractions, has become the de facto policy for dealing with school discipline (see Riestenberg this volume). Though zero tolerance expanded in the wake of school rampage shootings in predominantly white, suburban schools (Giroux, 2009), the 'bad apples' that are expelled at disproportional rates are those at the bottom of the barrel: minority students, whose families hold little power in the system. The evidence of disproportional representation is clear, it is students of colour and working-class students (Skiba *et al.*, 2008). The racial disparities in the school system are reflected in the criminal justice system, where black males are incarcerated at a rate six times that of white males.

At the same time, school suspensions have increased for all students, not just minority students. In the US, since 1973, the number of students suspended annually has more than doubled to 3.3 million students. Suspension increases the likelihood of a student being expelled, dropping out, and being incarcerated, a phenomenon dubbed the 'school to prison pipeline' (Wald and Losen, 2003, p. 11). Through zero tolerance and an increasing reliance on police presence in schools, many school officials are in effect helping to create an 'institutional link' between schools and prisons. Statistics about prisoners reveal further links between schools and prisons: in 1997, nearly 70 per cent of prisoners never graduated high school, and approximately 70 per cent of juvenile offenders had learning disabilities (Wald and Losen, 2003). What do these institutional links reveal about the character of our institutions, particularly schools, our primary developmental institution, through which we educate and socialise our children, and create the history of tomorrow?

Part of the answer may lay in our history of justice and institutional design, established, for worthy intention, in the name of the common good, and a just society (see Braithwaite and Pettit, 1990). Our institution of justice is built on three broad concepts of justice: distributive justice; adversarial justice and retributive justice. Simply put, distributive justice rests on a set of normative principles designed to guide the allocation of the benefits and burdens of economic activity, which are regulated by the state. These principles gave rise to our notion of just-desserts, wherein the fair distribution of rewards (benefits) and punishment (burdens) is thought to produce the best collective outcomes. The focus is on a strong external sanctioning system, regulated by a state-based institutional authority. Adversarial justice is based on the premise that impartial argument (typically between two parties) brings out the truth, through a focus on the facts of the case. It is a win/lose system of justice, wherein reason trumps emotion. Retributive justice operates on the premise that proportionate punishment is a morally acceptable response to crime and wrongdoing, regardless of whether the punishment causes any tangible benefits (see Zehr, 1990). Punishment is thought to re-enforce the rule of law, or the primacy of the institutional authority through a code of conduct.

Restorative justice grew out of concerns regarding how we institutionalise, and operationalise, these conceptual ideals of justice. Three broad concerns will be highlighted. First, Christie (1977) argued the case for conflict as property; specifically, that conflict is stolen by the state, for the state, and in that process, conflict is stolen from the people most affected; in particular, the victim. Conflict is not only stolen by the state, individuals are represented by third parties – lawyers, judges and juries – in the name of impartiality. Through that process, first party decision-making, by those most affected, is lost to third parties, who answer to the state. Second, and related to this first point, the third parties focus on the facts, as the system favours reason over emotion. Sherman (2003) argues that there is reason for emotion, that emotional engagement is the key to building common understanding, justice and behavioural change. Third, Zehr (1990) juxtaposed punishment (retributive justice) with repairing the harm done (restorative justice), as a response to crime, wrong doing and harmful behaviour, arguing that the system causes more harm than good when we punish. Instead of asking: 'What rules were broken?'; 'Who did it?' and 'What punishment do the offenders deserve?'; the questions should centre around 'Who has been hurt?', 'What are their needs?', and 'Who has the obligation to address the needs, to put right the harms, to restore relationships?' (Zehr, 2002).

Are these concerns relevant to the institutional power dynamics of schools? To answer this broad question we can break it down to the same basic three concerns: (1) To what extent do we punish (and reward) in the name of the common good of those in the care of the school? (2) To what extent do we send the problem, the 'bad apple', out of the classroom, out of the school, into the hands of third parties; thus, stealing conflict and opportunity from those most affected in classrooms and school yards? (3) To what extent do we focus on the facts, in the name of impartiality, referring to the student code of conduct to decide the just response? In other words, to what extent do we value reason over emotion, focusing on the traditional 3Rs, over building social and emotional intelligence? We can reframe these questions in reference to longitudinal school data from the United States, which indicates that connection to school is a strong protective factor for a range of behaviours of concern in schools: violence and delinquency; emotional distress; substance abuse; early sexual behaviour and pregnancy. The question then is: Do our institutional responses foster connection to school communities for students, themselves at risk, as a result of exhibiting these behaviours, (1) punishes? (2) steals conflict away from those most affected? (3) focuses on the facts, instead of emotional engagement? Has the cost of these institutional practices been the experience of belonging, of community, that we are striving to protect? Has the cost of these institutional practices been a loss of understanding and capacity to acknowledge and respond to our common humanity, to our common good?

A group of influential world leaders was recently asked: what is the greatest threat to humanity? While some answered terrorism, poverty and hunger, the Dalai Lama gave a distinctly different answer: 'We have raised a generation of passive bystanders'. Could this be the cost of state-based institutional justice, opposed to community-based justice within classrooms and schools? Imagine an institutional climate wherein we learn the skills to manage our own conflict, instead of sending the problem, and the person, out the door; wherein we learn the importance of telling the truth without fear of punishment; wherein we understand why social and emotional intelligence is as important, if not more important, than academic intelligence. These are the skills, processes and products that restorative justice seeks, in both its normative and operational ideals.

We must not lose sight of these broad concerns, grounded in strong normative and explanatory theory building, which converged to lay the foundation for the field of restorative justice. These broad theoretical concerns were building long before the field of study was born, and named, in the 1990s. As we seek to define the concept of restorative justice do we become myopic in perspective, focusing on the encounter, the value of reparation, the transformation of the individual, at the expense of broader systemic knowledge and understanding (see Van Ness and Johnstone, 2003; Van Ness, Cremin, this volume)? With a focus on these three broad levers of institutional design, what does restorative justice add to the justice equation in schools?

By way of illustration, we can take the problem of effectively addressing concerns over school bullying, as the study of bullying and restorative justice make a good conceptual fit. Bullying is defined at the 'systematic abuse of power'; in other words, domination. As a response, restorative justice values non-domination and deliberation, the aim is empowerment, as such restorative responses must be 'on guard against imbalance of power' (Braithwaite, 2002, p. 264). A range of ill-effects, associated with bullying, have been well documented (see Swearer et al., 2010). For students who have bullied others, this behaviour pattern has been associated with anger, violence, hyperactivity, externalising problems, delinquency, criminality, depression and suicidal ideation. For students who have been bullied by others, these students experience stress-related illness, school avoidance and disinterest, poor academic performance, increased fear and anxiety, emotional distress, depression and suicidal ideation. Interestingly, while the trajectories are distinct, both students who bully, and who are bullied, are on a path of alienation and social isolation. Given the concern about the ill-effects of bullying, a range of bullying intervention programmes have been developed. Given the fact that many bullying intervention programmes had poor effect sizes, Farrington and Ttofi (2009) carried out a meta-analysis of a number of these programmes, concluding: 'No anti-bullying programme was based on well-developed and tested theories of bullying such as defiance theory or re-integrative shaming theory. Research is needed to develop and test better theories of bullying and victimisation as a basis for new intervention programmes' (Farrington and Ttofi, 2009, p. 23). Each of these explanatory theories, in different ways, makes a case for restorative justice. Re-integrative shaming theory builds our understanding of the role of the moral emotion of shame and the process of shaming in understanding and responding to school bullying (see Ahmed *et al.*, 2001). Defiance theory (Sherman, 2003) builds our understanding of when punishment increases crime, decreases crime and has no effect.

These are not the only theories that make a case for restorative justice, other theories include: social identity theory (Tajfel and Turner, 1979); re-integrative shaming theory (Ahmed *et al.*, 2001; Braithwaite 1989); a theory of unacknowledged shame (Scheff, 1994); and procedural justice (Tyler and Blader, 2000). More recently, in an article on rule breaking, procedural justice and restorative justice, Tyler also concludes that a shift from regulation by external sanctions, to self-regulation, is important:

> Sanctioning-based models, which dominate current thinking about managing criminals, have negative consequences for the individual wrongdoer and for society. It is argued that greater focus needs to be placed on psychological approaches whose goal is to connect with and activate internal values within wrongdoers with the goal of encouraging self-regulatory law-related behaviour in the future.
>
> (Tyler, 2006, p. 309)

Explanatory theories, such as re-integrative shaming theory, social identity theory, and self-categorisation theory provide a broad theoretical framework for understanding the psychological mechanism of internal sanctioning systems, which underpin self-regulatory law-related behaviour. It is building understanding of the fit between internal sanctioning systems and external sanctioning systems that holds promise for the development of progressive theory building and practice in the area of restorative approach in schools.

While it is often claimed that practice has driven theory-building in the field of restorative justice, others have claimed that 'nothing is as practical as a good theory' (Lewin, 1951, p. 169). Both are important for research and development in this emerging field of study, particularly in schools. Practice, and training, without theoretical understanding can produce more harm than good; theory building, without practice, limits external validity and levers to build capacity. Comparative studies, such as the re-integrative shaming experiments, currently limited to a criminal and juvenile justice context (see Sherman and Strang, 2007), which test theory and practice concurrently offer a rich medium for further research and development. Together, they can help navigate the paradigm shift of institutional design and culture.

Building on Zimbardo's (2007) analysis, the paradigm shift must embrace all levels of influence, and power imbalances: individual, situational, institutional. At an individual level, teaching healthy social and emotional skills is a step in the right direction (see Jennings and Greenberg 2008); at a situational level, developing healthy group norms and social connections that empower bystanders will empower the community to act and not to be passive bystanders (see Cowie this volume); at an institutional level, a shift from the reliance on external sanctioning systems, of rewards and punishment, that foster and promote power imbalances to a system that promotes healthy self-regulation and social engagement is vital (Tyler, 2006). Together, the challenge is to create socially and emotionally intelligent individuals, and peer-cultures, within institutional conditions that acknowledge, develop and nurture self-regulatory behaviour, and respond to harmful behaviour, such as bullying, in a manner that addresses the underlying issues, while affirming the moral values of the institution.

Many schools have struggled with this transition to restorative justice within schools. I believe that part of the reason this is the case is that we have been myopic in our understanding and analysis. We focus our lens too narrowly in defining the field, which is problematic in such a broad paradigm shift, and we continue to measure the results in relation to outcomes important to the paradigm we seek to be shifting from, such as reducing the suspension rates of the 'bad apples'.

We must learn from the experience of Phil Zimbardo by examining our own failures to embrace the difficult conversations in building theory that upholds practice, and practice that upholds theory. We must expand our levels of analysis from individual, to situational, to institutional; beyond the 'bad apple' through broad systemic studies. At the same time, we must acknowledge and celebrate the anecdotal evidence that is often cursorily to our lens of analysis. For example, acknowledging who stopped the Stanford Prisoner Experiment and by what process of influence? It was not the institutional authority who stopped the experiment; it was the person closest to Phil Zimbardo, the person who became his wife. She held him accountable for his own behaviour, and questioned his moral stance. It was the social and emotional relational dimension that produced the influence and leverage for change. What we need is a shift from institutional mechanisms of social control to institutional mechanisms that bring out the best in us, to connect us to each other, to something greater than ourselves. Restorative justice challenges us to move beyond the 'bad apple', beyond passive bystanders, to take responsibility for our own behaviour and the behaviour of others.

As individuals and communities we hold our common humanity in our hands. The time is ripe for a paradigm shift from institutions of social control, born of the Age of Reason (wherein reason was separated from emotion), to institutions of social engagement that embrace both reason and emotion, each of which underpin our common humanity.

This new horizon may be characterised as a shift:

- From a myopic focus on punishing the 'bad apple' to widening the lens to a relational culture of well-being and belonging.
- From isolating positions of fear, fault and retribution to embracing the gifts of generosity, abundance, and compassion.
- From accountability through law and authority to fostering accountability through want not fear.
- From a focus on strong institutions to a focus on strong communities.

References

Ahmed, E., Harris, N., Braithwaite, J. and Braithwaite, V. (2001) *Shame Management through Reintegration*. Cambridge: Cambridge University Press.

Braithwaite, J. (1989) *Crime, Shame and Reintegration*. Cambridge: Cambridge University Press.

Braithwaite, J. and Pettit, P. (1990) *Not Just Deserts: A Republican Theory of Sentencing*. Oxford: Clarendon Press.

Braithwaite, J. B. (2002) *Restorative Justice and Responsive Regulation*. Oxford: University Press.

Christie, N. (1977) 'Conflicts as Property', *The British Journal of Criminology* 17, 1–15.

Farrington, D. P. and Ttofi, M. M. (2009) *School-based Programs to Reduce Bullying and Victimization*. Campbell Systematic Reviews, 2009: 6.

Giroux, H. (2009) *Youth in a Suspect Society: Democracy Or Disposability?* Toronto: Palgrave Macmillan.

Haslam, A. and Reicher, S. (2003) 'Beyond Stanford: Questioning a role-based explanation of tyranny', *Dialogue (Bulletin of the Society for Personality and Social Psychology)*, 18, 22–25.

Jennings, P. and Greenberg, M. (2008) 'The prosocial classroom: Teacher Social and Emotional Competence in Relation to Student and Classroom Outcomes', *Review of Educational Research*, 79(1), 491–525.

Lewin, K. (1951) *Field Theory in Social Science; Selected Theoretical Papers*. D. Cartwright (ed.). New York: Harper & Row.

Pranis, K., Stuart, B. and Wedge, M. (2003) *Peacemaking Circles: From Crime to Community*. St. Paul, MN: Living Justice Press.

Reicher, Stephen and Haslam, S. Alexander (2006) 'Rethinking the psychology of tyranny: The BBC Prison Study', *British Journal of Social Psychology*, 45, 1–40.

Scheff, T. J. (1994) *Bloody Revenge: Emotions, Nationalism and War*. Boulder, Co.: Westview Press.

Sherman, L. (2003) 'Reason for emotion: Reinventing justice with theories, innovations, and research', *Criminology*, 41, 1–38.

Sherman, L. W. and Strang, H. (2007) *Restorative Justice: The Evidence*. London: The Smith Institute.

Skiba, R., Reynolds, C. R., Graham, S., Sheras, P., Conoley, J. C. and Garcia-Vazquez, E. (2008) 'Are Zero Tolerance Policies Effective in the Schools?', *American Psychologist*, 63, 852–862.

Swearer, S., Espelage, D. L., Vaillancourt, T. and Hymel, S. (2010) 'What can be done about school bullying? Linking research to educational practice', *Educational Researcher*, 39(1), 38–47.

Tajfel, H. and Turner, J. C. (1979) 'An integrative theory of intergroup conflict' in S. Worchel and W. G. Austin (eds) *The Social Psychology of Intergroup Relations*. Monterey: Brooks/Cole.

Tyler, T. (2006) 'Restorative Justice and Procedural Justice: Dealing with Rule Breaking', *Journal of Social Issues*, 62(2), 307–326.

Tyler, T. R. and Blader, S. (2000) *Cooperation in Groups: Procedural Justice, Social Identity, and Behavioral Engagement*. Philadelphia: Psychology Press.

Van Ness, D. and Johnstone, G. (2007) *Handbook of Restorative Justice*. Devon: Willan Publishing.

Wald, J. and Losen, D. J. (2003) (eds) *New Directions for Youth Development: Deconstructing The School to Prison Pipeline,* No. 99, Fall.

Zehr, H. (1990) *Changing Lenses: A New Focus on Crime and Justice.* Scottsdale, PA: Herald Press.

—— (2002) *The Little Book of Restorative Justice.* Intercourse: Good Books.

Zimbardo, P. G. (2007) *The Lucifer Effect: Understanding how Good People turn Evil.* New York: Random House.

Chapter 13

Challenges to education

Restorative Practice as a radical demand on conservative structures of schooling

Gillean McCluskey

Introduction

Bells that ring to time work and control play, rules that govern movement round and between buildings, regulated access to toilet facilities, uniform codes, public address systems, electronic absence monitoring, systematised rewards and punishments, high security perimeter fences, CCTV, alarm systems and swipe access, short rests and long periods of work.

These are all features more often associated with incarceration than with education. However, teachers and students, particularly in the senior stages of schooling, are often subject to such measures, in ways that may both reflect and shape the concerns of local community and wider society. This chapter sets out to examine the challenges and opportunities for schools wanting to work holistically and dynamically as learning communities committed to Restorative Practice (RP). These will be schools seeking to move beyond an assumption that RP is simply about improving children's behaviour or reducing disciplinary exclusion rates. They will recognise that RP offers the opportunity for a radical re-imagining of the relationship between school, teacher and student but they will also understand that this brings significant challenges to school structures which are often deeply conventional and resistant to innovation.

Findings from research (Lloyd and McCluskey 2009; Skinns *et al.*, 2009; Kane *et al.*, 2007; Bitel 2005) indicate that RP has most impact when the whole school community embraces its principles, values, strategies and skills. There has clearly been success for RP and there have been many examples of significantly positive change in school communities with fundamental improvement in the relationships between teacher and child, child and child, home and school, even teacher and teacher. However, findings to date also indicate that RP has often only been implemented in part and that the focus has frequently been on addressing poor or inappropriate behaviour of children, rather than on rethinking how the school community as a whole can work to enable active engagement with learning. With only partial implementation, there has been only partial success for RP.

This chapter argues against partial implementation of RP and the notion that a 'weak' or diluted version of RP is adequate for schools. It sets out a rationale for a radical, holistic version of RP and the potential benefits for all members of the school community. It acknowledges the pressurised nature of the current working context for teachers and others working with children in these troubled and turbulent times. It goes on to identify the key gains for a school community that embraces a 'strong' version of RP and sets that alongside the known outcomes where this has not happened. Finally, drawing on research, policy and practice, it suggests some ways to take forward ideas that teachers and other practitioners may find useful.

Setting the context for children and young people

The first *UK Children's Commissioner Report* to the United Nations Committee on the Rights of the Child (UNCRC) (2008) noted that, among other 'bad things about being a child in England':

> Children feel increasingly pressurised, in particular, by school, exams and commercial marketing.
> Child mental health has deteriorated over the last thirty years.
> Children feel increasingly unsafe in their local area, with one in four concerned about violence, crime and weapons.

In Wales, it noted:

> Child poverty is still very high.
> Child and adolescent mental health services are struggling to cope with demand for their services.
> Disabled children's experiences are worse than those of their peers.

In Northern Ireland it noted:

> While many of today's children have not lived through the Troubles, their parents and relatives have, and this has resulted in residual 'after effects' for many children and young people. Sectarianism, paramilitary control, loss and bereavement result in an inability to cope or to access opportunities which all children should enjoy as their right. For example, access to play and leisure, access to adequate health care, access to education etc, are often more difficult to achieve for those living with the trauma of the conflict.

And in Scotland, amongst other key points, it noted:

> Scotland shares with the rest of the UK a public attitude towards children and young people that tends to demonise them and often seems to wish to exclude them from public spaces. At the same time, there is evidence of an over-protective attitude towards children that reduces their opportunities for

play, leisure, recreation and healthy development. This may be fuelled by parental fears or by institutional avoidance of any risk that might lead to liability. In Scotland, research has shown that adults fear contact with children in case they are accused of harming a child. This very widespread and significant fear has created an unhealthy climate that limits opportunities and hampers child development.

This assessment of the experience of childhood in the UK is significant because it represents the first time that the four Children's Commissioners in the UK produced a joint report to the UNCRC. The evidence it contains has the power of cumulative impact, but the report is not alone in its recognition of the difficulties facing children and young people in present times. The Cambridge Primary Review (2009), conducted by Alexander and colleagues, represented the most comprehensive enquiry into primary education in England in 40 years, and it too highlighted important challenges facing schools, teachers and students. The UNICEF Reports, *Child Poverty in Perspective* (2007) and *The Children Left Behind* (2010) also highlight the current difficulties facing children, setting this in an international context. The emerging picture is one that gives cause for deep concern and demands a thorough and careful response. It is important to be clear that education is only one possible site for change and improvement. Nonetheless, it is also clear that education has a responsibility and also a right to expect to play an integral part in bringing about such change.

A rationale for radical RP

RP has the capacity to bring about change and respond to these issues but, crucially, only where it is more than a rewording of a school discipline or behaviour management policy. A typical definition of RP on a school website may read: 'Restorative Approaches are a range of practices used to manage behaviour in school'. This suggests that RP is often construed as a behaviour management practice, merely another 'tool in the tool box' for teachers dealing with disruption, disengagement and disaffection. This can only serve to neutralise and weaken the potential impact of RP, leading to dilution, assimilation and its eventual demise. If, on the other hand, the warnings from international bodies such as UNICEF (2010; 2007), and research such as that undertaken by Alexander and others (2009), are taken seriously, then a 'strong' version of RP may offer a highly effective way forward. It must include a focus on children's behaviour and relationships but just as importantly, it can take full account of the ambitions of teachers to innovate, communicate and inspire; the very aspects of teaching that draw people into the profession but which can then become difficult to hold on to in the face of other pressures and demands. It can also respond to an emerging and significantly helpful body of evidence about the developmental and psychosocial needs of adolescence and the mismatch with structures, in particular, of most secondary schools, in terms of the need for young people to develop individual and social identity, the need for academic self-regulation, the importance of peer relations, autonomy, and support from adults beyond the family (Skiba *et al.*, 2006).

Setting the context for teachers

Teachers work in a stressful environment. Society expects much, expectations are many and their roles and responsibilities have expanded as the demands placed on education itself have expanded. Today, their responsibilities are complex and often conflicted. These pressures place expectations on schools and teachers to achieve hugely varying and competing goals: to focus on inclusion and also prioritise academic excellence, to nurture competition but also develop communities that are caring and careful of each other, to punish inappropriate behaviour but also to encourage the development of individual self-regulation. At the same time, scrutiny of teachers' work has never been greater. Quality assurance, improvement, audit and inspection mechanisms often exert undue pressure even when intended to offer support.

In the classroom, the professional task of teaching is also under great pressure. In difficult economic times where competition for both employment and places in further and higher education courses is fierce, the teacher's role as judge or adjudicator can become paramount. It is easy to understand why there may be little time for risk taking or experiment. It is generally acknowledged that the rate of policy innovation connected with these different goals and demands means that schools have found the context of their work increasingly stressful and challenging. It is hardly surprising that, in the face of such pressure, school leaders and teachers may come to see compliant students as good students, a quiet class as a good class, and a good school as one where there is no conflict.

What are the challenges for schools which embrace RP in full?

RP demands that schools are well led, that they have teams of adults that talk with each other and that question and listen in equal measure. A restorative school is led by adults who model positive ways of working and communicating with each other across school stage or subject boundaries. Such a school has high academic aspirations for its students and ensures that pedagogy and curriculum are influenced by restorative principles. It is characterised by openness to challenge and risk, to authentic collaboration with its students (McCluskey 2012), with parents and other carers, the local community and with other professionals. Its ethos is characterised by the idea of school as a place where change is possible and regard for itself as a community rather than as an institution or organisation. It values time spent on reflection and 'slow knowing' (Claxton 1999) and this reflection takes account of the inherent power differentials in school communities and the effect of asymmetrical relationships between and among different members of the school community as a whole; that is, not only among its students.

It takes account too, of the continuing impact of inequality and discrimination within educational experience in general, evident in national and international statistics on attainment and disciplinary exclusion. It rejects the assumption that schools need to maintain the right to exclude or expel students. Bauman's definition of democracy has resonance here:

> Democracy is not an institution, but essentially an anti-institutional force, a 'rupture' in the otherwise relentless trend of the powers-that-be to arrest change, to silence and to eliminate from the political process all those who have not been 'born' into power...Democracy expresses itself in a continuous and relentless critique of institutions; democracy is an anarchic, disruptive element inside the political system; essentially a force for dissent and change. One can best recognise a democratic society by its constant complaint that it is not democratic enough.
>
> (Bauman 2001: 54–55)

RP, like Bauman's democracy, needs to be disruptive and unsettling: disruptive in the sense that it interrupts ineffective custom and practice and traditional ways of doing things that have outlived their usefulness. This demands a fundamental reappraisal in many schools of what teachers do and what students are.

The conservative structures of schooling

This chapter began with a list of features found in many schools. It was suggested that this list might also describe a prison rather than the ideal school. Reading that list, a teacher in a primary or elementary school setting might feel that it does not accurately reflect the educational experience of younger children. And indeed teaching practices in early years or foundation phase have benefited hugely from research evidence about the need for play, outdoor learning, adventure and the importance of relationships in learning. In some ways, this has returned the early stages of schooling to its original principles. But children in the UK now enter the formal education system earlier than they did 10 to 15 years ago and earlier than their counterparts in many other countries. They often wear uniforms and are subject to school rules from age three. Though teachers do their best to adapt these rules, they are still more likely to be based on a simplified version of primary school rules than on a guide derived from professionally-informed understanding of child development processes, and what can reasonably be expected from a girl or boy aged three, four or five years old. So, although the structures of primary or elementary schools have many excellent aspects and many teachers may quite legitimately feel they are 'half-way there' (McCluskey *et al.* 2008), their work is still bound by problematic structures.

Day-to-day life of secondary schools is perhaps much more easily recognisable in the list referred to at the beginning of the chapter. Again, a secondary school teacher may respond by saying that within these strictures there is still room for innovation and the exercising of professional autonomy, and that without such rules a large organisation such as a secondary school would not be able to operate effectively. These are important points and the discussion that follows sets out some key considerations in response.

What happens if radical RP is not implemented?

In times of stress schools and teachers may tend to 'default' to rule following, a more punitive approach and more conventional ways of teaching. However, there is growing evidence that this may be counter-productive. According to Skiba *et al.* 'Recent research indicates a negative relationship between the use of school suspension and expulsion and school-wide academic achievement, even when controlling for demographics such as socio-economic status' (2006: 5). The authors of this important review of the literature for the American Psychological Association are careful to say that such findings do not show a causal effect, but they do suggest that 'it becomes difficult to argue that zero tolerance creates more positive school climates when its use is associated with more negative achievement outcomes' (2006: 5). This finding is particularly pertinent to secondary schools, where rates of exclusion and expulsion are known to be highest. In a wider context it relates to what has been called the 'school to prison pipeline' and the ways in which young people who do least well in school are also most likely to come in to contact with criminal justice systems in later life (McAra and McVie 2010; Smith 2004).

Much has been written about how to improve schools and/or make them more effective but some problems seem particularly resistant to change. Analysis of educational attainment and exclusion statistics across the UK has, over a long number of years, consistently pointed to disproportionate over-representation of some groups (DfE 2012; Scottish Government 2011; Welsh Government 2012). While political concern has led to initiatives to reduce exclusion or raise attainment from time to time, this has had relatively little impact on this disproportionality. The experience of boys and young men in school, for example, and their high rates of exclusion, often at a ratio of 4:1 in secondary schools, is rarely challenged by policy and often seems to be tacitly accepted as a natural consequence of 'masculinity'. The experience of some minority groups, for example, black boys in England and Wales and Gypsy, Roma, Travellers in Scotland, England and Wales, have been more often highlighted, but change still seems to be slow in coming. The continued under-achievement of children from poorer families and of 'looked after' children also poses an uncomfortable question for RP. Earlier it was noted that among the list of demands that RP makes of schools is that it reflects on the power differentials in a school community and the effect of asymmetrical relationships between and among different members of the school community (not only among its students). It went on to suggest that RP needs to consider the continuing impact of inequality and discrimination within educational experience in general, evident in UK and international statistics on attainment and disciplinary expulsion. Translating the principles of RP into practice asks for reflection on the kinds of explanations given by schools for inappropriate behaviour, for failure to achieve academically or for early drop out, disengagement or disaffection. In this context, Hopkins offers a very helpful reflection on a common contrast between attitudes to learning needs and behavioural needs (2011) adapted from Porter (2007).

Academic errors	Behavioural errors
Errors are accidental	Errors are deliberate
Errors are bound to happen	Errors should not happen
Learning requires exploration – students learn by questioning and challenging what they are told	Students should not explore limits, nor question and challenge what they are told – they should accept and obey
Academic learning difficulties signal a need for additional learning or modified teaching	Behavioural difficulties should be suppressed and signal a need for sanctions

Box 13.1 Academic and behavioural errors

Much of the most effective restorative work in schools has been successful because it acknowledges that an event or incident does not happen in isolation. It is more likely to be the 'tip of the iceberg', and a symptom of a long-held misapprehension or unresolved conflict. Those working in a restorative way have often noted that a single incident, whether it occurs in the staffroom or playground may involve many people beyond the one or two most obviously involved (McCluskey *et al.* 2011). It may impact on a group of peers or involve families, or even extended family networks. It may involve principles and deeply-held views. This is one reason why it becomes important to avoid the use of simplistic terms such as 'offender' and 'victim' in the school setting, terms which underestimate the complexity of relationships in school.

A 'strong' version of RP must also include reflection on issues of 'race', language, age, religion and belief, gender, socio-economic status, disability and sexual orientation. Such reflection helps scope the ways in which a school can respond to a problem and seek to identify solutions, building a positive ethos and meeting crises when they occur. It will always be important to understand 'within-child' explanations of behaviour, but it is equally important to consider the school's own institutional contribution to that behaviour and the wider social and political contexts. If this 'strong' version of RP is not embraced, and as long as behaviour is merely pathologised, schools cannot expect to see a shift in the over-representation of some groups of students in these key statistics.

Finding a way forward

As the economic climate continues to dominate decisions about public expenditure, local authorities and schools are being asked to make large budget cuts. This may seem a difficult time to look for a radical version of RP, but may also present a key opportunity to acknowledge that schools need to do things differently. If budget restraints mean fewer classroom assistants, teaching assistants or specialist teachers or support staff, fewer opportunities for collaborative and inter-professional working, and potentially fewer additional resources or places to refer young people on to when mainstream school seems inappropriate, then it is likely that there will be more pressure on schools. It was noted earlier that teachers already work in a very pressurised environment. If budget restraint also means lower levels of financial support overall for vulnerable groups, then schools and teachers will encounter children affected by this. Research has demonstrated that RP can produce a calmer school, where staff feel valued and listened to and where students feel they have a voice. Finding a way forward is challenging but it is also possible. The 'wheel' (Figure 13.1) sets out the demands that a strong version of RP makes of schools.

Becoming restorative means...

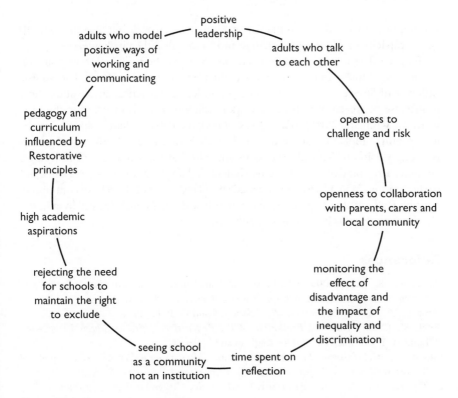

Figure 13.1 Restorative practices

It is important to look again at the demands of a strong version of RP in the wheel (Figure 13.1). The challenges will always include the need to 'seed' and grow a way of speaking about/with children and young people based on an understanding of them as active citizens with lives beyond school; and the need for teachers to 'seed' and grow RP in their daily interactions with colleagues, parents and partner agencies. In terms of school structures and systems, this may also necessitate the introduction of more formalised systems of support and supervision for school staff working with the most vulnerable and challenging children and young people. It will necessitate a concentration on clarity about roles and responsibilities.

In all this, it is also essential to bear in mind the following:

- Schools are all different and may need to start from different places.
- Becoming more restorative takes time – allow 3–5 years for change to be embedded in a way that is sustainable.
- Becoming restorative is a process, not a goal.
- Look for 'quick wins' and accept that some parts of the process take longer.
- Change needs to include times of no change; i.e. times for reflection and consolidation.

It is important to understand that these are major demands but also that schools have a capacity to advocate for change and to mobilise the challenge.

Hendry offers a helpful way for schools to assess their own starting point on this journey (2009: 141) using a self-evaluation toolkit. Blood and Thorsborne (2006) and Drewery (2003) also offer grounded and practical advice about how to increase the reach of restorative work in schools. It is also worth recalling the words of Bauman (2001), that 'One can best recognise a democratic society by its constant complaint that it is not democratic enough' (2001: 55) noted earlier. A strong version of RP will mean constant calls that the school is not restorative enough. A restorative school will be vigilant and alive not only to these calls, but to their source. When these calls are made by all members of the school community equally; staff, students, parents, and when heard with equal respect by all, it is clear that a school is becoming radically restorative.

References

Alexander, R. (ed.) (2009) *Children, their World, their Education: Final Report and Recommendations of the Cambridge Primary Review*. London: Routledge.

Bauman, Z. (2001) *The Individualized Society*. London: Polity Press.

Bitel, M. (2005) *National Evaluation of the Restorative Justice in Schools Programme*. London: Youth Justice Board for England and Wales.

Blood, P. and Thorsborne, M. (2006) 'Overcoming Resistance to Whole-School Uptake of Restorative Practices'. Paper presented to *International Institute of Restorative Practices. The Next Step: Developing Restorative Communities, Conference*, Bethlehem, PA.

Claxton, G. (1999) *Hare Brain, Tortoise Mind. Why Intelligence Increases when you Think Less.* Hopewell, New Jersey: Ecco Press.

Department for Education (2012) *Permanent and Fixed Period Exclusions from Schools in England 2010/11.*

Drewery, W. and the Restorative Practices Development Team (2003) *Restorative Practices for Schools: A Resource.* Waikato: University of Waikato.

Hendry, R. (2009) *Building and Restoring Respectful Relationships in Schools: a guide to using Restorative Practice.* Abingdon: Routledge.

Hopkins, B. (2011) *The Restorative Classroom: Using Restorative Approaches to Foster Effective Learning.* London: Optimus.

Kane, J., Lloyd, G., McCluskey, G., Stead, J., Riddell, S. and Weedon, E. (2007) *Restorative Practices in Three Scottish Councils: Evaluation of Pilot Projects 2004–2006.* Edinburgh: Scottish Executive.

Lloyd, G. and McCluskey, G. (2009) *Restorative Practice Pilots and Approaches in Scotland – Follow Up.* Edinburgh: Scottish Government.

McAra, L. and McVie, S. (2010) 'Youth crime and justice: Key messages from the Edinburgh Study of Youth Transitions and Crime', *Criminology and Criminal Justice,* 10 (2): 179–209.

McCluskey, G. (2012) 'Youth is Present Only When Its Presence is a Problem': Voices of Young People on Discipline in School. *Children & Society.*

McCluskey, G., Lloyd, G., Kane, J., Stead, J., Riddell, S. and Weedon, E. (2008) 'Can Restorative Practices in Schools make a Difference?', *Educational Review: Special Issue: Truancy, Disaffection, Anti-social Behaviour and the Governance of Children,* 60(4): 405–417.

McCluskey, G., Kane, J., Lloyd, G., Stead, J., Riddell, S. and Weedon, E. (2011) '"Teachers are Afraid we are Stealing their Strength": A Risk Society and Restorative Approaches in School', *British Journal of Educational Studies,* 59(2): 105–119.

Porter, L. (2007) *Behaviour in Schools.* Maidenhead: Open University Press.

Scottish Government (2011) *Summary Statistics for Schools in Scotland.* Edinburgh: Scottish Government.

Skiba, R., Reynolds, C., Graham, S., Sheras, P., Conoley, J. and Garcia-Vasquez, E. (2006) 'Are Zero Tolerance Policies Effective in the Schools? An evidentiary review and recommendations. A Report by the American Psychological Association Zero Tolerance Task Force', *American Psychologist,* 63(9): 852–862.

Skinns, L., Du Rose, N. and Hough, M. (2009) *An Evaluation of Bristol RAiS.* London: Institute for Criminal Policy Research, Kings College London.

Smith, D. (2004) *The Links between Victimisation and Offending (No.5).* Edinburgh: The Edinburgh Study of Youth Transitions and Crime.

UK Children's Commissioners (2008) *UK Children's Commissioners Report to the United Nations Committee on the Rights of the Child.*

UNICEF (2007) *Child Poverty in Perspective: An Overview of Child Well-being in Rich Countries.* Florence: UNICEF Innocenti Research Centre.

—— (2010) *The Children Left Behind.* Florence: UNICEF Innocenti Research Centre.

Welsh Government (2012) *Exclusions from Schools in Wales 2010–11,* SDR 33/2012. Cardiff: Welsh Government.

Chapter 14

Effective evaluation of restorative approaches

Gillean McCluskey, Jean Kane, Gwynedd Lloyd,
Sheila Riddell, Joan Stead and Elisabet Weedon[1]

Introduction

Restorative Approaches in schools have developed out of growing interest in Restorative Justice in the community. Schools looking for strategies to address disaffection, behaviour difficulties and violence were attracted by the key ideas: the need to restore good relationships when there has been conflict or harm and to develop a school ethos, policies and procedures that reduce the possibilities of such conflict and harm. In 2004, the Scottish Executive funded a pilot project on Restorative Approaches (RA) in three local authorities, commissioning a team based at Edinburgh and Glasgow Universities to carry out a two-year evaluation in 18 pilot schools. This evaluation (Kane *et al.* 2007) and its follow up (Lloyd and McCluskey 2009) together comprise the largest evaluation of RA undertaken to date in the UK. The methods were negotiated throughout the research period with a range of stakeholders, including the funders, the local authorities and key school personnel. This chapter focuses on the process of that evaluation, some methodological questions arising from the evaluation, and the issue of the relationship of the research to policy and practice development in restorative approaches.

The policy context

Scotland covers nearly a third of the total land area of the UK but has a population of only 5.12 million. It is a semi-autonomous part of the UK: it established its own parliament and government in 1999, which are responsible for domestic legislation and policy on education, social welfare, justice and the environment. The government in London remains responsible for international affairs, defence, broad economic aspects and equal opportunities. Recent elections in Scotland returned a Scottish Nationalist Government, creating the possibility of disagreements with the Conservative administration in the UK Parliament. Earnings in Scotland are generally lower than in the UK as a whole and one third of Scottish children live in families whose average income is less than 50 per cent of the British average income.

The Standards in Scotland's Schools (etc.) (Scotland) Act 2000 enshrined in statute the presumption of mainstream education for all children, while recognising that there may be some children for whom special provision may be more appropriate, either because of their need for very specialised resources or because their challenging behaviour may be detrimental to those around them. The legislation also retained the right of schools to exclude students.

Funding was initially provided for a 30-month pilot project in three local authorities. The overall aim was to learn more about the impact of RA on school cultures and to look at whether there could be a distinctive national approach, an approach that both complemented and offered something additional to practice.

The aim of this chapter is not to discuss the value of RA in schools; the findings of the pilot and follow-up Scottish evaluations are available in the reports, *Restorative Practices in Three Scottish Local Authorities: Final Report of the Evaluation of the First Two Years of the Pilot Projects 2004–2006* (Kane *et al.* 2007) and *Restorative Practice Pilots and Approaches in Scotland – Follow Up* (Lloyd and McCluskey 2009). Consideration here is given to the methods of the evaluation, in particular, to the relationship between the commissioners of the research, the researchers and the researched in this project. The nature of the collaboration between stakeholders in the RA pilot and the evaluation team will be outlined and probed with a view to identifying the benefits and problems of a collaborative approach to research such as this. The endeavour throughout the research was to combine methodological rigour with responsive support for the developing situation in schools and local authorities. An important aspect for consideration here is the relationship between the evaluation methods and the focus of the investigation, that is, to the formative effect of RA itself on the enquiry. Before that discussion, the next section will offer a brief account of the pilot RA project.

The pilot project

Restorative Approaches have their roots in Restorative Justice, the history and development of which has offered some key aspects that seemed to be useful to schools. These features included:

- the importance of fair process;
- the recognition of the rights, and involvement where possible, of all parties in dispute or conflict resolution;
- the notion of restoration or reparation instead of retribution;
- the importance of developing empathy for others in preventing and responding to conflict or violence;
- the valuing of the views of all parties in open discussion;
- the effectiveness of circles for exchanging views, expressing feelings or resolving issues; and
- the importance of the language (often scripted) used in addressing conflict and resolving disputes.

These features of RA were very attractive to policymakers and others seeking ways of improving, or developing further, the ethos of Scottish schools. Alongside the pilot project, the Scottish Executive commissioned a formative evaluation of the work to be conducted by the Universities of Edinburgh and Glasgow and completed at the end of October 2006 (Kane *et al.* 2007). In each of the three participating local authorities, six schools were identified as pilot schools; these included 10 secondary schools, seven primary schools and one special school, variously situated in urban, suburban and rural areas and in areas of severe economic poverty as well as areas of relative economic wealth. The 18 pilot schools had varied histories in terms of existing approaches that could be described as restorative. In addition, schools had different reasons for joining the pilot project. Some schools had already demonstrated a commitment to the implementation of RA and were enthusiastic about participation in the pilot whilst other schools, especially those with newly appointed head teachers, were judged by the local authority to be ready to develop school ethos using RA. A third group of schools had been encouraged by local authorities to join the project as a means of responding to critical aspects of school inspection reports. Their participation was voluntary but originated in extrinsic accountability pressures. An evaluation had always been envisaged as part of the project; its main function to ensure that participants were assisted to learn more about RA in schools as a result of their participation in the pilot. Thus, the evaluation team was encouraged to focus on the processes of implementation, to gauge the effectiveness of these processes in different schools and local authorities and to support the implementation by providing feedback derived from data collected. Beyond the school-based implementation, it was envisaged that the evaluation would contribute to a collective and developing understanding of RA in education contexts. There were issues in the implementation of RA in schools that could helpfully be explored and even resolved through the evaluation, for example, the place of conferencing in school practices. The objectives of the pilot project and the evaluation together were:

- to identify the training and support which staff felt were required to enable them to implement the initiatives effectively;
- to explore the different situations, contexts and areas of the curriculum where the new approaches were employed;
- to analyse the ways in which different participants (teachers, classroom assistants, students, parents) responded to the innovative approaches and the conditions which appeared to produce beneficial outcomes;
- to identify the characteristics of schools, staff or others which contributed to positive or negative outcomes;
- to identify the support required from local authorities to promote and support school-level implementation.

The evaluation project was designed to take account of these objectives, as well as the broad purposes of the pilot indicated above. The RA evaluation was from its inception an integral part of the pilot project, an 'insider' position that afforded the evaluation team opportunities, advantages and potential pitfalls.

Evaluation method

The two-year pilot project and its evaluation were closely tied to each other, ensuring that the evaluation engaged local authority and school-based staff on a continuing basis at all stages of the project. When researching policy or practice it has been *de rigueur* in recent years to locate such an analysis within the rubric of 'what works'. The pragmatics of such an approach are particularly attractive to those involved in both developing and evaluating projects and policy initiatives. This project was clearly located within this rubric but it also went well beyond judgements of outcomes and narrow measurements of progress. During the tendering process it became apparent that there was already considerable input and participation from the three local authorities who were piloting the initiative, and from some of the schools. This participation pervaded the project and demanded of the research team particular methods and approaches to funders and stakeholders in schools and in local authorities. In outlining how the evaluation proceeded, particular attention will be given to the aspects of the project that underline its claims to participative research.

The design of the evaluation itself emerged from discussions with those piloting RA in local authorities and in schools. The evaluation team worked throughout with a national development and advisory group consisting of key managers from the local authorities, schools and educational psychology services within each of the three local authorities. This group met about three times a year and was convened and chaired by representatives from the Scottish Government. These meetings reported on developments in the three local authorities, discussed emerging ideas and worked on policy and practice statements. In the early stages, part of each meeting was devoted to discussion of the evaluation and feedback on the emerging evaluation framework. This framework was also shaped through meetings and discussions with individual schools. The active involvement of schools and authorities in the evaluation allowed different definitions and criteria for success to be developed, acknowledged and applied. The criteria for judging success were clearly stated at the outset but, importantly, were to apply differentially across the participating local authorities and schools to accommodate local differences in aims and approaches to RA. For example, discussions on local and national steering groups identified the more complex and compartmentalised departmental structures of secondary schools as likely to have bearing upon the implementation of RA. There were, therefore, overall differences in the aims for RA in primary and secondary schools, with primary schools tending to see RA as permeating school culture and providing a vehicle for the development of school ethos. On the other hand, secondary schools generally emphasised RA as a means of resolving particular incidents where relationships had broken down or conflict had arisen.

The evaluation was designed to allow schools to judge practices in relation to the school's own aims for the innovation. The framework for the evaluation accommodated these differences, taking account of the different contexts in which RA were developed but also trying to enable comparison of progress and outcomes as the development proceeded across Scotland. Some performance indicators were therefore used in all local authorities, whereas others were specific to a given context.

The participation of stakeholders was also evident in a long process of discussion and negotiation around the nature of data to be collected. All parties involved in the pilot and its evaluation favoured a multi-method approach, that is, an approach which contained both formative and summative dimensions, which drew on a range of research strategies and techniques and which generated both qualitative and quantitative data. Local authority and school-based staff favoured both 'hard' and 'soft' outcome measures. 'Hard' measures would explore the impact of the initiative by monitoring a range of quantitative outcomes such as disciplinary referrals, recorded incidents of bullying and exclusions. 'Soft' measures would examine actors' perceptions of and responses to the pilots. There was a reluctance by the government funders (unusually) to see the collection of 'hard' data as the most important, coupled with a commitment to the evaluation of the particular aims and outcomes being developed in each school. Data collection involved:

- interviews with a range of local authority and school staff (over 400 interviews/162 individuals);
- interviews, individual and group with students (138 primary and 93 secondary students);
- interviews with parents (31);
- school staff survey (627 returns/response rate 45 per cent);
- student survey (1163 – administered to students aged 9–11 years and aged 13–15 years;
- documentary analysis;
- participation in a range of government, local authority and school-based meetings;
- collection of statistical data at school and local authority level;
- observation in classrooms, playgrounds and meetings.

There was a strong sense from Government and from the advisory group that the main purpose of the evaluation was to identify and record a sense of process of how the pilot schools were working to develop their projects and how learning about their progress towards change might ultimately help other schools to also think about the issues. The evaluation of the initiative was to take place alongside the pilot during its formative stages. The aims therefore expanded from a description and analysis of 'what' works to include attention to process and elements of 'how' it worked, resulting in both a formative and summative evaluation (Bennett 2003). However, what also needed to be taken into consideration was a particular request from one local authority (which was then applied to all the local authorities in the pilot) to explore the context and the prevailing factors that need to be present for the initiative to be successful and effective: not just what works and how it works, but also what prior conditions are necessary for it to work. This was later developed into a 'readiness tool' for wider use (Hendry 2009). The evaluators were seen as helpful to the pilot projects in feeding back their observations and on-going analysis, thus affecting directly, as well as responding to, the projects as they progressed.

Understandings of evaluation usually revolve around monitoring, auditing, assessing and inspecting, in order to establish value, utility, relevance, practicality, generalisability and causality. Scriven (1996) describes evaluation as either formative (to support the process of improvement by identifying strengths and weaknesses) or summative (reporting on a programme). The distinction between 'formative' and 'summative' provides a useful framework in which to locate the many different ways in which evaluation takes place, but this is less helpful in making sense of evaluation that is aimed towards generating knowledge about the basic principles underlying effective programme development and implementation (Simon 1987; Clarke 1999). This evaluation was formative in that it took place alongside, and as part of, the development of the initiative over the initial two-year period, but there was also considerable emphasis throughout on a summative exploration of 'what worked', as well as on reciprocal processes of development and evaluation. The researchers' impact on the development operated on two levels. First, in each school they offered comment and interim feedback to schools as the development proceeded. They were described at one point by a school-based participant as fulfilling the role of 'critical friend'. Secondly, the research team offered an important conduit through which the experiences of the 18 pilot schools could be disseminated, considered and acted upon as the project developed. Thus schools could learn from not just their own experience but also from each other as the project progressed. In describing the evaluation as formative, its aims and processes can be linked to what has been termed 'action research', which is generally described as monitoring, observing and changing rather than investigation, interpretation and analysis. Action research differs starkly from conventional social research in that action researchers insist that research process, research outcomes and the application of results to problem solving are inextricably linked (Greenwood and Levin 1998: 93).

The purpose of this chapter is not to discuss the findings of the project. Those are available in the full report (Kane *et al.* 2007) but a brief indication of the findings will serve to provide some background for discussion of issues raised by the participative nature of the research. The evaluation indicated that greatest success was achieved where schools aimed to improve school ethos by creating and sustaining positive relationships throughout the school community. Primary schools had been more likely than secondary schools to have implemented RA in these permeating ways so it was in the primary sector where higher levels of successful implementation were apparent, although two secondary schools were notable exceptions to this general finding. When introduced with commitment, enthusiasm, leadership and significant staff development there was a clear positive impact on relationships in school, identifiable through the views and actions of staff and students, as well as evident in measurable reduction of playground incidents, discipline referrals, exclusion and use of external behaviour support (McCluskey *et al.* 2007). The evaluation highlighted the length of time and the difficulties involved in changing school processes and cultures (Blood and Thorsborne 2005; Kane *et al.* 2007). Other significant issues included the challenge of RA for school discipline systems still strongly underpinned by punishment (McCluskey 2012; Parsons 2005).

The main success of RA was judged to be in its capacity to improve relationships within the school community. This strength of RA impacted upon the evaluation itself – across the project a high value was placed upon trust and collaboration between all those involved in the pilot and its evaluation. There was a commitment in the research team to enabling participation in research, as well as a recognition of many practical advantages accruing from such methods. In addition, the focus of enquiry in this project – RA – itself generated commitment to maximising participation amongst stakeholders. Within the pilot, RA was increasingly viewed as a vehicle for transforming school ethos, crucially through the involvement of all those within the school community. Many schools used RA to create a space to allow students especially, to be listened to and to be involved in the management of relationships, for example, through peer mediation. Coming from the pilot schools and local authorities was an impetus to ensure the same engagement with the processes of the evaluation. Ideals of collaboration, and recognition of the many practical benefits it afforded, also brought risks to the robustness of the research. Collaboration did not always sit easily with the task of monitoring performance and reaching a judgement of the success and effectiveness of the initiative, a tension explored in the next section.

Discussion of methods

The broad aim of the pilot was to change schools for the better; the purpose of the evaluation was not just to offer judgement as to whether or not this was happening, but to work with local authority and school staff to support progress towards that aim. Working towards these goals demanded that the researchers developed close affinity with schools and maintained relationships with key staff in ways which could be seen as jeopardising the rigour of the research. Commitment to school improvement and participation in change processes are core aspects of teachers' professionalism but how do these features relate to researchers' professionalism? Issues of the role and contribution of the evaluation team are addressed in this section; first, by offering a rationale for the kind of participation described here; second, by probing how participation affected the rigour of the RA research and finally, by discussing the limits of participation in this project and in research on RA more generally.

Why collaborate?

The main rationale for collaboration between researchers and the fields researched rests upon commitment to change as the overriding purpose of social research. By this account, the likely impact of research is increased where there is shared purpose between the researchers and those researched (Huxham and Vangen 2005). More than this, Edwards has commented that educational researchers share with the field researched:

> ... a set of value-laden concerns about individual, community, and societal well being. These concerns mean that much of educational research is and should be a site of continual meaning-making and they mark educational research as an activity in which engagement with its fields of study is crucial.
>
> (Edwards 2002: 158)

The commonality between researchers and the fields researched is such that they may be seen as belonging to the same community of practice. Simon (1987: 251) viewed this aspect, amongst others, as a feature of democratic evaluation shaped by 'a rhetoric of community, reciprocity, partnership'. Hammersley (2005) detects danger in shifting research into professional communities of practice, arguing that the role of educational research would thus be limited to shaping directly the activities of educators.

The RA evaluation was intended to enhance understandings of RA in school contexts, and to generate knowledge about how implementation could improve schools in and beyond the pilot. In pursuing the former aim, the purpose of the researchers was closely aligned with the purpose of school-based participants who were motivated by a desire to effect improvement, particularly in their own setting. In addition, where there was common cause between the researchers and participants, research processes were likely to be more relevant to school practices. Outcomes were more likely to be 'owned' by school-based participants, increasing the likelihood of follow-up action in the school. In addition, the collaborative research model offered major strengths in its facilitating of ready access to the sites of investigation and depth of discussion with participants. These advantages yielded rich data, and multiple interpretations of that data, valuable to researchers, professionals and policymakers concerned to understand more about school cultures. Countering these advantages, though, was the possibility that the relationships created through this process militated against dispassionate, objective enquiry and tended to promote a partisanship by the research team in relation to the promotion of the project, leading to a crossing of the fine line between evidence-gathering and advocacy. The relevance of the research for the pilot schools was assured by the close tie to the development of practice, but was the rigour of the research compromised by these ways of working with schools? The next section will consider how the evaluation attempted to blend collaboration and rigour.

Participation and rigour

Kemmis and McTaggart (2003) describe action research as setting in motion processes by which participants collectively make critical analysis of their practices, their understandings and the settings in which they practise in order to change the practice settings and the consequences of their practices in these settings. Often, this is through individual practitioner research/reflection. This project, however, involved not only teachers/practitioners but also researchers and funders, and may therefore be described as having elements of participatory action research. The research enabled knowledge about RA to be constructed in ways that had a formative effect on practice. The task of the evaluation team was to take account of different constructions of RA in school settings and in local authorities, to represent 'multiple realities', that is, by attempts to access and understand different constructions of knowledge and by giving particular voice to those whose voices were not usually heard. Student perspectives of the impact of RA were gathered through observation, in interviews and by large student surveys in each of the pilot schools. This data, especially in secondary schools, occasionally but not surprisingly conflicted with the views coming from senior staff who were themselves advocates of RA. For example, RA were cited in some schools as permeating school ethos, positively affecting relationships across the school. Students in some of those schools did not report so positively, offering their experience of unfair and/or disrespectful behaviour. This kind of data was discussed with staff leading the initiative in schools and sometimes challenged their assumptions about the processes of change and helping to shape the development as it proceeded.

Researchers' assumptions were also challenged at times. Openness to different perspectives on RA in schools was sometimes painful when participants were very occasionally aggressively hostile to the initiative in their school. One researcher's discomfort with those views led her to consider her own partisanship but also the ethics of allowing a teacher to make some comments about students that she found objectionable. Researchers' strong identification with schools' endeavours to implement RA may have rendered them less open to alternative perspectives, less inclined to represent 'multiple realities' where particular constructions of reality were very obstructive to the implementation of RA and challenging generally to the researchers' own value system.

All those actively involved in this study (researchers, local authorities and school representatives and funder) thought that RA was a good idea, that it 'made sense' and should be encouraged. But as well as the overall interest in RA, there were layers of disagreement and debate. For example, within the research team members did not always share the same views about the value of particular practices in schools and this led to internal debate; strong discussions were held within the team, for example, about the place of punishment in school. Similarly, schools and local authorities endorsed different practices under the broad RA banner. In comparing and contrasting understandings of RA, and experience of establishing them, views of participants and researchers alike shifted and more robust understandings emerged. Kemmis and McTaggart (2003) comment that 'participatory action research offers an opportunity to create forums in which people can join one another as co-participants in the struggle to remake the practices in which they interact...' (Kemmis and McTaggart 2003: 382).

Such forums were a key element of this project. A network of groups and sub-groups (national steering groups, local authority networks and steering groups, research teams, school staff) met throughout the two-year period enabled the sharing of experience about the pilot and its evaluation. Such opportunities were crucial in enabling the production of 'knowledge for practice' – knowledge which guided subsequent activity. Thus, for all those involved in the project, knowledge production and the pursuit of change in schools were not easily separable.

The methods here could not be called participatory action research, although they had elements of such methods. The research team aimed to produce knowledge about RA in school settings for an audience beyond the pilot schools, including policymakers, professionals working on the pilot and the academic community. In this aim the purposes of the researchers were to some extent differentiated from school-based participants, although even here there was commonality of purpose across the whole group involved in the pilot initiative. In furthering this aim, the participation of 'stakeholders' was of central importance in ensuring, not just the relevance of the work, but also its rigour. Stronach and McClure argue that 'the redefinition and re-location of negotiation, placing it at the heart...of a consciously hybrid research process, offers more open possibilities and more educative futures' (1997: 112).

Discussions, interviews and initial findings were negotiated with those involved through regular written and verbal feedback. This continuous feedback allowed for critical reflection on the highs and lows of the intervention, and provided opportunities to change and adapt accordingly. Interim reports were provided for each school and comments were received and acted upon by the research team. Researchers were given on-going feedback about the scope of their methods, for example, where school staff believed particular perspectives had been missed or others had been over-emphasised. This was not a process whereby claims made by the research were amended by school-based participants. Sometimes data revealed the existence of practices denied by senior staff. The use of punishments alongside RA was one such contentious issue. One pilot school professed to have abandoned punishment in favour of restorative approaches but evidence of punishment subsequently emerged in the data and informed judgements about that school's effectiveness in moving towards its own goals for RA.

The approaches outlined above required certain attitudes from the researchers. A researcher adopting participative approaches has an obligation to underpin knowledge claims with constant critical reflection. The effective researcher in the participatory model is not so different from a model of the effective teacher – the work of both is shaped by combining action with reflection in an on-going process. This requires reflexivity, a responsiveness to emerging issues and a preparedness to shape the process as it proceeds, rather than simply a launching of a pre-designed project onto a school community. Critical self-scrutiny featured at all stages of the process for the research team; using evidence as feedback about the research process and the researchers, and not just as comment about the development of the RA project. The regular feedback of interim findings and discussion with schools inevitably meant that the research process and the development process were reciprocally influential, again with the advantages and disadvantages that this implies. The subjectivity of the interpersonal processes of research was mitigated by the multi-layered collaborations it included, some of them challenging for those involved. In addition, the collection of more objective outcome data, for example exclusion figures and discipline referrals supported the rigour of the research.

Limits of participation

For the kind of educational research discussed here, it is feasible and desirable to embrace participative approaches but there were limits to what was possible. Two features of the research, in particular, constrained its participative nature. The first was the impact of government funding on the three-way relationship between the evaluators, the evaluated and the funders. The second limiting factor related to the capacity of schools to enable staff's active participation in research studies. These two factors are considered in turn.

In participatory research, the dichotomy between the researcher and the researched begins to break down. The researcher is no longer the expert whose interpretations are the only ones that matter, but, instead, is a facilitator. The construction of knowledge becomes a collective process for all of the participants, including the researchers (Edwards 2002). Although the methods adopted by the RA evaluation team were partly founded upon these understandings, there were features that limited the extent to which the project could be called participatory. First, the research was an external evaluation funded and directed by the Scottish Executive. The imperative for academics to gain and sustain funding from commissioned projects, combined with the pressures of a 'performativity' culture, have been noted by a number of commentators as potentially jeopardising researchers' impartiality (Simon 1987; Stronach and McClure 1997). Griffiths, Cotton, and Bowbrick (2006) comment that in research into policy, the relationship between researchers and policymakers is a complex one: 'on both sides, careers, credibility and cash are at stake, as well as professional identities...in informal settings further tales abound about the tensions in the relationship between researchers and policymakers' (Griffiths, Cotton, and Bowbrick 2006: 1).

In the RA project, relationships between the evaluators and the evaluated, however cordial and constructive, were nevertheless ultimately unequal. Schools chose to participate and outcome measures were negotiated but researchers retained the right to produce and report, in the end, their own evaluative findings.

The relationship between the researchers and the funders in this project was very constructive, with government representatives on the national steering group articulating an interest in RA and a commitment to supporting schools and local authorities in pursuit of their implementation. The RA evaluation did not demonstrate the tensions noted by commentators including Griffiths, Cotton, and Bowbrick (2006). What would account for a lack of such tension in this project? Torrance (2003: 172) advocates that: '[researchers] ...have a wealth of knowledge to contribute to public debate, and an expertise in designing and conducting studies which ought to be used to hold policy to account, as well as promote its development'.

The knowledge and expertise of the evaluation team were recognised. Early on in the project, queries about the robustness of the proposed evaluation, and suggestions to enhance its rigour, came entirely from the research team. Some of these, for example a proposal to increase the use of outcome measures in the evaluation, were resisted by an alliance between Government, local authority and school representatives on the grounds that an emphasis on outcomes would not necessarily reflect school development. Neither could tension arise from the evaluation team's attempt to hold policy to account for there was no specific policy commitment to RA. The RA initiative was exploratory, arising from a broad policy commitment to improve behaviour in schools. Lack of tension could be attributed to the focus of the enquiry; national and local government officers professed themselves to be personally and professionally influenced by restorative principles, as were the researchers, and this is likely to have enhanced relationships within the project and to have created a positive tone. More generally, the experience of members of this research team in Scotland is of a relationship with policymakers that is much less adversarial than seems to be the case, for example, in England. And yet, for participatory research, a possible disadvantage of this positive relationship is that, from the perspective of schools, government-sponsored evaluators may be viewed as an arm of government, as quasi-inspectors whose role is to police the implementation of policy initiatives. For schools of which participation was required by the local authority, for example, following a critical report by government inspectors, the evaluation team may have seemed not as helpful co-problem-solvers but as a means of ensuring increased pressure for change in the school. The question about how research is funded continues to be an issue in the field of Restorative Approaches, where much of the research is small scale, qualitative and undertaken by those with an interest in the outcomes.

A further constraint on the participative qualities of this project was that participants themselves were not all equal; some enjoyed greater influence and impact than others. For participants such as central and local government officers, conventional data-gathering techniques such as one-to-one interviewing were a familiar and appropriate means of allowing them to share their views of the topic under consideration. Some were confident enough to take a measure of control over the process, for example, by stipulating the conditions and circumstances under which they were prepared to be interviewed. For other participants, though, such as the children and young people, and their parents, the methods used to enable expression of their knowledge were more problematic. There were limits to the participative nature of the project in that all participants could not be said to have equal ownership of the project, for example, those leading the pilot in schools and local authorities were highly engaged, whilst some teacher participants professed to know very little about the project. And even where commitment to and interest in the project was very strong the practical constraints of, for example, school organisation, may have prevented professional participants from engaging fully with the research processes at all stages.

Participation in research offers the potential for change in the participants as well as change in the site being researched (Oliver 1992; Powell 2002). By this account, the research process provides the means for all involved to develop and learn through the collective construction of knowledge. The research process is formative of the research site, of the researchers and of all other participants. One of the consequences of fostering broad participation in school-based educational research is a fuller integration of teaching and research activity in those sites. Orme comments on the challenge of enabling more fully participative social research:

> Those who are at times deemed subjects or objects of the research have to be involved as full participants. This requires more than giving informed consent: participants are active agents within the research process. This in turn necessitates that they are receptive to research, both its findings and its nuances, and that they are themselves research literate. A consequence of this for social sciences is an educational role, making research accessible both as an outcome and as an activity.
>
> (Orme 2000: 212)

This would better equip professionals to participate more effectively as researchers but, until schools themselves are constructed as sites for the learning of everyone involved, it is unlikely that the broader range of participants in research would be fully empowered to take control of research processes and outcomes. For example, the young people in this study and, to a lesser extent, their parents, cooperated with the study but it is not possible to claim that they were sufficiently engaged with the school, nor experienced enough in participation in the organisation, to become co-owners of the project. Neither could many of the school-based staff who contributed to the study be called participants if that term denotes ownership of the project. Principles of participatory research might be hard to follow through where the research is into organisations which have low levels of participation amongst their constituency, or very hierarchical forms of organisation. Restorative Approaches themselves, with their emphasis on student voice and engagement, could have the potential to improve schools as sites of more fully participative research.

Conclusion

The relevance of the research for the pilot schools was assured by its close tie to the development of practice but was the rigour of the research compromised by these ways of working with schools? Funded research related to policy priorities carries particular challenges for researchers who pursue collaborative methods, for alongside obvious gains – ease of access, breadth of participation, relevance of findings, likelihood of impact – are risks of a loss of autonomy. Collaboration within this project afforded various opportunities for participation to students, school staff and local authority officers. The evaluation was positioned 'inside' the pilot project and so its processes and outcomes were, to a considerable extent, owned by the pilot group. The advantages of this were an increase in the relevance of the research for each school and for schools not in the pilot but interested in learning from the experience of pilot schools. In addition, the researchers benefited from the restorative tone and ethos of the whole pilot group with its emphasis on respectful relationships, cooperation and validation of different perspectives. In summary, this study was successful in developing an evaluation method which was congruent with its restorative aims and which can therefore offer a basis for future evaluations in this important field.

Note

1 The authors wish to acknowledge work of the Scottish Restorative Practices team. An earlier version of this chapter appeared in Kane, J., Lloyd, G., McCluskey, G., Maguire, R., Riddell, S. and Weedon, E. (2009) 'Generating an Inclusive Ethos? Exploring the Impact of Restorative Practices in Scottish Schools'. *International Journal of Inclusive Education*, Vol. 13(3): 231–253.

References

Bennett, J. (2003) *Evaluation Methods in Research*. London: Continuum.

Blood, P. and Thorsborne, M. (2005) 'The challenge of culture change'. Paper presented to the *6th International Conference on Conferences, Circles and other Restorative Practices*, March 3–5, in Sydney.

Clarke, A. (1999) *Evaluation Research*. London: Sage.

Edwards, A. (2002) 'Responsible research: Ways of being a researcher', *British Educational Research Journal* 28 (2): 157–68.

Greenwood, D.J. and Levin. M. (1998) *Introduction to action research*. London: Sage.

Griffiths, M., Cotton, T. and Bowbrick, P. (2006) 'Educational researchers doing research on educational policy: Heroes, puppets, partners, or...?'. Paper presented to the British Educational Research Association Annual Conference, Warwick.

Hammersley, M. (2005) 'Communities of practice and educational research', *International Journal of Research & Method in Education* 28 (1): 5–21.

Hendry, R. (2009) *Building and Restoring Respectful Relationships in Schools: A Guide to Restorative Practice*. Abingdon: Routledge.

Huxham, C. and Vangen, S. (2005) *Managing to Collaborate*. Abingdon: Routledge.

Kane, J., Lloyd, G., McCluskey, G., Riddell, S., Stead, J. and Weedon, E. (2007) *Restorative Practices in Three Scottish Local Authorities: Final Report of the Evaluation of the First Two Years of the Pilot Projects 2004–2006*. Edinburgh: Scottish Executive.

—— (2008) 'Collaborative evaluation: balancing rigour and relevance in a research study of restorative approaches in schools in Scotland', *International Journal of Research and Method in Education* 3 (2): 99–111.

Kemmis, S. and McTaggart, R. (2003) 'Participatory action research' in N.K. Denzin and Y. Lincoln (eds) *Strategies of Qualitative Enquiry*. London: Sage.

Lloyd, G. and McCluskey, G. (2009) *Restorative Practice Pilots and Approaches in Scotland – Follow Up*. Edinburgh: Scottish Government.

McCluskey, G. (2012) 'Youth is present only when its presence is a problem: Voices of young people on discipline in school', *Children & Society*.

Oliver, M. (1992) 'Changing the social relations of research production'. *Disability, Handicap and Society* 7 (2): 101–14.

Orme, J. (2000) 'Interactive social sciences: Patronage or partnership?', *Science and Public Policy* 27 (3): 211–9.

Parsons, C. (2005) 'School exclusion: The will to punish', *British Journal of Education Studies* 53 (2): 187–211.

Powell, J. (2002) 'The changing conditions of social work research', *British Journal of Social Work* 32, (1): 17–33.

Scriven, M. (1996) 'Types of evaluation and types of evaluator', *Evaluation Practice* 17 (9): 151–61.

Simon, H. (1987) *Getting to Know Schools in a Democracy: The Politics and Process of Evaluation*. London: Falmer.

Stronach, I. and McClure, M. (1997) *Educational Research Undone: The Postmodern Embrace*. Buckingham: Open University Press.

Torrance, H. (2003) 'When is an "evaluation" not an evaluation? When it's sponsored by the QCA? A response to Lindsay and Lewis', *British Educational Research Journal*, 29 (2): 169–73.

Part III

Catalytic?

Chapter 15

Restorative approaches in schools

Necessary roles of cooperative learning and constructive conflict

David W. Johnson and Roger T. Johnson

Introduction

The need to repair the harm caused by destructively managed conflicts or deliberate offences against others is one of the most fundamental issues facing the world today. This chapter will discuss how cooperative learning and constructive experiences of conflict can enhance restorative approaches in schools and help meet this broader agenda. Further afield, restorative procedures are being used in National Truth and Reconciliation Commissions where the historically oppressed face their previous oppressors and the two groups strive to establish an ongoing cooperative, equalitarian relationship (Vora and Vora, 2004), to negotiate ends to civil wars so that the various sides will work together for the country to function (Druckman and Albin, 2011), to national reconciliations between majority and minority groups for past injustices (such as Australia's efforts to reconcile with its Aborigines), to crime situations where offenders and victims meet to repair the damage created by the crime (Braithwaite, 1989; Umbreit, 2001) and to schools where restorative practices are used to create a 'just' educational community. What makes schools such a key setting for restorative approaches is that such experiences train students for a lifetime of seeking equity and fairness in their relationships. Schools have the power and the opportunity to make restorative approaches a habit and a way of life.

In order for restorative approaches to be effective, cooperative learning and constructive conflict resolution must be the cultural norm in schools. In order to understand the implications of such a statement, it is necessary to review: (a) the nature of restorative approaches and how these fit into an overall view of justice; (b) social interdependence theory as a theory underlying restorative approaches, cooperation and constructive conflict; (c) the need for a cooperative context in order for restorative approaches to occur; (d) the use of integrative negotiations and peer mediation as a restorative approach; (e) the use of constructive controversy to make intellectual decisions about how justice may be achieved; and, finally, (f) the development of civic values.

Types of justice

Restorative justice can be best understood in relation to other types of justice. As this is the first chapter in the section on the potential catalytic properties of restorative approaches in schools, it may be helpful to revisit a few key concepts. Justice as a whole encompasses distributive justice (i.e. ensuring that benefits are distributed justly), procedural justice (i.e. the same procedures are applied fairly to all members), moral inclusion (i.e. everyone is perceived to be part of the same moral community) and restorative justice (i.e. repairing the harm done by an offence) (Deutsch, 2006; Johnson and F. Johnson, 2012; Johnson and R. Johnson, 1989, 2005a, 2009a).

Distributive justice

Justice involves the distribution of benefits (and sometimes costs and harm) to a group or organisational members (Deutsch, 1985). Benefits may be distributed in three ways. First, the **equity (or merit) view** is one where a person's rewards should be in proportion to his or her contributions to the group's effort. This view is inherent in competitive situations. Second, the **equality view** is that all group members should benefit equally. It is inherent in cooperative situations. Third, the **need view** suggests group members' benefits should be awarded in proportion to their need. Cooperators typically ensure that all participants receive the social minimum needed for their well-being. Whichever of these approaches is used, it has to be perceived as 'just', as perceived unjust distribution of rewards or benefits tends to result in low morale, high conflict and low productivity (Johnson and F. Johnson, 2012; Johnson and R. Johnson, 1989, 2005a, 2009a).

Procedural justice

In addition to the distribution of rewards and benefits, the procedures used to determine the benefits each person receives must be perceived as just. **Procedural justice** involves perceived fairness of the procedures that determine the benefits and outcomes a person receives. Fair procedures require that the same procedures are applied equally to everyone and also that they are implemented with polite, dignified and respectful behaviour. Typically, fairness of procedures and treatment are a more pervasive concern to most people than fair outcomes (Deutsch, 2006). The more frequent the use of cooperative learning, the more students tend to believe that everyone who tried has an equal chance to succeed in class, that students get the grades they deserved and that the grading system is fair (Johnson and R. Johnson, 1989, 2005a, 2009a). Even when their task performances are markedly discrepant, members of cooperative groups tend to view themselves and their group-mates as being equally deserving of benefits and rewards.

Scope of justice

Justice tends to be given only to individuals who are perceived to be included in one's moral community, that is, who fall within the scope of justice (Deutsch, 1985; Opotow, 1990). Individuals and groups who are outside the boundary of one's moral community may be treated in ways that would be considered immoral if people within the moral community were so treated. The scope of justice is the extent to which a person's concepts of justice apply to specific others (Deutsch, 1985, 2006). Moral considerations guide our behaviour towards those individuals and groups who are inside our scope of justice. The concept of moral inclusion therefore, is applying considerations of fairness and justice to others, seeing them as entitled to a share of the community's resources and seeing them as entitled to help, even at a cost to oneself (Opotow, 1990, 1993). Moral inclusion includes the values of fairness, equality and humanitarianism. Moral exclusion permits and justifies derogating and mistreating outsiders and is perpetuated primarily through denying that it has harmful effects. Those outside the scope of justice can be viewed as nonentities (e.g. less than human) who can be exploited (e.g. undocumented immigrants, slaves) or enemies who deserve brutal treatment and even death. The denial includes minimising the duration of the effects; denying others' entitlement to better outcomes; and seeing one's mistreatment as negligible (Opotow and Weiss, 2000).

Restorative justice

While distributive justice focuses on the perceived fairness of the distribution of benefits and rewards, and procedural justice focuses on the perceived fairness of the procedures used to determine outcomes, restorative justice focuses on repairing the harm caused by an offence or a destructively managed conflict. Restorative approaches become applicable after a conflict has taken place in which one party was harmed by another or another type of justice was violated. Restorative justice involves bringing together all parties affected by harm or wrongdoing (e.g. offenders and their families, victims and their families, other members of the community and professionals), discussing what happened and how they were affected and agreeing on what should be done to right any wrongs suffered (Morrison and Ahmed, 2006; Umbreit, 1995). RJ is both a process that encourages individuals to meet, problem solve and negotiate with each other whilst adhering to a set of values that emphasise the importance of healing, repairing, restoring, reintegrating the relationships and preventing harm to others.

Restorative approaches deal with at least two issues. The first is the resolving of past conflicts to restore justice among parties and within the community as a whole. The second is to create the conditions for maintaining long-term, ongoing cooperation among parties in the future (given that future contact will occur). In most cases, the shadow of the future is almost always present when restorative approaches take place in educational contexts, as it re-establishes the membership of the 'offender' and 'victim' in a moral community in which they may continue to interact in an on going, long-term relationship. There are a number of characteristics necessary for a restorative approach to be created: (a) there must be identifiable disputants with different views on a matter of conflict; (b) their participation must be voluntary; (c) they must have the capacity to engage fully and safely in dialogue and integrative negotiations; and (d) a facilitator or mediator must be present to provide the help and support that the participants need.

Process and outcomes

Once disputants agree to a restorative approach, there is a process in which individuals meet, engage in a problem-solving dialogue and negotiate with each other. The 'victim' is given the opportunity to express his or her needs and feelings resulting from being harmed and to help determine the best way for the 'offender' to repair the harm he or she has created. The 'offender' is expected to take responsibility for his or her actions and realise that the actions had real consequences for the 'victim' and the community. Since the responsibility for reconciliation is partially theirs, the community (i.e. faculty, administrators, families) is given the opportunity to participate in the discussion. The process is based on a set of values that emphasise the importance of healing, repairing, restoring and preventing harm to others, as well as reintegrating the relationships among the relevant parties. The outcomes of restorative justice include an agreement reflecting: (a) restoration and reparation (i.e. restitution agreed on by offender, victim and community); and (b) the establishment or re-establishment of constructive relationships among offender, victim and the community as a whole (given that they will interact in the future). In many ways, the process of restoring justice may be more important than the outcomes per se for preventing harm in the future, repairing relationships and re-establishing cooperation among the parties involved.

Aspects of restorative approaches

Three important aspects of restorative approaches are reconciliation, remorse and forgiveness. *Reconciliation* is an emotional reattachment and affiliation between former opponents after conflict-induced separation (de Waal, 2000; Roseth, Pellegrini, Dupuis, Bohn, Hickey, Hilk and Peshkam, 2010). It reaffirms and restores the positive, cooperative relationship among the parties in a conflict. In some cases it ends the negative sanctions placed on the offender, which often include social exclusion. In all cases it involves an emotional reattachment among the parties involved in the conflict. Reconciliation usually includes an apology, institutes a sense that justice has prevailed, recognises the impact of the acts perpetuated, restores respect for the social identity of those formerly demeaned, validates and recognises the suffering undergone by the victim and relevant community members, establishes trust between victim and offender and removes the reasons for either party to use violence to 'right' the wrongs of the past.

Remorse is an emotional expression of personal regret felt by a person after he or she has committed an act that they deem to be shameful, hurtful or violent. Remorse is a negative, conscious and emotional reaction to personal past acts and behaviours that is often expressed by the term 'sorry'. Remorse reflects such feelings as sadness, shame, embarrassment, depression, annoyance or guilt. The offender accepts responsibility and hopefully feels genuinely sorry for his or her actions. He or she commits to not repeating the actions in the future.

Forgiveness occurs when the victim pardons the offender and lets go of any grudge, desire for revenge, or resentment toward the offender for the wrongdoing (Enright, Gassin and Knutson, 2003). Forgiveness conveys the victim's hope and expectation that the offender can be trusted in the future to not repeat the offence and take responsibility for the well-being of the victim.

Necessary conditions

There are at least four conditions that influence the effectiveness of the implementation of restorative approaches. The first is creating a cooperative context within which the disputants can reconcile and repair their relationship. This includes establishing the membership of all parties in the same moral community. The second is the use of integrative (e.g. problem-solving) negotiations to ensure that disputants seek outcomes that are mutually beneficial. The third is to ensure that difficult decisions in implementing agreements are made utilising the constructive controversy procedure. The fourth is to affirm civic values and ensure that they underlie the process and outcomes of restorative approaches. To discuss these conditions, it is first helpful to review social interdependence theory, which we argue underpins each of these elements.

Social interdependence theory

Underlying the nature of cooperation, integrative negotiations, constructive controversy and civic values is social interdependence theory. **Social interdependence** exists when the accomplishment of each individual's goals is affected by the actions of others (Deutsch, 1949, 1962; Johnson, 1970, 2003; Johnson and Johnson, 1989, 2005a, 2009a). There are two types of social interdependence, positive (cooperation) and negative (competition). **Positive interdependence** exists when individuals perceive that they can reach their goals if and only if the other individuals with whom they are cooperatively linked also reach their goals. Participants, therefore, promote each other's efforts to achieve the goals. **Negative interdependence** exists when individuals perceive that they can obtain their goals if, and only if, the other individuals with whom they are competitively linked fail to obtain their goals. Participants, therefore, obstruct each other's efforts to achieve the goals. **No interdependence** results in a situation in which individuals perceive that they can reach their goals regardless of whether other individuals in the situation attain or do not attain their goals.

The basic premise of interdependence theory is that how goal interdependence is structured determines how individuals interact, which in turn determines outcomes. When positive goal interdependence is structured, **promotive interaction** results (i.e. one's actions promote the goal achievement of others). When negative goal interdependence is structured, **oppositional interaction** results (i.e. participants' actions obstruct the goal achievement of others). When no goal interdependence is structured, there is no interaction. Promotive interaction tends to result in a wide variety of outcomes that may be subsumed into the categories of high effort to achieve, positive relationships and psychological health. Oppositional interaction tends to result in low effort to achieve by most students, negative relationships and low psychological health. No interaction tends to result in low effort to achieve, an absence of relationships and psychological pathology.

Cooperation and competition provide contexts in which restorative approaches will either be effective or ineffective. Individualism is by definition generally not a desirable option, as it means no interaction between disputants.

Cooperative context

In order for restorative approaches to be effective, they should ideally occur within a cooperative context. In a cooperative context (Deutsch, 1973; Johnson, 2003; Johnson and Johnson, 1989, 2005a, 2009b; see Figure 15.1 and Box 15.1 also):

1   Individuals focus on mutual goals and shared interests.
2   Individuals are concerned with both self and others' well-being.
3   Individuals adopt a long-term time orientation where energies are focused both on achieving goals and on building good working relationships with others.
4   Effective and continued communication is of vital importance in resolving a conflict. Within a cooperative situation, the communication of relevant information tends to be open and honest, with each person interested in informing the other as well as being informed. Communication tends to be more frequent, complete and accurate.
5   Perceptions of the other person and the other person's actions are far more accurate and constructive. Misperceptions and distortions such as self-fulfilling prophecies and double standards occur less frequently and are far easier to correct and clarify.
6   Individuals trust and like each other and, therefore, are willing to respond helpfully to each other's wants, needs and requests.
7   Individuals recognise the legitimacy of each other's interests and search for a solution to accommodate the needs of both sides. Conflicts tend to be defined as mutual problems to be solved in ways that benefit everyone involved.

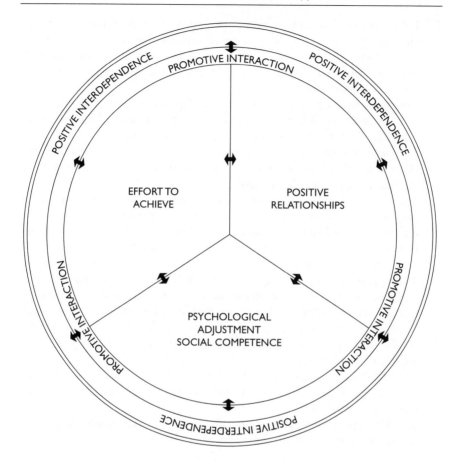

Figure 15.1 Outcomes of cooperative learning

Restorative approaches encounter problems and challenges in competitive contexts. Within a competitive context (Deutsch, 1973; Johnson and Johnson, 1989, 2005a):

1   Individuals focus on differential benefit (i.e. doing better than anyone else in the situation). In competitive situations, how well a person is doing depends on how his or her performance compares with the performances of the others in the situation. There is a constant social comparison in which the value of one's outcomes depends on how they compare with the outcomes of others.
2   Individuals focus on their own well-being and the deprivation of the other participants. In striving to 'win', individuals focus not only on what is good for them but also what will deny others what they need to win. There is a vested interest in others doing less well than oneself.

3   Individuals adopt a short-term time orientation where all energies are focused on winning. Little or no attention is paid to maintaining a good relationship. In most competitions, there is an immediate finishing line on which all attention is focused with little or no concern for the future relationship with the other competitors.

4   Communication tends to be avoided and when it does take place it tends to contain misleading information and threats. Threats, lies and silence do not help individuals resolve conflicts with each other. Competition gives rise to espionage or other techniques to obtain information about the other that the other is unwilling to communicate and 'diversionary tactics' to delude or mislead the opponent about oneself.

5   There are frequent and common misperceptions and distortions of the other person's position and motivations that are difficult to correct. Individuals may engage in self-fulfilling prophecies by perceiving another person as being immoral and hostile and behaving accordingly, thus evoking hostility and deceit from the other person. Individuals may see the small misbehaviours of their opponents while ignoring their own misbehaviour (this is known as the 'mote-beam mechanism'). Double standards may exist. Because preconceptions and expectations influence what is perceived and because there is a bias toward seeing events in a way that justifies one's own beliefs and actions, and because conflict and threat impair perceptual and cognitive processes, the misperceptions are often difficult to correct.

6   Individuals have a suspicious, hostile attitude toward each other that increases their readiness to exploit each other's wants and needs and refuse each other's requests.

7   Individuals tend to deny the legitimacy of others' wants, needs and feelings and consider only their own interests.

When disputants are brought together to reconcile and restore balance and harmony to their relationship, they would ideally perceive and experience a cooperative context and understand that they will jointly engage in cooperative efforts in the future. A cooperative context ensures that disputants have a stake in: (a) each other's well-being; (b) the future of the relationships; and (c) the common good. It includes both cooperative goals (resolutions of a conflict are based on common goals and interests) and cooperative processes (e.g. procedures, rules, criteria for success, boundaries) that are understood and followed. Within schools, the easiest way to establish a cooperative context and to teach students the nature of cooperative efforts is to use cooperative learning throughout the majority of the school day.

Moral community and social interdependence

In order to be effective, restorative approaches must unite offenders and victims in the same moral community, which could be the classroom, the school, the city or town, or the society. The word 'community' is derived from the Latin 'communis', which means 'shared'. Community is a group of people who live in the same locality and share common goals and values and a common culture. The heart of a community is positive interdependence where members work together to achieve common goals and maintain common values and culture. A community is threatened by negative interdependence in which members work against each other to achieve goals only one or a few can attain.

Research results

The many diverse dependent variables examined in studies on social interdependence over the past century may be subsumed within three broad categories: cooperation tends to promote higher achievement, more positive relationships and greater psychological health than competitive or individualistic efforts (Johnson, 2003; Johnson and Johnson, 1989, 2005a, 2009a; see also Box 15.1). In addition, there is a cluster of behaviours and attitudes that occur within cooperative endeavours that are especially relevant to restorative approaches in schools. This cluster includes pro-social behaviour, perspective taking, high levels of cognitive and moral reasoning, the development of a moral identity, basic self-acceptance, moral inclusion and a wider scope of justice and an understanding of fairness.

Nature of Cooperative Context	Nature of Competitive Context
Mutual goals	Differential goals
Concern for self and other's well-being	Concern for own well-being, others' deprivation
Liking and trust	Hostility and distrust
Others' needs/interests seen as legitimate	Denial of legitimacy of others' needs/interests
Long-term time perspective	Short-term time perspective
Promotive interaction pattern	**Oppositional interaction pattern**
Accurate communication	Inaccurate or no communication
Accurate perceptions	Misperceptions
Trusting and trustworthy	Distrusting and untrustworthy
Constructive problem-solving	Destructive 'Going for the win'

Box 15.1 Context of restorative justice

The nature of cooperative learning

Cooperative learning is the pedagogical use of small groups so that individuals can work together to maximise their own and each other's learning (Johnson, Johnson and Holubec, 2008). Within cooperative learning groups, individuals discuss the material to be learned, help and assist each other to understand it and encourage each other to work hard. Any assignment in any curriculum for any age student can be done cooperatively.

Effective cooperation requires that five basic elements be carefully structured into the situation (Johnson and Johnson, 1989; Johnson, Johnson and Holubec, 2008). First, there must be a strong sense of positive interdependence so individuals believe they are linked with others such that they cannot succeed unless the others do (and vice versa). Individuals must believe that they sink or swim together. Positive interdependence may be structured through mutual goals, joint rewards, divided resources, complementary roles and a shared identity. Second, each collaborator must be individually accountable to do his or her fair share of an activity. Third, collaborators must have the opportunity to promote each other's success by helping, assisting, supporting, encouraging and praising each other's efforts to achieve. Fourth, working together cooperatively requires interpersonal and small group skills, such as leadership, decision-making, trust-building, communication and conflict-management skills. Finally, cooperative groups must engage in group processing, which exists when group members discuss how well they are achieving their goals and maintaining effective working relationships.

There are three types of cooperative learning: formal, informal and base groups. *Formal cooperative learning* consists of students working together, for one class period to several weeks, to achieve shared learning goals and complete jointly specific tasks and assignments (Johnson, Johnson and Holubec, 2008). In formal cooperative learning groups, teachers consider cooperation when planning activities, explain the task and the positive interdependence required, monitor and support the learning groups, assess student learning and encourage groups to process how well they are working together.

Informal cooperative learning consists of having students work together to achieve a joint learning goal in temporary, ad-hoc groups that last from a few minutes to the length of a lesson (Johnson, Johnson and Holubec, 2008). The procedure for using informal cooperative learning during a lecture entails having three-to-five minute focused discussions before and after the lecture (i.e. bookends) and two-to-three minute interspersing pair discussions throughout the lecture.

Cooperative base groups are long-term, heterogeneous cooperative learning groups with stable membership whose primary responsibilities are to provide support, encouragement and assistance to make academic progress and develop cognitively and socially in healthy ways as well as holding each other accountable for striving to learn (Johnson, Johnson and Holubec, 2008).

These three types of cooperative learning may be used together. A typical class session may begin with a base group meeting, followed by a short address by the teacher in which informal cooperative learning is used. A formal cooperative learning lesson is then conducted. Near the end of the class session a plenary may take place, which could also make use of informal cooperative learning. The class could end with a base group meeting.

Teaching students to be peacemakers

Within a community there are conflicts based on individuals' differing interests within a situation. **Conflict of interests** exist when the actions of one person attempting to maximise his or her wants and benefits prevents, blocks or interferes with another person maximising his or her wants and benefits (Deutsch, 1973; Johnson and Johnson, 2005b). Such conflicts are ideally resolved through problem-solving (integrative) negotiation. When negotiation does not work, mediation could be attempted in place of direct involvement by a teacher.

Conflict resolution and peer mediation programmes have their roots in at least four sources (Johnson and Johnson, 1996a, 2005b, 2009b): researchers in the field of conflict resolution, advocates of non-violence, anti-nuclear war activists and members of the legal profession. Research-based peer mediation programmes began in the 1960s with the Teaching Students To Be Peacemakers Program (Johnson and R. Johnson, 2005b). The lessons focus on the following themes:

1 Students are taught to recognise that conflicts are inevitable, healthy and potentially valuable.
2 Students are trained to keep two concerns in mind when resolving conflicts: (a) the importance of the goals they are trying to achieve; and (b) the importance of the relationship with the other person. When those two concerns are present, there are five strategies available for managing a conflict: withdrawal, forcing, smoothing, compromising and problem-solving negotiations.
3 All members of the school community need to know how to negotiate constructive resolutions to their conflicts. There are two types of negotiations: distributive or 'win-lose' and integrative or problem solving ('win-win'). In ongoing relationships, only a problem solving approach is constructive. The steps in using problem-solving negotiations are: (a) describing what you want; (b) describing how you feel; (c) describing the reasons for your wants and feelings; (d) taking the other's perspective; (e) inventing three optional plans to resolve the conflict that maximise joint benefits; and (f) choosing one and formalising the agreement with a handshake.
4 Once the problem-solving negotiation procedure is learned, all members of the school community need to then learn how to mediate conflicts of interests. A mediator is a neutral person who helps two or more people resolve their conflict, usually by negotiating an integrative agreement. Mediation consists of four steps: (a) ending hostilities; (b) ensuring disputants are committed to the mediation process; (c) helping disputants successfully negotiate with each other; and (d) formalising the agreement.

5   Once students understand how to negotiate and mediate, the peacemaker programme can be implemented. Each day the teacher selects two class members to serve as official mediators. Any conflicts students cannot resolve themselves are referred to the mediators. The role of mediator is rotated so that all students in the class or school serve as mediators an equal amount of time. If peer mediation fails, the teacher mediates the conflict. If teacher mediation fails, the teacher arbitrates by deciding who is right and who is wrong. If that fails, the head teacher mediates the conflict. If that fails, the head teacher arbitrates.

6   Additional lessons are needed to refine and upgrade students' skills in using the negotiation and mediation procedures. Negotiation and mediation training may become part of the fabric of school life by integrating them into academic lessons. Literature, history and science units typically involve conflict. Almost any lesson in these subject areas can be modified to include role playing situations in which the negotiation and/or mediation procedures are practised.

The Teaching Students to be Peacemakers Program is a 12-year spiral programme that is re-taught each year in an increasingly sophisticated and complex way. It takes years to become competent in resolving conflicts. Twelve years of training and practice will result in a person with considerable expertise in resolving conflicts constructively.

The benefits of conflict resolution and peer mediation programmes

We have conducted 17 studies on implementing the Peacemaker Program in schools involving students from kindergarten through the tenth-grade and several other researchers have conducted relevant studies (Johnson and Johnson, 2005b). The benefits include students and teachers developing a shared understanding of how conflicts should be managed, students learning the negotiation and mediation procedures and retaining their knowledge throughout the school year and the following year, students applying the procedures to their own conflicts as well as other people's conflicts, transferring the procedures to non-classroom settings such as the playground and lunchroom and transferring the procedures to non-school settings such as the home. Students' attitudes toward conflict tended to become more positive. Students tended to resolve their conflicts without the involvement of faculty and administrators and, therefore, classroom management problems decreased by about 60 per cent and referrals to adults dropped by about 90 per cent. Students generally liked to engage in the problem-solving negotiation and mediation procedures. Finally, when integrated into academic units, the conflict resolution training tended to increase academic achievement and long-term retention of the academic material.

Constructive controversy

A 'controversy' exists when one person's ideas, opinions, information, theories or conclusions are incompatible with those of another and the two seek to reach an agreement (Johnson and Johnson, 2007, 2009b). Controversies are resolved by engaging in what Aristotle called 'deliberate discourse' (i.e. the discussion of the advantages and disadvantages of proposed actions) aimed at synthesising novel solutions (i.e. creative problem-solving). Teaching students how to engage skilfully with a controversy begins with randomly assigning students to small but heterogeneous cooperative learning groups (typically four members). The groups are given an issue on which to write a report. Each cooperative group is divided into two pairs. One pair is given the 'con' position on the issue and the other pair is given the 'pro' position. Each pair is given the instructional materials needed to define their position and point them towards supporting information. The cooperative goal of reaching a consensus on the issue (by synthesising the best reasoning from both sides) and writing a quality group report is highlighted. Students then: (a) research and prepare a position; (b) present and advocate their position: (c) refute opposing position and rebut attacks on their own: (d) reverse perspectives: and (e) synthesise and integrate the best evidence and reasoning into a joint position.

The process of engaging with controversy consists of reaching a tentative conclusion, being exposed to an opposing position ('the disputed passage'), being uncertain as to the correctness of one's position, searching for new information and alternative perspectives (known as epistemic curiosity) and reaching a new, more thoughtful conclusion. This process may be repeated several times before a final reasonable judgement is made. The considerable research available indicates that intellectual 'disputed passages' create higher achievement (characterised by longer retention, more frequent use of higher-level reasoning and metacognitive thought, more critical thinking, greater creativity and continuing motivation to learn), more positive interpersonal relationships and greater psychological health when they: (a) occur within cooperative learning groups; and (b) are carefully structured to ensure that students manage them constructively (Johnson and Johnson, 1979, 1989, 2007, 2009b). Finally, engaging in a controversy can also be fun, enjoyable and exciting.

Civic values

The value systems underlying competitive, individualistic and cooperative situations are a hidden curriculum beneath the surface of school life (Johnson and Johnson, 1996b, 2000). Whenever students engage in competitive efforts, for example, they learn the values of: (a) commitment to getting more than others (there is a built-in concern that one is smarter, faster, stronger, more competent and more successful than others so that one will win and others will lose); (b) success depends on beating, defeating and getting more than other people (triumphing over others and being 'Number One' are valued); (c) what is important is winning, not mastery or excellence; (d) opposing, obstructing and sabotaging the success of others is a natural way of life (winning depends on a good offence – doing better than others – and a good defence – not letting anyone do better than you); (e) feeling joy and pride in one's wins and others' losses (the pleasure of winning is associated with others' disappointment with losing); (f) others are a threat to one's success; (g) a person's worth (own and others) is conditional and contingent on his or her 'wins', (a person's worth is never fixed, it depends on the latest victory); (h) winning, not learning, is the goal of academic work; and (i) people who are different are to be either feared (if they have an advantage) or held in contempt (if they have a disadvantage).

The values inherently taught by individualistic experiences are: (a) commitment to one's own self-interest (only personal success is viewed as important, others' success is irrelevant); (b) success depends on one's own efforts; (c) the pleasure of succeeding is personal and relevant to only oneself; (d) other people are irrelevant; (e) self-worth is based on a unidimensional view that the characteristics that help the person succeed are valued (in school that is primarily reading and maths ability); (f) extrinsic motivation to gain rewards for achieving up to criteria is valued; and (g) similar people are liked and dissimilar people are disliked.

In contrast, the values inherently taught by cooperative efforts are: (a) commitment to own and others' success and well-being as well as to the common good; (b) success depends on joint efforts to achieve mutual goals; (c) facilitating, promoting and encouraging the success of others is a natural way of life (a smart cooperator will always find ways to promote, facilitate and encourage the efforts of others); (d) the pleasure of succeeding is associated with others' happiness in their success; (e) other people are potential contributors to one's success; (f) your own and other people's worth is unconditional (because there are so many diverse ways that a person may contribute to a joint effort, everyone has value all the time); (g) intrinsic motivation based on striving to learn, grow, develop and succeed is valued (learning is the goal, not winning); and (h) people who are different from oneself are to be valued as they can make unique contributions to the joint effort.

Constructive conflict resolution promotes the values of subjecting one's conclusions to intellectual challenge, viewing issues from all perspectives, reaching agreements that are satisfying to all disputants and maintaining effective and caring long-term relationships. In other words, constructive conflict resolution inherently teaches a set of civic values aimed at ensuring the fruitful continuation of the community.

Conclusion

Effective restorative approaches are implemented on solid foundations in schools and we have argued that this bedrock is constituted of cooperative learning, social interdependence and constructive experiences of conflict. One of the major purposes of restorative approaches is to right past wrongs in a way that allows for the involved parties to work cooperatively in the future. The easiest way to create a cooperative context is for teachers to use cooperative learning throughout the majority of the school day. Doing so will create positive relationships in which students frequently engage in pro-social actions, accurate perspective taking, higher levels of cognitive and moral reasoning and more moral inclusion. They feel better about themselves, develop a stronger moral identity, and care more about justice and fairness for everyone.

In order to maintain positive relationships and cooperative endeavours, it is necessary to resolve conflicts constructively. Students need to learn how to resolve conflicts of interests through problem-solving negotiation and peer mediation. Students also need to learn how to resolve intellectual disagreements through constructive controversy. Being competent in resolving conflicts of interests and controversies gives students a developmental advantage that will benefit them throughout their lives. It also ensures that when individuals who have experienced a destructive conflict come together they are experienced and skilled in restorative processes.

Finally, engaging in cooperative efforts and resolving conflicts constructively fosters civic values in students. Cooperation promotes commitment to others' success and well-being, commitment to the common good and taking joy in other's success and well-being. Constructive conflict resolution promotes the values of subjecting one's conclusions to intellectual challenge, viewing issues from all perspectives and reaching agreements that maximise joint gain.

It is the combination of cooperative experiences, constructive conflict resolution and civic values that most effectively develop the positive relationships and pro-social behaviours that create the conditions under which restorative approaches will be most effective.

References

Braithwaite, J. (1989) *Crime, shame and reintegration*. Cambridge, UK: Cambridge University Press.

De Waal, F. B. M. (2000) 'The first kiss' in F. Aureli and F. B. M. de Waal (eds.) *Natural conflict resolution*. Berkeley, CA: University of California Press, pp. 13–33.

Deutsch, M. (1949) 'A theory of cooperation and competition'. *Human Relations*, 2, 129–152.

—— (1962) 'Cooperation and trust: Some theoretical notes' in M. R. Jones (ed.) *Nebraska symposium on motivation*. Lincoln, NE: University of Nebraska Press, pp. 275–319.

—— (1973) *The resolution of conflict*. New Haven, CT: Yale University Press.

—— (1985) *Distributive justice: A social psychological perspective*. New Haven, CT: Yale University Press.

—— (2006) 'A framework for thinking about oppression and its change', *Social Justice Research*, 19(1), 7–41.

Druckman, D. and Albin, C. (2011) 'Distributive justice and the durability of peace agreements'. *Review of International Studies*, 37, 1137–1168.

Enright, R. D., Gassin, E. A. and Knutson, J. A. (2003) 'Waging peace through forgiveness education in Belfast, Northern Ireland: A review and proposal for mental health improvement of children', *Journal of Research in Education*, 13(1), 51–61.

Johnson, D. W. (1970) *Social psychology of education*. New York: Holt, Rinehart & Winston.
—— (2003) 'Social interdependence: The interrelationships among theory, research, and practice', *American Psychologist*, 58(11), 931–945.
—— (2009) *Reaching out: interpersonal effectiveness and self-actualization* (10th ed.). Boston: Allyn & Bacon. First edition 1972.
Johnson, D. W., and Johnson, R. (1979) 'Conflict in the classroom: Controversy and learning'. *Review of Educational Research*, 49, 51–61.
—— (1989) *Cooperation and competition: Theory and research*. Edina, MN: Interaction Book Company.
—— (1996a) 'Conflict resolution and peer mediation programs in elementary and secondary schools: A review of the research', *Review of Educational Research*, 66(4), 459–506.
—— (1996b) 'Cooperative learning and traditional American values', *NASSP Bulletin*, 80(579), 11–18.
—— (2000) 'Cooperative learning, values, and culturally plural classrooms' in Leicester, M., Modgil, C. and Modgil, S. (eds.). (2000) *Classroom issues: Practice, pedagogy and curriculum*. London: RoutledgeFalmer.
—— (2005a) 'New developments in social interdependence theory'. *Psychology Monographs*, 131(4), 285–358.
—— (2005b) *Teaching students to be peacemakers*. 4th edition. Edina, MN: Interaction Book Company.
—— (2007) *Creative controversy: Intellectual challenge in the classroom* (4th edition). Edina, MN: Interaction Book Company.
Johnson, D. W. and Johnson, R. T. (2009a) 'An educational psychology success story: Social interdependence theory and cooperative learning', *Educational Researcher*, 38(5), 365–379.
—— (2009b) 'Energizing learning: The instructional power of conflict', *Educational Researcher*, 38(1), 37–52.
Johnson, D. W. and Johnson, F. P. (2012) *Joining together: group theory and group skills* (11th Ed.). Boston: Allyn & Bacon. First edition 1975.
Johnson, D. W., Johnson, R. and Holubec, E. (2008) *Cooperation in the classroom*. (7th edition). Edina, MN: Interaction Book Company.
Morrison, B. and Ahmed, E. (2006) 'Restorative justice and civil society: Emerging practice, theory, and evidence', *Journal of Social Issues*, 62(2), 209–215.
Opotow, S. (1990) 'Moral exclusion and injustice: An introduction', *Journal of Social Issues*, 46, 1–20.
—— (1993) 'Animals and the scope of justice'. *Journal of Social Issues*, 49, 71–85.
Opotow, S. and Weiss, L. (2000) 'Denial and exclusion in environmental conflict'. *Journal of Social Issues*, 56, 475–490.
Roseth, C. J., Pellegrini, A. D., Dupusi, D. N., Boh, C. M., Hickey, M. C., Hilk, C. L. and Peshkam, A. (2010) 'Preschoolers' bistrategic resource control, reconciliation, and peer regard', *Social Development*, 19, 1–27.
Umbright M. S. (1995) *Mediating interpersonal conflicts: A pathway to peace*. West Concord, MN: CPI Publishing.

Chapter 16

Peacebuilding through circle dialogue processes in primary classrooms

Locations for restorative and educative work

Kathy Bickmore

Introduction

Conflict management approaches in schools range from one-dimensional post-incident intervention (addressing symptoms) to comprehensive prevention and transformation (addressing causes). Peace*keeping* involves monitoring and disciplinary interventions to enforce temporary cessation of violence. Peace*making* also involves intervention after incidents arise, but uses dialogue to resolve disputes. Peace*building* is comprehensive transformation: it includes peacemaking dialogue, education, and longer-term processes to redress injustice and rebuild healthy social relationships (Bickmore, 2011a; Galtung, 1996; Harris and Morrison, 2003). Many schools emphasise peacekeeping (reasserting control through punishment and exclusion) rather than peacemaking or peacebuilding (guiding thoughtful, respectful dialogue for self-governing conflict resolution and to nurture healthy relationships) (Morrison, 2007; Skiba, Rausch, and Ritter, 2004). When they can, schools often avoid facing underlying conflicts, although relatively peaceful moments could present ideal opportunities for constructively critical education to rebuild social ties and redress injustices (Davies, 2004; Gladden, 2002). Comprehensive peacebuilding is least often implemented in under-resourced schools, where poor and racialised students are especially disadvantaged by standardised curriculum and testing (also Harber and Sakade, 2009; Morrison, Thorsborne, and Blood, 2005).

While the typical hidden curriculum in state-funded schools tends to avoid conflict and to reinforce uncritical deference, it is possible instead to encourage equitable, constructive dialogue about conflicts, such as in restorative peacemaking circle processes. One challenge is location: many restorative opportunities are relegated to the marginal curriculum of discipline, involving a few students outside the classroom rather than engaging a wider range of students, consistently, in discussing conflicts openly as learning opportunities. This chapter is drawn from a study in progress, called Peace-Building Dialogue in Schools, which involves case studies of professional development and teacher-implemented curricula.[1] The goal is to learn what dialogic peacebuilding learning opportunities may look like when they are implemented in state-funded schools (in classrooms and beyond), and their consequences for diverse students. Specifically, this chapter examines the ways three elementary teachers infused restorative talking-circle dialogues and related conflict education into regular, implemented curriculum and classroom practices.

Conflict, democratic peacebuilding and education

Social conflict, i.e. opposing or incompatible needs and demands, is inevitable in any community, including schools. Violence, aggression and harmful ways of dealing with conflict may be enacted or confronted but are not inevitable. All schools address conflict, implicitly or explicitly, relatively democratically or relatively coercively. Through contrasting perspectives and problems, conflicts are embedded in any school subject area and may be brought into the light through classroom dialogue (Johnson and Johnson, this volume; see also: Avery, Johnson, and Johnson, 1999; Bickmore, 2008b; Frankenstein, 1987; K. Simon, 2001; Stevahn, 2004).

Dialogue is constructive communication for understanding, problem-solving and building relationships (Schirch and Campt, 2007). Comprehensive peacebuilding transformation means creating mechanisms, capacities, and habits for democratic dialogue about conflict, in the context of social diversity. It includes peace and justice education, and restorative approaches – before, during, and after the eruption of visible disagreements or aggression. This requires different types of conversation at different levels; negotiation and decision-making about conflict in relation to discipline, governance and classroom pedagogies to contest currently-typical punitive approaches that are both inequitable and ineffective (Bickmore, 2004; Jull, 2000; NYCLU, 2011; Skiba and Peterson, 1999).

Whole-school restorative peacebuilding reduces the need for intensive conflict repair work by transforming school climates to prevent aggression and to build healthy relationships, skills and mechanisms to handle conflicts constructively before they escalate (Amstutz and Mullet, 2005; Claassen and Claassen, 2004; McCluskey, Lloyd, Stead, *et al.*, 2008; Palazzo and Hosea, 2004). Building on social learning theories, restorative approaches are intended to create 'contexts for learning in which the voice of the other may be heard, and where dialogue and reflective enquiry prompt learning that is inclusive and socially informed' (Macready, 2009, p. 218).

There is a rich history of research on conflict resolution in education. A particularly well-researched peacemaking dialogue initiative is peer mediation, in which trained students facilitate problem-solving negotiation to help peers to autonomously resolve disputes. Like any restorative approach, peer mediation can be implemented in classrooms, giving all students an opportunity to participate (Cremin 2007; Johnson and Johnson, 1996; Sellman 2008). However, it is more commonly implemented as a co-curricular 'cadre' leadership initiative, in which selected students mediate on call or in the schoolyard, outside of regular classroom curricula. Quality peer mediation programmes reduce aggressive behaviour and develop mediators' and peer participants' reasoning, social skills and willingness to handle conflict constructively (Bickmore, 2002; Burrell *et al.*, 2003; R. Harris, 2005; Jones, 2004). Inclusive programmes with diverse peer mediators are the most sustainable and effective (Bickmore, 2001; Day-Vines, Day-Hairston, Carruthers, Wall, and Lupton-Smith, 1996).

Peer mediation and restorative circles are forms of self-governance, in that students share responsibility for addressing the consequences of their own choices and participate in making decisions to help resolve problems. Other kinds of student self-governance also constitute opportunities to practise constructive conflictual dialogue (Angell, 2004; Cotmore, 2004). Regular implementation of dialogic class meetings seems to facilitate student participants' learning to cooperate, communicate and resolve some classroom problems (Miller, 1997; Porro, 1996; Triplett and Hunter, 2005). Self-governance activities encourage students' development of agency, through voicing ideas and the feedback of 'give-and-take' with peers (Davies, 2002; Howard and Kenny, 1992; Osler and Starkey, 2006).

A key element of peacebuilding is preparation for dialogue – conflict resolution education rather than only conflict resolution in education. Preparation includes developing knowledge and understanding of diverse stakeholders' perspectives rooted in their social contexts, interests and needs (e.g. Hess, 2009; Prutzman and Johnson, 1997) and guided practice in skills and processes for talking about conflict (e.g. Bickmore, 2008a; Finn, 1999; I. Harris, 2004; Pranis, 2005; Skiba, 2000).

Preparatory learning opportunities may help to facilitate equity. Diverse students often have unequal access to the communicative conventions of dominant groups (Delpit, 1995), and unequal opportunities to have their voices perceived as convincing and valuable (Ellsworth, 1989; Gordon, 2006; R. Simon, 1992).

> Just as diversity can be a deliberative strength, it can also re-inscribe social divisions if students feel they are being silenced or do not want to voice opinions that differ from the majority.
>
> (Hess and Avery, 2008, p. 514)

Thus, when conflict surfaces, the lowest-status participants face the most risk, because their ways of being and thinking may be most unfamiliar or unpopular. However, pedagogical approaches make a difference: competitive debates marginalise less-confident students more than cooperative open discussions (Aronson, 2000; Hemmings, 2000).

So, preparation and practice in constructive, equitable dialogue about social and interpersonal conflicts is an important component of peacebuilding, which can occur in classrooms. Unfortunately, such education is not very common, especially for less-privileged students (Bickmore and MacDonald, 2010; Dull and Murrow, 2008; Kahne and Middaugh, 2008; Sears and Hughes, 2006). My research examines dialogic learning opportunities – both conflict 'resolution' (restorative peacemaking) and conflict 'education' (part of peacebuilding) – that have been implemented inside public elementary school classrooms in urban Canada.

Restorative peacebuilding dialogue: Who and where in the school?

The literature reviewed previously shows that various kinds of student dialogue about conflict may be feasibly and effectively implemented in school settings, and that through this practice students can develop relationships and the capacity to handle conflicts non-violently and democratically. However, it also shows that such sustained, inquisitive, carefully-facilitated communicative talk about difficult issues is not often sustained in state-funded schools. A major difference among conflict dialogue opportunities is whether they are implemented in core classroom curriculum, in explicit co-curricular spaces such as student councils or peer mediation or in the (hidden and marginal) co-curricular spaces of administration and discipline. These institutional locations have important implications for who participates, how sustained the dialogue may be and what kinds of conflict issues are (and are not) usually taken up in these conversations.

Clearly, restorative and transformative justice approaches, in their justice system and social movement origins outside schools, were designed primarily as post-incident problem-solving processes, not primarily as spaces for education, discussion of public issues or even proactive community building (Lederach, 2003; Zehr, 2002). As restorative approaches have been applied inside schools, they have been re-theorised to include proactive educative and community-building elements at other points in the conflict cycle (Morrison, 2007; Vaandering, 2009). This has been framed as a whole-school philosophy as well as an individual conflict management approach.

Although the theory and professional development resources for restorative practices in schools emphasise proactive, educative practices (extended across schools and classrooms) as well as post-incident problem-solving, it appears that most of the school practices taken up in the name of restorative justice, and most of the empirical research on those practices, have focused mostly on more limited, post-incident cessation of violence through transforming discipline and conflict management practices outside of regular classroom curriculum – comparable to the ways restorative justice practices are used in justice systems beyond schools (Ashworth *et al.*, 2008; Drewery and Winslade, 2003; Hamilton, 2008; McCluskey, Lloyd, Kane, *et al.*, 2008; Stinchcomb, Bazemore, and Riestenberg, 2006; Varnam, 2005).

In many school policy guidelines, for instance Caring and Safe Schools in Ontario (Ministry of Education, 2010), 'peace' itself in the school is conceptualised as an absence of problems, not as redress of structural problems or as on-going presence of processes and roles for teaching and practising peacemaking and peacebuilding (what Galtung [1969] calls 'positive' peace) that would be part of the on-going daily work of enacted curriculum and pedagogy. To locate restorative dialogue approaches primarily in the 'discipline' arena of human relations control and conflict management tends to focus energies on individual 'problem' students and situations, after episodes of harm (Bickmore, 2011b). In contrast, to take up restorative dialogue in the enacted curriculum would focus energies on building skills, understanding and relationships in 'whole' communities and on proactive as well as responsive initiatives throughout the conflict cycle.

Classroom pedagogies are viable alternative institutional entry points for restorative approaches in schools that might pull restorative justice practice less toward the peacekeeping end of the continuum (in discipline) and more toward comprehensive peacebuilding. Within these classroom spaces, what formats of dialogue and what skills and strategies facilitate constructive, respectful expressions of diverse identities, viewpoints and emotions by the widest possible range of participants? My research examines a range of ways in which teachers may open such opportunities for frequent dialogue inside classrooms, and make it both constructive and inclusive in mixed groups.

'Peace-building dialogues in schools': The research aims

This research project, Peace-Building Dialogues in Schools, examines how restorative circles and other conflict dialogue may be feasibly learned and implemented, in both classroom and co-curricular settings, with what consequences for educators and diverse students – through participant observation, document analysis and semi-structured interviews. This is exploratory research about a diversity of approaches and participants, not an evaluation study of closely comparable cases.

All of the case study sites are located in one large urban Canadian school district with a diverse student population. The classrooms profiled in this chapter relate to one group of five to six year olds and another group of 12–14 year olds from two state-funded 'alternative' schools within that district (pseudonyms 'Primary' and 'Intermediate'), whose missions emphasise democratic social justice education. Teachers from these two schools had participated in a full-day teacher professional development workshop (February 2010) about how to conduct peacemaking dialogue circle processes for interpersonal problem-solving. Primary school teachers also attended a half-day restorative preparation session and a half-day follow-up professional development workshop that demonstrated how the peacemaking circle process could be used as a pedagogical tool, infusing constructive conflict dialogue learning opportunities into academic curriculum.

As is somewhat typical for such schools, students in the classrooms studied here were ethnically and economically diverse, but in general somewhat more privileged than students in nearby neighbourhood schools. These schools were required to cover the same mandated curriculum, but retained flexibility that allowed them to create innovative interdisciplinary thematic units using different-sized blocks of time. Teachers applied to work in these schools and sometimes made themselves available for a little more collaborative work with colleagues than typical in regular schools. While this sampling limited initial study scope, these alternative school sites were an ideal place to begin this research, in that the teachers' commitment to democratic social justice education dovetailed with restorative peacebuilding research goals.

The following elements, informed by the previous literature review, were examined at each case study school:

- Preparation 'for' conflict dialogue and peacebuilding – building knowledge and understanding 'about' conflicts and skills and processes 'for' dialogue about conflict.
- Locating selves 'in relation to' conflicts – individual reflection and writing to articulate one's own perspectives and choices in conflicts, pair and small group dialogue to articulate and listen to contrasting perspectives and choices, and physical task structures requiring participants to take a stand on conflicts (communicating non-verbally, for example, standing in an opinion spectrum line or in corners representing different decisions).
- Entering 'into' conflicts – perspective-taking 'in role' (as fictional characters or as actors in actual scenarios), articulating one's own viewpoint, debating (trying to persuade or 'win over' others' views), sharing (communicating diverse views to develop mutual understanding, as in a seminar or talking circle) or free-flowing issues discussion (explaining one's own and responding to others' views).
- Conflict decision-making (agency) – deliberation (discussion to build agreement) and negotiation (jointly assessing opposing viewpoints to resolve conflict), perhaps interspersed or completed with decision check-ins (such as majority-rule voting or group consensus polls).

Within each of these elements, the research examines how diverse students were enabled to participate in different ways, in relation to different kinds of interpersonal and social conflict topics and different dialogue processes.

Findings

The data analysed below include classroom observations and a 40–60 minute interview with each teacher. The examples are chosen to represent the range of learning experienced by teachers and children.

Teacher T3

Teacher T3 taught 18 students (five to six years old) at Alternative Primary School (A4): six boys (one African heritage, one East Asian heritage, four white) and 12 girls (two Asian heritage, 10 white). Observed lessons included class meetings in a peacemaking circle format and infused into language arts lessons, various community building, conflict education and problem-solving goals. From the first day of school, T3 explicitly taught non-violent communication and cooperation.

For instance, she had children talk in partners to reinforce skills and norms (attend to instructions, focus on the speaker, make eye contact, speak with respect in ways that people will understand you) and to facilitate class community building. T3 explained that she and all teachers at school A4 had introduced a three-step conflict resolution process ('say how you feel, say what you heard and say what you need'), but that her most important teaching was to model inclusive language and 'I' messages (speak for yourself, no-blame) to encourage her students to incorporate these into their own 'natural language' (interview June 2010).

T3 reported that her students experienced interpersonal conflicts throughout the day, often around tangible disputes such as sharing stationery or choosing where to sit. In the playground, their conflicts sometimes involved aggressive play and social exclusion (who would play with whom). For example, soon after initial professional development workshops, during our first observation in T3's classroom, there was a problem-solving dialogue after an incident in the playground between an African-American boy and a white girl. The boy had accidentally poked the girl in the eye during play and told her he was sorry but the girl had either not heard or not accepted the apology. The boy was angry to be still blamed after he had apologised so he pushed the girl to the ground. When playtime ended the two students each told their side of the story to T3 while all the students came inside and sat on the carpet. T3 asked whether this was a problem to be solved as a class or only with the people involved. The girl involved in the incident asked that the problem be addressed as a class, to which T3 agreed; the boy did not respond. He may not have heard or understood, although he did join the circle. The children sat in a circle to share perspectives about this conflict in an open, teacher-guided format, without circulating a talking piece. T3 asked questions and some students volunteered to answer by raising their hands. First, T3 asked for an account of what had happened. While a girl (bystander) told the class what she had seen happen on the playground, the boy who had been directly involved moved to the side of the circle and lay on the ground. T3 moved to sit beside him and asked the class to imagine why he might want to move away from the circle (that is, to empathise) and how they could make this boy feel part of their circle. T3 asked the boy if he knew he had poked the girl in the eye: he said yes, and that he had apologised to her. T3 asked the class if they thought the problem could have been an accident: a female student voiced agreement that it was. T3 asked questions to elicit further descriptions of the situation, and again asked the students to put themselves in the boy's shoes: 'Has there ever been a time where you made a mistake and got caught, or were embarrassed, making the mistake? Was there ever a time when you felt like you [wished you] could disappear?' T3 concluded the circle by asking the girl (who had been pushed) what the boy could do to make her feel better. She requested an apology: he agreed and did so.

After the follow-up professional development on circle processes mentioned above, T3 started using circles regularly in her classroom, often circulating a talking piece to give every student an explicit opportunity to speak and talking with the students about why this was important.

The first few times we all came together in a circle, I asked the students to review...How does sitting in a circle help us to communicate? Because we can see each other, it allows us to take turns. And they had a sense that we would go around the circle, everyone would have a turn...you could always pass if you needed to. So, those things were in place before we tried to...use circles to intentionally unpack conflict.

(T3 interview)

This class discussed post-incident conflict issues such as peer aggression (pushing) in the playground and, in another instance, the exclusionary ways the class had been treating one unpopular student. In the first instance above, T3 managed the post-incident problem-solving in a manner similar to the way she would have done before the professional development session; sometimes addressing individual students whose experiences she wanted to bring into the conversation, sometimes ceding the floor to whichever students volunteered to speak up (without circulating a talking piece, many remained silent). In contrast, in a later class meeting she described, T3 had passed a talking piece around the circle, inviting each student to talk about, 'What can we do to have a safe class, with [the targeted student as well as themselves] included in it?' Then, 'What do you do if someone in the class is behaving in a different way? Like, what are some of the ways we can respond and support each other?' While students had the option to pass without speaking, T3 described all students as highly engaged in these circles, because they had strong feelings about these conflicts. She encouraged students to name frustrations and validated their feelings. She distinguished feelings from behaviour, telling the children that, 'not liking is OK, but [not] doing mean things and sharing that with other people...' Problems discussed in these circles also sometimes addressed issues children had suggested anonymously.

A few weeks later, T3 facilitated a peace education dialogue about conflict solving choices, preparing children by inviting them to share, 'Something you've learned about solving problems'. Six male and seven female students offered responses; two males and three females passed. In small groups, the children then created scenarios based on interpersonal aggression conflicts they had experienced in the school or on the playground. T3 instructed them to: 1) show the problem: who is the victim, bystander, and who is causing the problem?; 2) show how not to solve the problem (a poor choice); 3) then the group would 'rewind' their scenario to the beginning and show a positive way to solve the problem. After a few minutes' practise, the class gathered and each group performed their scenario, including disputes about butting in line and sharing toys, and one relational conflict in which three boys would not allow two girl peers to play with them during break time. First-round scenarios showed escalating aggression, whereas 'rewind' versions showed simple non-violent problem-solving and sharing (such as agreeing to take turns or play together). Afterwards, T3 paraphrased how the children had solved each problem presented.

Teacher T3 said it generally took 15–20 minutes for a talking piece to go around the circle, to give every child a chance to speak and she reflected that this could be 'too much sitting...very hard [for such young children] to wait your turn' (interview, June 2010). Therefore, she interspersed circle dialogue with activities such as talking to a partner, moving to a new place in the circle, sharing ideas, role play or physical movement. With this modification, these young students showed aptitude and interest in discussing and suggesting constructive responses to interpersonal disputes, including complex issues of social exclusion and fairness. When T3 passed a talking piece to every student, this elicited involvement of more students in dialogue than when students volunteered or were called upon. T3 concluded:

> I think it's important to not be so afraid of conflict, because it's such a natural part of this collaborative work we do. But hopefully it says to kids that conflict's okay, and let's just figure out ways that we can learn about each other and learn about ourselves through our discussion of conflict.

Teacher T5

At the Alternative Intermediate School, Teacher T5 taught a group of 12–14 year olds an integrated English Language, Arts, Health, and Social Studies class. During the study, we conducted 12 classroom observations. Over the past ten years, T5 had frequently taught dialogue-based lessons on social conflict issues. These typically engaged students in conversation about issues, both 'in role' (dramatic improvisations to voice the perspectives of imagined or historical characters) and 'out of role' (preparing and debriefing in their own voices). T5 had facilitated some class meeting circles in past years, but not recently.

T5 taught an extended unit based on a short story about a racism-related school bullying situation (*The Staircase* by William Bell). It culminated in peacemaking circles 'in role' about the central problem in the story: being excluded and excluding others. Students improvised to express characters' divergent perspectives on the social conflict as they imagined them. T5 invented a few roles (beyond those in Bell's story), to involve all students and to pro-actively re-balance the conflict dialogue by inserting viewpoints that would re-humanise Akmed, the visible minority Muslim target of bullying in the story. Although the unit topics were relevant to these students' lived experiences, in class discussions they were guided to speak of the issues in conceptual terms and from the perspectives of imagined characters and not required to reveal their personal conflicts. In private journal writing, T5 invited students to apply unit concepts to their own experience.

To prepare students for peacemaking dialogue T5 taught key concepts for understanding complex social conflicts. She guided the students, step by step, to imagine alternate points of view and to analyse conflicts distinguishing wants from needs. For example, early in the unit she facilitated a simulation on social power, inclusion and exclusion (March 22). Then she applied these concepts in a role-play activity (March 23) to an early moral dilemma in *The Staircase* story: one character wants another to retaliate for a perceived offence by Akmed (the bullying target). Students assigned the role of Jason worked together to discern his perspective; others who would play Megan did the same. T5 had students reflect independently in writing (locating themselves 'in' the conflicts) and later share aloud what the 'other' character wanted, what their own character would do, predict consequences and name feelings and then (out of role) to reflect on their own views about peer pressure and fitting in.

Mid-unit, the class had developed a negative attitude about Akmed (comparable to the views of his classmates in the story – describing him as unfriendly, rude, and strange). To elicit more critically reflexive engagement with the conflict issues in the story, T5 introduced a character she invented. After students worked in pairs to develop questions to ask, she 'visited' the class in role as Akmed's aunt to present a re-humanising perspective about Akmed. This caused an evident change in many students' perspectives about the situation. Later, a series of lessons taught how to distinguish human 'wants' from 'needs', as part of understanding divergent viewpoints and assessing conflict solution options. After facilitating a consensus-building process on a list of 'most important' human needs, T5 had students discern the needs and wants of various characters in *The Staircase*.

Near the end of the unit, T5 assigned each student a character from the story (including invented additional characters) – three to each of seven characters for three peacemaking circle role-plays. As in a 'real' post-incident restorative problem-solving dialogue, preparation phases were prominent in T5's unit: both teaching skills and expectations for the circle process and discerning the wants and needs of each party. Scaffolding students' discernment of their characters' divergent viewpoints, students were grouped into sub-sets: perpetrators, Akmed's allies and bystanders. T5 also reviewed the circle facilitator role with the students who would co-facilitate ('listen and summarise what everyone says...See if there are any patterns that come up and identify any patterns'). Students were expected to know their roles so deeply so they could improvise in answering the circle dialogue questions and responding to the contributions of peers.

Pairs of student facilitators each led two circle processes, one at a time, in a 'fishbowl' format with the rest of the class observing. The first student facilitator asked circle participants to describe a time they had been excluded. She modelled answering the question 'in role' as a teenager not involved in the conflict scenario. She mentioned a time when she hadn't had any friends, then passed the talking piece to the person sitting beside her who spoke in role as a bystander student Teresa. All students, in role, spoke to the question in turn, then the facilitator summarised. The second facilitator invited circle participants to describe a time when they had been part of a group that excluded another; again all replied. Most students contributed general stories about a range of different situations and time ran out before circles could take up more direct dialogue on the conflicts in the story. This circle process was followed by a further peacemaking circle role-play two weeks later. This time, building on T5's facilitation experience and the earlier lessons, most students spoke more directly to the perspectives of their characters in the conflict in *The Staircase*. Thus, this circle more closely imitated a restorative dialogue on the bias-based social aggression conflict at the heart of the story. For example, one student in role said, 'I don't get excluded, because I'm popular'. The student playing Akmed's Aunt Souhila said, 'I didn't get a job because they were racist and I wasn't white'. After the simulation, T5 debriefed the experience in open whole-class discussion, with students now 'out of role', expressing their own perspectives. T5 explained, 'It's harder to talk with people who are on the other side of the problem, and that's why these two questions [above] are so important to have at the beginning'. T5 told students they would complete the final peacemaking circle simulation in a future lesson – probing the perspectives of perpetrators, allies of Akmed, and bystanders, and developing solution ideas.

Thus, to prepare students for constructive dialogue about real conflicts in the future, T5 taught academic skills such as interpreting characters' frames of reference and points of view in texts, and conflict analysis and communication skills such as recognising wants and needs, perspective taking, listening carefully to contrasting viewpoints and following steps of dialogue processes such as the peacemaking circle. T5 explained that she usually addressed conflictual curriculum content both in role (often in small groupings) and (out of role) in whole-class discussions, to give diverse students multiple points of entry. She argued that exploring issues through taking on the perspectives of characters (in fiction, history or news scenarios), instead of asking students to disclose their own 'real life' situations, inspired maximum engagement and depth of understanding among her adolescent students: 'I start where it's not about them…One of the fastest ways to break down those barriers is when they can go into role. The kids that don't participate suddenly become the kids that participate the most'. In our observations, when T5 invited students to volunteer responses in open whole-class discussions, a third to half of the class was typically silent and a few voices tended to dominate. In contrast, during pair work and role-play exercises including the circles (using a talking piece) every student participated.

T5 acknowledged that the drama work in her implemented curriculum took a lot of time, but was "worth it" because it provoked deep awareness of multiple perspectives on complex social justice questions. Infusing conflict dialogue education into the academic curriculum is what made the necessary time available for complex restorative dialogue learning. Circles that proactively included formerly silenced perspectives and that passed a talking piece (giving every participant equal opportunities to speak), facilitated inclusion and power-balancing contributing to peacebuilding as well as peacemaking.

What facilitated and impeded restorative conflict dialogue in classrooms?

Routine aspects of school institutions sometimes impeded thoughtful enacted curriculum, in particular conflict dialogue. For example, announcements over the PA system, once lasting nearly five minutes, interrupted T1's class during two observations. The teachers explained the importance of creating regularised spaces and structures for peacebuilding learning, inside their regular implemented classroom curricula, in order to create the developmental time for sustained deep learning and transformation of classroom relationships. T3 described the learning opportunities embodied in classroom dialogue circles:

> It's your oral language, it's your drama…So, you sell it to teachers by saying there's value in this work because you can report on it in these areas. But there's also value in this work beyond the report card: because it helps you to create a culture in your classroom that will enable you to do more group work or…where kids can be working more independently…because the kids will know how to support each other… I will put it into my timetable so that it becomes part of my program.

T5 reflected that she felt lucky to be working in an alternative school, where there was flexibility to adjust the timetable and team-teach, to do sustained, integrated curriculum work. Even in this school, she and others felt that the demands of curriculum coverage often impeded sustained, dialogue-driven peacebuilding education. All teachers participating in this study expressed the need for more on-going professional dialogue and support, including opportunities to directly experience peacemaking circles, to build capacity to implement proactive conflict dialogue education and restorative circle meetings in their own classrooms.

Discussion

These teachers in similar kinds of schools, working with children of different ages, chose different paths to incorporate conflict dialogue as a proactive learning opportunity in their classrooms. At the Primary School, after follow-up professional development on how to do so, the teacher (T3) also began infusing peacemaking dialogue education into academic curricula. At the Intermediate School, the teacher (T5) used conflict dialogue, sometimes open-ended, occasionally circulating a talking piece, primarily as a way to encourage emotional engagement and critical awareness of justice issues in academic subject matter. T5's simulated post-incident restorative circle, based on conflict in a story where students acted out the characters' roles, was preparation for future restorative peacemaking. T3, in contrast, sometimes used peacemaking circles to address actual conflict among the children in their classes, sometimes using an open, informal conferencing model and other times passing a talking piece. In some instances, the dialogic learning opportunities that arose were instigated by episodes of harmful social behaviour, as is typical in restorative justice practices. In more instances, however, these teachers initiated proactive opportunities for constructive conflict dialogue; teaching new ways of communicating about conflict and/or guiding students to probe and respond to the conflicts embedded in literature and social life.

In their restorative circle processes, these teachers did not use a standard script for circle guidelines or dialogue questions. However, they did follow broad principles for restorative circle processes: beginning with reinforcing and confirming agreement on guidelines, then asking lower-risk community-building questions before proceeding to riskier questions about participants' conflict behaviour. The alternative school settings made it more feasible for all three teachers to adjust their implemented curricula in these ways, although they still felt pressure to fulfil curriculum mandates.

An interesting theme that emerged was how teachers tapped into students' imaginations, by inviting them to play the roles of characters in peer conflicts or in literature that addressed relevant conflicts at some distance from students' actual lives. These teachers found ways to make conflict dialogue safer, especially for student participants closer to the 'issues' at hand, by encouraging them to voice and listen to the perspectives of others (with whom they might or might not identify), rather than only speaking about conflict that would expose their own identities and experiences. Sometimes they role-played characters in literature; other times the younger students acted out scenarios based on their school experiences. In debriefing those learning activities – privately in writing, with a partner or in larger groups – students could choose to apply those perspectives and insights to specific conflict situations in their own lives or to remain at a distance. Either way, they were practising the skills and knowledge-building associated with restorative communication.

Because these educators focused their restorative dialogue work on peacemaking meetings (student input in governance) and implemented academic curriculum in classrooms, all of their students had frequent, on-going opportunities to practise recognising, communicating about, and creating resolutions to conflicts, not only in relation to simple disputes, but also in relation to complex instances of social exclusion/inclusion and (in)equality. The management of conflict was not relegated to the margins of school processes, nor limited to those individuals considered 'at fault' for destructive behaviour, nor limited to those conflicts that had escalated into major disruptions. These teachers attempted to practise 'positive peace', in which all members of the community were expected and invited to participate in interpreting, discussing and discerning appropriate responses to conflicts in daily school life. Clearly, making restorative conflict dialogue part of regular, whole-class learning activities increased the time to experience and take part and the opportunities to observe diverse peer and adult models participating in proactive, inclusive dialogue about questions of conflict and justice for essentially all students in these classrooms.

There is already much theory and research about what could be done to improve the democratic and peacebuilding learning opportunities of students in schools and it is clear that conflict dialogue is an important part of that picture. What is missing, and is still needed, is a well-grounded theoretical framework for understanding why those promising democratic peacebuilding pedagogies are so rare, especially in under-resourced state schools serving diverse populations, and what can be done about it in particular social (and national) contexts. Describing and analysing specific instances, like those in this chapter, in which teachers facilitate democratic and restorative conflict dialogue (peacebuilding) learning opportunities in regular classroom activity, helps to make visible the factors that help and hinder that important work.

Note

1 Acknowledgement: The Peace-Building Dialogue in Schools project is funded by the Social Sciences and Humanities Council of Canada.

References

Angell, A. (2004) 'Making peace in elementary classrooms: A case for class meetings', *Theory and Research in Social Education*, 32(1): 98–104.

Aronson, E. (2000) *Nobody Left to Hate: Teaching Compassion after Columbine*. New York: Worth Publishers.

Ashworth, J., Van Bockern, S., Ailts, J., Donnelly, J., Erickson, K. and Woltermann, J. (2008) 'The restorative justice center: An alternative to school detention', *Reclaiming Children and Youth*, 17(3): 22–26.

Avery, P., Johnson, D. and Johnson, R. (1999) 'Teaching an understanding of war and peace through structured academic controversies' in A. Raviv and D. Bar-tal (eds) *How Children Understand War and Peace*. San Francisco: Jossey-Bass, pp. 260–280.

Bickmore, K. (2001) 'Student conflict resolution, power 'sharing' in schools, and citizenship education', *Curriculum Inquiry*, 31(2): 137–162.

—— (2002) 'Peer mediation training and program implementation in elementary schools: Research results', *Conflict Resolution Quarterly*, 19(4): 137–160.

—— (2004) 'Discipline for democracy? School districts' management of conflict and social exclusion', *Theory and Research in Social Education*, 32(1): 75–97.

—— (2008a) 'Education for Conflict Resolution and Peacebuilding in Plural Societies: Approaches from Around the World' in K. Mundy, K. Bickmore, R. Hayhoe, K. Madjidi and M. Madden (eds) *Comparative and International Education: Issues for Teachers*. Toronto and New York: Canadian Scholars Press and Teachers College Press, pp. 249–272.

—— (2008b) 'Social studies for social justice: learning/navigating power and conflict' in Linda Levstik and Cynthia Tyson (eds) *Handbook of Research in Social Studies*. Mahwah, NJ: Lawrence Erlbaum, pp. 155–171

—— (2011a) 'Keeping, making, and building peace in school', *Social Education*, 75(1): 42–46.

—— (2011b) 'Policies and programming for safer schools: Are 'anti-bullying' approaches impeding education for peacebuilding?', *Educational Policy*, 25(4): 648–687.

Bickmore, K. and MacDonald, A. (2010) 'Student leadership opportunities for making "peace" in Canada's urban schools: Contradictions in practice', *Interamerican Journal of Education for Democracy/Revista Interamericana de Educación para la Democracia*, 3(2): 126–152.

Burrell, N., Zirbel, C. and Allen, M. (2003) 'Evaluating peer mediation outcomes in educational settings: a meta-analytic review', *Conflict Resolution Quarterly*, 21(1): 7–26.

Claassen, R. and Claassen, R. (2004) 'Creating a restorative discipline system: Restorative justice in schools', *The Fourth R* (Winter), 9–12.

Cotmore, R. (2004) 'Organizational competence: A student council in action', *Children and Society*, 18: 53–65.

Cremin, H. (2007) *Peer Mediation – Citizenship and Social Inclusion Revisited*, Milton Keynes, UK: Open University Press.

Davies, L. (2002) 'Possibilities and limits for democratisation in education', *Comparative Education*, 38(3): 251–266.

—— (2004) *Education and Conflict: Complexity and Chaos*. London: Routledge/Falmer.

Day-Vines, N., Day-Hairston, B., Carruthers, W., Wall, J. and Lupton-Smith, H. (1996) 'Conflict resolution: The value of diversity in the recruitment, selection, and training of peer mediators', *School Counselor*, 43: 392–410.

Delpit, L. (1995) *Other People's Children: Cultural Conflict in the Classroom*. New York: New Press.

Drewery, W. and Winslade, J. (2003, December). 'Developing restorative practices in schools: Flavour of the month or saviour of the system?' Paper presented at the *Australian Association for Research in Education/New Zealand Association for Research in Education*, Auckland, NZ.

Dull, L. and Murrow, S. (2008) 'Is dialogic questioning possible in social studies classrooms?', *Theory and Research in Social Education*, 36(4): 391–412.

Ellsworth, E. (1989) 'Why doesn't this feel empowering? Working through the repressive myths of critical pedagogy', *Harvard Educational Review*, 59(3): 297–322.

Finn, P. (1999) *Literacy with an Attitude: Educating working-class children in their own self-interest*. Albany, NY: SUNY Press.

Frankenstein, M. (1987) 'Critical mathematics education: An application of Paulo Freire's epistemology in Ira Shor (ed.), *Freire for the Classroom: A Sourcebook for Liberatory Teaching*. Portsmouth, NH: Boynton-Cook, pp. 180–210.

Galtung, J. (1969) 'Violence, peace, and peace research', *Journal of Peace Research*, 6(3): 167–192.

—— (1996) *Peace By Peaceful Means: Peace and Conflict, Development, and Civilization*. London: Sage Publications and International Peace Research Assn.

Gladden, R.M. (2002) 'Reducing school violence: Strengthening student programs and addressing the role of school organizations', *Review of Research in Education* 26: 263–299.

Gordon, T. (2006) 'Girls in Education: Citizenship, Agency and Emotions', *Gender and Education*, 18(1): 1–15.

Hamilton, M.V. (2008) *Restorative Justice: Reconceptualizing School Disciplinary Theory and Practice*. Pacific University. Proquest Dissertations and Theses Database database.

Harber, C. and Sakade, N. (2009) 'Schooling for violence and peace: how does peace education differ from "normal" schooling?', *Journal of Peace Education*, 6(2): 171–187.

Harris, I. (2004) 'Peace education theory', *Journal of Peace Education*, 1(1): 5–20.

Harris, I. and Morrison, M. (2003) *Peace Education*. 2nd edition. Jefferson, NC: McFarland.

Harris, R. (2005) 'Unlocking the learning potential in peer mediation: An evaluation of peer mediator modeling and disputant learning', *Conflict Resolution Quarterly*, 23(2): 141–164.

Hemmings, A. (2000) 'High school democratic dialogues: Possibilities for praxis', *American Educational Research Journal*, 37(1): 67-91.

Hess, D. (2009) *Controversy in the Classroom: The Democratic Power of Discussion*. New York: Routledge.

Hess, D. and Avery, P. (2008) 'Discussion of controversial issues as a form and goal of democratic education' in J. Arthur, I. Davies and C. Hahn (eds), *Sage Handbook of Education for Citizenship and Democracy*. Los Angeles and London: Sage Publication, pp. 508–518.

Howard, R. and Kenny, R. (1992) 'Education for democracy: Promoting citizenship and critical reasoning through school governance' in A. Jarred (ed.), *Learning for Life: Moral Education Theory and Practice*. Westport, CT: Praeger, pp. 210–227.

Johnson, D. and Johnson, R. (1996) 'Conflict resolution and peer mediation programs in elementary and secondary schools: a review of the research', *Review of Educational Research*, 66(4): 459–506.

Jones, T. (2004) 'Conflict resolution education: the field, the findings, and the future' *Conflict Resolution Quarterly*, 22(1-2): 233–267.

Jull, S. (2000) 'Youth violence, schools and the management question: A discussion of zero tolerance and equity in public schooling'. *Canadian Journal of Educational Administration and Policy* (17). Available at: <http://www.umanitoba.ca/publications/cjeap%3E>.

Kahne, J. and Middaugh, E. (2008, February) 'Democracy for some: The Civic opportunity gap in high school'. Retrieved July 20, 2010. Available at: <http://www.civicyouth.org>.

Lederach, J.P. (2003) *The Little Book of Conflict Transformation*. Intercourse, PA: Good Books.

Macready, T. (2009) 'Learning social responsibility in schools: a restorative practice', *Educational Psychology in Practice*, 25(3): 211–220.

McCluskey, G., Lloyd, G., Stead, J., Kane, J., Riddell, S. and Weedon, E. (2008) '"I was dead restorative today": From restorative justice to restorative approaches in school', *Cambridge Journal of Education*, 38(2): 199–216.

McCluskey, G., Lloyd, G., Kane, J., Riddell, S., Stead, J., and Weedon, E. (2008) 'Can restorative practices in schools make a difference?', *Educational Review*, 60(4): 405–417.

Miller, F. (1997) 'A class meetings approach to classroom cohesiveness: Perspectives', *Social Studies and the Young Learner*, 9(3): 18–20.

Ministry of Education, Ontario (2010) *Caring and Safe Schools in Ontario*. Toronto: Ministry of Education, Province of Ontario.

Morrison, B. (2007) *Restoring Safe School Communities: A Whole School Response to Bullying, Violence and Alienation*. Leichhardt, New South Wales, Australia: Federation Press.

Morrison, Br., Thorsborne, M. and Blood, P. (2005) 'Practicing restorative justice in school communities: The challenge of culture change', *Public Organization Review: A Global Journal*, 5: 335–357.

NYCLU (2011) *Education Interrupted: The Growing Use of Suspensions in New York City's Public Schools*. New York: NY.

Osler, A. and Starkey, H. (2006) 'Education for democratic citizenship: a review of research, policy and practice 1995–2005', *Research Papers in Education*, 21(4): 433–466.

Palazzo, D. and Hosea, B. (2004) 'Restorative justice in schools: a review of history and current practices', *The Fourth R* (Winter), 1 and 7–8.

Porro, B. (1996) *Talk it Out: Conflict Resolution in the Elementary Classroom*. Harrisburg: Association for Supervision & Curriculum Development.

Pranis, K. (2005) *The Little Book of Circle Processes: A New/Old Approach to Peacemaking*. Intercourse, PA: Good Books.

Prutzman, Pr. and Johnson, J. (1997) 'Bias awareness and multiple perspectives: Essential aspects of conflict resolution', *Theory Into Practice*, 36(1): 26–31.

Schirch, L. and Campt, D. (2007) *The Little Book of Dialogue for Difficult Subjects*. Intercourse, PA: Good Books, Inc.

Sears, A. and Hughes, A. (2006) 'Citizenship: education and indoctrination', *Citizenship Teaching and Learning*, 2(1): 3–17.

Sellman, E. (2008) *Mediation Matters – Creating a Peaceful School through Peer Mediation*, Cambridge: LDA.

Simon, K. (2001) *Moral Questions in the Classroom*. New Haven: Yale University Press.

Simon, R. (1992) *Teaching Against the Grain*. Toronto: OISE Press.

Skiba, R. (2000) *Violence Prevention and Conflict Resolution Curricula: What Works in Preventing School Violence*. Bloomington, IN: Indiana University.

Skiba, R. and Peterson, R. (1999) 'The dark side of zero tolerance: Can punishment lead to safe schools?', *Phi Delta Kappan*, January, 372–382.

Skiba, R., Karega Rausch, M. and Ritter, S. (2004) 'Discipline is always teaching: Effective alternatives to zero tolerance in Indiana's schools', *Education Policy Briefs* 2: 3.

Stevahn, L. (2004) 'Integrating conflict resolution training into the curriculum', *Theory Into Practice*, 43(1): 50–58.

Stinchcomb, J.B., Bazemore, G. and Riestenberg, N. (2006) 'Beyond zero tolerance: Restoring justice in secondary schools', *Youth Violence and Juvenile Justice*, 4(2): 123–147.

Triplett, C.F. and Hunter, A. (2005) 'Talking circle: Creating community in our elementary classrooms', *Social Studies and the Young Learner*, 18(2): 4–8.

Vaandering, D. (2009) *Towards the Effective Implementation and Sustainability of Restorative Justice in Ontario Public Schools: A Critical Case Study*. PhD, University of Western Ontario, London, Ontario.

Varnam, S. (2005) 'Seeing things differently: Restorative justice and school discipline', *Education and the Law*, 17(3): 87–104.

Zehr, H. (2002) *The Little Book of Restorative Justice*. Intercourse, PA: Good Books.

Chapter 17

Challenging the punitive turn in youth justice through restorative approaches in schools?

Natasha Du Rose and Layla Skinns

Introduction

The climate and well-being of staff and pupils within educational institutions are shaped and framed by their wider social and political contexts, as well as the leadership and educational practices within them. During the last quarter of the twentieth century in Western Europe and the US, this context has been one of a 'punitive turn' in criminal justice and a new culture of control (Garland 2001, 1996, Hallsworth 2000, Waquant 1999) and the youth justice system has featured significantly in this development (Muncie 2008, Benekos and Merlo 2008, Goldson 2005). This punitive climate permeates educational institutions and contributes to the mentalities of staff and pupils; mentalities which restorative approaches aim to transform. This chapter explores the significance of the punitive climate for the implementation of restorative approaches in schools and the tension between traditional punitive approaches and restorative ones.

The punitive turn

The application of restorative justice in schools in the UK since the 1990s has occurred in a markedly punitive cultural climate, particularly for young people. According to Garland (2001) we have witnessed a new culture of control in criminal justice policy or a 'punitive turn' in the UK and US since the 1980s, characterised by the re-emergence of punitive sanctions and expressive justice. Crime policy is profoundly politicised and populist and the language of condemnation and punishment has re-entered official discourse. The image of a 'disadvantaged, deserving subject of need' engaging in delinquent or criminal activity has disappeared and instead images of dangerous offenders who are beyond reform predominate (Garland 2001).

In support of the punitive turn thesis, commentaries on juvenile justice emanating from the US, UK and Western Europe have outlined how traditional principles of juvenile protection, welfare and support that dominated in the late nineteenth century and up to the 1960s, have been eroded and replaced with punitive values in support of retribution, incapacitation and individual responsibility (Muncie

2008). In the UK, increases in juvenile incarceration rates, the failure to separate children from adults in custody, the use of secure training centres for 12 year olds, the lowering of the age of criminal responsibility, the use of curfews, zero tolerance, dispersal zones, 'Anti-Social Behaviour Orders' (ASBOs), naming and shaming, electronic tagging, fast tracking and the abolition of *doli incapax* (whereby young children were deemed incapable of committing a criminal act) contribute to the notion that there has emerged 'an American-inspired institutional intolerance towards those aged under 18' (Muncie 2008, p. 109). Media constructions of youth offending distort public perceptions fuelling fear and anxiety. Young people are constituted as having become increasingly out of control, anti-social, dangerous, delinquent and criminal than was previously the case and their behaviour more serious (Goldson 2005, Allen 2002). The behaviour of children in schools has also been constructed as having got worse and is accompanied by suggestions that school discipline should be improved (MORI 2001).

The culture of control focuses on the protection of the public from crime through identifying, assessing and managing risk (Garland 2001). The concern is with the potential for harm, disorder and anti-social behaviour, and pre-emptive and early intervention strategies. Risk factors for young people are constructed as poor parental supervision, hyperactivity, divorce, low family income, poor housing and low educational attainment (Farrington 2000, 1996). Those constructed as posing the most 'risk' in the criminal justice system are invariably the most disadvantaged, neglected, vulnerable and damaged young people (Goldson 2005, Muncie 2005). However, constructions of those considered at 'risk' increasingly appeal to notions of wilful irresponsibility and individual failure (Goldson and Jameison 2002). Issues of social exclusion and deprivation are transferred from the auspices of welfare and child protection agencies to the criminal justice system (Muncie 2005). Access to children's services is no longer based on need; rather, on whether children and families are seen to be 'failing', 'posing risk' or to be a 'threat'. This qualifies them to be 'targeted' by an 'intervention' (Goldson 2005, p. 39). One such 'intervention' that may be used is that of restorative justice. What is the place of restorative justice in the youth justice system in the UK and what can be learnt from this relevant to the school context?

Restorative youth justice

Restorative approaches in schools in the UK have been adopted in the wider context of restorative developments in youth justice. Some commentators have suggested that the engagement with restorative justice indicates that counter-vailing tendencies are in operation in youth justice systems across the world and thus the punitive turn thesis provides an incomplete picture (Muncie 2005). Restorative justice is not easily defined as it includes a variety of practices and is used in a diverse range of contexts (Daly 2002). However, the basic tenet of restorative justice is that the response to harm should be to put right the harm, as far as possible, and not to inflict further harm on the offender. It emphasises the responsibility and accountability of offenders to make amends for their actions, and provide support to the victims. Its objectives are healing the harm done and the reintegration of the victim and offender in their communities.

Australia and New Zealand have the most advanced restorative justice schemes integrated into their youth justice system. Restorative justice processes and practices, in particular conferencing, are established in statutes and constitute part of a coherent response to young offenders (Gelsthorpe and Morris 2002). In England and Wales, elements of restorative justice were formally introduced as a supposedly mainstream response to youth offending in the Crime and Disorder Act 1998 and the Youth Justice and Criminal Evidence Act 1999. This included court ordered reparation or action plan orders, diversionary measures to youth offending teams or court referrals to youth offender panels all involving reparative or restorative activities (ibid). Gelsthorpe and Morris (2002) discuss whether an engagement with restorative justice principles is indicative of a re-enchantment with social welfare based principles. However, they conclude that restorative principles are not core components of the youth justice system but are rather additions to a system that continues to be centred on notions of punishment and retribution. They highlight the limits or 'pitfalls' in implementing restorative practices in a system driven by punitive, exclusionary and coercive values. They suggest that the full potential of restorative justice cannot be realised in such a context but what has emerged is a rather diluted version involving, for instance, coercive reparation orders that are imposed on offenders without their consent and restorative processes that simply deal with low level offenders. In 2006, the Youth Justice Board of England and Wales stated it was committed to giving restorative justice a more central position in the youth justice system (Youth Justice Board 2006). With recent political changes in positions such as the Minister of Justice, one can only imagine that more punitive approaches are set to ensue for children and young people.

Critics of the adoption of restorative practices in youth justice in the UK have argued that rather than being at odds with current trends in crime control, restorative practices complement them. Muncie (2005, p. 44) argues it is no accident that restorative justice and neo-liberal ideologies have emerged alongside one another as 'both proclaim an end to state monopoly and a revival of community responsibilisation'. Restoration 'can simply be used to enforce neo-liberal notions of individual responsibility' (ibid). He states: 'The burden tends to fall on individuals to atone or change their behaviour, rather than on the state to recognise that it also has a responsibility' (Muncie 2006, p. 780). Restorative practice may simply be perceived by governments as yet another tactic to adopt to reduce the crime rate and, as some commentators have suggested, lead to net widening (Hudson and Galaway 1996, Walgrave 1992).

A growing number of proponents of restorative justice have challenged the restorative/retributive justice dichotomy (Cunneen and Hoyle 2010, Daly 2002, Barton 2000). This is a significant issue, as this opposition was played out in the Restorative Approaches in Schools initiative discussed forthwith (RAiS hereafter).

For example, Daly (2002) discusses how the restorative justice and criminological literature tends to depict retributive justice as the opposite of restorative justice. 'Retributive justice' comes to stand for everything that is bad and restorative justice for all that is good. Retributive justice is characterised as exclusively about punishing an offence, adversarial relations between parties, hostility towards and social exclusion of the offender. Restorative justice takes on a mythical position delivering extraordinary occurrences of repair, reconciliation and personal transformation. She questions the usefulness of advocates telling the 'mythical true story' of restorative justice in this way and suggests that 'the politics of selling justice ideas may *require* people to tell mythical true stories' (Daly 2002, p. 72). Nevertheless, Daly (2002, p. 59) contends that the contrast is 'a highly misleading simplification', which is used to caricature criminal justice and it also assumes that 'an ideal justice system should be of one type only, that it should be pure and not contaminated by or mixed with others'. When observing restorative youth justice conferences Daly (2002, p. 59) further argues that participants 'engaged in a flexible incorporation of multiple justice aims' including elements of retributive justice in the form of censure for past offences. Reparation and censure are part of the restorative process and both can be experienced as punishment even if this is not what is intended. She argues that retribution and reparation should not be seen as contradictory principles but rather as dependent on one another.

Similarly, Cunneen and Hoyle (2010) argue that retributive justice can comprise some restorative measures and restorative justice can and does punish offenders. They state that as restorative processes can impose considerable burdens on offenders, they undeniably deliver punishment. Furthermore, it is not necessarily the case that punishment is experienced as painful. They make a case for restorative justice to be used for serious offences and state that according to the empirical evidence 'restorative justice is most effective when it is used *in addition* to retributive justice' (Cunneen and Hoyle 2010, p. 47; see also Sherman and Strang 2007). This debate raises a number of important questions for schools, i.e. how to incorporate restorative approaches in a punitive climate, whether they will be diluted, whether they can be seen to be at odds with one another, or as complementary, whether they will be seen as a tough enough response to harms caused and whether they will indeed be adopted in response to serious incidents and if all are mirrored in the literature on restorative approaches in the school setting. They were also mirrored in the findings of the research conducted by the authors in four schools in Bristol that were in the process of implementing restorative approaches.

Restorative justice in schools

In the case of young people in schools, the theory that has developed is that restorative approaches can offer an effective alternative to the use of traditional discipline (Malouf 1998, Krygier 1997, Cox 1995). Restorative approaches in schools, it is argued, are essential to the development of conflict resolution skills and the building of responsible citizenship (Morrison *et al.* 2006). While bad behaviour in schools is often viewed as symptomatic of a wider culture of an out of control youth, schools 'have the potential to curb behavioural problems and front-end the process of social regulation' (Morrison 2001, p. 204). When traditional disciplinary measures are used in schools, troubled/troublesome school pupils are often excluded. While there is the concern that restorative justice in the criminal justice system may lead to net-widening, in the school setting there is the possibility of diverting some young people from the criminal justice system (Cunneen and Hoyle 2010).

The Restorative Approaches in Schools (RAiS) programme was implemented in four schools in south Bristol in 2007. The programme was set up by the community interest company, Restorative Solutions and funded by the Esmée Fairbairn Trust and the Paul Hamlyn Foundation. South Bristol was selected because of the high levels of deprivation in this area. An independent evaluation was conducted to examine: (a) how school leaders and teachers incorporated restorative approaches into the development of school policies and processes; and (b) whether and how restorative approaches impacted on the pupil and staff perceptions of the climate for learning, school attendance, school term exclusions (permanent and fixed-term) and on educational attainment (see Skinns *et al.* 2009 for more detail). Quantitative and qualitative data were collected. Thirty-four interviews were conducted with staff and 26 were conducted with pupils to evaluate the implementation of restorative approaches and perceptions of the climate for learning. Local authority data from four RAiS schools and four non-RAiS schools before and after the implementation of restorative approaches were used to analyse pupils' attendance, exclusions and attainment rates.

There have been high hopes for restorative approaches in schools, but problems frequently arise in implementation. Cameron and Thorsborne (2001) discuss the limited potential of restorative approaches in schools due to 'tensions between existing philosophies and practices and restorative interventions' (p. 180). In the participating Bristol schools, all the school managers provided a different account of why they decided to implement restorative approaches, how they fitted into the school, how they were used and the difficulties encountered. There were, broadly two different approaches to implementation; (i) whole-school; and (ii) pockets of restorative approaches (often referred to as a 'cadre' approach). The whole-school approach meant that restorative approaches were incorporated into policies and procedures and used throughout the school from the outset of the programme. The intention was to change the culture of the school from the top down and allow teachers and pupils to quickly adjust to the new way of doing things. The 'pockets' approach meant that restorative approaches were concentrated in parts of the school, for example, one year group, though the nature of implementation and issues faced varied from pocket to pocket. In the schools that implemented restorative approaches in pockets, traditional disciplinary approaches continued to dominate the culture of the school. This is also an issue that has been identified in previous research (Sherman and Strang 2007). It was only in one school ('School 2'), which employed a whole-school approach to implementation, that staff attempted to incorporate restorative approaches into existing school policies, had stopped using detentions in favour of a graduated system of restorative approaches and routinely used restorative conferences as an alternative to exclusions. This suggests that in School 2 only, disciplinary approaches such as exclusions were not the dominant modus operandi; instead, they co-existed alongside restorative approaches.

Regardless of whether the school had aimed to implement restorative approaches on a whole-school basis or in pockets, the implementation process was not straightforward as they were seen to be at odds with traditional sanctions and classroom management styles. Staff in both types of schools stated that restorative approaches were resisted by colleagues because they threatened the existing climate for learning in which they had power to discipline and punish badly-behaved pupils with detentions and exclusions. Interviewees in all the schools reported there were a minority of staff who remained opposed to restorative approaches, did not want to try them and preferred to continue to use traditional sanctions. Restorative approaches were seen as a form of disenfranchisement that undermined their authority and threatened long-established practices, as this 'Champion' from School 3 explained:

> They will see, this is what I've done for X amount of years, you know, duty worker comes along, they pick them up…whatever, it's not my problem, somebody else should be dealing with their behaviour, that kind of thing, and you're going to get staff like that.

The research did not investigate the views of teachers who were opposed to restorative approaches. However, the fact that oppositional voices exist in schools is perhaps unsurprising given the punitive climate that permeates the wider society.

Hybridised approaches

Given this resistance, unsurprisingly, participating staff in all the schools said that punishment was still a necessary aspect of school culture and that restorative approaches should be used alongside sanctions, such as detentions and exclusions, rather than instead of them. Staff provided numerous reasons why exclusion in particular should be valued and continued. Many asserted that one of the fundamental roles of punishments was to send a message to all pupils about acceptable and unacceptable forms of behaviour. There seemed to be a broad consensus that permanent or fixed-term exclusions were a necessary response to serious incidents, particularly when the perpetrator showed no remorse: 'If someone's going to deny it, then it doesn't work, so you've still got to have exclusions there for the kids that say, "No, I didn't do it. I didn't hurt anyone. I don't care"' (Head of Year, School 2). Some pupils voiced the same opinion:

If the people actually don't care about what the other person is thinking, and don't really care if they're being horrible to someone, and if they're sort of winning, in a way, then it doesn't work, maybe they should get in trouble.

(Pupil 9, aged 13, School 2)

Some also suggested that traditional punishments still had a place alongside restorative approaches and following restorative justice conferences, as this pupil explained: 'Me writing on a piece of paper [following a restorative justice conference] isn't going to stop me from hitting her again. It's just making them shut up basically' (Pupil 11, aged 15, School 2). In instances such as this the restorative justice conferences failed to change perpetrators' perspectives and they continued to view their actions as just 'having a laugh' or as a justified response to mistreatment e.g. verbal abuse. Several pupils who had been bullied also thought that punishment may be more effective than restorative approaches in dealing with the pupils who had harmed them and were disappointed when punishment was not used, as this pupil noted: 'If they were punished, they'd probably learn a bit more, and then it will all stop'. (Pupil 1, aged 14, School 3). For some pupils the option to take part in a restorative conference was perceived as 'getting away with it' and/or an easier option: 'It's easier than being punished because all we have to do is kind of sit there, and just talk about stuff' (Pupil 6, aged 15, School 2). Conversely, staff suggested that pupils did not necessarily experience exclusion as a sanction. This reflects the position of Cunneen and Hoyle (2010) that punishment is not necessarily experienced as painful. 'Exclusion, per se, isn't a punishment. You and I know that, you know, it's a duvet day, isn't it?' (Senior Manager, School 3). The interviews with pupils showed that this was indeed the case and that in some cases punishment was not a deterrent either. Several pupils stated that they were not bothered about being excluded and having days off school. 'Them keeping me outside of school, it's just nothing. It's just like being home all weekend. She has to sit in school doing lessons, and I'm at home, nice, in my pyjamas'. (Pupil 11, aged 15, School 2).

There is no doubt that whether young people perceive it to be or not, excluding them from access to and opportunities for education *is* punitive. The aim of restorative approaches, if implemented to their full potential, is to prevent a young person reaching the point of exclusion in the first place. In addition, the notion of a restorative approach as an easier option for pupils was resisted by some staff who contrasted it with the young person's experience of exclusion:

You exclude kids for two days, what do they care? They get to sod about with their mates and they're not bothered in any way. Whereas…this [a conference] is serious. They have to sit down in front of that person and really feel what they're feeling and apologise.

(Behaviour Support Assistant)

Some pupils similarly indicated that a restorative conference was not an easy experience. 'Sometimes even if things have been sorted out, you leave there like even more pissed off because you're like, I've wasted a whole day talking to people I hate' (Pupil 6, aged 15, School 2). The fact that restorative approaches were only implemented in pockets in three out of four of the schools meant that their potential was limited. The use of restorative approaches was described by a 'Champion' in one of the schools as 'another tool in the box'; that is, as an additional strategy in a broad spectrum of practices for managing behaviour, rather than a change in philosophy. This of course means that there is a risk that traditional sanctions such as detentions and fixed-term exclusions will remain the predominant, automatic or 'easier' response to pupil behaviour rather than a last resort. This was found in the accounts of several staff. For instance, one Head of Year stated:

> Being completely truthful, sometimes I will just put them in the inclusion room, because it's easier to fill in a form, and phone the parents and say they're in the inclusion room, because I simply have not got the time to do the background 'RJ', and then do the 'RJ' itself.
>
> (Head of Year, School 3, 'RJ' meaning restorative justice)

This was also found in research by the Youth Justice Board (2004).

Staff in the schools that had implemented restorative approaches in pockets, felt that people were forgetting to use them, people were 'getting rusty' and the approaches had already been 'diluted'. This was seen to do with the reality of the competing demands of school life.

> It's like if it's not something that you do as a standard thing every day, and everyone's doing it, then it kind of gets forgotten, and it gets diluted, and then some people are doing it, some people aren't, and, oh what was that restorative thing we did once?
>
> (Head of Year, School 3)

Staff in all the schools pointed out that for restorative approaches to avoid being forgotten altogether, to continue to be used and to grow, staff needed continued input and encouragement in the form of refresher sessions and training, continued consultation with the RAiS project worker and/or stronger leadership.

In the three schools that did not use a whole-school approach, there were examples of how seemingly well-intentioned staff had compromised the integrity of the programme. First, in School 1, conferences were conducted with harmers who had not admitted they had done anything wrong, as this interviewee explained:

> The perpetrators, there were three of them, they hadn't actually been asked if they wanted to have a conference, they hadn't actually admitted they'd done anything wrong, so they were coming into a room with a victim but they hadn't admitted to it.
>
> (Support Worker 1, School 1)

Secondly, there were also accounts of staff finding it difficult or thinking it unnecessary to keep to the set script. For example, staff would tell pupils to apologise or tell them what they had to do to make amends or generally chip in with their own prescriptive opinions. This Head of Year at School 3 said of staff using restorative approaches: 'They're not actually using the script properly, and they're putting their own opinions in' (Head of Year, School 3). One pupil described how he had been shouted at in what was supposed to be a conference. 'You've got the support kind of people, they do like proper conferences but the other ones, they say they're conferences but they're just going to sit you down and shout at you' (Pupil 6, aged 15, School 2). Thirdly, some pupils at School 1 reported that they were given little choice about taking part in conferences. When asked whether he was asked to attend a conference, one pupil said 'we didn't really have a choice to go down and speak about it'.

There were also cases of management using restorative approaches which, despite good intentions, could not be described as 'restorative'. For example, one school adopted a strategy for dealing with pupil reintegration, which involved a 'quiet day' spent in the internal exclusion room to prepare them for going back into the school. During the day, they were asked to do a piece of restorative writing in which they reflected on what had happened, who they affected and what they could do to put things right. Pupils were asked to talk about what they had written with the facilitator and the other pupils in the exclusion room. The written sheet was then given to their teacher with the idea that a restorative conversation would take place between them and the pupil. However, the extent to which the use of 'quiet days' was restorative was questionable, as pupils were not given a choice. There was also little in place to ensure that the restorative conversation between the pupil and teacher took place. This mirrors the limits Gelsthorpe and Morris (2002) identified in implementing restorative practice in a youth justice system driven by punitive, exclusionary and coercive values. What emerged was a diluted version of restorative approaches involving hybridised and coerced restorative practices.

As restorative approaches were used in a limited capacity whereby only one school adopted the use of conferences instead of detentions and exclusions, so their impact and potential was inevitably limited. As in the youth justice system, restorative conferences were not seen as a suitable response to serious incidents in the school setting in three out of four of the schools and both staff and pupils expressed the desire for exclusions to remain available for such incidents. As one 'Champion' stated, the pupils responsible for serious incidents would continue to be immediately excluded: 'I don't think it will replace punishment, it shouldn't anyway, and I don't think it will here in the school, because the most serious ones are out, straightaway, like I said, it's the RJs after'.

If restorative approaches are not adopted for serious incidents their potential in preventing exclusions and crime are likely to be limited. Significantly, the most at risk, vulnerable and disaffected school pupils will continue to be excluded and the possibility of diversion from the criminal justice system impeded. At the same time, the question remains whether restorative approaches could offer an alternative for such pupils. There were two pupils who had taken part in conferences in School 2 who had histories of truancy, frequent detentions and fixed-term exclusions. They said that they also experienced difficulties with a parent or guardian at home. They expressed disillusionment with what their schools had to offer them, school policies and procedures and how they were treated by staff. Significantly, these were amongst the pupils who saw conferences as 'getting away with it' and an easier option. Their accounts raise questions about the ability of restorative approaches to deal with the most disaffected for whom nothing seems to work. Restorative approaches may only tackle the symptoms of deeper underlying issues such as family problems linked to social exclusion and deprivation. At the same time, these two pupils described how they appreciated the input of particular staff who had listened to them and helped them.

The transformative potential of restorative approaches

Notwithstanding the limits of restorative approaches and the hybridised form that they took in most of the schools in the research, as well as the fact that the programme was at a relatively early stage in its implementation, there was evidence of its transformative potential. According to staff and pupils, the restorative approaches adopted improved the climate for learning in numerous ways and challenged pupil and staff perceptions of the usefulness of existing mechanisms for punishing pupils. Staff described restorative approaches as better than punishment because they could be used to resolve behavioural issues for good by getting to the bottom of them. For pupils, restorative approaches meant they did not feel as if they were 'in trouble', which could be beneficial given the negative implications of labelling. In addition, they felt as if they were treated in a more reasonable and adult way and that they had to face up to being in the 'wrong'. This could bring about real changes to their behaviour.

> After that thing that happened and the meeting I realised that I would change. I just thought bad things are not really fun. In the school, I thought everyone would like me better. I'd be respected if I was kinder and everyone would appreciate me more.
>
> (Pupil 17, aged 12, School 4)

Restorative approaches encouraged a fairer approach to dealing with bad behaviour which moved beyond simplistic bully/victim categories. They improved communication between staff and pupils, encouraging people to talk calmly, rather than shouting, as well as improving relationships. Pupils got on better with their peers and conferences gave pupils a voice and helped to redress the power imbalance in staff–pupil relationships, humanising staff in the process. There was some evidence that restorative approaches had partly contributed to a calmer atmosphere in school, emanating from staff to pupils. Restorative approaches reportedly improved the emotional literacy of staff, but especially pupils, in their ability to reflect on their behaviour, empathise and to take responsibility for their actions. Some staff experienced the development of pupils' emotional literacy as a 'time-saver' because they could sort out problems for themselves. Restorative approaches also helped improve the well-being of staff and pupils. Staff had the confidence and skills to deal with pupils without relying on support staff or senior teachers.

The transformative potential of restorative approaches in schools could also be seen in terms of its impact on two key outcomes, attendance and fixed-term exclusions. In the research, three types of schools were compared with each other on these two outcomes measures: those with high levels of participation in restorative conferences, low levels of participation and with no participation at all (as two comparator schools were included in the research which did not implement the RAiS programme). In terms of attendance, staff and pupils reported that restorative approaches helped increase the attendance rate because they reduced the likelihood of conflicts and victimisation that may have, otherwise, kept pupils at home. Quantitative analysis confirmed staff and pupils' perceptions of the benefits of restorative approaches for attendance rates. Analysis of mean attendance rates between high, low and non-RAiS schools and between 2005/6 and 2007/8 showed that attendance rates were significantly higher in RAiS schools compared to non-RAiS schools. Regression analysis confirmed this picture. It showed that attendance rates in 2007/8 were significantly predicted by a number of factors, including the type of school (high or low use of restorative approaches). This suggests that restorative approaches offer a promising way of increasing school attendance rates.

As for fixed-term exclusions, there were reductions in the absolute numbers of fixed-term exclusions in the schools implementing restorative approaches. This reduction was noted by staff in all four RAiS schools. Staff believed that restorative approaches impacted on fixed-term exclusions either: (i) directly (i.e. when a conference was used for a serious misdemeanour instead of an exclusion); or (ii) indirectly (i.e. when a restorative conference was used to address less serious misdemeanours, meaning that low-level incidents were prevented from escalating into bigger incidents that could result in exclusion). That said, there were also reductions in the number of fixed-term exclusions in non-RAiS schools too. This is a reason to be cautious in interpreting the drop in the number of fixed-term exclusions in schools with high and low use of restorative approaches as being causally linked. As one interviewee noted, all schools are under pressure to reduce exclusions and it may be that restorative approaches are one of only a number of tools that contribute to a reduction. However, it is likely that restorative approaches were a contributing factor to reductions in fixed-term exclusions, particularly in the schools where conferences were routinely and explicitly used as an alternative to fixed-term exclusions.

Conclusion

Regardless of the school, and therefore the approach, to implementing restorative approaches, the programme made a sufficient impact in challenging at least some pupils' and staff's perceptions of the existing mechanisms for punishing pupils; for example, pupils began to realise that they wanted to feel fairly treated and that they were treated in a reasonable and adult manner and that they wanted to face up to their wrong-doing, but without feeling as if they were 'in trouble'. These are the founding principles of restorative justice and re-integrative shaming. That is, an offender can be made to acknowledge their wrong-doing and be shamed in front of their peers and significant others such as their family, but also be allowed to make amends and be punished in a way that they can be re-integrated and accepted back into their communities. It is an achievement that staff and pupils had begun to grasp these principles in only two years, particularly when the successful implementation of a whole-school approach is generally agreed to take up to five years (Blood 2005, Blood and Thorsborne 2005, Morrison 2005, Hopkins 2004).

Restorative approaches do have transformative potential in schools but issues that have emerged in the implementation of restorative justice in the criminal justice system are mirrored in school settings. Firstly, as has been found in research in criminal justice settings, the dichotomy between restorative justice and punitiveness is far from clear-cut. In the present study, traditional forms of punishment such as exclusion from school were not necessarily seen as punitive, whilst restorative conferences were seen as more onerous. Secondly, similar to the adoption of restorative justice in the youth justice system, restorative approaches were implemented in hybridised forms and in a limited capacity. The idea that implementation should be approached on a 'whole-school' basis is good in theory, but theory and practice have been shown to be different. Restorative approaches were implemented in pockets only in all but one of the four schools and restorative approaches were used *alongside* traditional punitive sanctions in all of them. As in the youth justice system, restorative approaches were not considered by staff in the schools as appropriate for dealing with serious incidents. Traditional punishments continued to be regarded as a necessary aspect of school culture by pupils as well as staff. Thirdly, as in criminal justice settings restorative approaches may fall short in terms of its capacity for transformative politics. As Cunneen and Hoyle (2010, p. 186) argue about restorative justice in general:

> Restorative justice lacks praxis – in the sense of a constantly reflexive, dialectical relationship between theory and action. It lacks an analysis of its own significant shortcomings; it lacks an analysis of political power and social power; it lacks a transformative politics.

Restorative approaches in schools do appear to currently lack 'praxis'. This is understandable given the frequent reports that a minority of school staff and pupils remain resistant to the implementation of these approaches. Consequently, training providers and amenable staff will be preoccupied with promoting it, showcasing its effectiveness, trying to win over sceptics and changing the culture of the school. This forecloses the space for providers and advocates to reflect fully upon and share the shortcomings of restorative approaches, or to celebrate the many hybrid forms it may take in practice. However, perhaps a more open and balanced dialogue about both the benefits and limitations of these approaches may in fact help to win over the hearts and minds of sceptics.

For restorative approaches to develop their potential in schools more understanding is needed of the perspectives of staff and pupils who are opposed to them, preferring to opt for more traditional punitive methods, and the pupils who do not want to take part; the kind of incidents these approaches are seen as unsuitable for, the pupils for whom it does not appear to help or that it completely excludes. In other words, research is needed not only into whether restorative approaches in schools can offer particular positive outputs and outcomes, which evidence shows it can, but also a critical analysis of how it is applied in practice, its limitations and what can be learnt from this. While stories of hybrid forms of restorative approaches in schools should not be left untold, continuing to tell the 'mythical true story' (Daly 2002) of restorative approaches transforming school cultures is perhaps still important in order that we remain open intellectually and emotionally to new experiences and change. And as Daly (2002) argues tales of repair, reconciliation and personal transformation is necessary to provide inspiration to policymakers and those experimenting with alternative justice forms.

At the same time, if implemented and practised effectively, restorative approaches have potential to counterbalance punitive forms of school discipline and, in a small but significant way, to challenge and circumvent the punitive turn in youth justice through education. First, in its transformation of traditional punitive forms of schools discipline, they may help to soften the impact of the punitive turn on young people. That is, restorative approaches may provide young people with the skills and the language to handle challenging situations in schools more effectively and avoid truancy and exclusions which are associated with involvement in crime. The use of such skills could extend to young people's interactions outside schools and enable them to avoid series of events leading to criminality and criminal justice intervention. Second, given that the Youth Justice Board have stated a commitment to giving restorative justice a more central position in the youth justice system, restorative approaches in schools might also 'set the tone' for what young people might come to expect in their dealings with the criminal justice system. Third, restorative approaches have the capacity to re-educate and transform the way adults i.e. school staff and parents see punishment in schools and in the wider society, and how best to respond to the behaviour of young people. The building of restorative social capital in schools could have far-reaching effects, contributing to the transformation of how young people are seen and treated, whereby strategies of detention and exclusion come to be seen as a last resort not only in schools but in the criminal justice system.

References

Allen, R. (2002) 'There Must be Some Way of Dealing with Kids', *Young Offenders, Public Attitudes and Policy Change* 2: 3.

Barton, C. (2000) 'Empowerment and Retribution in Criminal Justice' in H. Strang and J. Braithwaite (eds) *Restorative Justice: Philosophy to Practice* pp. 55–76. Aldershot: Ashgate/Dartmouth.

Benekos, P. and Merlo, A. (2008) 'Juvenile Justice: The Legacy of Punitive Policy', *Youth Violence and Juvenile Justice* 6(1): 28–46.

Cameron, L. and Thorsborne, M. (2001) 'Restorative Justice and School Discipline: Mutually Exclusive?' in H. Strang and J. Braithwaite (eds) *Restorative Justice and Civil Society*. Cambridge: Cambridge University Press.

Cox, E. (1995) *A Truly Civil Society*. ABC Boyer Lectures. Sydney: ABC Books.

Cunneen, C. and Hoyle, C. (2010) *Debating Restorative Justice*. Oxford: Hart Publishing.

Daly, K. (2002) 'Restorative Justice: The Real Story', *Punishment and Society* 4: 55.

Farrington, D. (2000) 'Explaining and Preventing Crime: The Globalisation of Knowledge', *Criminology* 38(1): 1–24.

Garland, D. (1996) 'The Limits of the Sovereign State: Strategies of Crime Control in Contemporary Society', *The British Journal of Criminology* 36 (4): 445–471.

—— (2001) *The Culture of Control: Crime and Social Order in Contemporary Society*. Oxford: Oxford University Press.

Gelsthorpe, L. and Morris, A. (2002) 'Restorative Justice; The Last Vestiges of Welfare?' In J. Muncie, G. Hughes and E. McLaughlin (eds) *Youth Justice: Critical Readings*. London: Sage, pp. 238–54.

Goldson, B. (2005) 'Taking Liberties: Policy and the Punitive Turn' in H. Hendrick (ed.) *Child Welfare and Social Policy: An Essential Reader*. Bristol: Policy Press, pp. 225–268.

Goldson, B. and Jameison, J. (2002) 'Youth Crime, the "Parenting Deficit" and State Intervention: A Contextual Critique', *Youth Justice* 2(2) 82–99.

Hallsworth, S. (2000) 'Rethinking the Punitive Turn Economies of Excess and the Criminology of the Other'. *Punishment and Society* 2(2): 145–160.

Hudson, J. and Galaway, B. (eds) (1996) '*Introduction*' in *Restorative Justice: International Perspectives*, New York: Criminal Justice Press 1–14.

Krygier, M. (1997) *Between Fear and Hope: Hybrid Thoughts on Public Values*. ABC Boyer Lectures. Sydney: ABC Books.

Malouf, D. (1998) *A Spirit of Play: The Making of Australian Consciousness*. ABC Boyer Lectures. Sydney: ABC Books.

MORI (2001) *Public Attitudes Towards Prisons: Report to Esmée Fairburn Foundation*. London: Esmée Fairburn Foundation.

Morrison, B. (2001) 'The School System: Developing its Capacity in the Regulation of a Civil Society' in H. Strang and J. Braithwaite (eds) *Restorative Justice and Civil Society*. Cambridge: Cambridge University Press.

—— (2006) *Restoring Safe School Communities: A Whole School Response to Bullying, Violence & Alienation*. Sydney: Federation Press.

—— (2005) 'Restorative Justice in Schools' in E. Eliott, and R. Gordon, (eds) *New Directions in Restorative Justice*. Cullompton, Devon: Willan Publishing.

Muncie, J. (2005) 'The Globalisation of Crime Control: The Case of Youth and Juvenile Justice', *Theoretical Criminology* 9(1): 35–64.

—— (2008) 'The "Punitive Turn" in Juvenile Justice: Cultures of Control and Rights Compliance in Western Europe and the USA', *Youth Justice* 8: 107.

—— (2006) 'Governing Young People: Coherence and Contradiction in Contemporary Youth Justice', *Critical Social Policy*, 26(4): 770–793.

Sherman, L. and Strang, H. (2007) *Restorative Justice: The Evidence*. London: The Smith Institute.

Skinns, L., Du Rose, N. and Hough, M. (2009) 'An Evaluation of Bristol RAiS', ICPR, Kings College London.

Walgrave, L. (1992) 'Mediation and Community Service as Models of a Restorative Approach: Why Would It Be Better? Explicating the Objectives as Criteria for Evaluation' in H. Messmer and H. Otto (eds) *Restorative Justice on Trial: Pitfalls and Potentials of Victim-Offender Mediation: International Research Perspectives*. Dordrecht: Kluwer Academic Publishers, pp. 343–354.

Waquant, L. (1999) 'How Penal Common Sense Comes to Europeans: Notes on the Transatlantic Diffusion of the Neo-liberal Doxa', *European Societies* 1(3): 319–352.

Youth Justice Board (2006) *Developing Restorative Justice: An Action Plan*. London: Youth Justice Board.

Chapter 18

Creating the restorative school part 1

Seeding restorative approaches in Minnesota

Nancy Riestenberg

Introduction

This is the first of three chapters engaging with issues concerning the effective implementation of restorative approaches in schools. In the next part, Edward Sellman examines the impact of restorative approaches on relationships and communicational practices as such approaches are implemented. In the third part to this section, McCall asks us to reflect on hierarchy in schools and whether it is possible, even desirable, for facilitators to exercise neutrality when supporting restorative approaches in schools. In this chapter however, once the context has been set, attention is focused upon examining the regional and institutional political contexts that enable and/or constrain restorative approaches in the earlier stages of their implementation.

Restorative approaches as both a way of 'doing' and as a way of 'being' in schools, can be both resilient and adaptive. They are characterised by several key elements that make them attractive to practitioners: they promote positive relationships, encourage people to consider their moral obligations to one another and possess the ability to augment other prevention programmes. These characteristics will be briefly presented. There are, however, numerous and continuing challenges to implementation warranting further attention. These will be discussed at two levels of policy: regional and institutional. Somewhat inevitably, the first level concerns such matters as security of funding, training and resources, which require economic and philosophical commitment from school leaders and regional policymakers. The second level focuses on the institutional context of the school itself and the frequent encounter between restorative approaches and a persistent attitude amongst professionals that punishment is an effective solution for controlling student behaviour, a theme that also overlaps with several other chapters in this and other sections. A review of how these challenges have been met in Minnesota, drawing upon interviews with and anecdotes from colleagues, may provide insight to others intent on a whole-school implementation of restorative approaches.

Context – Minnesota's restorative journey

Minnesota, home to the headwaters of the River Mississippi, has a population of 5.2 million people, 900,000 of whom are school age and are drawn from diverse ethnic and linguistic origins, within both longstanding and recent migrant communities. Minnesota has a history of innovation within its services for children and young adults with prevention education programmes, curriculum development projects and training for schools on a range of issues including chemical dependency, sexual violence and domestic abuse alongside pioneering pedagogical approaches such as theatre education. It was the first state in the United States whose education authority actively promoted the use of restorative approaches in schools as both a response to issues concerning student discipline and as a strategy for preventing violence. Between 1998–2001, the authority allocated funding to demonstrate the implementation of these approaches alongside the publication of guidance materials for schools. These initiatives developed interest and professional networks, encouraged experimentation and offered training to schools, their communities and criminal justice workers.

'Restorative justice', well-discussed in previous chapters, is a term originating from criminal justice and law enforcement to describe programmes and practices that conceptualise 'crime' as a violation of people, interpersonal relationships and communities. These violations then create obligations to repair damage (Zehr 2002). In the Minnesota educational community, 'restorative approaches' inform both preventative and responsive disciplinary processes by seeking to address any harm caused, alongside the teaching of problem-solving skills. By viewing conflict as an inevitable and potentially constructive human experience, in fact necessary for social and emotional development, it is positioned as part of the learning process, as an educational entitlement (Stutzman et al. 2005).

The impetus to use the principles and approaches of restorative justice came from a public policy shift in the 1990s requiring the criminal justice system to respond to crime and for schools to manage disciplinary issues in alternative ways. State funds supported pilot projects that introduced model practices in court services, community organisations and schools, and trained key leaders. Inter-agency relationships between state Departments of Education, Public Safety and Corrections, resulted in grant provision for a range of restorative approaches: the use of circles, curriculum development, conferencing and technical training in implementing both school- and workplace- based restorative programmes. Community organisations, advocates and entrepreneurs helped develop an infrastructure of knowledge, practice and training that continues to serve people interested in implementing restorative approaches.

From 1998–2001, The Minnesota Department of Education (MDE) conducted a three-year evaluation of the implementation and use of restorative approaches; focusing particularly on the introduction of social, emotional learning and community building in the classroom and the use of circles to repair harm. The latter involves those with a stake in a conflict sitting in a circle, taking turns to talk and employing problem-solving and solutions-focused techniques to reach mutually acceptable agreements (see Bickmore, this volume for a detailed overview of this process). The findings from this research were promising, indicating that:

- Consistent application of restorative approaches, such as circles to repair harm and behaviour management techniques influenced by restorative processes, resulted in significant yearly reductions of student referrals to senior leaders and suspensions in one school for 7–11 year olds.
- A resource room implementing problem-solving strategies with students experiencing emotional and/or behavioural difficulties resulted in increased academic achievement at one school for 11–16 year olds.
- Teachers reported higher rates of satisfaction with their own behaviour management approaches.
- Strategies introduced through teacher training were widely applied in the classroom at five schools for 7–11 year olds, where 50–70 per cent of teachers used circles, and classroom/behaviour management skills influenced by restorative principles (MDE 2001).

Further grants followed between 2001–2003, designed to provide state-wide training and evaluation on restorative approaches. The previous evaluation made two things apparent: 1) restorative approaches showed great promise in reducing behaviour-related referrals and suspensions; and 2) after the grant money runs out, a programme can, and often does, end. In response to the latter point, the next round of funding aimed to build capacity and sustainability by training as many people as possible, as the following report extract indicates:

> Given the uncertainty of grant awards and general funding for education, as well as the natural mobility of teaching staff, it seemed to be more cost effective to teach a lot of people 'how to fish,' rather than have them depend on a guide with a good boat for a limited amount of time.
>
> (MDE 2003, p. 14)

The evaluation of the second round of funding also showed reductions in behaviour-related referrals and a striking reduction in suspensions at two schools within a year (45 and 63 per cent respectively). Both of these schools trained staff to use circles in the classroom on a daily basis as well as using them as a disciplinary response to repair harm. It was noted that the initiative at both schools benefitted from support from administrative staff and the leadership.

During 2007–2008, the state Department for Education conducted a retrospective student discipline study, and attempted to compare the impact of restorative approaches against suspensions, in relation to educational outcomes, recidivism of school offences and adult criminal records. As the study was retrospective, going back four, five and in some instances six or seven years, it rather unsurprisingly proved difficult to obtain information on students who had participated in a restorative process some time ago at school. The study was therefore inconclusive regarding the sample's adult criminal record, attendance and graduation, and various restrictions to data systems prohibited access to test scores. However, it was possible to compare disciplinary records in some detail.

The analysis of referral and suspension data indicated that students who went through a restorative process were less likely to repeat an incident resulting in a disciplinary response. For the group who had experienced a restorative approach, the rate for repeat of an incident was 40 per cent. For the group who had only been suspended, the rate was 57 per cent. The students who had experienced a restorative approach and did repeat an incident requiring a disciplinary response also had a longer delay between incidents. As the chapter by McCluskey *et al.* (this volume) indicates, evaluating the impact of such approaches is difficult and caution is needed when extrapolating impact from such data but nonetheless, these figures were encouraging, especially when seeking to justify extra resources to professionals making funding decisions.

Indeed, the results of this evaluation, combined with advocacy drawn from international research provided evidence to justify allocating resources and further training across the state. For over a decade, an intensive weeklong seminar has been offered to up to seven new school teams per annum alongside workshops and training sessions for all schools throughout the year. In addition, a network of experienced community and school-based trainers provide staff development to anyone willing to explore alternatives to suspension and initiatives underpinned by restorative principles. As a result, restorative approaches have proliferated in Minnesota schools from the initial four pilot sites in 1998 to about one-third of Minnesota school districts at the time of writing.

The key strengths of restorative approaches

Support staff, teachers, school leaders and administrators may consider using restorative approaches for a variety of practical reasons: grant funds make it viable to try, cultural practices resonate with restorative philosophy and/or because other approaches have not worked in the past. In my experience of working with practitioners, I see three key strengths that make the use of restorative approaches in schools particularly attractive. They promote positive relationships, encourage moral awareness and demonstrate the ability to augment other prevention programmes and each of these characteristics will be discussed in turn.

Positive relationships

Relationships occupy the core of restorative philosophy and there is mounting evidence to support the importance of social and emotional aspects of learning (Gerhardt 2004, Zins *et al.* 2004). Restorative processes dovetail well with a humanistic educational agenda, recognising that emotional security and belonging to a community are integral to effective education. Bernare (2010, online source) summarises the connection between emotional safety and learning, arguing 'there is a good amount of neurological evidence to promote the idea that if students do not feel comfortable in a classroom setting, they will not learn; physiologically speaking, stressed brains are not able to form the necessary neural connections'.

Moral awareness

Restorative approaches are rooted in mutuality and help those involved with a conflict understand the moral aspects of complex issues, the interdependency of roles and a way to untangle any mess caused by harm. Stephanie Haider, a trainer and director of Lakes Area Restorative Justice Project located in Central Minnesota, explained what drew her to Restorative Justice work. She was a probation officer, working with adolescent girls.

> These girls were in trouble – run-aways, assault, etc., – because of abuse, sexual abuse. It was predictable. And in the 1970s, there was no training for how to work with these very mixed up families – I'd either be punitive or too lenient in dealing with these girls. This caused me a lot of stress. In the 1980s I learned about victim-offender mediation and the idea of restitution. So, we developed the Dakota County restitution program. We wrote in the manual, 'If you have wronged someone, it is your responsibility to make it right with that person and your community as a whole and it is your responsibility to improve yourself with personal achievements and goals.' This is what it's about – it is not about being punitive or lenient, but being accountable. Not by me, but by the victim and the community – they could do my job for me. It was a revelation. It was a relief.

Restorative approaches enable two contradictory ideas to be held at the same time – a person can be both an 'offender' and a 'victim', may have both obligations and needs, and we need not ignore either status. Given the multiple experiences some children have with victimisation, this notion is enormously useful when a child hurts someone else. Their community can acknowledge both truths and in doing so, provide real support and foster genuine accountability (see McCall's chapter, this volume, for an interesting discussion of facilitators being on both sides at the same time).

Augmentation of other preventative programmes

Restorative approaches are often congruent with other programmes that have humanistic values and objectives, including bullying prevention, emotional literacy and pupil empowerment initiatives. They can complement whole-school approaches to positive relationships and sympathetic approaches to behaviour management. The synergy between behaviour management and restorative approaches, as discussed in the next two chapters, is crucial. When students make mistakes with their academic learning, the educational response is to offer them further instruction and support. However, when students make 'behavioural' mistakes, educators all too often retort to punitive measures, ignoring the skills both students and teachers have acquired for resolving conflict in more participatory and sustainable ways. For expedience, teachers 'do' to them (detain, suspend, exclude) rather than working 'with' them to solve a problem.

This latter point is one of the main challenges schools face when implementing restorative approaches. This and other challenges will be discussed in the next section.

The challenges of funding, training, resources and policy

Every innovation encounters challenges on the way to its demise or institutionalisation. The main challenges to restorative approaches in schools identified by MDE (1997) are still its challenges today: funding, training, resources and school policies underpinned by a belief in punishment and an ingrained socio-political desire for retribution. The educational landscape of the United States, like other international contexts, has faced common challenges concerning economic instability and inconsistent funding, performative pressures and what Du Rose and Skinns (this volume) call a 'punitive turn', the latter particularly evident in the frequent use of zero tolerance policies in schools and their communities. These challenges can be found at both levels of regional and institutional policy, each will be discussed in turn.

Regional policy

Funding

State education requires substantial public resources and is, therefore, significantly affected by the ebb and flow of the national and state economies and political agendas. In Minnesota, 40 per cent of the state budget is designated for education, which constitutes 80 per cent of the monies available to individual schools to fund their activities. School districts may levy additional taxes to boost funding with the federal government only contributing less than five per cent of the total funding needed. There is a clear relationship between the level and consistency of funding of school-based programmes and related matters such as the availability of trained personnel. New initiatives are particularly vulnerable to high staff turnover when it occurs, which impact upon the sustainability of programmes when key professionals and/or resources are lost and not replaced.

Inconsistent funding and staff mobility have been addressed by creative responses to these challenges in Minnesota:

1   Schools look beyond their walls for community restorative programmes with which to partner. The Lakes Area Restorative Justice volunteer conferencing programme, for example, provides restorative conferencing to several school districts and county court services. Similarly, Minneapolis Schools have a vetting process for their community restorative programmes, so a principal may easily contact a community facilitator to help with an incident in school where harm needs to be repaired.
2   Districts prioritise training current employees rather than hiring someone paid by time-limited grant money, meaning restorative approaches are distributed across the skill sets of a wide number of personnel.
3   Educators trained in restorative approaches are strategically placed, seeding these approaches in new schools.

These strategies may be replicable in other regional contexts.

Training

As discussed, funding is closely related to the issue of training. It has been a regional strategy to provide a steady flow of training, keeping it affordable and sometimes free. Community organisations, individual trainers and the Minnesota Departments of Corrections and Education work collaboratively to provide training and seminars. There are also a growing number of books, blogs, online videos and websites on restorative approaches in schools to supplement and reinforce training provided. A particularly successful strategy has been the introduction of coaching, whereby individuals interested in restorative approaches can request to be apprenticed to an experienced and skilled facilitator. In both our research (e.g. Joyce and Showers 2002) and our initial evaluations, we have observed that coaching increases the likelihood that a person will actually use the skills they have acquired.

The reluctance to participate

Some schools and personnel within schools may be reluctant to participate with restorative approaches. This may change slowly as the term 'restorative' and opportunities to participate in restorative approaches become more common. There is some progress in this direction. For example, a bill introduced in the United States Congress in January 2012, the Restorative Justice in Schools Act, allows local education authorities to use Elementary and Secondary Education Act funding for teachers and school-based counsellors to receive training in restorative justice and conflict resolution.

Time

Teachers in the US and further afield are under enormous performative pressures, which place considerable pressure on the time allocation of activities during the school day. As a consequence, teachers may omit morning circles because they feel they need to spend more time on content. This is a false economy though as the neglect of social and emotional aspects of learning only results in the long-term in greater time being spent on discipline. Administrators frequently admire the outcomes of restorative approaches with their students but then bemoan the amount of time it takes (two hours for a restorative conference for example). When the positive outcomes (regular school attendance, homework completion, low levels of recidivism and successful graduation) of a juvenile community circle process run by a county court are reported, people are delighted. When it transpires that the participants have met on a fortnightly basis with their community circle for five months to two years, they sigh: 'Really? That long?' When these terms are fully appreciated, it becomes clear that restorative approaches are not a soft option as they require serious time commitments from all involved. However, the length of participation results in benefits extending well beyond the school career. Some participants have even gone on to study restorative justice and returned to their schools some time later to advocate its impact on their lives.

Institutional policy

The year 2000 marked a significant change in United States' education policy. The education funding bill, entitled 'The No Child Left Behind Act', was passed by Congress and signed by the President. This Act sought to raise educational standards by measuring student outcomes and implementing consequences for schools not making 'annual yearly progress', determined by student test scores. Hence, schools focused almost all of their attention on reading and maths academics. Anderson (2007) highlights this moment as the time that set back any implementation of restorative approaches in schools more than any other factor. Rather suddenly, schools were under financial pressure to focus on teaching students to perform well in tests. Concurrently, there was a further drive towards zero tolerance as a means of controlling behaviour in the classroom.

Zero tolerance

The policy of zero tolerance for guns on school property affected dissemination of restorative approaches in schools. First set in federal law in 1994, some states and school districts expanded the policy. Zero-tolerance policies result in suspension, expulsion or police arrest of students of all ages for alcohol, possession of drugs, possession of firecrackers or, that euphemism for challenging teacher authority, insubordination. Although the No Child Left Behind Act attempted to raise educational standards, when merged with zero-tolerance policies it had the unintended outcome of increased rates of exclusion for many marginal, special education and minority students and essentially creating a school-to-prison pipeline. (Anfinson *et. al.* 2010, Losen and Skiba 2010, The Advancement Project 2010). Such policies were underpinned by a return to more punitive models of discipline in schools and a pervading view that 'wrongdoers' deserved retribution.

The belief in punishment

As other chapters in this volume (McCluskey, Du Rose and Skinns, Sellman) have highlighted (and will highlight) punitive models of discipline in schools at best undermine, and more probably, thwart the potential benefits of restorative approaches in schools. Punitive measures do not have a particularly successful track record. Research indicates that school exclusion has a deleterious effect on youth including: high levels of repeat offending (Costenbader and Markson 1998, Skiba and Knesting 2001), school dropout rates (Ekstrom 1986), acceleration of misbehaviour (Tobin *et al.* 1996), entry into criminality (Christle, Nelson, and Jolivette 2004, Advancement Project 2005) and decreased academic achievement, (Townsend 2000, Arcia 2007). The tendency toward punitive ways of thinking is perhaps best countered by initial participation in a conference or circle, so that one can see and feel how the process works. This can then be followed by incorporation of restorative approaches within the daily activities of classrooms (see Bickmore, Johnson and Johnson this volume) for detailed discussion on such matters. Both of these suggestions potentially increase the empathy experience in classrooms, which is the antidote of wishing harm upon others.

Conclusion

I work for a state agency to ensure public funds are used appropriately and provide technical assistance and training. I liken my job to that of a gardener collecting seeds from each new plot implementing restorative approaches – in some instances, heirloom seeds and in others, hybrids of innovation. I see the work of others and I share the seeds of their insight, successes and failures. For more than a decade, I have been part of a cadre of public servants who have worked with schools and their communities, professionals from the criminal justice sector and social services to implement restorative approaches in a range of settings. As discussed in this chapter, there are considerable challenges, particularly those placing economic and narrow educational demands on schools. Yet, for every obstacle encountered I have witnessed creative solutions to these problems. To seed restorative approaches in schools requires steadfast commitment, willingness to collaborate and adaptability.

References

Advancement Project. (2005) 'Education on Lockdown: The schoolhouse to jailhouse Track'. Available at: <http://www.advancementproject.org/publications/opportunity-to-learn.php>. Accessed 15 June 2009.

Anderson, C. (2007) *Restorative Measures: Respecting Everyone's Ability To Resolve Problems*. Minnesota Department of Children Families and Learning (Minnesota Department of Education).

Anfinson, A., Autumn, S., Lehr, C., Riestenberg, N. and Scullin, S. (2010) 'Disproportionate Minority Representation in Minnesota Public Schools', Minnesota Department of Education. Available at: <http://education.state.mn.us/mdeprod/groups/SafeHealthy/documents/Report/017654.pdf>. Retrieved 4 January 2011.

Arcia, E. (2006) 'Achievement and enrollment status of suspended students', *Education and Urban Society, 38*, 359–369.

Bernard, S. (2011) 'To Enable Learning, Put (Emotional) Safety First'. Available at: <http://www.edutopia.org/print/node/35436 published 12/1/2010>. Accessed 6 January 2011.

Christle, C., Nelson, M. C. and Jolivette, K. (2004) 'School characteristics related to the use of suspension', *Education and Treatment of Children 27*, 509–526.

Costenbader, V. and Markson, S. (1998) 'School suspension: A study with secondary students', *Journal of School Psychology, 36*, (1), 59–82 (24).

Federal Policy, ESEA Reauthorization, and the School-to-Prison Pipeline. A joint position paper of: Advancement Project, Education Law Center– PA, FairTest, The Forum for Education and Democracy, Juvenile Law Center, NAACP Legal Defense and Educational Fund, Inc.

December 2010. Available at: <http://www.jlc.org/images/uploads/Federal_Policy_ ESEA_Reauthorization_and_the_School-to-Prison_Pipeline_-_01_18_11.pdf>

Gerhardt, S. (2004) *Why Love Matters: How Affection Shapes a Baby's Brain.* London: Routledge.

Joyce, B. and Showers, B. (2002) *Student Achievement through Staff Development.* Alexandria, VA: Association for Supervision and Curriculum Development.

Konopka, G. (1973) 'Requirements for healthy development of adolescent youth', *Adolescence,* Volume VIII Number 31, Fall 1973, 1–26.

Losen, D. and Skiba, R. (2010) *Suspended Education: Urban Middle Schools in Crisis.* Southern Poverty Law Center. Available at: <http://www.splcenter.org/sites/default/ files/downloads/publication/Suspended_Education.pdf>. Accessed 9 January 2011.

Minnesota Department of Education (2001) *In School Behavior Intervention Grants Final Report, 1998–2001.*

—— (2003) *Restorative School Grants Final Report, January 2002–June 2001.*

—— (2007) *Title IV: Safe and Drug Free School End of the Year Report Summary 2005-2006 School Year.* Available at: <http://education.state.mn.us/MDE/Learning_Support/ Safe_and_Healthy_Learners/Safe_Learners/Safe_and_Drug_Free_Schools/index. html>. Retrieved 15 January 2011.

—— (2010) *School Discipline: A Study of Approaches and Outcomes: A focus on Restorative Practices.* Contact Nancy Riestenberg, nancy.riestenberg@state.mn.us.

—— (2011) *Minnesota Student Survey on Bullying: An Analysis of Associations.*

'No Child Left Behind Act' of 2001, Pub. L. 107–110 (H.R.1).

Skiba, R. J. and Knesting, K. (2001) 'Zero tolerance, zero evidence: An analysis of school disciplinary practice' in R. J. Skiba and G. G. Noam (eds.) *New Directions for Youth Development.* San Francisco: Jossey-Bass.

Skiba, R. J. and Peterson, R. L. (1999) 'The dark side of zero tolerance: Can punishment lead to safe school?' *Phi Delta Kappan,* 80, 372–376.

Stutzman Amstutz, L. and Mullet, J. H. (2005) *The Little Book of Restorative Discipline for Schools: Teaching Responsibility, Creating Caring Climates.* Intercourse, PA: Good Books.

Townsend, B. (2000) 'The disproportionate discipline of African American learners: Reducing school suspensions and expulsions', *Exceptional Children,* 66(3), 383–391.

U.S. Department of Justice, (1999) '1999 National Report Series: Minorities in the Juvenile Justice System'. Available at: <http://www.ncjrs.gov/pdf>. Retrieved 15 January 2011.

Wachtel, T. and McCold, P. (2001) 'Restorative justice in everyday life: Beyond the formal ritual' in H. Strang and J. Braithwaite (eds), *Restorative Justice and Civil Society.* Cambridge: Cambridge University Press.

Zehr, H. (2002) *The Little Book of Restorative Justice.* Intercourse, PA: Good Books.

Zins, J. E., Weissberg, R. P., Wang, M. C. and Wahlberg, H. J. (2004) *Building Academic Success on Social and Emotional Learning: What Does the Research Say?* New York: Teachers College Press.

Chapter 19

Creating the restorative school part 2

The impact of restorative approaches on roles, power and language

Edward Sellman

Introduction

This chapter, positioned between two others focusing on implementing restorative approaches across whole school culture, discusses the impact effective implementation can have upon roles, power and communicational practices. It focuses on peer mediation (Sellman 2008) as a specific example of a restorative approach and presents the findings from research conducted at nine schools (seven primary, two secondary) in England, which had previously implemented a mediation service as an alternative to teacher arbitration for students experiencing 'difficult' interpersonal conflict. This analysis was informed by themes from a previous stage of research conducted at one additional primary school, where the intervention process had been observed longitudinally.

The analysis draws upon post-Vygotskian theory in order to understand and describe the cultural processes affecting the implementation of peer mediation services. The findings of this research highlight the need for realistic anticipation of the degree of cultural transformation required to fully support approaches that offer some form of empowerment to students in schools, as peer mediation does. The chapter discusses how such empowerment is limited and how this issue can be illuminated by greater scrutiny of the roles, power relationships and language adopted by schools attempting to implement restorative approaches. Peer mediation was most successful in schools where there was a considerable shift in roles and perceptions of power, accompanied by the production of new cultural tools that promoted new ways of thinking, speaking and acting with regard to conflict.

Peer mediation and learning about conflict

By now, most readers will be familiar with the principles of restorative approaches and how they differ to contrasting approaches, the text will therefore move swiftly to the discussion of the research. However, it may be useful at the beginning to re-emphasise how restorative approaches, such as peer mediation in schools, are distinctive to other educational approaches to conflict.

1   The *pedagogy* of mediation training is very different to other forms of education about conflict. Most children learn about conflict informally in their relationships with their peers, siblings and authority figures. Analysis of conflict is rarely deep as conflicts are frequently avoided or resolved rather quickly in favour of the disputant with the greatest power in that context. In contrast, mediation training is underpinned by humanistic values though it is actually quite formal; there are rules, stages and communicational practices to be followed. Superficially at least, parties are equal in power and status.

2   Engaging with restorative approaches as either a 'client' or mediator is different to learning about conflict via a curriculum topic such as citizenship. Curriculum approaches have considerable merit of course (see Johnson and Johnson this volume), though if not accompanied by an experiential element can construct students as citizens 'to be' rather than citizens 'in situ'. As a result, issues relating to conflict management are taught in lessons, representing knowledge to be taken into the adult world in the future, rather than organisational affordances made to facilitate democratic engagement in the present (Hicks 2001, Rudduck and Fielding 2006). There is, of course, also education about conflict through the hidden curriculum (certain views of history in taught subjects, models of moral behaviour implicit in school rules, for example). Restorative approaches contain their own hidden curriculum (e.g. humanistic values), which may complement, clash with or be affected by the 'hidden messages' of other areas of schooling, a point that will be revisited.

The research shared in this chapter will highlight that restorative approaches such as peer mediation frequently underestimate the degree, and complexity, of cultural transformation required for such services to be maintained and have any impact. One aspect of such transformation often shared in a limited literature is the need to reassess power relations between teachers, other adults in schools, and students (McCluskey this volume, Tyrrell 2002, Wyness 2006) – which will be a recurring theme for further discussion in this chapter. Researchers and educationalists may therefore benefit from a more refined analysis of the problematic practices between traditional approaches to management and innovations planned.

Research design

The design of this research commenced with a desire to better understand the relationship between cultural and interactional levels of analysis in schools. Post-Vygotskian theory was selected as an approach suitable for achieving this (e.g. Daniels 2001a, Engestrom 1999, 2007) as it seeks to understand the relationship between interactional and institutional levels of analysis and is methodologically attracted to intervention-based research. It is particularly alert to 'contradictions' and how these can both obstruct and propel transformative practice. The aggravation and analysis of such contradictions during periods of transformation is a central feature of post-Vygotskian research. As an example, 'traditional' approaches for resolving more difficult conflict in schools by adult arbitration is built upon radically opposing principles of power and control that 'contradict' those of peer mediation, a point for extended discussion throughout the chapter.

The research reported here also draws upon Bernstein's (2000) theory of cultural transmission as a means of enriching the description of cultural practice and transformation. Bernstein's concepts of classification and framing are thus useful here (see Daniels *et al.* 1996, Daniels 2001b for an introduction). Briefly, 'classification' refers to the degree of insulation between categories (curriculum subjects, teachers/pupils). These are said to be strong or weak depending on the explicitness of boundaries between them and the degree of specialisation within. 'Framing' refers to the regulation of communication between social relations and their physical organisation within the school. Overall, where classification and framing is weak, practice is more seamless and order is regulated more horizontally. Where classification and framing is strong, there will be clear demarcations and relations between parties will be more hierarchical. Bernstein's (2000) language of description informed the analysis of the strength of classification reported by interviewees between people enacting certain roles when resolving conflict and the explicitness of rules framing the approach. The research was thus able to focus upon whether forms of social organisation (e.g. who resolves conflict and how) are transformed by intervention (peer mediation training) and subsequent impact.

In Vygotsky's (1978) consideration of method, he argued the need to artificially provoke development as a means to its study. Engestrom (1999) describes how Sylvia Scribner has demonstrated that Vygotsky's ideas concerning appropriate method cannot be reduced to a single technique. Instead, she suggests four steps in conducting research, these are:

1   Observation of behaviour in the current context. This is sometimes referred to as 'rudimentary' behaviour, meaning behaviour that has lost its history such as professional practice that is reproduced in an unquestioned or non-reflective manner.
2   Reconstruction and description of historical behaviour and how behaviour in the current context came to be.
3   Experimental production of change from rudimentary behaviour through intervention.
4   Observation of the actual development.

To investigate the implementation of peer mediation services and subsequent processes of school transformation a two-stage approach to research was adopted, influenced by these four steps. In the first stage, these four steps were incorporated into a case study where a peer mediation service was implemented at a primary school that served a socially and economically diverse community in England. Pupils, teachers, lunchtime supervisors and the peer mediation trainers from this school were interviewed both pre- and post-intervention. The emphasis of these interviews was to explore how a selection of conflict scenarios typical to schools (such as peers arguing, fighting, calling each other names, as well as challenges to teacher authority) would be responded to before and after the training. The peer mediation training was also observed. Cumulatively, these data were used to construct an account of the transformation process, with a focus on whether communicational and conflict management practices had been modified in any way some time after the intervention.

This account was then contrasted in a second stage to the historical accounts of nine other schools (seven primary, two secondary) that had attempted to implement peer mediation with mixed success two years previously (one secondary and six primary schools were still running a service). Teachers from the nine other schools and peer mediation trainers were interviewed retrospectively during stage two. The focus of these interviews was to reflect upon the impact peer mediation may have had since its implementation and any processes that enhanced or impeded any such impact. Themes identified in both stages inform the analysis made and are reported in the next section.

Findings: The cultural transformation required for effective implementation of restorative approaches in schools

Analysis of the interview data identified three main themes, these were:

- Theme 1: A contradiction between traditional and innovative approaches to resolving conflict (between arbitration and mediation).
- Theme 2: The need of substantial support for transformative practice.
- Theme 3: The production and endorsement of new cultural tools.

The distribution of these themes across the 10 schools from both stages can be seen in Table 19.1.

The table indicates a clear relationship between each of these themes being positively reported and the status of their peer mediation service. In the two schools where peer mediation training had taken place and a service subsequently introduced but then abandoned, interviewees reported significant issues concerning staff members modifying their perceptions of power and control (theme 1), the degree of support for students to exercise responsibility in this way (theme 2) and changes in communicational practices that would have supported the intervention (theme 3). The inverse pattern can be seen to be generally applicable to schools both sustaining a service and reporting a positive impact. Each of these themes will now be discussed in turn and will include extracts from the interviews to illustrate key points.

Table 19.1 The distribution of themes across schools from both stages 1 & 2.

School	A	B	C	D	E	F	G	H	J	K
Stage	1	2	2	2	2	2	2	2	2	2
Pri/Sec	Pri	Pri	Pri	Pri	Sec	Pri	Pri	Pri	Sec	Pri
Service Status	Running with a positive impact	Running with a positive impact	Running with a positive impact	Running with a positive impact	Running with a positive impact	Running with a positive impact	Running with a limited impact	Running with a limited impact	Abandoned – little/no impact	Abandoned – little/no impact
Theme 1	+	+	+	+	+	+	0	0	0	0
Theme 2	–	+	+	–	+	+	+	0	0	0
Theme 3	+	+	+	+	+	+	0	–	0	0

Key: +: theme reported positively, 0: theme reported negatively, –: theme not reported/insufficient evidence

Theme 1: A contradiction between traditional and innovative approaches to resolving conflict (between arbitration and mediation)

At the school studied in stage one, where peer mediation had been successfully implemented, a clear contradiction between the roles and their inherent power relationships underpinning traditional and innovative approaches for resolving conflict (arbitration and mediation) was observed. In schools implementing restorative approaches more effectively, this contradiction had been resolved to modify roles in ways harmonious with mediation and a number of characteristics serve as evidence of this transformative process:

1   Teachers and lunchtime supervisors interviewed about the scheme at the school observed that the service had been popular with pupils and this was connected to the pupil's perception of authority. Pupils could volunteer to have minor conflicts mediated by peers without the threat of sanctions, as one pupil stated, 'If we ask the teacher, one of us might be upset because one of us might get into trouble. With peer mediators, you know you're not going to get into trouble' (Peer mediation client, School A).

2   Changing roles meant that minor conflicts were frequently prevented from escalating and members of staff had greater time free for other activities (which with some irony included arbitrating 'more serious' conflicts) as this teacher's comment elucidates, 'Dinnertimes seem easier because lunchtime supervisors are not having to deal with the small problems, they're going to peer mediation. They are now able to spend more time with the deeper problems that peer mediation doesn't deal with' (Teacher, School A).

3   The peer mediators visibly distinguished themselves (by wearing red caps) to identify themselves on the playground, which communicated a different role and status to other pupils.

4   The pupils exercised some autonomy in maintaining the service for themselves, even drawing up a rota.

5   To sustain the service, it was planned that the pupils would pass their skills onto replacement peer mediators before they left school at the age of eleven. This form of 'peer apprenticeship' would provide the trainees with additional responsibilities.

Similar changes in teacher and student roles were reported by each school that successfully sustained a peer mediation service (Table 1). If peer mediation is effectively implemented in schools there appears to be a radical reconfiguration of roles. The 'innovative' approach of peer mediation is underpinned by principles of power and control in which pupils have a greater role in the regulation of their own and their peers' conflicts. In contrast, more traditional approaches to conflict resolution, arbitration by teachers for example, are underpinned by principles of teacher-control and authority. The modification of traditional approaches can be understood as a process in which teachers' perceptions of power and control are re-evaluated (Tyrrell 2002). Such a shift represents a translation of some teacher power to some pupils, who use such tools as peer mediation scripts to help their fellow students.

This isn't a straightforward transference of power from adults to all pupils however. More accurately, it is the wider distribution of power to a sub-group of pupils, the mediators, and to a much lesser extent, their clients. As a result, when pupils encounter conflicts that are difficult to resolve independently through negotiation, they now have a greater opportunity to resolve the dispute between themselves and to ask peers to help them in this process rather than adults.

Arbitration	Peer Mediation	Negotiation
Strong classification	Weaker classification between teachers and pupils, stronger classification between pupils and peer mediators	Weak classification
Strong framing	Strong framing	Weak framing

Box 19.1 Arbitration, mediation and negotiation in terms of classification and framing

Bernstein's (2000) theory of cultural transmission is helpful in elucidating this process. The traditional approach, teacher arbitration, is characterised by strong 'classification and framing', where strict rules for acceptable behaviour apply and sanctions for breaking these rules are enforced by adults. The relationships between subjects are clearly defined (arbitrator and arbitrated) and the structure of communication reveals the power of one to judge the other and administer appropriate sanctions. In contrast, classification and framing when negotiation takes place between equal parties is weak, where horizontally related parties agree a solution between themselves. The innovative approach of peer mediation represents a median between these contrasting approaches (as shown in Box 19.1). One can understand the transformation of the traditional activity as a process in which there is relinquishment of some teacher power to peer mediators and hence a weakening of 'classification and framing' between teachers and some pupils.

Although horizontal relations underpin the process of peer mediation, peer mediators are trained to halt the process if ground rules are not kept and they often use a script to facilitate the process according to pre-determined stages (Sellman 2008). The script used by peer mediators serves as a framing device, which delineates sequential steps in exploring the problem and generating potential solutions. This process is more formally controlled than in negotiation but less formally controlled than in arbitration. It is noteworthy that the scripts commonly used by child mediators are similar in how they delineate the order and manner of questioning to those used in adult contexts (e.g. legal- and community-based mediation). Although mediators may modify or re-write their scripts, this guise of 'pupil empowerment' is not pupils exercising their own voice but rather they are learning to apply the voice of adults (with certain values) when resolving conflicts.

Thus, the implementation of peer mediation: i) weakens the classification of social relations between teachers and pupils as arbitration is de-formalised in certain situations; and ii) strengthens the relations between some pupils by creating a division of labour in which pupils assume the roles of peer mediators and disputants. The clearest indication of this is the coloured caps or other identifying features worn by peer mediators on the playground. Whereas such visual demarcations solve a number of practical problems (e.g. how to find a peer mediator on the playground) they also symbolise the creation of a sub-group. These mediators are no longer 'peers', they stand out to others because they have certain skills, roles and responsibilities that are different to others.

Pupil empowerment therefore, in the case of peer mediation at least, does not involve a subversion of the traditional teacher–student power relation but rather a re-organisation of power. Wisely or not, the teachers at all schools interviewed in stages one and two regarded peer mediation as having less utility for resolving serious conflicts. This represented a tension between staff members who were and were not prepared to 'trust' pupils sufficiently (Tyrrell 2002). Hence, the principles of power and control underpinning the activity of resolving 'serious' conflicts usually remains strongly classified and framed.

Theme 2: The need of substantial support for transformative practice

For roles to be transformed in the way described in relation to theme 1, there needs to be a 'critical mass' of support for such change, as a peer mediation trainer observes,

> If there's only one committed member of staff it's not enough for the work to survive. In the end they find it too difficult to maintain what they have started. There needs to be a definite commitment in senior management plus a reasonable number of other supporters. It's the concept of critical mass; it doesn't have to be everyone but a mass large enough so that the others will sway their way rather than overwhelm them with indifference and hostility.
>
> (Peer mediation trainer)

In schools where a critical mass of support is achieved, greater coherence and consistency for resolving conflict in more dialogic ways is achieved throughout the school. In such cases, new ways of thinking and talking about conflict are more pervasive. When this doesn't happen, which may sometimes be compounded by curriculum and organisational issues, the school encounters problems in implementing and/or sustaining innovative approaches, such as peer mediation. This appeared to be the case in those schools that assumed they could develop conflict resolution skills via teaching such skills as a solitary addition to the curriculum, without sufficient attention to cultural processes. Kenway and Fitzclarence (1997) argue that interventions often focus their attention on the behaviour of individuals rather than social and cultural practices. Yet, such factors are crucial ingredients in whether initiatives are successful or not (Cowie and Jenifer 2007).

One deputy headteacher, reflecting on the failure to sustain peer mediation at a secondary school was forthright with his analysis:

> The aims were isolated…and to try and do it for one hour a week when for the other twenty hours a week, the regime was totally different…teachers react to small groups of disruptive children by exerting their influence and control. Discipline across the school was teacher-led and then they came to this one PHSE lesson where that didn't apply, where they were given responsibility for their own behaviour and they didn't cope with it very well.
> (Deputy headteacher, School J)

Similarly, another teacher drew attention to similar contradictions at his school, when asked, 'What are the differences and similarities between the school culture and the intervention?' 'All the systems of reward and punishment are teacher led and mediation isn't and the two things really are (knocks fists together) going to clash. They're mutually exclusive' (Teacher, School H, author's comment in brackets).

These extracts highlight the need for consistency between the principles of power and control underpinning peer mediation and ways of managing behaviour throughout schools. When the cultural tools produced by peer mediation training are not reproduced and distributed in a school because they contradict the traditional approach, any attempt at pupil empowerment risks becoming either tokenistic and/or fragmented (it only happens at certain times, in certain places, for limited purposes). In these schools, peer mediation is often a 'bolt on feature' (Cremin 2001) and soon dissipates. However, when such issues are resolved, transformative practice is often accompanied by the introduction of new linguistic and psychological possibilities, as the next section will discuss.

One could argue that an emphasis on intervention (and intervention-based research) detracts attention from cultural change. Van Ness (this volume) discusses the relationship between restorative approaches and world view, alerting us to the need to move away from an instrumental conceptualisation of restorative practice, which focuses on approaches and techniques. Instead, he suggests greater attention needs to be paid to the context in which restorative approaches are located, and in schools this concerns the cultural characteristics of institutions. In this regard, a great deal can be learned from indigenous communities and their broader respect for the environment they inhabit and the community to which they belong. Many such cultures have been associated with restorative principles, however, such approaches are not seen as a technique for controlling the disorder of an individual in such communities but rather as a principle binding the community together in a cohesive and sustainable manner.

Similar observations were apparent in the contexts of New Zealand and South Africa, which were reported by Drewery (this volume) and Lephalala (this volume) respectively. In New Zealand, restorative approaches are much more established in the education and youth justice systems than in the UK. Drewery (this volume) emphasises the need for a whole school culture supportive of restorative approaches. This is frequently challenged by the school's focus on the individual. Hence, there is a need for a paradigm shift from a modernist perspective that focuses on fix to a more humanistic, restorative or even ecological paradigm, emphasising community and the individual's role and dignity within that community. The research reported here is perhaps limited by its emphasis on intervention 'after' culture rather than a 'culture first' conceptualisation, where culture represents the context in which restorative approaches almost appear as the 'natural' way of doing things in light of the types of relationships encouraged in such cultures. Nonetheless, elements of culture supporting restorative approaches will certainly include many of the features reported here, notably around relationships and language, discussed further in the next section.

Theme 3: The production and endorsement of new cultural tools

In stage one, trained peer mediators and their class-teacher reported that they found the peer mediation script to be a useful tool. Those interviewed recounted the sections of the script and suggested that the script was also used in other situations, as with the following sequence from a pupil interview.

R: What kinds of conflict did you experience before being trained as a peer mediator?
P: Usually a lot of people arguing and shouting at each other and everybody else not knowing what to do, usually just standing in the background not knowing what to do so the fight would go on and get worse.
R: Would you have been one of those standing in the background?
P: Yes, because I wouldn't know what to do.
R: And has that changed at all?
P: I'm now trying to sort out the problems before it gets too violent.
R: How do you do that?
P: Well, I go in and ask them to calm down and ask them the different questions and try to make them see that its not what they think it is and that its different and then they should see that its not a fighting matter and should make friends.
R: And what questions do you use?
P: <u>I ask them what's happened and who's doing it with them if the others have gone off, and then we go and find them and ask them to explain what's happened, the other person explains what's happened and then think about the two things that they've said and then give them a few ideas and think about what to do next.</u>

R: Where do those questions come from?
P: The scripts, I use some of the words that are on the script.
R: When do you use those scripts?
P: When we're peer mediating at the moment, but we usually remember them and we use them outside as well.

The underlined segment in this sequence outlines the stages of the peer mediation script, minus a question about feelings. It is possible that the pupil is using the voice of the script. Her account suggests that many characteristics of this new tool have been internalised. If her own account is accepted, the tool has shaped some of her thought processes but now she reports beginning to apply the tool in familiar situations.

The accounts of pupils and teachers at schools where peer mediation had been successful suggest that peer mediation training produced new forms of social relations, which involved the use of new cultural tools such as the peer mediation script. The use of these new tools creates opportunities for new ways of thinking and acting with regard to conflict. The previous sequence showed how one pupil used the script to regulate her own thinking, speaking and acting in conflict situations. Such appropriation was not restricted to pupils however. One class-teacher described how she now used a 'talking-stone' (initially used as part of the peer mediation training) to encourage turn-talking between students if they were arguing, whilst another described how he used the peer mediation script to regulate his own behaviour management in the classroom. Talking about the impact of the intervention on his own practice, he stated:

> I think I am better now at talking with the children over a problem. I actually do use the peer mediation script when I'm dealing with two children. I don't read it out but I know the sorts of, the way to talk, to get one child saying something and then saying to the other and making more of a tennis match, if you like, between the two children. Whereas originally, I would have spoke individually to the one with them standing in front of me and individually to the other. Instead now, I'm more, we'll hear the one side, we'll hear the other side and then we'll hear what that person's going to do and what the other person's going to do instead of doing it in big blocks. And I think they've got that better now because they immediately hear how each other is feeling.
>
> (Teacher, School B)

Here again, the teacher alludes to ventriloquising the stages of the peer mediation script but shows how he has made the tool serve his own ends. In this example, the language used by the teacher, when he would have once arbitrated the conflict, has been modified. The teacher uses the new tool in a way that is reminiscent of the relationship between speech and tool use described by Vygotsky (1978). When individuals encounter a difficult task, they often resort to externalised speech and the use of semiotic tools (social in origin) to structure their speech. In this particular case, the teacher uses the peer mediation script, which translates a certain set of social relations into principles of communication. By replicating the tool in his own classroom practice, he helps to reinforce the innovative approach (mediation rather than arbitration), a step that is perhaps central to establishing a new form of practice across the school. If mediation techniques are also used as everyday management techniques, a peer mediation service will have a far greater chance of success as the principles of power and control underpinning both approaches are more consistent.

When students used these tools effectively, teachers commented that it introduced a new stage to their thinking processes:

> A big problem here is that the children's background encourages them to think of physical retaliation as their first response. If you said 'Why did you do that?', expecting some deep rooted problem, he'll say 'He was in front of me, or he looked at me'. We noticed that the impact of the course and the work teachers did before and after could extend the pause, the gap between action and reaction.
>
> (Headteacher, School E)

Tentatively, such observations suggest that pupils connected with peer mediation may be adopting a more pro-active identity in the conflict management process. Sfard and Prusak (2005) define 'identity' as the stories an individual agent tells, about a subject, to an audience. When a conflict is arbitrated, the 'story' of a pupil's conflict is told to them by an adult. This reinforces the notion that their conflict is something over which they have little or no control or authority. When a conflict is mediated, as the headteacher testifies, there is a potential identity shift. Instead, the pupil participates in creating and proposing a shared 'story' about the conflict, of which they feel greater ownership and ability to participate in its resolution.

The transformation the headteacher suggests is taking place here indicates that if pupils are given the opportunity for greater and more meaningful involvement, particularly in those areas of school life traditionally reserved for teacher regulation, students can demonstrate potentially significant gains in learning and identity development, i.e. they acquire the *skills* to resolve conflict constructively and they *expect* to be involved in the process. If students are to be able to manage their own conflicts effectively, not only do they need to be given the tools to do this but school organisation also needs to be sufficiently transformed in order to allow them to genuinely employ these tools. As well as being trained in restorative approaches and having genuine opportunities to use them, critical literacy may have a role to play here. Cultures offering students the opportunity to develop such skills also offer them the opportunity to analyse both interpersonal and structural conflicts.

Conclusion

The findings reported in this chapter suggest that the frequent shortcoming of peer mediation services can be explained by a school's failure to modify traditional management approaches to incorporate the new rules, roles and cultural tools produced by an innovative approach such as peer mediation. Schools perhaps underestimate the degree to which principles of power and control underpinning traditional approaches have to be transformed in order for new innovative approaches to be implemented. In research by Tyrrell (2002), this was a psychological issue concerning teachers' perception of authority rather than a practical issue concerning resources. Broadwood (2000) states that a successful peer mediation service has to be compatible with a school's vision and its approach to regulating social relations. This is characterised by clear and consistent means for dealing with conflict, which are modelled by all teachers and reproduced in their management style. Schools that implement initiatives as if they can be 'bolted upon' existing structures, determined by adults, are unlikely to both sustain the initiative and reap any benefits without radical appraisal and transformation of existing structures (McCluskey this volume).

Those schools where peer mediation has been both successful and sustained for several years are underpinned by consistent principles of power and control, as embodied by communicational practices, between management strategies used by adults and the philosophy underpinning mediation. It would appear then that a key feature of pupil empowerment may not be schools with pupil empowerment initiatives but rather schools that create the conditions in which pupil empowerment initiatives thrive.

References

Bernstein, B. (2000) *Pedagogy, Symbolic Control and Identity*. 2nd Edition. London: Rowman & Littlefield Publishers.

Broadwood, J. (2000) 'Leap confronting conflict', *Development Education Journal*, 6 (2), 18–19.

Cowie, H. and Jenifer, D. (2007) *Managing Violence in Schools*. London: Paul Chapman.

Cremin, H. (2001) *Peer Mediation Training for Young People*. Bristol: Lucky Duck Publishing.

Daniels, H. (2001a) *Vygotsky and Pedagogy*. London: Routledge.

—— (2001b) 'Bernstein and activity theory' in A. Morais, I. Neres, B. Davies and H. Daniels (eds) *Towards a Sociology of Pedagogy: The Contribution of Basil Bernstein to Research*. New York: Peter Lang.

Daniels, H., Holst, J., Lunt, I. and Johansen, L. U. (1996) 'A comparative study of the relation between different models of pedagogic practice and constructs of deviance', *Oxford Review of Education*, 22 (1), 63–77.

Engestrom, Y. (1999) 'Activity theory and individual and social transformation' in Y. Engestrom, R. Mietinnen, R. and R. J. Punamaki (eds) *Perspectives on Activity Theory*. Cambridge: Cambridge University Press.

—— (2007) 'Putting Vygotsky to Work: The Change Laboratory as an Application of Double Stimulation' in H. Daniels, J. Wertsch and M. Cole (eds) *The Cambridge Companion to Vygotsky*. Cambridge: Cambridge University Press.

Hicks, D. (2001) 'Re-examining the future: the challenge for citizenship education', *Educational Review*, 53 (3), 229–240.

Kenway, J. and Fitzclarence, L. (1997) 'Masculinity, violence and schooling: challenging 'poisonous pedagogies', *Gender and Education*, 9 (1), 117–133.

Sellman, E. (2008) *Mediation Matters: Creating a Peaceful School through Peer Mediation*. Cambridge: LDA.

Sfard, A. and Prusak, A. (2005) 'Telling Identities: In search of an analytic tool for investigating learning as culturally shaped activity', *Educational Researcher*, 34 (4), 14–22.

Tyrrell, J. (2002) *Peer Mediation: A Process for Primary Schools*. London: Souvenir Press Ltd.

Vygotsky, L. S. (1978) *Mind in Society: The Development of Higher Psychological Process*. Cambridge MA: Harvard University Press.

Wyness, M. (2006) 'Children, young people and civic participation: regulation and local diversity', *Educational Review*, 58 (2), 209–218.

Chapter 20

Creating the restorative school part 3

Rethinking neutrality and hierarchy

Shelagh McCall

Introduction

Within previous chapters in this section, it has been argued that restorative approaches in schools are more successfully implemented and demonstrate greater impact when they are accompanied by the following: a financial commitment to long-term sustainability; support from school leaders, regional policymakers and training providers; a position within daily organisational and pedagogic structures in addition to the marginal curriculum of discipline and pastoral care; and when they are accompanied by changing perceptions of authority and disciplinary roles often embodied in different ways of communicating.

As discussed by Bickmore (this volume), restorative approaches in schools can be underpinned by contrasting objectives, understood as reactive or proactive strategies for dealing with difficult conflict. The reactive model is closely allied with well known practices of 'behaviour management', whereby a range of values and practices are applied after an incident to encourage students to take responsibility for what has happened and what may need to happen next to repair any harm before moving forward. Responsive approaches are therefore those that attempt to keep or make peace after an incident. In some contrast, proactive approaches are related to a development model of education, emphasising the need for students to acquire and practise a range of civic skills, both in the here and now as well as in the future. Proactive strategies hence are more concerned with peacebuilding.

This chapter begins by discussing these two models, recognising that the objective of each has merit but that they are best seen as interconnected and inter-serving models. It is suggested that neither, however, can be satisfactorily implemented without necessary attention to whole-school transformation, which in turn demands a proactive vision. The chapter then focuses upon two particular barriers to whole-school implementation of restorative approaches based on that proactive vision: the issues of neutrality and hierarchy. Neutrality is identified as an issue because teachers are often placed in situations where it is, in reality, difficult to be impartial and objective. Recognising this difficulty, an argument is made for teachers to occupy the role of '*omni-partiality*', being on both or all sides at the same time. Secondly, the issue of hierarchy is seen as a barrier because restorative approaches raise expectations of how people will be involved and treated in post-incident decision-making and conflict prevention. For such involvement to be genuine, challenging questions may need to be addressed concerning existing school structures. In discussing both of these issues, reference is made to Ury's (2000) 'third-side' approach to managing conflict, offering some ideas for how these issues may be resolved. In so doing, links are made to some of the key themes contained within this volume.

The reactive and proactive as interconnected restorative models

One of the most widespread and easily recognised applications of restorative approaches in schools is the reactive model, embodied in such approaches to conflict resolution as peer mediation and restorative conferencing. These specific approaches are often attractive to schools as they have a clear training element, end-product and promise an impact on behavioural incidents such as repeated rule breaking, escalated inter-pupil conflicts and even exclusions from school. They are characterised by a response to rule breaking popular with progressive and liberal educators as the process involved does not ascribe blame or impose sanctions, rather it emphasises a collaborative approach to understanding and repairing the harm caused by the rule breaking. Participation in such conflict resolution processes requires a certain set of skills, including collaboration, consensus-building and active listening. Such processes are also (or should be) built upon a range of common values, including equality, respect and inclusion, which might be described as 'democratic' or 'heterarchic' values. When such processes are used solely as a behaviour management tool, there is the risk (well observed by Sellman, this volume) that these values may clash with other elements of school organisation and pedagogic practice. Thus any behaviour management function of restorative approaches in schools immediately raises questions about whole-school transformation, which may be most coherently resolved by consideration of the proactive model.

The development of the skills and the assimilation of a heterarchic value system, seemingly required by student participation with a reactive restorative model, goes well beyond the purpose of behaviour management. The skills and values employed are the ingredients of respectful relationships, equally essential for harmonious citizenship in the here and now, and the future. This is what Drewery has called a 'developmental approach' (Drewery, this volume). This can be *ad hoc*, where students learn and assimilate the skills and values through participation in conflict resolution processes, often at the margin of school experience; or more systematically such as when dealing with conflict constructively is at the heart of daily school organisation and pedagogic practice.

Drewery (this volume) asks us what we are employing restorative approaches in schools for? This is a helpful challenge as it recognises the potential for both responsive and preventative objectives, reflected in behaviour management and developmental functions respectively. These interests are clearly interconnected. A school's vested interest in the success of behaviour management processes is not just about tackling specific incidences of misconduct. Its long-term hope is also educative, a hope that the student will learn from the experience and not repeat previous mistakes. Similarly, the interest of the school in educating students as future citizens is also about capacitating students with the skills for respectful relationships in the here and now (Hendry 2009, Wyeness 2006). Where students are better equipped to respect diversity and difference and act co-operatively in that context, there should be less need to employ behaviour management processes.

It is at best unpredictable, and rather unlikely that restorative approaches solely serving a reactive or behaviour management function can by themselves achieve the broader goals of reduced recidivism at school or beyond. This is because such long-term success depends upon the capacity of the particular individuals involved to understand and integrate the lessons contained within the process. It will be harder for students to understand and integrate such learning if the values and skills associated with the process are not reflected and reinforced in wider school culture. By the same token, whether a school can succeed in developing the caring culture necessary to equip students as both citizens of the here and now as well as the future depends on whether such lessons are reflected and reinforced by the school's behaviour management system. A student who learns and expects to be involved with decision-making will quickly become disillusioned if their behaviour is responded to arbitrarily and punitively.

Research (McCluskey this volume, Sellman this volume, Du Rose and Skinns this volume) shows that a school's resistance to change its traditional activities and power structures is a real impediment to implementing effective restorative approaches. In order to achieve and sustain the long-term success of restorative approaches in schools, it will be necessary to engage with organisational change, including some questioning of hierarchical structures. Clearly, this could be daunting and challenging for those involved as it requires stakeholders to become open to the potential of both systemic and intrapersonal change. Such a demand is made by Hopkins when considering whether mediation in schools should extend to mediation between teachers, students and colleagues:

> The notion of general accountability, and the possibility of acknowledging mutual contribution when there have been difficulties involving adults and young people – these are both potentially threatening ideas. The challenge for restorative justice enthusiasts is to make the case for restorative dialogue to be just that – a process that restores good relationships, goodwill and well-being – and that must be a good thing for young and old in a school, or indeed in any community where people need to be working in proximity to each other day after day.
>
> (Hopkins 2004, p. 109)

For some, such a step may seem radical. Yet, if the commitment to restorative approaches in schools is to extend beyond lip-service and marginal 'interventions', then a restorative culture will place demands upon both individual and organisational transformation.

Management of conflict

In every community conflict is inevitable and a school is no different. Deutsch's work (1973) has been helpful in conceptualising conflict in education as something that should be managed rather than eliminated. Choices then need to be made about when we engage in conflict management (in other words, how much conflict is tolerable), how we engage with the people and issues involved and what lessons are learned from both the conflict and how it was managed. The approach to conflict resolution adopted will ultimately influence what kind of community we have.

For example, we can choose to deal with conflict only when it becomes destructive – that is, when the system of rules has broken down and specific harm has been caused. In a school setting where traditional discipline methods are employed, the most likely process employed in conflict management is the use of arbitrary power by the teacher, usually the administration of a standardised punishment. This approach is 'arbitrary' because no deep inquiry is made into what has occurred, why and what the real harm is. The potential consequence of deciding to intervene only when conflict becomes destructive is mere containment of that conflict, where latent issues unresolved by the management process and tension will remain. The use of arbitrary power is also likely to engender a disrespectful and disenfranchised community, where young people struggle to understand the relationship between sanctions and rule breaking, and do not feel they exercise a stake in the system.

The philosophy underpinning restorative approaches in schools aims at stopping conflict from becoming a destructive cycle by helping to build a respectful and more egalitarian community, and repairing any harm caused by conflict in a deeper and more satisfactory manner to those involved. The resolutions sought by restorative approaches are not arbitrary as they should be based on an assessment of the true harm caused, with reparation linked to a mutual agreement of the action necessary to repair this harm. One purpose of repairing the harm would seem to be returning the community to a place where the conflict is well below the threshold where it becomes potentially destructive. So in response to the question often asked about restorative approaches – 'Restoring what?' – I would suggest restoring a community in which conflict is non-destructive, or restoring conflict to a non-destructive level. What restorative approaches have in common, be they reactive or proactive in objective, is that they do not call upon an arbitrary power to achieve a desired outcome. Instead, they offer a collaborative and consensus-based alternative. I will now outline Ury's third-side approach to managing conflict as a way of discussing the roles of non-conflict parties in facilitating restorative approaches in schools, and as a way of raising questions about neutrality and hierarchy during such processes.

A 'third-side' approach to managing conflict

Ury (2000) has suggested that there are three major opportunities to channel a conflict's vertical momentum, that being its tendency to escalate from underlying tensions into a destructive struggle, into a horizontal momentum instead, characterised by constructive change. In summary, these three opportunities are:

1   To prevent destructive conflict emerging in the first place by addressing latent tensions.
2   To resolve any overt conflicts which do develop.
3   To contain any escalating power struggle that temporarily escapes resolution.

In each of these stages, 'third-siders' fulfil different roles. In schools, these roles can be enacted by anyone with a responsibility for maintaining conflict below the level at which it becomes destructive, including teachers who convene restorative conferences, peer mediators who help resolve playground disputes, or children with a befriending or buddying brief. They need not be those formally responsible for resolving conflict, so could also include bystanders. The proactive use of restorative approaches may aim to build social capacity in order that all school community members are able to assist with the management of conflict.

Ury (2000, p. 190) elaborates the nature of the role, describing ten different ways in which the third-sider roles help de-escalate or contain a conflict, represented in Box 20.1.

Why conflict escalates		Ways to transform conflict
	PREVENT	
Frustrated needs	→	The provider
Poor skills	→	The teacher
Weak relationships	→	The bridge-builder
	RESOLVE	
Conflicting interests	→	The mediator
Disputed rights	→	The arbiter
Unequal power	→	The equaliser
Injured relationships	→	The healer
	CONTAIN	
No attention	→	The witness
No limitation	→	The referee
No protection	→	The peacekeeper

Box 20.1 Third-sider roles

One can readily see both reactive and proactive strategies for dealing with conflict amongst these roles and a comparison with the objectives of peacebuilding, peacemaking and peacekeeping outlined by Bickmore (this volume). Ury's (2000) specification of third-sider roles reinforce the inter-relationships and interdependence between behaviour management and developmental education previously discussed. But how can we achieve the characteristics of peacebuilding cultures described by Bickmore in order to reduce the demand on peacekeeping roles in the long-term future. Thus follows a discussion of two issues affecting third-sider roles, neutrality and hierarchy and an argument that each issue needs to be fully understood and reconceptualised in order to achieve such long-term systemic change.

The issue of neutrality

Restorative approaches place a high value on the neutrality and impartiality of the third-sider (for example, the mediator or facilitator). Whereas neutrality may be a desirable value in theory, research (e.g. Mayer 2004) has observed that it is difficult to implement in practice and can present an obstacle to the success of mediation and similar processes. As one example, some restorative approaches are prone to what could be called the 'inauthentic apology' (Acorn 2004), where participants reluctantly volunteer to partake in the process but still perceive the approach as an exponent of institutional order and justice. Neutrality means different things in different contexts. When mediators talk about being neutral, they often mean that they are neutral within a procedure, they are there to see that the rules of the process are followed and that both sides have equal opportunities to participate. But parties to a conflict may perceive the 'neutrality' of the mediator quite differently. For example, in a conflict where one student has hit another, the 'victim' may far more readily accept the neutrality of the peer or adult convening the process than the 'perpetrator' will. The third-sider may, for the perpetrator, represent the very system against which they experience frustration and express resistance and therefore are incapable of genuine 'neutrality'. Although the 'perpetrator' may recognise a neutral process (in the sense that there is consistency of approach and each participant has equal opportunity to engage), the suspicion may well be of substantive partiality on the part of the third-sider. In other words, no matter how 'fair' the process appears to be, the third-party 'sides' with the 'victim' on the question of who has been harmed and who is responsible for making amends.

In reality, no-one is truly neutral or impartial, even those trained in mediation. Everyone has experienced conflicts which have shaped their perspectives, priorities and biases. Concerning intense conflict, neutrality is perhaps non-desirable. More neutral spaces, like courts, should be places of last resort. The danger of a system of extreme neutrality, equality and fairness is that 'the harsh reality of bias, inequality and unfairness must be formally disregarded, neutrally rephrased or denied' (Cloke 2001, pp. 148–149). Being a 'third-side' is not the same as being neutral. According to Mayer (2004) third-siders are not people who approach conflict from a neutral stance or primarily from a procedural point of view. Cloke (2001) further posits that parties do not want mediators or third-siders who are actually neutral. Instead, what they want is only the appearance of neutrality.

Furthermore, what they want is a third-sider who is honest, empathetic and on everyone's side at the same time – someone who is 'omni-partial'. In relation to the transformative potential of conflict, Cloke argues that much is lost in an over-emphasis on neutrality, he elaborates:

> Because neutrality implies objectivity and distance from the source of the conflict, it cannot countenance empathy or give the mediator room to acknowledge or experience grief, compassion, love, anger, fear or hope. Neutrality can paralyse emotional honesty, intimate communication, vulnerability, and self-criticism. It can undermine shared responsibility, prevention, creative problem-solving, and organisational learning. It can ignore the larger systems in which conflict occurs. It can fail to comprehend spirit, forgiveness, transformation, or healing, which are essential in mediation. As a result, it can become a straitjacket and a check on our ability to unravel the sources of conflict.
>
> (Cloke 2001, p. 14)

The 'omni-partiality' proposed by Cloke (2001) can appear threatening because it requires the mediator to open to the possibility that not only will the process transform the conflict under scrutiny and those involved, it may also transform the mediator themselves by exposing their prejudices and empathetic skills. A challenge is made to all third-siders. The challenge is to establish and sustain a restorative approach that not only fulfils a reactive function (repairing harm) but also has the capacity to transform individuals and the context in which they are located, hence proactively shaping the likelihood of future conflict. This challenge can be understood as a shift from an instrumental application of restorative approaches, characterised by educational goals, to a transformative application capable of conveying important feedback for individual and institutional change. This of course requires individuals to abandon the notion that anyone can or should be neutral. 'Omni-partiality' helps ensure that the process is seen to be fair but does not simultaneously restrict wider transformation by allowing third-siders to acknowledge their own stake in the process and outcome as well as those directly affected. 'Omni-partiality' encourages the development of the skills of restorative approaches (consensus building and collaboration) whilst assimilating its values (equality, inclusion, respect) and potential for change into the wider community, acknowledging that no participant can actually stand outside of the context in which they are located.

The issue of hierarchy

Conflict has considerable learning potential for institutions. What may at first seem to be an interpersonal conflict may also raise issues for the whole school community and may even be a by-product of how that community operates. All conflict is contextual and schools are diverse places, constituted by people with differing needs, ideas and personalities. 'Harmony' can be achieved from the top-down by imposing structures, rules, processes on community members or, more democratically and collaboratively, it can be built from the ground up. As previously discussed, restorative approaches can be implemented in different ways too, with varying emphasis on hierarchy and democracy.

For example, victims may feel pressurised into co-operating in the rehabilitation of the perpetrator when there is an emphasis on hierarchy and a reactive application of restorative justice in schools. If the wider school culture is actually autocratic and does not reflect the values underlying restorative conflict resolution processes then it will be difficult for participants to view such processes as truly democratic and voluntary. In such contexts, there may be greater emphasis on securing apologies at the cost of young people genuinely empathising and collaborating with one another. If authentic and honest communication is not a feature of the wider school culture processes such as conferencing will be undermined. The conflict under scrutiny may be superficially resolved but there will be no deeper opportunity for positive transformation – either of the individuals or the institution. Similar contradictions may occur if there is greater attention to peacebuilding activities but only tokenistic commitment to ideas such as inclusion and collaboration when real-life problems are encountered. In such contexts, students may learn the theory of restorative approaches but the practice of sub-ordinance to hierarchical power structures.

So, how do we go about beginning to create a restorative school culture with comparable qualities of democracy, collaboration and participation? Culture is what everyone knows and nobody talks about, hence, the first step is to get everybody to begin talking about these attributes. Everyone in the school community will have a view on the merits and limitations of their existing culture and a vision of how they would like their new culture to be. This has to be a multi-party process, characterised by a shift in language from 'How *do* we do things around here?' to 'How *can* we do things around here?'. Through such dialogue a facility for identifying and agreeing shared values is created. Such an initiative sits easily with those advocating greater pupil voice and participation with decision-making on important school matters (Wyness 2006). In doing so, the heterarchy is able to influence the hierarchy. A feedback loop is created enabling democratisation.

There will, of course, be the practical necessity of preserving roles essential for the school to function. The proposal here is not to dismantle the hierarchy. Clearly, effective leadership and decision-making remain essential. Rather, it is to propose the creation of the necessary communicational practices for both horizontal and vertical dialogue with opportunities for feedback and change. As a component of such dialogue there is understanding and agreement concerning how decisions will be made and by whom, accompanied by an expectation of leadership characterised by consent and co-operation.

Culture change is not a static process and therefore it is important that dialogue remains continuous and multi-directional. It is important to create multiple feedback systems that allow members of the school community to comment on and influence both their relationships and structures. It is also important that those in positions of responsibility accept the feedback as collaborative and constructive, and that those giving the feedback do so from a position of sympathetic values and vision.

Conclusion

In order to contribute to the creation of a restorative school culture, it seems important that those with responsibilities recognise they are a constituent part of that culture, they cannot stand apart from, or above, their community and expect restorative approaches to fulfil their potential. Democratic or heterarchic values are therefore necessary. In this chapter, the role of omni-partiality has been suggested as an alternative to standing apart, remaining neutral. Such a position allows greater empathy and fosters shared responsibility for fair, inclusive and authentic responses to conflict. It promotes deeper engagement with the issues and the potential for broader transformation. It has also been suggested that dialogue rather than dictat enables those with responsibilities to stand alongside rather than above their community. Multi-party, collaborative processes for decision-making foster the democratic communication channels necessary for conceptual cohesion between ways of doing and ways of being, between the reactive and proactive objectives of restorative approaches in schools. In such cultures, restorative means are also restorative ends.

References

Acorn, A. (2004) *Compulsory Compassion: A Critique of Restorative Justice.* Vancouver: UBC Press.

Cloke, K. (2001) *Mediating Dangerously: The Frontiers of Conflict Resolution.* San Francisco: Jossey Bass.

Deutsch, M. (1973) *The Resolution of Conflict.* New Haven, CT: Yale University Press.

Hendry, R. (2009) *Building and Restoring Respectful Relationships in Schools: A Guide to Restorative Practice.* London: Routledge.

Hopkins, B. (2004) *Just Schools: A Whole School Approach To Restorative Justice.* London: Jessica Kingsley Publishers.

Mayer, B. S. (2004) *Beyond Neutrality: Confronting the Crisis in Conflict Resolution.* San Francisco: Jossey Bass

Ury, W. (2000) *The Third Side: Why We Fight and How We Can Stop.* New York: Penguin.

Wyness, M. (2006) 'Children, young people and civic participation: regulation and local diversity', *Educational Review,* 58 (2), pp. 209–218.

Chapter 21

Who misses out?

Inclusive strategies for students with communicational difficulties

Mary Meredith and Edward Sellman

Introduction

The restorative conference as conceived by O'Connell and Wachtel (1999) is critiqued as one example of a restorative approach in this chapter, on the grounds that the approach is not as inclusive as it could be and must become if it is to improve outcomes for a vulnerable and marginalised group; particularly young people with communicational difficulties.

Given the considerable number of studies which now highlight a link between language difficulties and youth offending, the fact that the restorative justice literature has not to date addressed the needs of this at-risk population would seem to be a surprising omission. Indeed, it is argued in this chapter that the restorative conference is, verbally, a challenging arena and paradoxically may therefore inadvertently discriminate against participants with both receptive and expressive language difficulties.

This is a situation that warrants scrutiny. Some multi-sensory adaptations to the conferencing process, well established in special education, time-tested in their capacity to strengthen engagement, are suggested as potential modifications to the process. The chapter begins, however, by highlighting the pressing need for such work. It would seem that the restorative conference is symptomatic of a much broader problem concerning identifying and meeting learning needs for those who find communication difficult. It is important to consider the restorative conference and its fitness for purpose within this wider context.

Communication difficulties and social exclusion

'The most effective way to reduce or prevent offending is to provide the right level of support at the time it is needed' (Dr. B. Lockhart OBE, cited in Youth Justice Agency Conference Report, 2009, p. 5). In a government commissioned review of services for young people with communication difficulties, Bercow (2008) makes a powerful case for early intervention by highlighting the 'multiple risks' that children face when their communication needs are not met. Although the notion of risk can be critiqued for shifting the blame from societal institutions to individuals (Daly, 2002), there are statistical relationships between communication difficulties and 'lower educational attainment, behaviour problems, emotional and psychological difficulties, poorer employment prospects, challenges to mental health and, in some cases, a descent into criminality' (Bercow, 2008, p. 7).

Youth Justice Agency statistics (2009) indicate over 60 per cent of young people in the criminal justice system have some form of language difficulty. Exacerbating this problem is the fact that, as highlighted in the Youth Justice Agency report just cited, current offender programmes are language-based and therefore difficult for the majority of young offenders to access. These young people are subsequently more likely to re-offend than those without communication difficulties (Davis *et al.*, 2004).

Clearly, there is an urgent economic and social imperative to prevent entry into the youth justice system, particularly of the most vulnerable. Describing communication as 'the missing link in the social exclusion chain', Beardshaw and Hosford outline a bleak and all too well-trodden path:

> This is a challenge that many young people are facing today. They don't have the language to express themselves, solve problems, support each other, or learn. Without this 'map', children are more likely to follow a well-trodden pathway of acronyms; from ASBO to NEET and from PRU to HMP via the YOI. As in the classroom, language is the conduit for interventions, support and help in these institutions. It is estimated that 60-90 per cent of vulnerable young people have communication difficulties. How can these young people progress without language skills?
>
> (Beardshaw and Hosford, 2009, p. 3)

Implicit in this argument is the notion that young people with limited language skills risk compromised outcomes, socially and academically, for as long as language is the 'conduit' for interventions. It follows then that interventions generally, and restorative conferencing in particular, must become less language-based and more multi-sensory if outcomes for such vulnerable and marginalised groups are to be improved.

The hidden nature of communication difficulties

Unless articulation problems affecting speech are evident, communication difficulties are often a hidden difficulty. We may understand what learners with such difficulties say to us and we assume that they in turn can understand what we say to them. It is not surprising, therefore, that problems around identification of communication difficulties are a key issue in the field.

A study by Conti-Ramsden and Botting (1999) found that of an estimated five per cent of children aged five to six with speech and language difficulties, only one per cent were identified on special needs registers. The four per cent who did not have their primary learning needs met at this early stage in their education were instead referred to support services for other reasons, such as slow educational progress, poor reading comprehension and/or challenging behaviour (e.g. Beitchman, 2001). More recent research would suggest that the situation has improved little, if at all. According to Bercow, identification of language impairment remains, 'grossly inadequate' (Bercow, 2008, p. 18), with many young people never receiving support for their difficulties.

Misconceptions are, it seems, rife. Beitchman *et al.* (1999) suggest that communication difficulties are often misinterpreted as non-compliance, with practitioners failing to appreciate the difference between poor receptive language and inability to comprehend instructions. Vallance *et al.* (1999) report that around 50 per cent of children receiving services for a range of adjustment disorders actually display language impairments when specifically tested. In an investigation of a special unit for children with behavioural, social and emotional difficulties, Burgess and Bransby (1990) found that 16 out of 17 had communication difficulties, normally requiring speech and language therapy. Eleven of these were described as having severe difficulties, but they did not have the clearly identifiable problems with speech that would have alerted professionals to their needs at an earlier stage. As Bryan *et al.* explain, such misconceptions actively undermine the life-chances of children deemed to be 'high-risk':

> High-risk children may receive services aimed at ameliorating their behaviour problems, but there may be little or no attention paid to suboptimal development in the realms of expressive and receptive language competence. This in turn reduces the likelihood of school engagement, thus lessening the access that high-risk young people have to the protective effects of academic achievement.
> (Bryan *et al.*, 2007, p. 508)

When communication needs are undetected and unmet, young people are more vulnerable to experiencing disaffection with education and/or school exclusion. According to a recent inquiry into school exclusions by the Children's Commissioner (Atkinson, 2011) young people with 'special educational needs' are in fact eight times more likely to be permanently excluded from school than their peers. Whilst a multi-sensory approach to conferencing as an alternative to exclusion has the potential to improve this situation (and restorative approaches are recommended in the inquiry report) modifications can only be made when language deficit has been identified in the first place. A coherent national strategy to improve outcomes for language impaired young people must therefore begin by introducing a policy of screening and timely intervention for oral language deficit, particularly when such difficulties often co-exist and inter-relate with other difficulties.

The impact on social relationships

A range of factors conspire to render young people with communication difficulties more likely to experience destructive forms of conflict than their peers.

For most young children, language becomes a substitute for action as they begin to understand what is said to them and to express their needs verbally. However, as Gallagher (1999a, 1999b) found, language impaired children are more likely to use direct physical action to express needs and, in this way, a strong association between challenging behaviour and communication difficulties develops.

Problems with peer relationships therefore tend to begin early and may even be evident in pre-school settings. For example, Hadley and Rice (1991) reported that 'preschoolers behave as if they know who talks well and who does not and they prefer to interact with those who do' (1991, p. 342). Consequently, language impaired children have fewer opportunities to practice their skills and fall further behind peers. This is confirmed by many studies showing that they are, for example, less adaptive to the feelings and needs of their listeners (Bergman, 1987; Ford and Milosky, 2008), less able to be tactful (Bliss, 1992), less able to interpret social clues (Longoria et al., 2009) and more limited in their ability to negotiate (Marton et al., 2005).

Benner et al. (2002) cites several longitudinal studies that suggest the strength of the relationship between communication difficulties and challenging behaviour increases over time (e.g. Baker and Cantwell, 1987). The changes in expectations when a student makes the transition from primary to secondary school are well documented and can prove particularly demanding for students with unidentified communication difficulties. Whitmore (2000) characterises this transition as a move away from the student-centred environment to a subject-centred one. The increased social challenge of education beyond 11 years of age is therefore exacerbated by an increasingly academic environment with an increase in new terminology, much of it abstract, and greatly increased listening demands. Benner et al. (2002) also claim that secondary school students are expected to learn through listening 90 per cent of the time. Ehren (1994) produced a comprehensive list of the ways in which increased academic and social pressure can affect the language impaired learner. Difficulties include not following instructions; asking irrelevant questions; not participating in class discussions; relating poorly to authority figures; getting along poorly with peers and interacting in an irrelevant way in conversations with both peers and adults (Ehren, 1994).

Such behaviours further exacerbate difficulties and social isolation leading to potential withdrawal or physical expression of frustration. According to Benner et al. (2002), a range of studies suggest that those with expressive language difficulties are more prone to withdrawal whilst receptive language difficulties are more likely to externalise their frustration. Cohen et al. (1998), for example, found that children with unidentified difficulties with receptive language were rated as the most aggressive by their teachers. Heneker (2005) found that of 11 students in a pupil referral unit (PRU), 91 per cent had some difficulties with receptive language.

As a consequence of such difficulties, young people with communication difficulties are more likely to require restorative approaches than their peers. Yet the same lack of oral competence that drives the need for restorative intervention must also undermine its success. Indeed, outcomes may be far from those intended with Snow and Sanger (2011) suggesting that an impression of shallowness and low empathy for the 'victim' may further stigmatise the alleged perpetrator during a restorative process. When the verbal challenges of the restorative conference are unpicked, it becomes clear just how significant the barriers to access are and how stressful such a process may be for a participant with a communication difficulty. Here follows a discussion of several barriers to accessing the restorative conference that may be experienced by such students.

Barrier to access: Social isolation

Particularly relevant to this chapter is the impact that social rejection must inevitably have on restorative conferencing. The word itself, restorative, reflects the underpinning ideal of repair:

> Restorative justice in the school setting views misconduct not as school rule-breaking, and therefore as a violation of the institution, but as a violation against people and relationships in the school and wider school community.
> (Cameron and Thorsborne, 2009, p. 2)

However, if there are no existing relationships to violate, if the perpetrator of harm is in fact a socially-rejected individual, then how does this work? The literature provides few answers to this question, save its more pro-active emphasis on relationship-building as a vital part of a school's broader commitment to restorative approaches. 'Delinquency' has become an emotive and judgemental term, but Masters' (1998, p. 3) definition of it as 'non-existence of a link' is painfully relevant to the context of this discussion. For the adolescent without social links and without a robust sense of self, the restorative conference could be a deeply undermining place.

Barrier to access: Expressive language difficulties

Those accepting responsibility for harmful behaviour are the first to be questioned in the scripted conference. The perpetrator is asked:

- What happened?
- What were you thinking at the time?
- What have you thought about since the incident?
- Who do you think has been affected by your actions?
- How have they been affected?

After hearing from the 'victim' and supporters, there is then a final opportunity for the wrongdoer to speak: 'Is there anything you want to say at this time?'

Taking into account the emotionally charged and unfamiliar nature of the social context, this is a challenging agenda even for those without communication difficulties. For those with limited language skills, it can be excruciatingly uncomfortable. Such students often mask their word-finding difficulties by keeping verbal contributions to a minimum. Their struggles with fluency can be exacerbated when they are put under pressure, making the conference situation even more stressful (e.g. Ripley *et al.*, 2001).

Even the opening question is potentially problematic. Ripley and Barrett (2008) suggest that it is often difficult to explain events leading up to a confrontation that result in young people with communication difficulties taking an inappropriate amount of blame for incidents in the first place. They struggle to create a 'personal narrative' and 'are not as skilled as their peers at negotiating their way out of trouble' (Ripley and Barrett, 2008, p. 96). Subsequent conference questions become more challenging still since they are abstract and de-contextualised. Clearly, with no scaffolding (which would be 'tinkering with the script' and is therefore forbidden in O'Connell's *Conferencing Handbook*, 1999), 'What were you thinking at the time?' is a difficult, open-ended question. For many students with communication difficulties, closed questions or forced alternatives – crudely, 'Did you think this or did you think that?' are necessary (Ripley *et al.*, 2008). However, such scaffolding would obviously undermine the 'free expression' that O'Connell *et al.* (1999) describe as critical to the success of the process.

'How have they been affected?' is a question designed to promote empathy and to encourage the perpetrator to talk about the emotional impact of his or her behaviour on others. Again, students with expressive difficulties are likely to find this difficult because, as Denham (1992) explains, the language of emotions – learned in the early years – is often one that many students with communication difficulties fail to master. Indeed, this constraint above all others threatens to undermine the entire conference process since its success hinges on the principle of 'affective resonance' (Nathanson, 1992). This is achieved when, through the free expression of feelings, a transition is experienced and participants are able to 'feel each other's feelings' (O'Connell *et al.*, 1999, p. 25). It follows that young people with expressive difficulties and therefore without this essential language for feeling, will struggle to produce the affective statements that are essential in creating the necessary emotional bonds central to the process, not to mention conflict resolution processes more generally.

Shortcomings can in turn make the next phase more challenging than it might otherwise be since 'victims', not satisfied by the account just offered, may respond by demanding further explanation:

> Victims may directly ask the offender questions, which the facilitator should allow. Victims often want to know why offenders committed the offence and why the offenders chose them to victimise, and want to be assured it will not happen again. If the offender was not forthcoming or remorseful, victims may have many challenging questions.
>
> (O'Connell *et al.*, 1999, p. 62)

Therefore, the more able the alleged 'perpetrator' is to express feelings during the opening interaction – or the more forthcoming – the less likely he or she is to be challenged a second time. For the participant with communication difficulties however, the expressive phase may well be extended, with 'victims' possibly frustrated by this stage asking many challenging questions, including demands for difficult explanations.

Barrier to access: Receptive language difficulties

Neither is the level of challenge necessarily reduced when the requirement to speak is replaced by one to listen. Difficulties with receptive language invariably underpin those with expressive language just discussed. As Ripley explains, 'problems in any one part of the language system will usually have implications for functioning in other parts of the system' (Ripley *et al.*, 2001, p. 7). The extended listening phase of the conference will therefore present just as great a barrier to meaningful participation as the first expressive phase for the language impaired participant: 'Victim', 'Victim Supporters' and 'Offender Supporters' are asked in turn the same set of four questions, with the exception of the final one:

- What was your reaction at the time of the incident?
- How do you feel about what happened?
- What has been the hardest thing for you?
- What do you think are the main issues (substituted in the case of 'Victim' with 'How did your family and friends react when they heard about the incident?').

Only the most competent listener would be able to process at least twelve consecutive responses of varying length and complexity without some degree of difficulty, particularly given the highly charged nature of the language. According to the *Conferencing Handbook*, 'Victims are generally forthcoming in describing their thoughts and feelings .... Facilitators should allow victims to vent their feelings ... Parents of offenders often express intense feelings of distress and shame' (O'Connell *et al.*, 1999, pp. 61–63). Even those with well-developed listening skills are likely to experience such persistency of language as challenging; those with receptive difficulties may well respond by simply tuning-out. Indeed, research shows that children with restricted receptive language learn to do this at an early age (e.g. Ripley *et al.*, 2008). By the time they begin secondary school, not listening and not expecting to understand has become an entrenched habit.

Barrier to access: Risk of failure and toxic shame

According to O'Connell *et al.*, Silvan Tomkins' psychological theory of human affect, helps explain why the scripted conference is so effective. He argues that, through the expression of true feelings, 'conference participants make an emotional journey together, feeling each other's feelings as they travel from anger and distress and shame to interest and enjoyment' (O'Connell *et al.*, 1999, p. 21). For O'Connell, the structured environment created by the script ensures that Tomkins' negative affects, forefront at the start of the process, are left behind as the conference reaches the agreement stage. However, this rests on several assumptions. First, that there has been a true expression of feelings, second that such expression has been processed by all participants and third that 'affective resonance' has therefore been enabled. When one or more of these essential components is missing, perhaps because of a communication difficulty, then there is surely a danger that the conference script does not carry participants seamlessly through Tomkins' affects but instead stalls at the dangerous stage of shame.

Not that shame is, by definition, a simply negative affect: Braithwaite (1989) explains that it occurs in all humans when confronted with their wrongdoing. He contends that provided shaming is reintegrative, it is positive by allowing wrongdoers to accept responsibility, to apologise and to make amends. The scripted conference ensures that 'perpetrators' move beyond their shame to be reintegrated back into their communities of support. Costello *et al.* (2010, p. 9) describe the process thus: 'Restorative conferencing, by its very nature, provides an opportunity for us to express our shame, along with other emotions, and in so doing reduce their intensity'. Here, an explicit link is made between expressive language and the successful discharge of shame. When such expression has not occurred because of the barriers described previously, then it follows that there may be no such catharsis and shame is only intensified. People are then, according to Nathanson (1992), liable to react in one of four ways, all of them damaging: by attacking self (e.g. self put-down); attacking other (e.g. blaming the victim, lashing out verbally or physically); withdrawal (e.g. isolating oneself, running and hiding) or avoidance (e.g. denial or distraction).

Tangney *et al.* (2002, p. 3) also dispute the notion that shame is ever positive, describing it as 'an extremely painful and ugly feeling that has a negative impact on interpersonal behaviour'. Furthermore, 'shamed individuals are inclined to assume a defensive posture, rather than take a constructive, reparative stance in their relationships', (Tangney, 2002, p. 181). At face value, this research finding would seem to undermine the whole notion of reintegrative shaming – according to Tangney, there can be no such thing. However, the distinction she draws between shame and guilt corresponds exactly with the one that Braithwaite (1989) draws between stigmatising and reintegrative shame; in this way, whilst the two theorists use different terms, they are not necessarily adopting fundamentally opposed stances in relation to shame. Both reintegrative shame (Braithwaite, 1989) and guilt (Tangney, 2002) render people better able to empathise with others and to accept responsibility for negative interpersonal events. Indeed, Tangney, applying her own terminology, actually recommends the 'guilt-inducing, shame-reducing philosophy and associated methods of the restorative justice approach' (Tangney, 2002, p. 193).

However, when a conference does not achieve its shame-reducing goal but rather the opposite, then its impact on both shamed individual and their community could be detrimental:

> Moderately painful feelings of guilt about specific behaviours motivate people to behave in a moral, caring, socially responsible manner. In contrast, intensely painful feelings of shame do not appear to steer people in a constructive, moral direction. Such intense moral pain about the self cuts to our core, exacting a heavy 'penance' perhaps. But rather than motivating reparative action, shame often motivates denial, defensive anger and aggression.
>
> (Tangney, 2002, p. 2)

Clearly then, when attempting to harness the potentially toxic emotion that is shame, practitioners are advised to proceed with the greatest caution. This is precisely why O'Connell emphasises the need for a carefully orchestrated shaming process. However, it has been argued from the outset that when language impaired young people are expected to manage the challenges of the scripted restorative conference unsupported, they are likely to flounder. As we have seen, they are a vulnerable group anyway – if their experiences of conferencing make them feel stigmatising shame as opposed to reintegrative shame, or shame as opposed to guilt, then well-meaning practitioners may have caused more harm than good.

Removing barriers through multi-sensory adjustments

There emerges a strong argument that the conference environment needs to be modified so that young people with communication difficulties are able to actively engage in the process and therefore learn from it. After all, within the school setting, the conference is fundamentally an educational strategy; one that is designed to provide opportunities for insight and learning (Cameron and Thorsborne, 2009).

Ever since Gillingham and Stillman (1956) devised their pioneering methods with struggling readers in the 1930s, there has been consensus in the field that multi-sensory input is essential for learners with special educational needs and is advantageous for all. In relying almost entirely on a single sensory pathway, the auditory, it follows that restorative conferencing cannot be regarded as an inclusive educational strategy. Restorative practitioners should therefore draw on good inclusive practice guidelines, such as those outlined in Westwood (2010).

Some of these might be most appropriately located within the pre-conference meeting that is strongly recommended in conferencing guidelines. This one-to-one discussion is of course designed to establish rapport and to ensure participants are fully aware of conference aims. However, it also provides an opportunity for what is often referred to in the special education field as 'pre-teaching'; that is, support which typically allows learners to become familiar – through multi-sensory approaches – with key words before encountering them in the classroom.

Ripley *et al.* (2001) underline the particular relevance of visual support in relation to learners with communication difficulties, explaining that 'images are a more direct route for instant understanding than words' (Ripley *et al.*, 2001, p. 21). In preparing students with communication difficulties for a restorative conference therefore, skilled practitioners could encourage students to express their thoughts and feelings visually. No attempt will be made here to suggest an exhaustive set of such approaches, but clearly questions like 'What were you thinking about at the time?' and 'What have you thought about since the incident?' could be answered through symbols and pictures drawn by the student. 'Who do you think has been affected by your actions?' invites the use of concentric circles with the inner circle representing the most affected 'victim' and the outer circle, the least (e.g. Warne, 2003). Students could also draw on Wilson and Long's *Big Book of Blob Feelings* (2010) to express how their actions affected others. Equally, a Likert five-point scale would enable learners to express subtleties of thought and shades of meaning not available to them through words alone.

Provided all participants are carefully briefed beforehand so that they do not feel that the process is trivialised, there is in fact no reason why participants with expressive language deficits should not respond to conference questions by sharing such pre-prepared visual materials. When in the alleged 'perpetrator' role, they are the first to respond to questions and so they do not at this stage have to take into account anything already said. The only priority is for them to communicate their thoughts and feelings clearly and openly, through the most effective channel, so that 'affective resonance' becomes possible. It is likely that they will do this more successfully visually than through language alone. If necessary, and depending on the severity of the communication difficulty, a commentary could be provided by an advocate.

The listening phase does, as already seen, present a different set of challenges. Again, however, conditions for listening could be improved without in any way compromising the integrity of the script. Ripley *et al.* (2001) suggest the use of a list of short questions, if necessary with picture support, that learners may be given prior to the delivery of an extended verbal explanation in a lesson. Listening for the answers, students are supported in focusing their attention. Such a strategy is clearly readily transferable into the restorative conference arena with participants invited to record any 'feeling' words on a template comprising conference questions. Furthermore, such templates could be differentiated according to the extent of the learner's difficulty. In this way, students might be provided with the opportunity to select from a menu of options – highlighting, perhaps, the most relevant word or image to capture a speaker's message. This level of interactivity also has the advantage of introducing a kinaesthetic element, argued by many (e.g. Hughes, 1999) as effective for a significant and disadvantaged group of learners. 'Disaffected' adolescents will not benefit from restorative interventions that simply offer more of the same – a one-dimensional pedagogy that may already have alienated them.

Available on the market at the time of press is an educational product, '*RJ 4 Teens*', specifically aimed at such young people. Introducing their resource, Anderson and Skeldon (2008, p. 2) rightly argue that,

The key to engaging young people effectively with the restorative process is reclaiming the frameworks of multi-sensory supported learning, which exist in early years development, and applying many of these basic principles to the restorative process itself.

Their resource comprises a set of graphical cards which are intended to provide a springboard into discussion. Participants select and arrange the most appropriate graphics to produce a 'picture framework' of what happened, who was affected by an incident and how it might be put right.

With visually appealing cards, the option of holding them and moving them around, its game-like quality and the underpinning restorative structure, RJ 4 Teens is potentially a useful resource. However, with no clear role for 'supporters', vital as we have seen in the triggering of guilt, it does lend itself to the impromptu conference situation rather than the formal meeting which has been the focus of this discussion. Moreover, when there has been serious harm and a formal conference is convened, the game-like approach of RJ 4 Teens might be considered inappropriate, particularly from the perspective of those victims whose needs must be considered paramount. As a step in what has to be the right direction however, and as a resource to support day-to-day restorative interactions, it constitutes an important and innovative development.

Conclusion

Restorative approaches in schools face a significant but surmountable challenge if they are to meet the needs of students with communication difficulties, and other students with similar needs. As highlighted in this chapter, it is this group that are simultaneously most likely to benefit from restorative approaches yet are also most likely to find the language-based processes exclusive. Perhaps there is a case for restorative practitioners working together with other professionals, such as speech and language specialists, in dynamic inter-agency partnerships to more fully utilise the potential of restorative approaches. Such partnerships could initially focus on two urgent areas for development: 1) the nature of support provided to young people before participating in restorative approaches; and 2) adjustments to the process itself, such as incorporating multi-sensory elements. The meaning of the words 'just' and 'adjust' can be traced back to common origins concerning law although the latter has evolved into a term closer in meaning to 'repositioning'. However, in this context it might be helpful to think of the word 'adjustment' as make fairer, more just, more inclusive. And unless restorative approaches are suitably adjusted for young people with communication difficulties, they will remain exclusive to many and that is clearly unjust.

References

Atkinson, M. (2011) *They Never Give Up on You*. School exclusions Inquiry. London.
Baker, L. and Cantwell, D. P. (1987) 'A prospective psychiatric follow-up of children with speech and language disorders', *Journal of the American Academy of Child Psychiatry* 26, 546–5, 3.

Beardshaw, V. and Hosford, A. (2009) 'Language and Social Exclusion', *I CAN Talk Series*, Issue 4. Available at: <www.ican.org.uk>.

Beitchman, J. H., Douglas, L., Wilson, B., Johnson, C., Atkinson, L., Escobar, M. and Tacack, N. (1999) 'Adolescent substance use disorders: findings from a follow up study of speech/language impaired and control children', *Journal of Clinical Child Psychology*, 28, 312–321.

—— (2001) 'Fourteen-year follow up of speech/language impaired and control children', *Journal of the American Academy of Child and Adolescent Psychiatry*, 40, 75–82.

Benner, G. J., Nelson, R. and Epstein, M. H. (2002) 'Language skills of children with EBD: A literature review', *Journal of Emotional and Behavioural Disorders* 10, 43.

Bercow, J. (2008) *The Bercow Report. A Review of Services for Children and Young People (0–19) with Speech, Language and Communication Needs.* Nottingham: DCSF Publications.

Bergman, M. (1987) 'Social Grace or Disgrace: adolescent social skills and learning disability subtypes', *Reading, Writing and Learning Difficulties*, 3, 161–166.

Bliss, L. (1992) 'A comparison of tactful messages by children with and without language impairment', *Language, Speech and Hearing Services in Schools*, 23, 343–347.

Braithwaite, J. (1989) *Crime, Shame and Reintegration.* Cambridge: Cambridge University Press.

Bryan, K., Freer, J. and Furlong, C. (2007) 'Language and communication difficulties in juvenile offenders', *International Journal of Language and Communication Disorders.* Vol 42. No. 5, 505–520.

Burgess, J. and Bransby, G. (1990) 'An evaluation of speech and language skills of children with BESD problems', *College of Speech and Language Therapy Bulletin*, 453.

Cameron, L. and Thorsborne, M. (2009) *Restorative Justice and School Discipline: Mutually Exclusive?* Available at: <http://www.iirp.org/library/schoolsdisc.html>.

Cohen, N. J., Barwick, M. A., Horodezsky, N. B., Vallance, D. D. and Im, N. (1998) 'Language, achievement and cognitive processing in psychiatrically disturbed children with previously indentified and unsuspected language impairments', *Journal of Child Psychology and Psychiatry*, 39, 865–877.

Conti-Ramsden, G. and Botting, N. (1999) 'Characteristics of children attending language units in England: a national study of 7 year olds', *International Journal of Language and Communication Difficulties*, 34, 359–366.

Costello, B., Wachtel, J. and Wachtel, T. (2010) *Restorative Circles in Schools.* International Institute for Restorative Practices, Bethlehem, Pennsylvania, USA.

Daly, K. (2002) 'Restorative Justice: The real story', *Punishment and Society.* Vol. 4, no. 1, pp. 55–79.

Davis, K., Lewis, J., Byatt, J., Purvis, E. and Cole, B. (2004) 'An Evaluation of the Literacy Demands of General Offending Behaviour Programmes', *Findings*, 233, 1–4. Available at: <http://www.publications.rds@homeoffice.gsi.gov.uk>.

Denham, S. A. (1992) 'Baby looks very sad: implications of conversations about feelings between mother and pre-schoolers', *Child Development* 61, 1145–1152.

Ehren, B. J. (1994) 'New directions for meeting the academic needs of adolescents with language learning disabilities' in Wallach, B. and Butler, K. (eds) *Language learning disabilities in school-age children and adolescents: some principles and applications.* New York: Macmillan.

Ford, J. A. and Milosky, L. M. (2008) 'Inference generation during discourse and its relation to social competence: an online investigation of abilities of children with and without language impairment', *Journal of Speech, Language, and Hearing Services in Schools* 32, 101–113.

Gallagher, T. M. (1999a) 'Interrelationships among children's language, behaviour, and emotional problems', *Topics in Language Disorders* 19(2), 1–15.

—— (1999b) 'Language skills and the development of social competence in school-age children', *Language, Speech and Hearing Services in Schools* 24 (4), 199–205.

Gillingham, A. and Stillman, B. (1956) *Remedial Training for Children with Specific Disability in Reading, Spelling and Penmanship.* Cambridge: MA Educators Publishing Service.

Hadley, M. and Rice, J. (1991) 'Predictions of interactional failure in preschool children', *Journal of Speech, Language and Hearing Research,* 34, 1308–1317.

Heneker, S. (2005) 'Speech and language therapy support for pupils with behavioural, emotional and social difficulties (BESD) – a pilot project', *British Journal of Special Educational Therapy,* Vol. 32, No. 2, 2005.

Hopkins, B. (2006) *Implementing a restorative approach to behaviour and relationship management in schools – the narrated experience of educationalists.* Unpublished doctoral thesis. Reading: University of Reading.

Hughes, M. (1999) *Closing the Learning Gap.* Stafford, UK: Network Educational Press.

Longoria, A. Q., Page, M. C., Hubbs-Tait, L. and Kennison, S. M. (2009) 'Relationship between kindergarten children's language ability and social competence', *Early Childhood Development and Care,* 179, 919–929.

Marton, K., Abramoff, B. and Rosenweig, S. (2005) 'Social cognition and language in children with specific language impairment', *Journal of Communication Disorders,* 38, 143–162.

Masters, G. (1998) *Reintegrative Shaming in Theory and Practice: Thinking about Feeling in Criminology.* Lancaster University: Department of Applied Science.

Nathanson, D. (1992) *Shame and Pride: Affect, Sex and the Birth of the Self.* New York: Norton and Company.

O'Connell, T., Wachtel, B., Wachtel, T. (1999) *Conferencing Handbook.* The Piper's Press: Canada.

Ripley, K. and Barrett, J. (2008) *Supporting Speech, Language and Communication Needs.* London: Sage Publications Ltd.

Ripley, K., Barrett, J. and Fleming, P. (2001) *Inclusion for Children with Speech and Language Impairments.* London: David Fulton Publishers.

Snow, P. C. and Sanger, D. D. (2011) 'Restorative justice conferencing and the youth offender: exploring the world of oral language competence', *International Journal of Communication Disorder.* Vol. 46. No. 3, 324–333.

Tangney, J., Dearing, R. (2002) *Shame and Guilt.* New York: The Guilford Press.

Turner, J. E. (1998) 'An investigation of shame reactions, motivation, and achievement in a difficult college course'. Unpublished doctoral dissertation. University of Texas: Austin.

Vallance, D. D., Im, N. and Cohen, N. J. (1999) 'Discourse deficits associated with psychiatric disorders and with language impairments in children', *Journal of Child Psychology,* 40, 693–704.

Warne, A. (2003) 'Establishing Peer Mediation in a Special School Context', *Pastoral Care in Education,* Dec 2003.

Westwood, P. (2010) *Commonsense Methods for Children with Special Educational Needs.* London: Routledge.

Whitmore, K. A. (2000) 'Adolescence as a Developmental Phase: A Tutorial', *Top Long Disord,* 20: 1–14.

Wilson, P. and Long, I. (2007) *The Big Book of Blob Feelings.* Milton Keynes: Incentive Publishing.

Youth Justice Agency. (2009) *Locked Up and Locked Out: Communication is the Key.* University of Ulster Conference Report.

Chapter 22

Speaking the restorative language

Richard Hendry, Belinda Hopkins and Brian Steele

Introduction

To conclude the final section, and indeed the book, we offer and reflect upon the writing of a short introductory pamphlet for educational settings, outlining some of the key ideas and issues underpinning restorative approaches in schools. As highlighted in the introduction, the same text can also serve as a useful glossary for any reader of this volume who is unfamiliar with terminology and some of the areas of debate. Before sharing the pamphlet itself, this chapter presents reflections by each of its authors on the process of writing the material and the issues it raised concerning its purpose, language and conceptual clarity. It is hoped that both the introductory text and the accompanying reflection will help those grappling with key issues concerning whether and how to implement restorative approaches in schools.

How the text came about

At the beginning of 2011, three people who had attended the ESRC seminar series, from which many of the chapters contained within this book were first presented, were invited to produce a brief, accessible text that would explain to interested practitioners what was meant by restorative approaches/practice in educational settings. We already knew each other, had done some work together in the past, and yet worked in geographically distinct places. Furthermore, in our day-to-day work as trainers and consultants, we were used to using different models of restorative practice. We were also used to having freedom to define our practice in our own way. The invitation to produce something we could all agree on was indeed quite a challenge.

It would undoubtedly have been easier for one person to have taken on the task alone, but then the resulting piece would have only reflected one person's perspective and if there is one thing we would probably all agree on it is that restorative practice involves listening to multiple perspectives on a given issue, and valuing them all. The advantage of working together, and over distance, is that our reflections on what we were doing are largely recorded in the e-mail exchanges we had. It was a truly collaborative process, embodying many of the values and skills we, as restorative practitioners, hold dear. Perhaps we would recommend after all, if you are contemplating writing something for your own school or district, working with others, modelling restorative practice and finding a way forward together that will produce something that is greater than the sum of the various parts. Perhaps the task did not necessarily totally transform our own individual outlooks or our practice but it was a very positive experience for all of us. It helped us think much more deeply about what it is we are actually doing when we seek to convey meaning to others on a subject about which we are all passionate.

What follows is a description of our three different perspectives on the experience of writing together, and what we learned from it. The chapter concludes with some recommendations for those who have the task of writing some kind of brochure, pamphlet or briefing about what a restorative approach in a school or educational setting might entail.

Belinda Hopkins

I welcomed the opportunity to work in collaboration with two practitioners who I greatly respect in order to see how, together, we could write about a subject we all hold dear. I had already written a lot about restorative justice and restorative approaches in the form of books, articles, a doctoral thesis, brochures, training manuals, website pieces and briefing papers (Hopkins, 2004, 2006, 2009, 2011, 2012). I was curious to see what constructs we shared in common and where we differed. I was also intrigued to see how others would tell the story – and learn from their fresh *re-storying* of restorative approaches to see how I could learn to re-story things for myself and others.

We all share a passionate conviction that restorative approaches or restorative practice can transform a school environment and impact positively on the lives of young people and adults alike. We would not be writing a document that was ambivalent about the benefits, nor would we flag up all the difficulties in overcoming resistance or implementing culture change. Of course we have written about such things as individuals and faced them in our work as trainers and consultants. However, this time I assumed that our task was to write not just an explanatory piece but a piece that was unashamedly positive about what a restorative approach can offer.

The task: To explain? to persuade? to convince?

Our brief then was to *explain* what restorative approaches or practice was all about, but perhaps also to be *persuasive* in order to *convince* possible sceptics. In this we would perhaps differ from some of the authors in this book whose job it is to engage with what is contested and to offer a balanced view and avoiding overt bias to one view or another.

How does one write to *bring people on board*? This is a question many school staff ask after an in-service introductory event, 'How can we bring parents and reluctant colleagues "on board?"' Different things work for different people – effective rhetoric; some underpinning or over-arching theory; some historical context; statistics and case studies; peer recommendations; a clear explanation and overview of what it would mean for individuals – 'Radio WIIFM' (what's in it for me?) as a colleague calls it. And some like to see a clear road map of how to get from where they see their school in the present to the 'nirvana' of the whole school restorative approach. What were we going to include in our piece – some of these things? All of them? Or a completely different approach?

Stumbling blocks: Readership and terminology

Over the nine months we were writing we drifted in and out of clarity on who our readership was – and I think this led to confusion at times. We accepted that we did need to write in ways that would be accessible to people who know nothing about the topic, but realised over time that it was unnecessarily complicated to try and write something that would meet the needs of all ages, all professions and the press – our original ambition.

We found we used different terminology for what we all do. I use the phrase 'restorative approaches', Brian uses the acronym RA and Richard refers to 'restorative practice'. Over the re-drafting process we changed terms several times. After Richard's first draft however I was encouraged to see that despite differences in terminology we had a broad agreement on what we were all talking about.

The very use of the word 'restorative' is opaque, meaning many things to many people and meaning nothing to many more. It is easy to fall into the trap of using the adjective 'restorative' in too self-referential a way. My own publicity materials often refer to 'restorative conversations' or 'responding restoratively' without really explaining what that means in 'lay terms'. I admit I have done this to keep under the 'restorative justice' umbrella. In fact other words would work just as well – active listening, emotional literacy, building relationships, assertiveness, community building, conflict resolution, putting things right, repairing relationships. So this tendency to use jargon begged another question for us to consider – what language would we use to explain what a restorative approach actually entails?

But what *were* we talking about? In addition to all the different skills introduced previously, I had been questioning the basic assumptions behind what a school is for, what a teacher's role is, and the messages implicit in what is taught, how it is taught, how mistakes are addressed, how learning is assessed and by whom. In a recent book (Hopkins, 2011) I had even coined the phrase 'Restorative Pedagogy', meaning an approach to teaching and learning that enshrined the values, principles and processes of restorative practice. Using the adjective 'restorative' before a word like 'pedagogy' outrageously stretches its meaning – but it was an attempt to give coherence to all I believed about educating young people in an inclusive and non-didactic manner for life as compassionate, caring, responsible citizens. I know Brian and Richard had been having similar thoughts in their own work.

It was inevitable therefore that we did confront the question of whether we needed to move away from the phrase 'restorative practice' or 'approach' altogether and choose another phrase. And yet that would be to cast us adrift from our intellectual home, the focus of this book and indeed the community within which we have all become quite well known. For me at least, it felt scary to give up terminology I have been using for many years. And so we stuck with the words we know – for now. However, when the word 'restorative' goes out of fashion I hope we will all still be here promoting the same values and principles in education, teaching the same essential skills and still challenging the reliance on extrinsic methods to teach young people self-regulation and pro-social attitudes and behaviours.

How to intrigue and inspire

The order in which a topic is explained, and the way it is explained is crucial. If the message is pitched in too bland and non-specific way that it fails to convey what is unique about a restorative approach, if it is too radical it comes across as unworkable, unrealistic or eccentric.

So the challenge for trainers and for writers is how to give their topic a special uniqueness and put this across in a way that inspires and intrigues people. I would say that the draft we finally sent for discussion at the ESRC seminar held in June 2011 failed to do either. What I remember from the seminar was the long silence that ensued when everyone on our table had read our piece. I later described this to Richard and Brian as a feeling of 'underwhelm'. Our piece, painstakingly worked on over many months and several drafts, had simply failed to 'wow' people.

I wondered if we needed to flag up the unique selling point of a restorative approach from the outset. I tentatively suggested starting at the 'sharp end' rather than starting with the foundations; talking about responses and reactions to behavioural and relational challenges first, rather than about how to prevent things happening in the first place. These ideas felt risky to me even as I suggested them. By starting with the sharp end stuff people might go away with the idea that a restorative approach was mainly about how one addressed harm and wrongdoing. On my own courses and presentations, I usually begin by explaining that what matters most is building strong relationships and also stress the importance of – to use Wachtel's (2011) mantra – 'working *with*' people rather than 'doing things *to* them'. When considering the task at hand, it occurred to me that the documentation one produces to explain something does not necessarily have to be arranged in the order of a training course, or an implementation plan. A pamphlet or brochure has a different function, and if it fails to grab the reader early on it has failed.

At what seemed like the eleventh hour Brian and Richard welcomed the new re-arranged version, with very minor amendments, and were complementary about it. All our shared hard work was still there – but re-arranged and compressed into the essentials. After a few more tweaks here and there, and having agreed on a short bibliography, we submitted our final draft, after nine months in gestation!

Let's hope others take it on and add to the hard work we have all done to create the foundational stones. The task was not an easy one and I learned a lot from it. I return to my own work and look at it with fresh eyes.

Brian Steele

In my section I would like to move from reflection on the process outlined by Belinda, to reflection about the content of the leaflet itself.

Reflecting on the process of preparing the original paper led me to identify a number of themes which focus upon key issues in my understanding of, and thinking about, restorative practice.

This piece explores these themes in some detail and its purpose is less about resolving the issues, but rather more about identifying them. This will, I hope, stimulate readers to consider these issues within their own context, and provide some 'scaffolding' for their own thinking.

Themes for exploration

Although I have identified five subsequent themes, these should not be seen as independent of each other, but rather as interconnected ideas which have been isolated from each other for clarity and to facilitate reflection.

The first theme to emerge about Restorative Practice was 'What is 'It'?' Until about halfway through the writing of the paper, we were still concerned with trying to understand what we each meant by restorative justice/restorative approaches/restorative practice. This was not just in terms of detailed definition, but more substantively 'what it is'. This lack of clarity around what was meant was not merely about semantics. In trying to communicate critical ideas we often found ourselves talking at cross purposes because of the lack of a shared, detailed conceptual framework and vocabulary.

It was remarkable that three people (each of whom has been involved in 'it' for many years and who are experienced practitioners) should have taken a considerable time to come to (a less than complete) shared understanding of 'it'. Our difficulties in establishing clarity, coherence, consistency and comprehensiveness around 'what it is', are reflected in other writings about restorative practice. It is clear when reading about the topic, that key concepts and vocabulary are not used synonymously across the literature, although there is often an implicit assumption made that there is an agreed set of structures and concepts. This is unhelpful for those pursuing a restorative 'agenda'.

The second theme to emerge was 'Scope of Focus' for restorative practice. Having determined what restorative practice means conceptually for us, and for our pamphlet, there seemed to be substantial debate around what it meant to be 'restorative' in practice. This, and following, debates are best framed by considering a number of questions:

- Is it mainly about the operation of a number of formal processes or distinct events – structured dialogues, meetings, restorative conferences?
- How does a school become a restorative school – does simply undertaking formal restorative processes automatically ensure that a school (or other organisation) becomes restorative?
- Can one be restorative on a day-to-day basis? How is this achieved?
- If there has been no identifiable 'harm' done, what is there to be restored? Is there an aspect of being 'restorative' which goes beyond repairing/restoring actual harm – ways in which 'restorative' can be conceived of as being preventative?
- Is there such a thing as a restorative culture? What does it comprise of? Is it important?

The next theme considered was 'What is Required?' What is necessary for individuals and organisations to be 'restorative'. Again consideration of key questions is a useful way to approach the theme.

- Does being restorative require the use of a script or if not a script then some kind of tightly structured model? Are there fundamental processes consisting of certain attitudes, values and skills which can be deployed in a more dynamic, freeform or interactive way? Are there certain forms of restorative practice which are best suited to certain situations or settings? What are they?
- Can it be assumed that individuals offered training in the delivery of various formal restorative practices will necessarily become restorative practitioners? Are there certain core skills which are required in order to operate restoratively beyond the structures and formats of restorative practice itself? What are these?
- Can it be assumed that all individuals who undertake training in restorative practices already possess these skills or will acquire them incidentally as a consequence of learning restorative practices? Should consideration be given to selecting individuals for training on the basis of them possessing such skills? Should restorative practices training always contain a consciously designed and delivered element of relevant skills training?
- Is there a distinct restorative philosophy underpinning the practices and can this be articulated?
- To what extent does such a philosophy extend beyond that which is formally tied in with ideas arising from consideration of harm/conflict etc? Is there a philosophy or set of beliefs, values and attitudes which, although related to restorative practice, has wider application, or is a sub-set of a wider or overarching philosophy or set of beliefs, values and attitudes?
- Would the existence of this philosophy and its operation be helpful in the application of restorative practices beyond the more formal/structured/'scripted' practices?

- To what extent has an 'implied philosophical underpinning' of restorative practice been made explicit? To what extent would making it explicit be useful?

The fourth theme was 'Consideration of Context'.

- How significant is the context within which restorative practice takes place?
- How true is the following statement? 'It is no use if a few of us are running restorative conferences if everybody else keeps on doing the same as we've always done?'
- A vital question: to what extent can there be genuine restorative practice in an organisation that has an essentially punitive culture?
- Can we assume that if an organisation undertakes restorative practices (in a formal sense) this, in and of itself, will lead to the development of a restorative culture in that organisation?
- To what extent does the very development of restorative practices inevitably require organisational development and change? Should restorative practice training assess the broader organisational culture within which the training is to be implemented and offer training or decline to offer training based on that assessment?
- Should an element of organisational development/change theory be integral to any restorative practice training?

The fifth and final theme was consideration of 'Links to Other Approaches or Practices'.

- To what extent does a restorative philosophy/set of beliefs/range of values connect to wider beliefs and values relating to 'what it is to be human'? Does the philosophical underpinning of humanistic psychology offer such a connection?
- Can it be assumed that all individuals who undertake restorative practices training already operate on the basis of such a philosophy or will begin to do so incidentally as a consequence of learning restorative practices? Should consideration be given to selecting individuals for training on the basis of their espousing such a philosophy or set of values, beliefs and attitudes? Should restorative practices training always contain a consciously designed and delivered element designed to develop/promote such a philosophy?
- If there are connected or related practices what are these? What is the overlap between them and restorative practices? How are restorative approaches distinct? Is there commonality of 'skill set' between restorative practice and such other approaches?

Richard Hendry

I want to use this opportunity to explore possible links between my experience of co-writing the pamphlet and some of the ideas and challenges inherent in restorative practice itself. Whilst I have, elsewhere, distinguished between 'proactive' and 'responsive' restorative approaches (Hendry, 2009), I am hoping here to draw inferences which apply to the full gamut of interactions that might be described as restorative. I aim to do this by exploring two specific aspects of our collaborative experience. Namely:

1   Perceptions of reality and the need (or otherwise) for shared definitions, and
2   The limits of communication.

Perceptions of reality

In all my work in restorative practice I hold dear a single question – one that I first came across in Carl Rogers' writing: That is, 'Do we need "a" reality?' (Rogers, 1980). I have found many of the ideas inherent in Person Centred Theory invaluable in developing my 'restorative' understanding and practice. In particular, I think the notion that each person's experience of reality is unique (and so never wholly accessible to others) begs fundamental questions about what restorative working is aiming to achieve.

Most theoretical frameworks for restorative interventions focus at an early stage in the process on the experiences and perceptions of those involved. This is sometimes described as the 'Facts' stage of the process. In reality, there is rarely complete unanimity about the 'facts' of what has happened amongst those involved in any situation of conflict or harm. Human cognition is too susceptible to 'trickery' through adaptive memory and flawed sensual perceptions for consensus to be the norm. Our feelings about difficult events can significantly influence the way in which we describe what are, apparently, the same experiences. And we can say with confidence that no two people will experience exactly the same emotional response to a shared event, particularly a conflict. So what is it we hope to achieve when, intervening restoratively, we give participants an opportunity to explore and share with others their experiences of past events?

Belinda, Brian and I came to the seminar series, and our subsequent shared task, with related but unique experiences of restorative practice. During the seminars we had taken part in many discussions which, for me, demonstrated some of these apparent or assumed differences. The experience of collaborating on the pamphlet highlighted a number of differences including different understandings of both the purpose of our task and the audience we were aiming to address. As Belinda has discussed previously, these relatively practical differences in perception were addressed through discussion and clarification.

What I found more interesting were the undercurrents of perception; the unspoken assumptions, based both on our prior understandings of each other and on our readings of the various draft texts that we shared. We each experience our own reality of what we think restorative approaches/practice are and the task of collaborating on its 'encapsulation' in a pamphlet allowed us to identify points of commonality in our thinking. For me, however, the process of identifying commonality was challenged by our unspoken needs and assumptions as we tried to balance our desires to both assert our ideas and to collaborate effectively. Of course, in writing this I am again making assumptions about others' experiences of reality, as the collaborative process did not include an opportunity to explore our underlying assumptions about each other's perspectives.

One example of this assumptive undercurrent emerged in our efforts to reach a shared definition of restorative practice/approaches. There was agreement regarding the broad nature of the term, encompassing both a philosophical perspective and a theoretical framework for interpersonal interactions and interventions. Nonetheless, there was considerable negotiation around the words we used to define terms as we struggled to balance our needs in the task.

The whole endeavour brings to mind a 'hour glass' process. We worked to bring together a fairly broad range of perspectives and understandings about restorative approaches, squeezing them into narrower definitions and descriptions that we could each accept as, in part at least, reflecting our experiences of reality. However, despite this 'tightening' process, those who read the pamphlet will absorb our definitions into their own reality. Each will make sense, and subsequent use, of the ideas in their own way.

In the end the valuable learning in the 'task' (whether collaborative or restorative) is, for me, in the striving to understand the other's experience. And the quality of that learning is often determined by the nature of the communication experienced in the task.

The limits of communication

If we accept the pretext that restorative working is fundamentally about the exploring and sharing of different realities then clearly, communication is the key that serves to unlock that experience. I think a valid criticism of much restorative work is that it relies too heavily on the quality of the verbal communication between participants. (There are interesting examples of restorative practitioners using symbolisation, graphic representation and other media to facilitate communication with and between participants.) Regardless of the medium, however, it is clear that the most effective, restorative experiences happen when people meet willingly, face-to-face and with the intention of communicating directly with each other about their experiences.

In collaborating on the pamphlet Belinda, Brian and I had to rely principally on e-mail exchanges. E-mail is a notoriously fickle medium through which to communicate nuance in meaning and emotion. And so I think we struggled to find a way of exploring the assumptions and perceptions described previously. Or rather, perhaps we chose not to try.

In our case the limitations of the communication led us to focus instead on more practical and pragmatic issues, leading perhaps to a greater sense of compromise and frustration around the whole process than I, at least, had hoped for. I wonder what we would have produced and, perhaps more importantly, what we would have *learned* if we had been able to spend at least a proportion of the time we spent on the task in face-to-face dialogue? Nonetheless, we worked together on a shared task and the outcome was, at least in our judgement, fit for its purpose.

So what has this experience taught me about restorative processes?

If we agree that an important task in any restorative intervention is to help one individual understand better how another individual experienced an episode in his or her life then, on the face of it, we should enter any restorative process with both trepidation and low expectations. The idea of empathy as an 'achievable state' has entered common parlance in recent years with, I would suggest, little critical understanding of the immensity of the challenge that faces anyone who wants to comprehend someone else's experience. 'I know exactly how you feel' is easily uttered, but ultimately deceptive. And yet the evidence of experience suggests that people not only want to but, at some level, *need* to engage in restorative processes. Regardless of how difficult that task can appear at times, and despite the limitations imposed by the communication methods available to us, people need to assert their reality and, at the same time, need to feel empathically connected to others. In the end perhaps it is not so much the 'mechanics' of the restorative process, the communicating of experience or the agreements reached, in themselves, but rather the *striving to achieve these* that brings about learning and change for those involved.

Further thoughts

Clearly, each of us has drawn different learning from the experience of co-writing the pamphlet. Nevertheless, we think we can offer the following practical pointers for those who want to engage in the process of conveying to others what is meant by restorative approaches and what it has to offer a school community. And so we offer these further questions for consideration:

What is the task?

Who is the intended readership? What is their role, age, prior knowledge and likely linguistic or conceptual understanding?

How long will the piece be?

What is its purpose? What will the content include?

What will the resulting piece look like? (e.g. pamphlet/booklet/website piece/video).

Consider the design – the importance of presentation, graphics, visual impact and accessibility.

Definitions, context and scope

What terminology will be used? Whose definitions are being drawn on?

Do we include pro-active as well as reactive processes?

Do we share the conflicts, questions and debates that exist in the field? How helpful is it to know, or indeed not to know, about these?

Are we being positive and persuasive, or do we take an impartial stance?

Do we include evidence, references and background reading?

What do we put in by way of explanatory diagrams and what do we miss out?

Do we use case studies or testimonials?

Models of practice; models of 'whole-school implementation'

To what degree do differences of model and practice matter at the level of individual practice?

The model and the approach to be used may already have been determined – but it is perhaps worth reflecting on this in the context of different training providers' approaches and the likelihood of staff turnover as this can lead to different models both of the practice itself, and also of the vision of what a 'whole-school approach' might look like.

Is it for the training provider or the project manager to impose their model of practice and their vision anyway?

Links to other initiatives and approaches

In what ways do restorative approaches complement the existing values, culture, ethos, curriculum, learning intentions, policies and procedures of the school?

What tensions or challenges might restorative approaches raise for the school community?

References

Hendry, R. (2009) *Building and Restoring Respectful Relationships at School: A Guide to using Restorative Practice*. Abingdon: Routledge.

Hopkins, B. (2004) *Just Schools*. London: Jessica Kingsley Publishers.

—— (2006) *Implementing a Restorative Approach to Behaviour and Relationship in School: The Narrated Experiences of Educationalists*. Reading: University of Reading.

—— (2009) *Just Care: Restorative Justice Approaches to Working with Children in Public Care*. London: Jessica Kingsley Publishers.

—— (2011) *The Restorative Classroom*. London: Optimus Publishing.

—— (2012) Restorative Justice as Social Justice, *Nottingham Law Journal*, 21 (2012), 121–132.

Rogers, C.R. (1980) *A Way of Being*. Boston: Houghton Mifflin.

Wachtel, P. (2011) *Therapeutic Communication: Knowing What to Say When*. London: Guilford Press.

Pamphlet

Restorative approaches in schools[1]

Richard Hendry, Belinda Hopkins and Brian Steele

If you work with, or care for, school-aged children and young people then this pamphlet is for you.

It will help you answer the following questions:

- What are Restorative Approaches?
- What is involved in a restorative response to harm or conflict?
- What is being 'restored'?
- What are the key elements of Restorative Approaches?
- Why are Restorative Approaches helpful?
- How can I find out more?

The pamphlet is not a substitute for appropriate staff development and training, which is an essential part of Restorative Approaches implementation in any setting.

What are Restorative Approaches?

The 'unique selling point' of a restorative approach is that it offers schools an alternative way of thinking about addressing discipline and behavioural issues and offers a consistent framework for responding to these issues. However, as this pamphlet will show, the approach is much more than a 'behaviour management tool'. In isolation, used as such, it will not be very effective.

The table on the next page compares different ways of thinking and responding in authoritarian and restorative models of discipline.

Schools that work restoratively find that relationships are stronger and learning is more effective, and so there is less need to resort to sanctions and punishments to try to 'manage' behaviour. There is a shift from one model of discipline to the other, at a pace appropriate to the school.

Authoritarian Approaches *The focus is on:*	Restorative Approaches *The focus is on:*
Rule-breaking	Harm done to individuals
Blame or guilt	Responsibility and problem-solving
Adversarial processes	Dialogue and negotiation
Punishment to deter	Repair, apology and reparation
Impersonal processes	Interpersonal processes
and, as a result;	*and, as a result;*
The needs of those affected are often ignored	The needs of those affected are addressed
The unmet needs behind the behaviour are ignored	The unmet needs behind the behaviour are addressed
Accountability = being punished	Accountability = putting things right

What is a restorative response to harm or conflict?

Those affected are invited to share:

1 What has happened.
2 What the impact has been on those involved: i.e. who has been affected and in what ways they have been affected.
3 What needs to happen to put things right or to make things better in the future.

This framework is based on sound learning theory regarding how people relate to each other and how best to meet the different needs that can arise from conflict or harm.
  To facilitate such a process requires the ability to:

* establish a respectful rapport with people;
* listen and respond calmly, empathically and without interruption or judgement to all sides of an issue;
* inspire a sense of safety and trust;
* encourage people to express their thoughts, feelings and needs appropriately;
* appreciate the impact of people's thoughts, feelings, beliefs and unmet needs on their behaviours;
* encourage those involved in the problem to find their own solutions.

This learning framework can be used in a wide range of contexts:

- a one way conversation, with one person listening and asking questions and the other talking;
- a two-way conversation, with both people taking turns to ask and answer questions;
- a small meeting when one impartial person – a facilitator – poses questions to two people who have had a difficulty, or where harm has been done, and who want to repair their relationship;
- a larger, facilitated meeting involving children, parents/carers, colleagues or others who have an important role to play (sometimes called a 'Restorative Conference');
- a facilitated circle involving part or all of a class, a staff team or a group of residents.

What is being restored?

This depends on the context and on the needs of those involved. What is being restored is often something *between* the people involved such as:

- effective communication;
- relationship, and even friendship;
- empathy and understanding for the other's perspective;
- respect;
- understanding the impact of one's own behaviour on others;
- reparation for material loss or damage.

However, something may also be restored *within* an individual – for example:

- a sense of security;
- self-confidence;
- self-respect;
- dignity.

Overall, the process often results in the restoration of someone's sense of belonging to a community (e.g. class, school, peer group or family).

What are the key elements of Restorative Approaches?

Restorative Approaches are *value-based* and *needs-led*. They can be seen as part of a broader ethos or culture that identifies strong, mutually respectful relationships and a cohesive community as the foundations on which good teaching and learning can flourish. In such a community young people are given a lot of responsibility for decision-making on issues that affect their lives, their learning and their experience of school.

Restorative Approaches build upon the basic principles and values of humanistic psychology:

- Genuineness – honesty, openness, sincerity.
- Positive regard for all individuals – valuing the person for who they are.
- Empathic understanding – being able to understand another's experience.
- Individual responsibility and shared accountability.
- Self-actualisation – the human capacity for positive growth.
- Optimistic perspectives on personal development – that people can learn and can change for the better.

Such principles and values not only underpin the more formal Restorative Approaches described previously, but they can also be practised in our informal, day-to-day interaction with others. Adults who do this 'model' effective ways of building and maintaining emotionally healthy relationships, and promote helpful, pro-social attitudes. In so doing, these adults may well be providing a positive 'social learning context' not readily available to some young people in other areas of their lives.

An 'iceberg' (Figure 22.1) metaphor can illustrate a whole-school restorative approach, it emphasises two points:

1 The ways in which the whole school community shares the responsibility to build, maintain and repair relationships are the more visible parts of Restorative Approaches. To be effective these processes need to be underpinned by sound knowledge, skills and shared values.
2 Schools that consciously focus the bulk of their effort on building and maintaining relationships will find that fewer things will go wrong and so there will be fewer occasions when relationships need to be repaired.

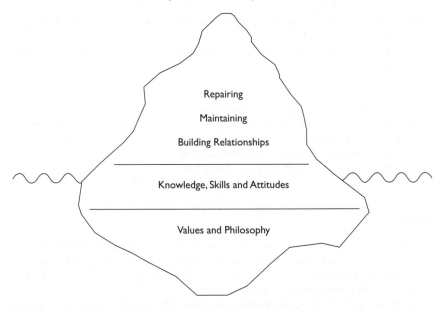

Repairing

Maintaining

Building Relationships

Knowledge, Skills and Attitudes

Values and Philosophy

Figure 22.1 Iceberg metaphor: Whole school restorative approaches

Why are Restorative Approaches helpful?

Staff, children and parents/carers who work restoratively report that this way of working leads to:

- a more respectful climate;
- a shift away from sanction-based responses that aim to 'manage' behaviour, toward a more relational approach;
- better relationships amongst children and staff;
- people being more honest and willing to accept responsibility;
- people feeling more supported when things go wrong;
- a calmer, quieter and more productive learning environment.

How can I find out more?

Here are some UK-based resources[2] that you should find useful.

Books:

Teresa Bliss (2008) *Mediation and Restoration in Circle Time.* Milton Keynes; Teach to Inspire: a division of Optimus Publishing.

Richard Hendry (2009) *Building and Restoring Respectful Relationships in Schools: A Guide to Restorative Practice.* Abingdon: Routledge.

Belinda Hopkins (2004) *Just Schools: A Whole School Approach To Restorative Justice.* London: Jessica Kingsley Publishers.

Belinda Hopkins (2011) *The Restorative Classroom: Using Restorative Approaches to Foster Effective Learning.* Optimus Education.

Colin Newton and Helen Mahaffey (2008) *Restorative Solutions: Making it Work.* Inclusive Solutions UK Limited.

Edward Sellman (2008) *Mediation Matters: Creating a Peaceful School Through Peer Mediation.* Cambridge: LDA.

Websites:

Restorative Justice Council: http://www.restorativejustice.org.uk/

Education Scotland – Restorative Approaches: http://www.ltscotland.org.uk/supporting learners/positivelearningenvironments/positivebehaviour/approaches/restorative/Index.asp

Transforming Conflict: http://www.transformingconflict.org

Sacro: http://www.sacro.org.uk/html/schools_work.html

The International Institute for Restorative Practices (UK): http://uk.iirp.edu/

Notes

1 This pamphlet was produced as a result of an international seminar series funded by the Economic and Social Research Council and organised by Cambridge, Edinburgh and Nottingham Universities in the UK in 2010 and 2011. The authors of the pamphlet were Richard Hendry, Belinda Hopkins and Brian Steele.

2 All correct 2013. These resources reflect the range of Restorative Approaches in the UK. Many excellent international resources also exist.

Index

Page references in *italics* indicate a figure and those in **bold** a table.